W9-DFO-346

Planet Ladder

Other 100% Authentic Manga Available from TOKYOPOP®:

COWBOY BEBOP 1 (of 3)
All-new adventures of interstellar bounty hunting, based on the hit anime seen on Cartoon Network.

MARMALADE BOY 1 (of 8)
A tangled teen romance for the new millennium.

REAL BOUT HIGH SCHOOL 1 (of 4+)
At Daimon High, teachers don't break up fights…they grade them.

MARS 1 (of 15)
Biker Rei and artist Kira are as different as night and day, but fate binds them in this angst-filled romance.

GTO 1 (of 23+)
Biker gang member Onizuka is going back to school…as a teacher!

CHOBITS 1 (of 3+)
In the future, boys will be boys and girls will be…robots? The newest hit series from CLAMP!

SKULL MAN 1 (of 7+)
They took his family. They took his face. They took his soul. Now, he's going to take his revenge.

DRAGON KNIGHTS 1 (of 17)
Part dragon, part knight, ALL glam. The most inept knights on the block are out to kick some demon butt.

Coming soon from TOKYOPOP®:

INITIAL D 1 (of 23+)
Delivery boy Takumi has a gift for driving, but can he compete in the high-stakes world of street racing?

SHAOLIN SISTERS 1 (of 5)
The epic martial-arts/fantasy sequel to Juline, by the creator of Vampire Princess Miyu.

PARADISE KISS 1 (of 3+)
High fashion and deep passion collide in this hot new shojo series!

KARE KANO: He Says, She Says 1 (of 12+)
What happens when the smartest girl in school gets competition from the cutest guy?

KODOCHA: Sana's Stage 1 (of 10)
There's a rumble in the jungle gym when child star Sana Kurata and bully Akito Hayama collide.

ANGELIC LAYER 1(of 5)
In the future, the most popular game is Angelic Layer, where hand-raised robots battle for supremacy.

LOVE HINA 1 (of 14)
Can Keitaro handle living in a dorm with five cute girls…and still make it through school?

Planet Ladder

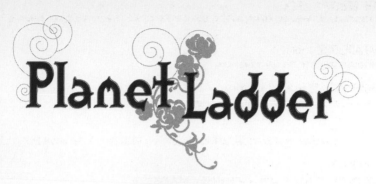

Volume 1

Written and Illustrated by
Yuri Narushima

TOKYOPOP®

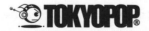

Los Angeles . Tokyo

Translator – Gabi Blumberg
Retouch and Lettering – Wilbert Lacuna and Santiago Hernandez, Jr.
Graphic Designer – Akemi Imafuku
Editors – Robert Coyner and Stephanie Donnelly
Associate Editors – Paul Morrissey and Trisha Kunimoto

Senior Editor – Jake Forbes
Production Manager – Fred Lui
Art Director – Matt Alford
VP Production – Ron Klamert
Publisher – Stuart Levy

Email: editor@TOKYOPOP.com
Come visit us online at www.TOKYOPOP.com

A  book

TOKYOPOP® is an imprint of Mixx Entertainment, Inc.

5900 Wilshire Blvd. Ste 2000, Los Angeles, CA 90036

© 1998 Yuri Narushima. All rights reserved. First published in
1998 by Soubisha Inc., Tokyo. English publication rights arranged
through Soubisha Inc., Tokyo. English text © 2002 by Mixx
Entertainment, Inc. TOKYOPOP® is a registered trademark and
the Robofish logo is a trademark of Mixx Entertainment, Inc.

All rights reserved. No portion of this book may be reproduced or
transmitted in any form or by any means without written permission
from the copyright holders. This graphic novel is a work of fiction.
Any resemblance to actual events or locales or persons, living or dead,
is entirely coincidental.

ISBN: 1-931514-62-3

First TOKYOPOP® printing: March 2002

10 9 8 7 6 5 4 3 2 1

Manufactured in Canada

Planet Ladder

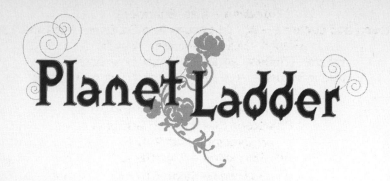

CONTENTS

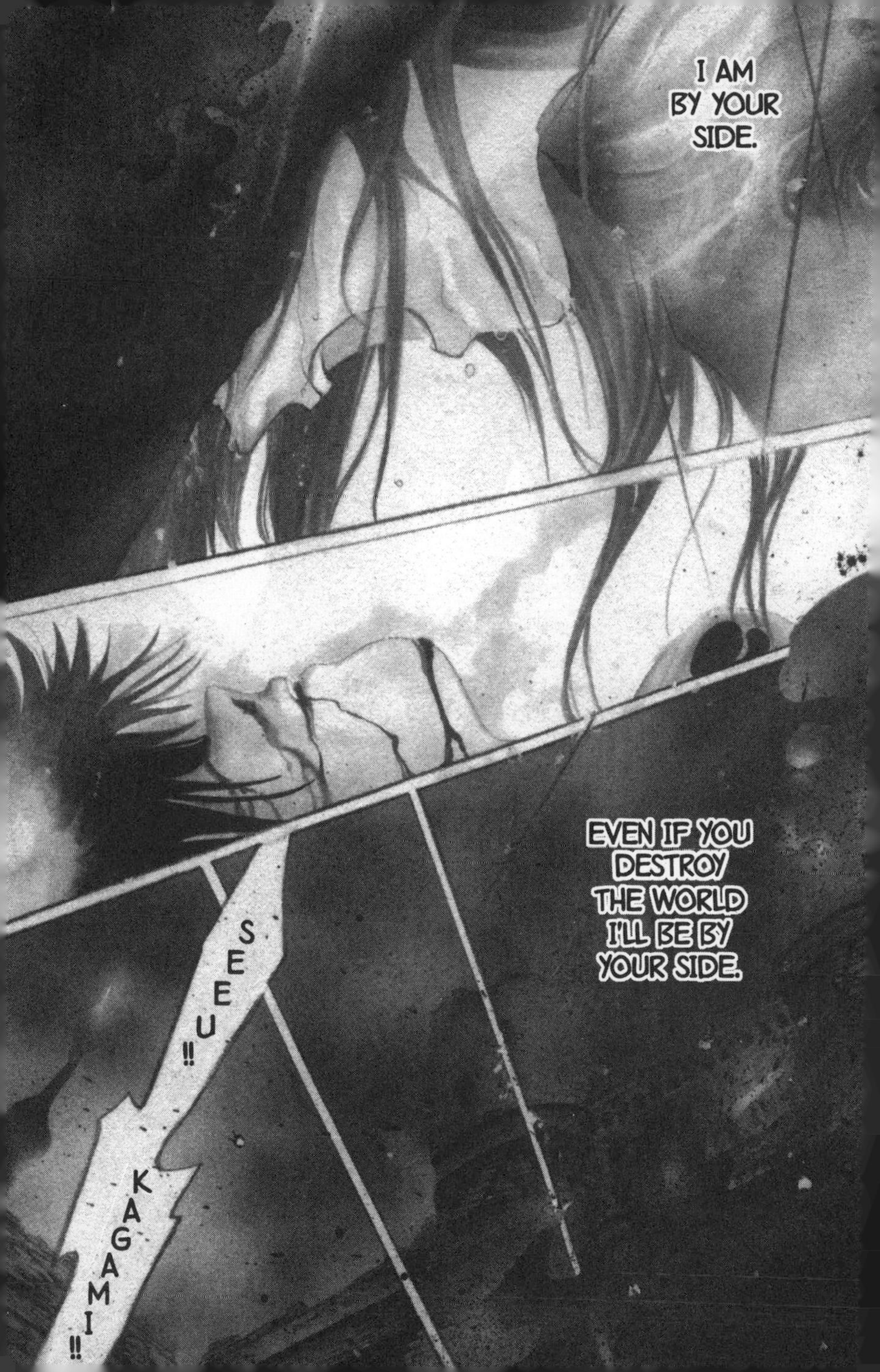
I AM BY YOUR SIDE.
EVEN IF YOU DESTROY THE WORLD I'LL BE BY YOUR SIDE.
SEEU!!
KAGAMI!!

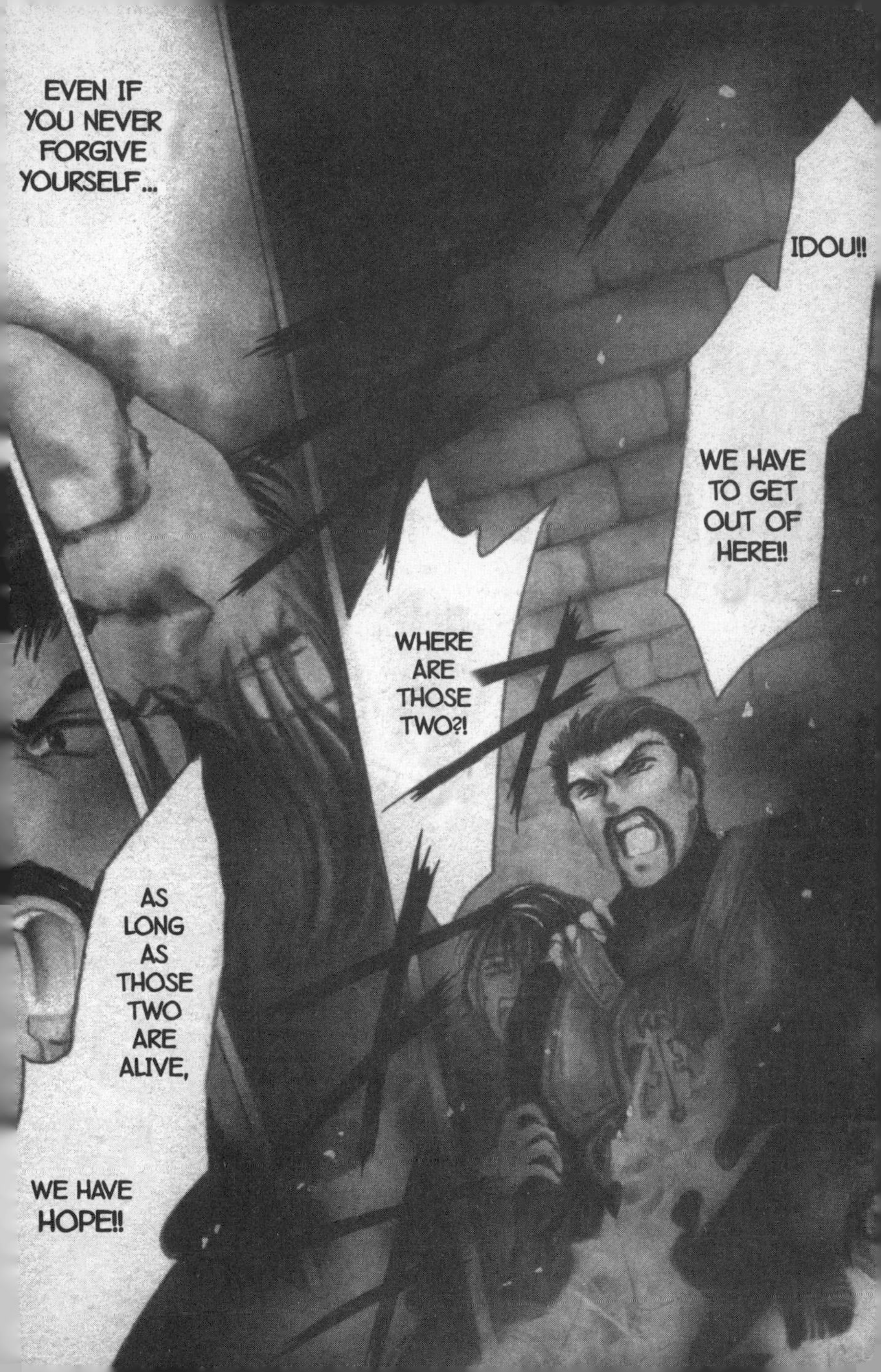
IDOU!!
WE HAVE TO GET OUT OF HERE!!
WHERE ARE THOSE TWO?!
EVEN IF YOU NEVER FORGIVE YOURSELF...
AS LONG AS THOSE TWO ARE ALIVE,
WE HAVE HOPE!!

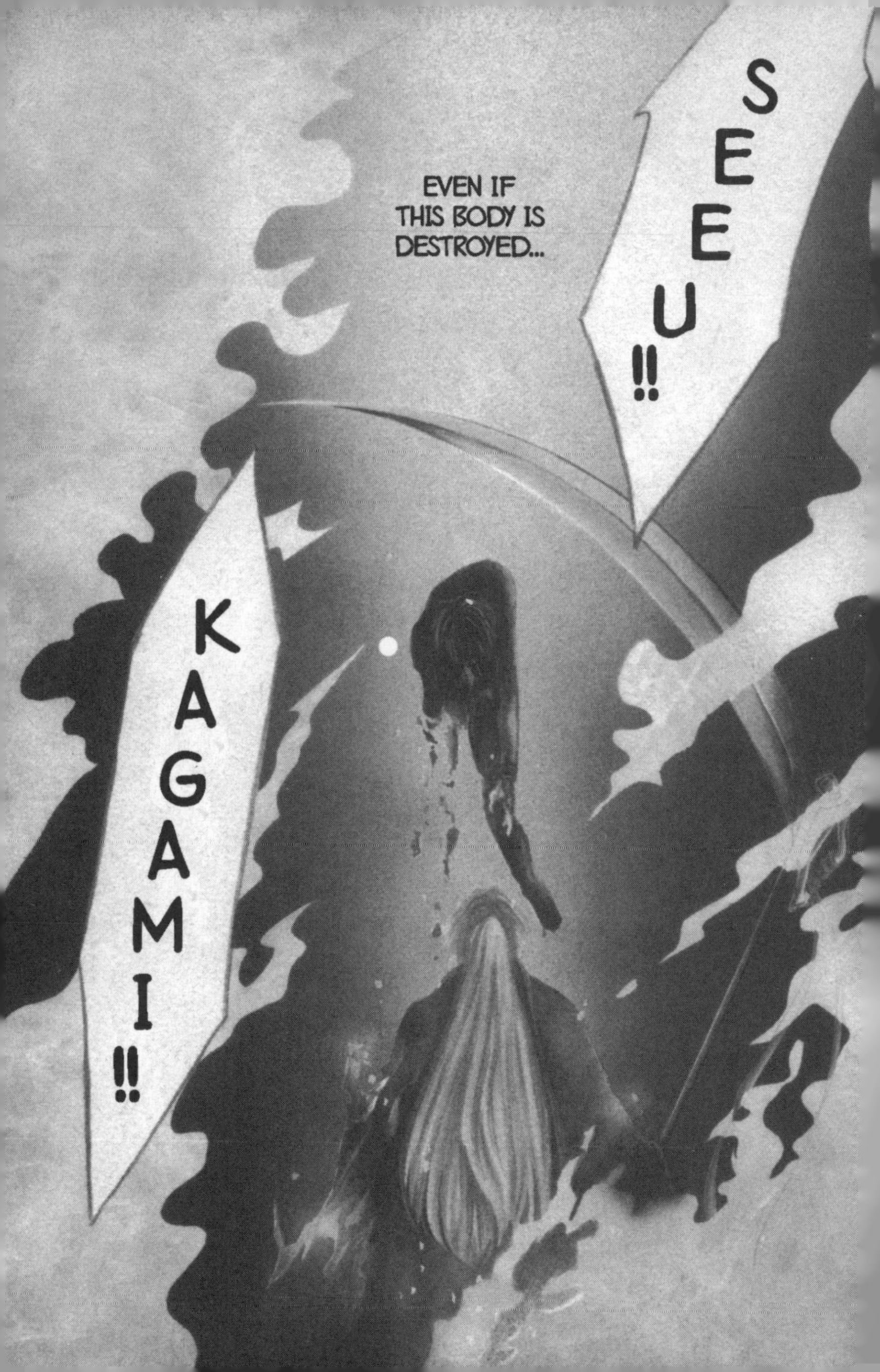
SEEU!!
EVEN IF THIS BODY IS DESTROYED...
KAGAMI!!

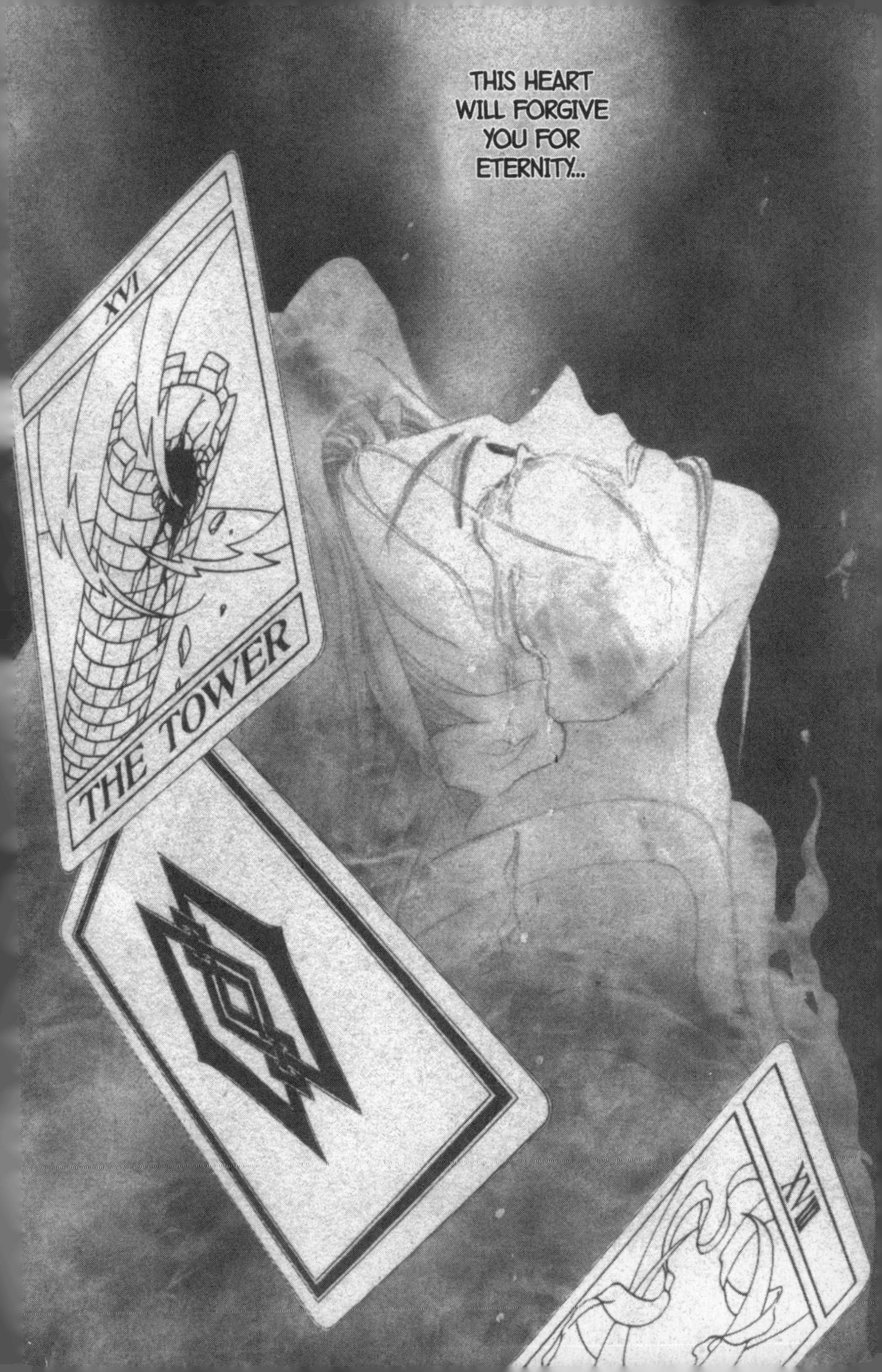
THIS HEART WILL FORGIVE YOU FOR ETERNITY...
XVI
THE TOWER

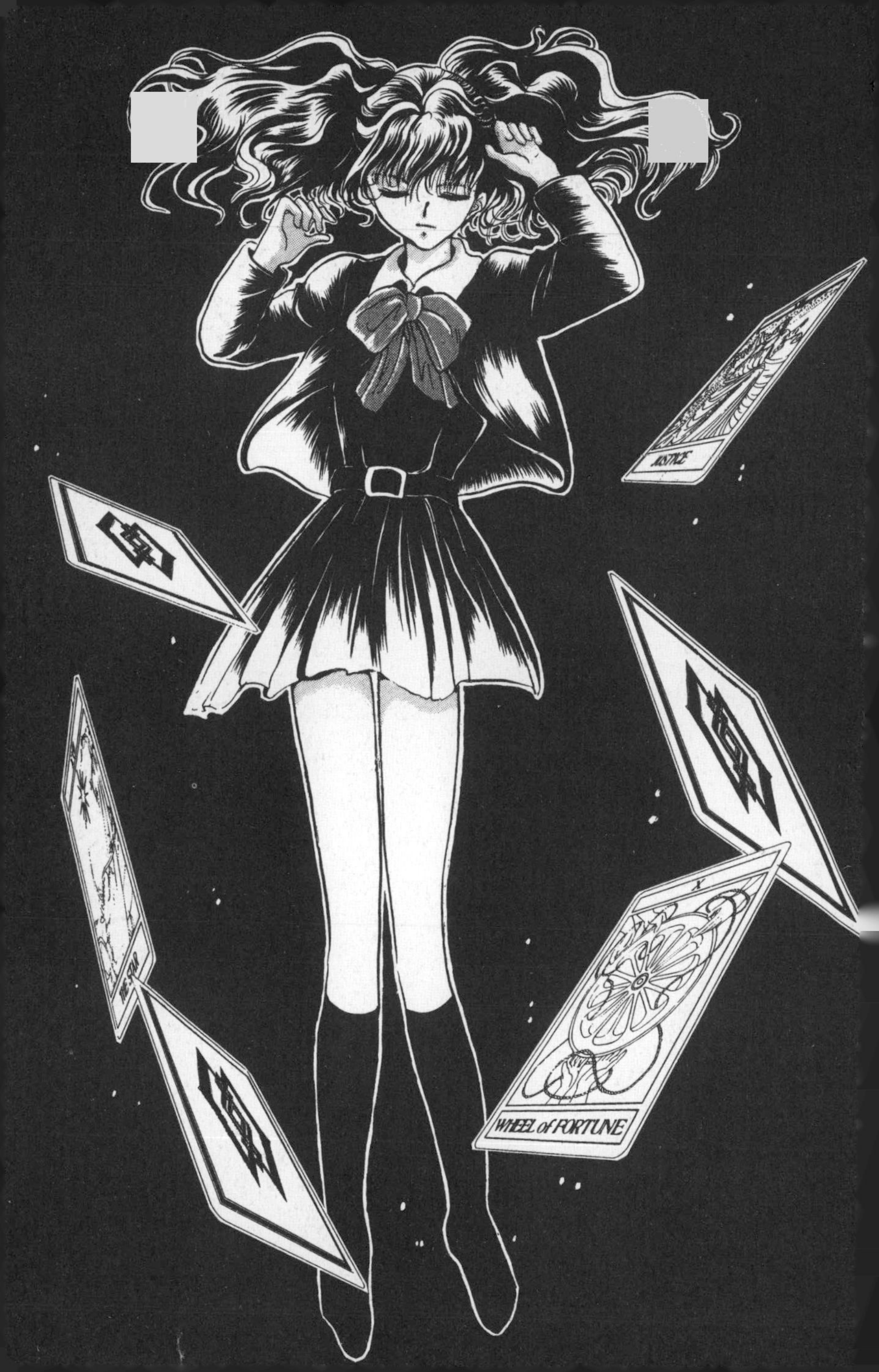
JUSTICE
X
WHEEL of FORTUNE
THE STAR

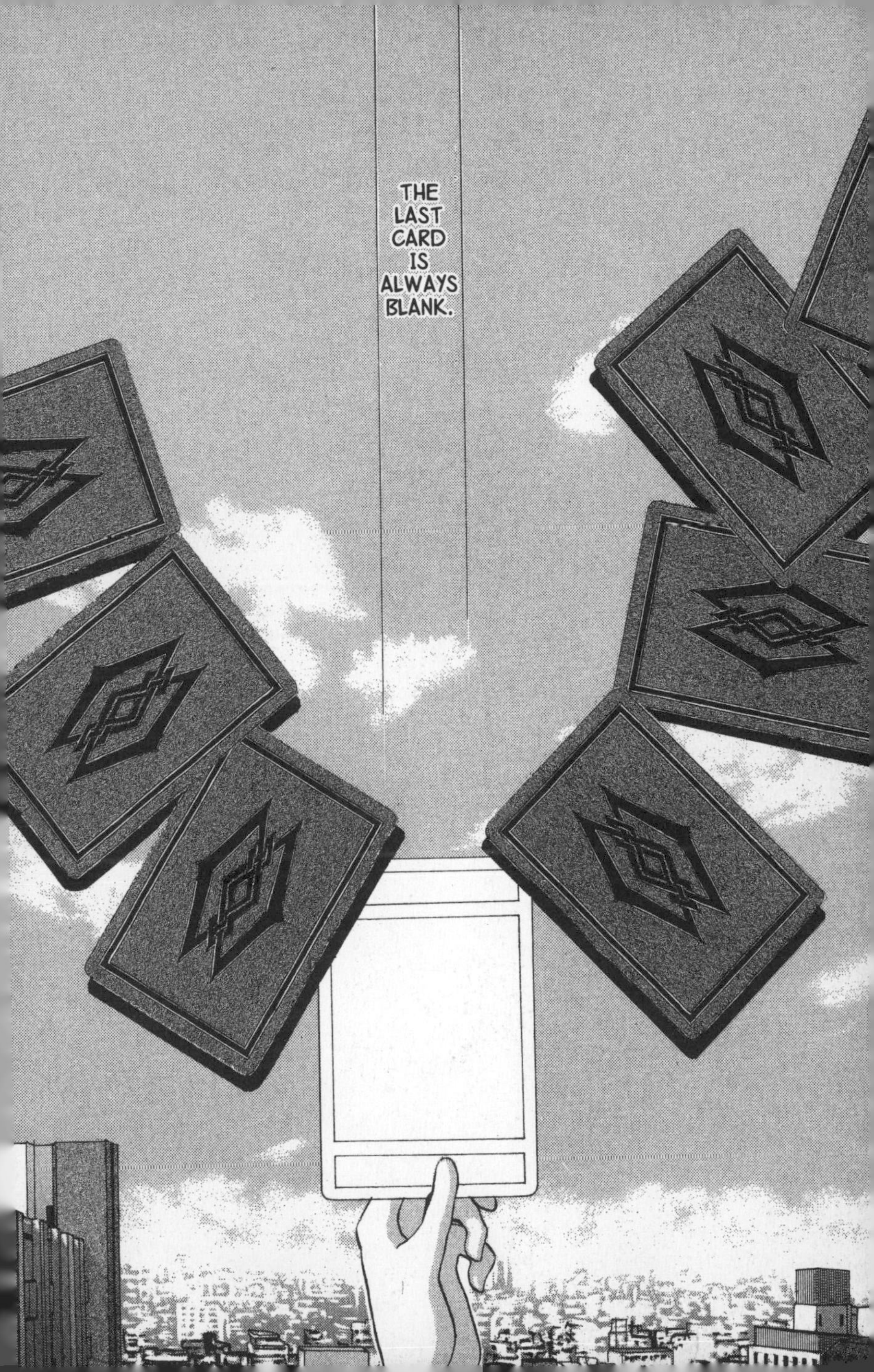
THE LAST CARD IS ALWAYS BLANK.

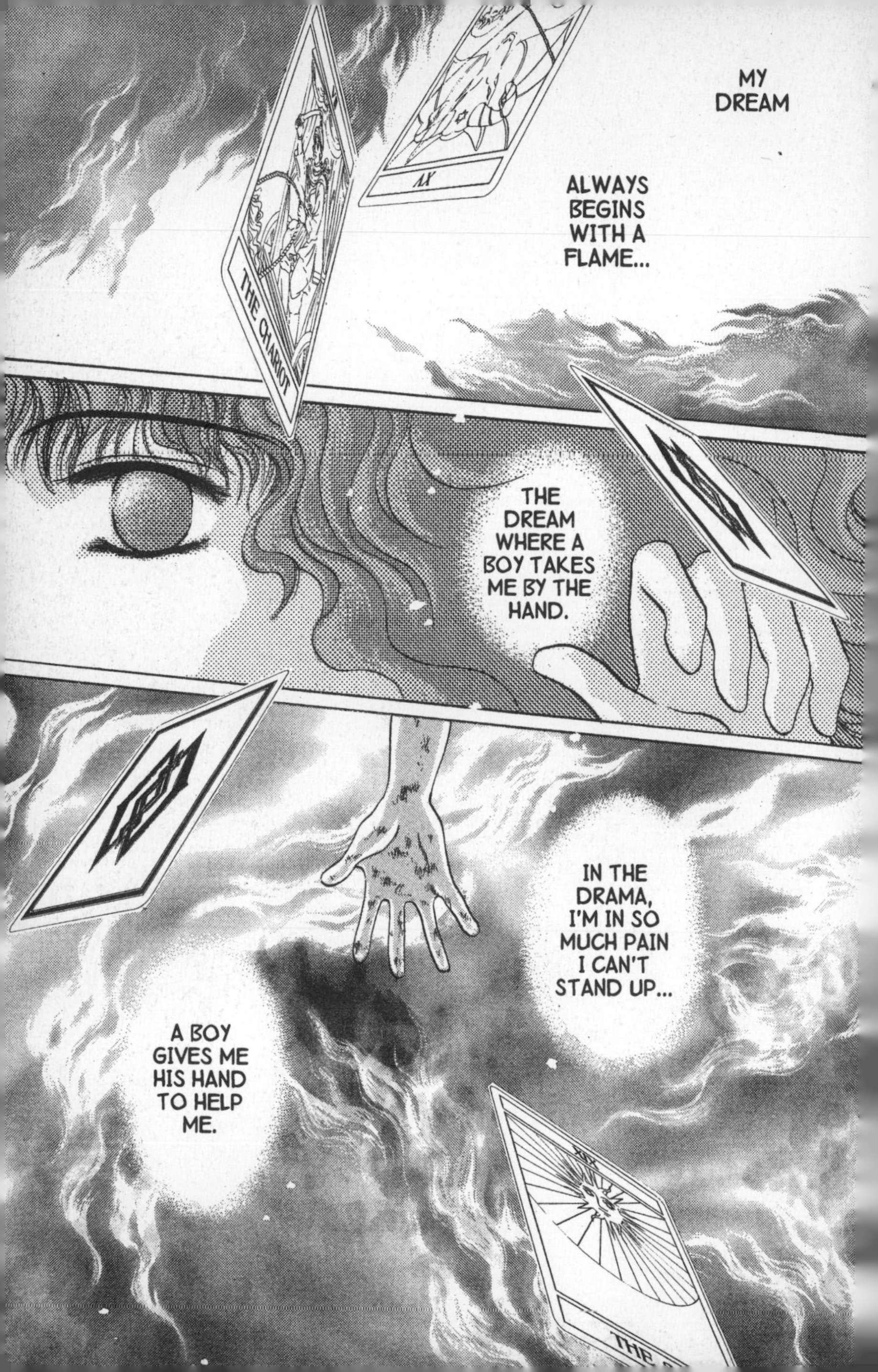
MY DREAM
ALWAYS BEGINS WITH A FLAME...
XV
THE CHARIOT
THE DREAM WHERE A BOY TAKES ME BY THE HAND.
IN THE DRAMA, I'M IN SO MUCH PAIN I CAN'T STAND UP...
A BOY GIVES ME HIS HAND TO HELP ME.

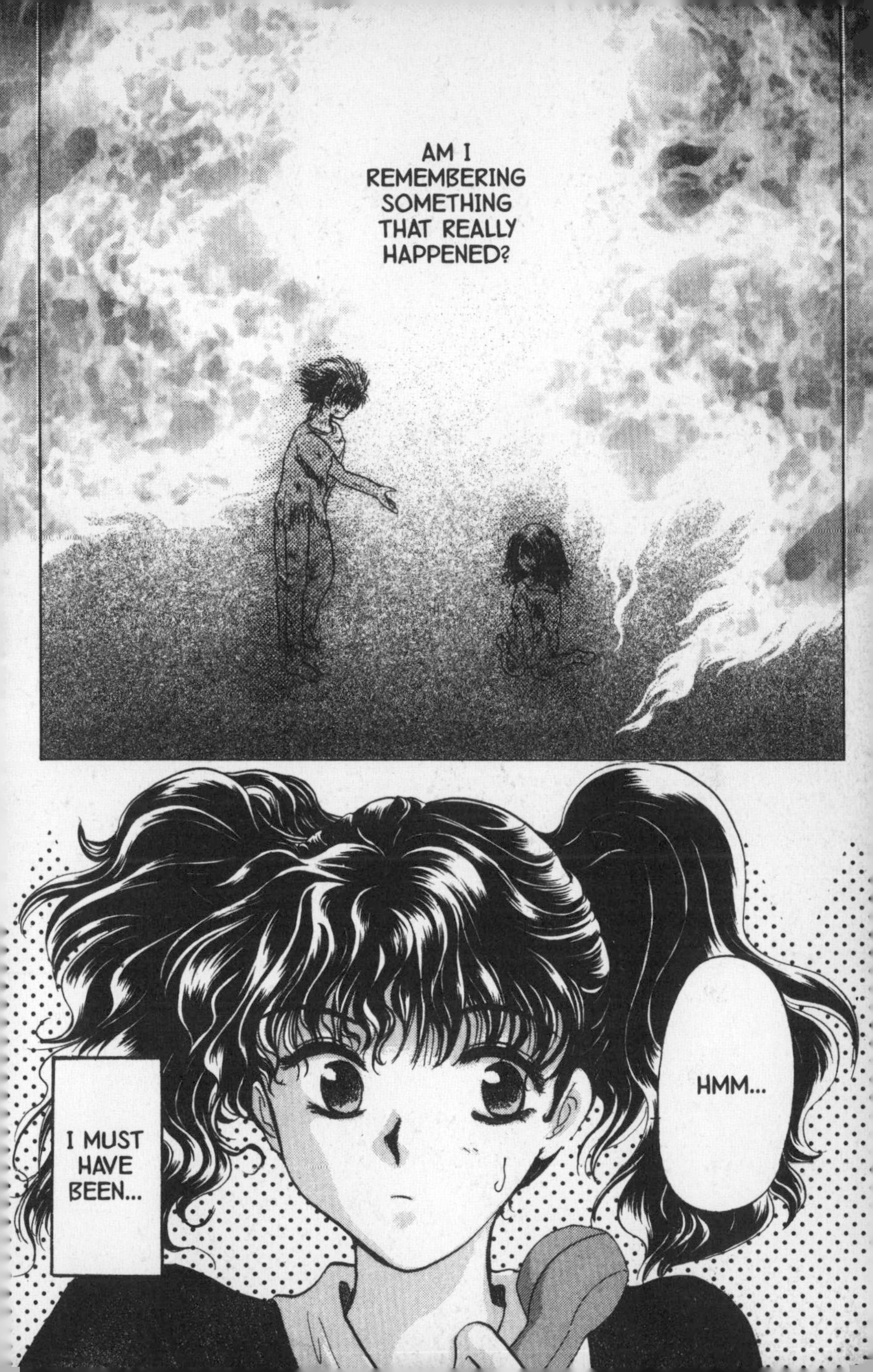
AM I REMEMBERING SOMETHING THAT REALLY HAPPENED?
HMM...
I MUST HAVE BEEN...

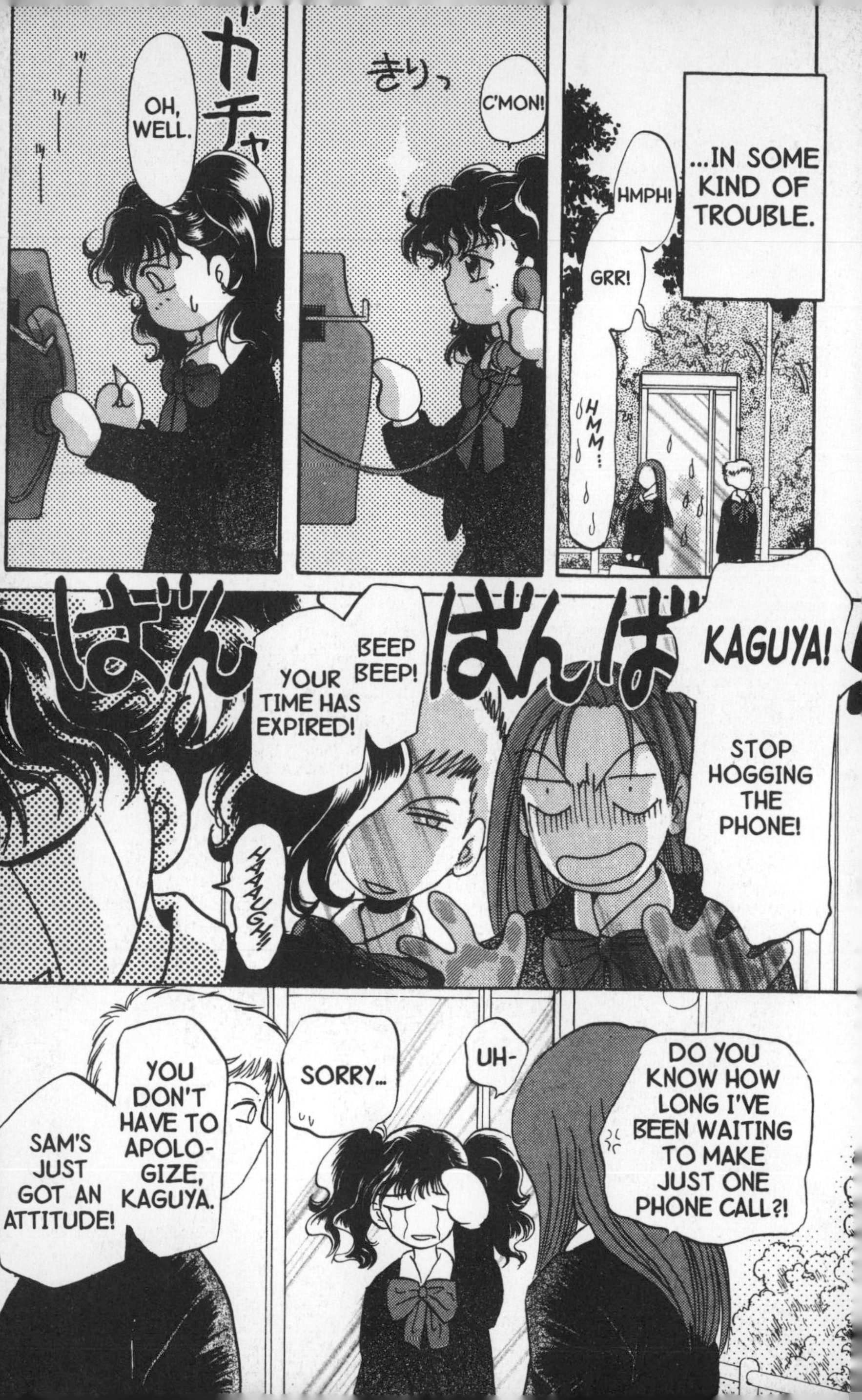
...IN SOME KIND OF TROUBLE.
HMPH!
GRR!
HMM...
きりっ
C'MON!
ガチャ
OH, WELL.
ツー ツー ツー
KAGUYA!
STOP HOGGING THE PHONE!
ばんば
BEEP BEEP!
YOUR TIME HAS EXPIRED!
ばん
HAAAUGH!!
DO YOU KNOW HOW LONG I'VE BEEN WAITING TO MAKE JUST ONE PHONE CALL?!
UH-
SORRY...
YOU DON'T HAVE TO APOLOGIZE, KAGUYA.
SAM'S JUST GOT AN ATTITUDE!

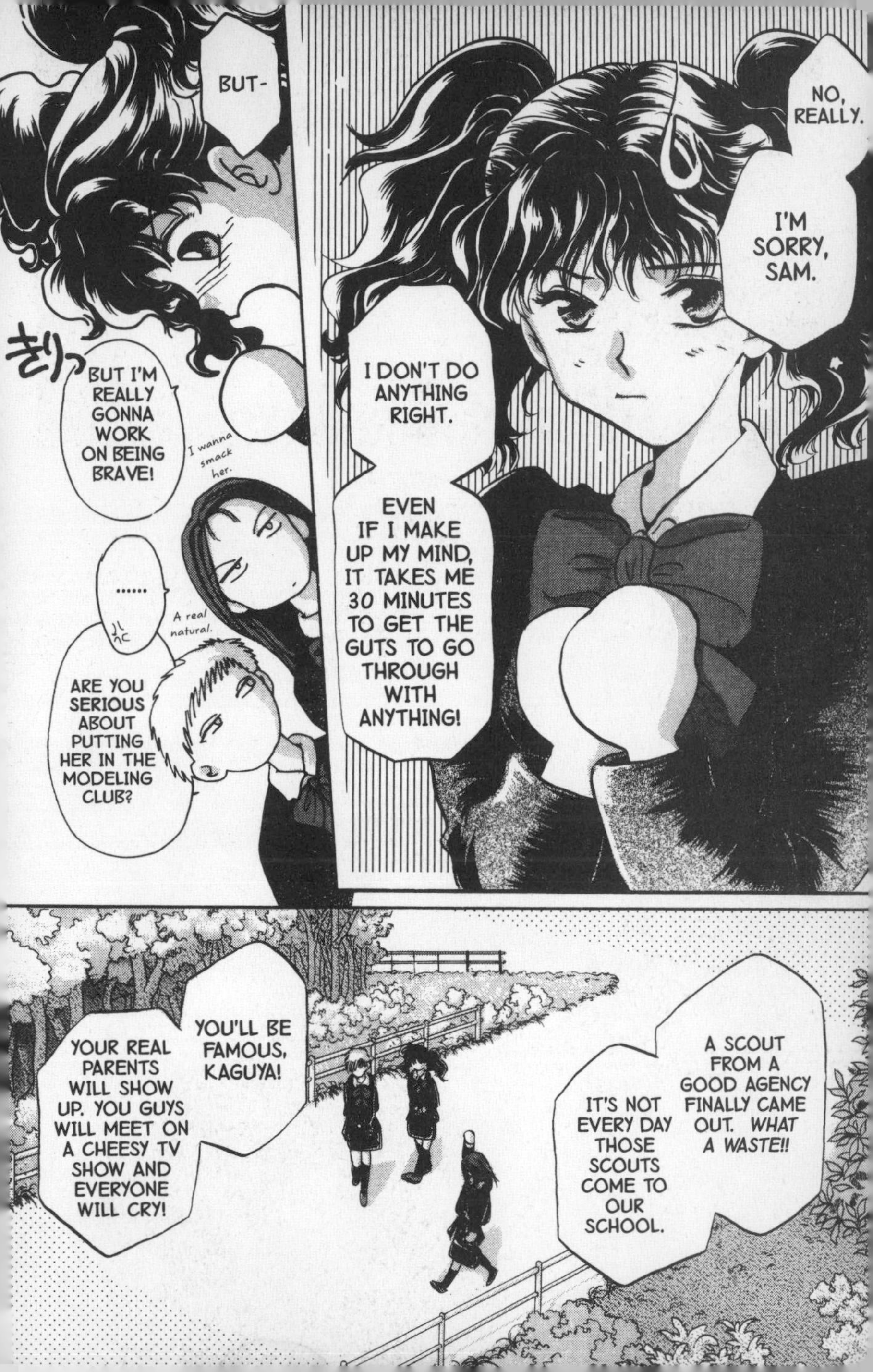
NO, REALLY.
I'M SORRY, SAM.
I DON'T DO ANYTHING RIGHT.
EVEN IF I MAKE UP MY MIND, IT TAKES ME 30 MINUTES TO GET THE GUTS TO GO THROUGH WITH ANYTHING!
BUT-
きりっ
BUT I'M REALLY GONNA WORK ON BEING BRAVE!
I wanna smack her.
......
A real natural.
ARE YOU SERIOUS ABOUT PUTTING HER IN THE MODELING CLUB?
A SCOUT FROM A GOOD AGENCY FINALLY CAME OUT. *WHAT A WASTE!!*
IT'S NOT EVERY DAY THOSE SCOUTS COME TO OUR SCHOOL.
YOU'LL BE FAMOUS, KAGUYA!
YOUR REAL PARENTS WILL SHOW UP. YOU GUYS WILL MEET ON A CHEESY TV SHOW AND EVERYONE WILL CRY!

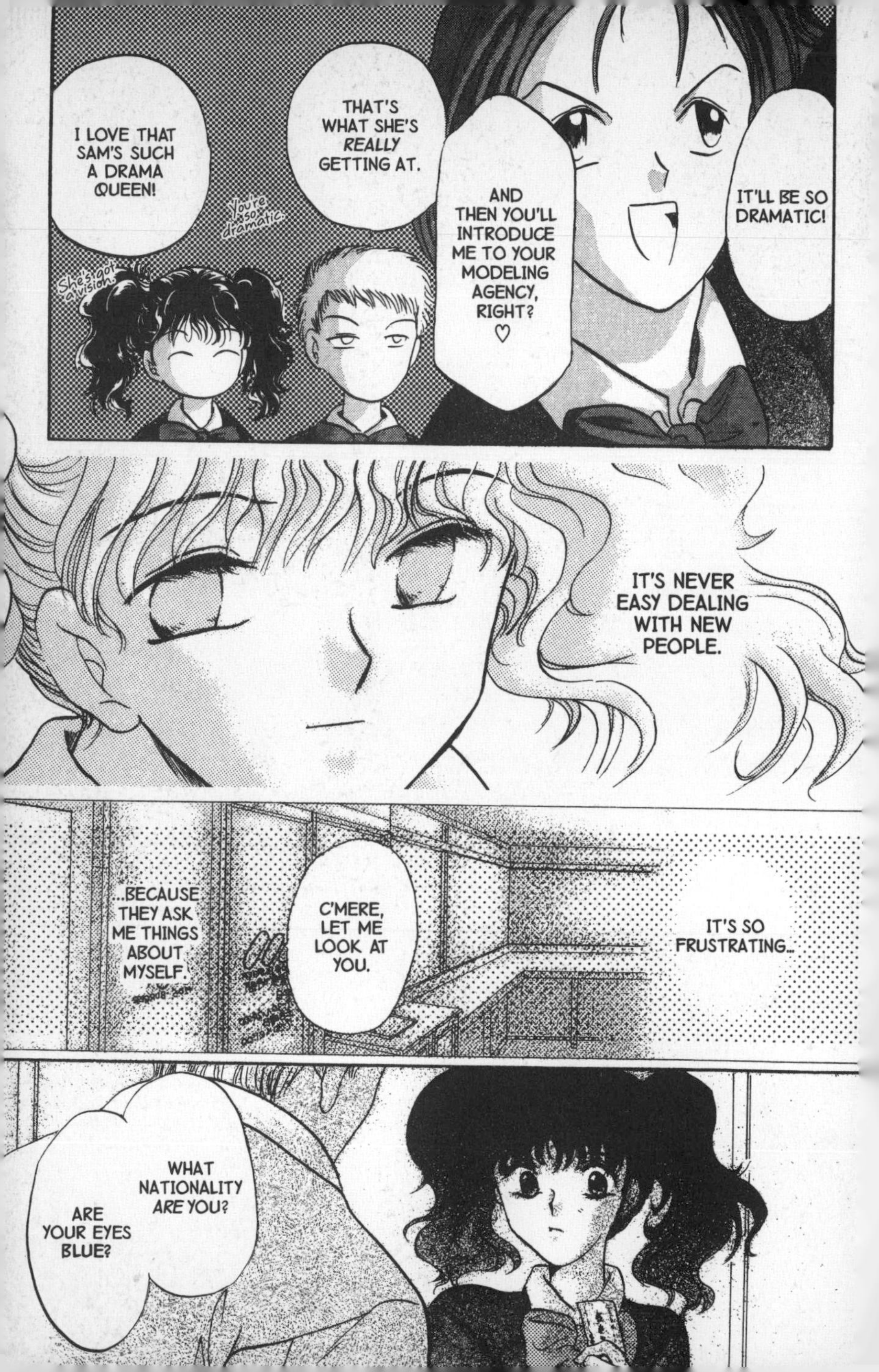
IT'LL BE SO DRAMATIC!
AND THEN YOU'LL INTRODUCE ME TO YOUR MODELING AGENCY, RIGHT? ♡
THAT'S WHAT SHE'S *REALLY* GETTING AT.
I LOVE THAT SAM'S SUCH A DRAMA QUEEN!
You're so dramatic.
She's got a vision.
IT'S NEVER EASY DEALING WITH NEW PEOPLE.
IT'S SO FRUSTRATING...
C'MERE, LET ME LOOK AT YOU.
...BECAUSE THEY ASK ME THINGS ABOUT MYSELF.
WHAT NATIONALITY *ARE* YOU?
ARE YOUR EYES BLUE?

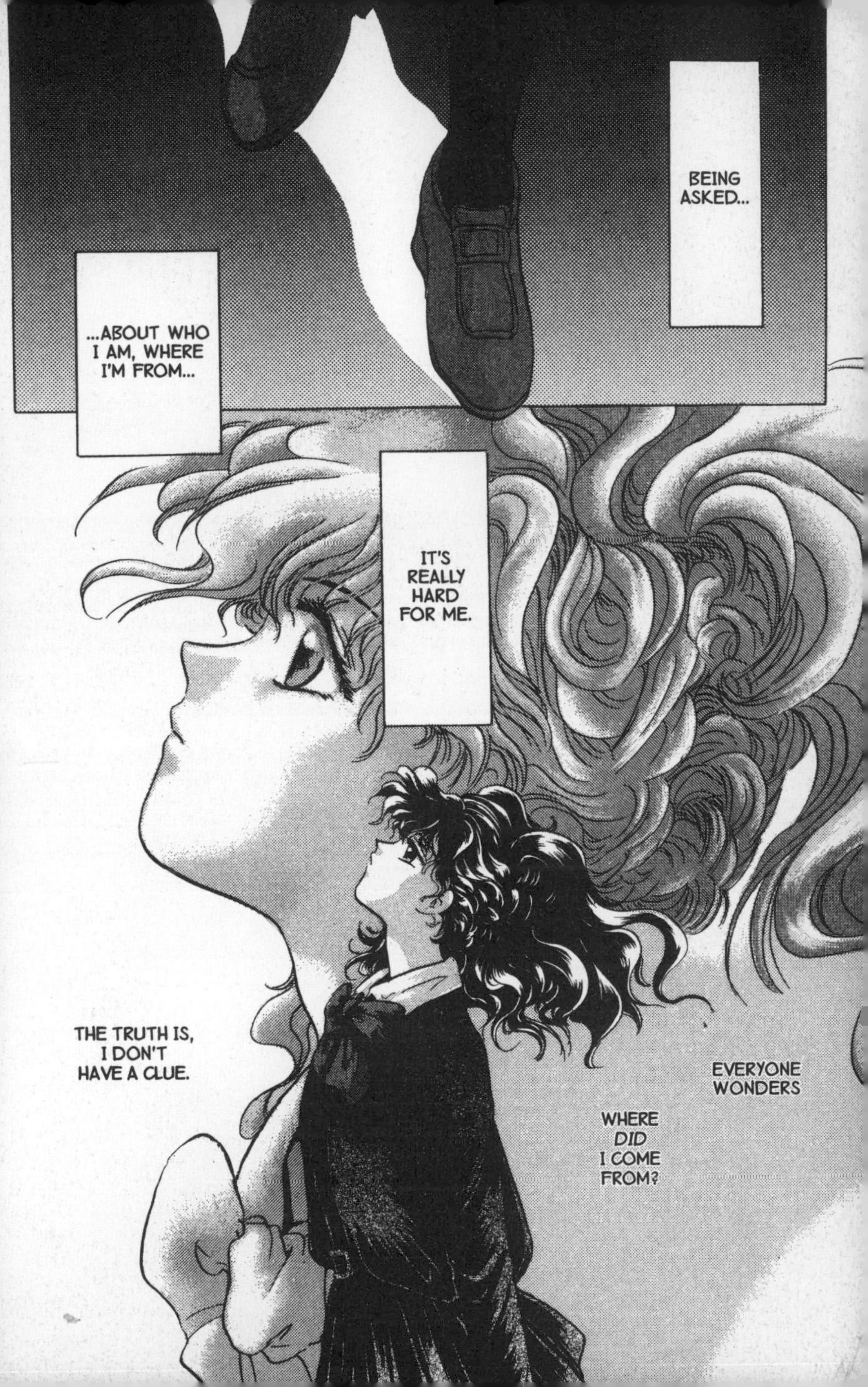
BEING ASKED...
...ABOUT WHO I AM, WHERE I'M FROM...
IT'S REALLY HARD FOR ME.
EVERYONE WONDERS
WHERE *DID* I COME FROM?
THE TRUTH IS, I DON'T HAVE A CLUE.

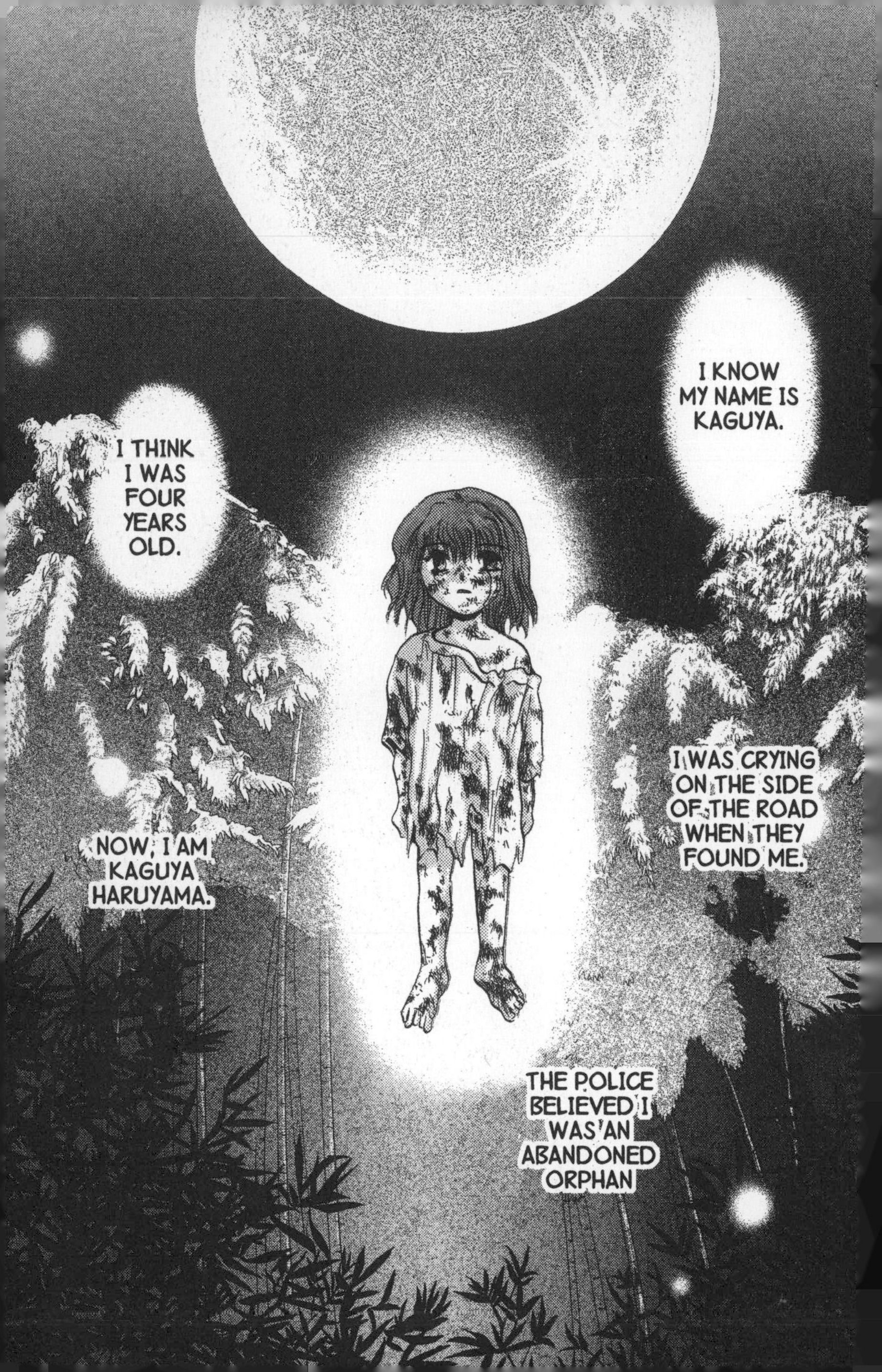

I KNOW MY NAME IS KAGUYA.
I THINK I WAS FOUR YEARS OLD.
I WAS CRYING ON THE SIDE OF THE ROAD WHEN THEY FOUND ME.
THE POLICE BELIEVED I WAS AN ABANDONED ORPHAN
NOW, I AM KAGUYA HARUYAMA.

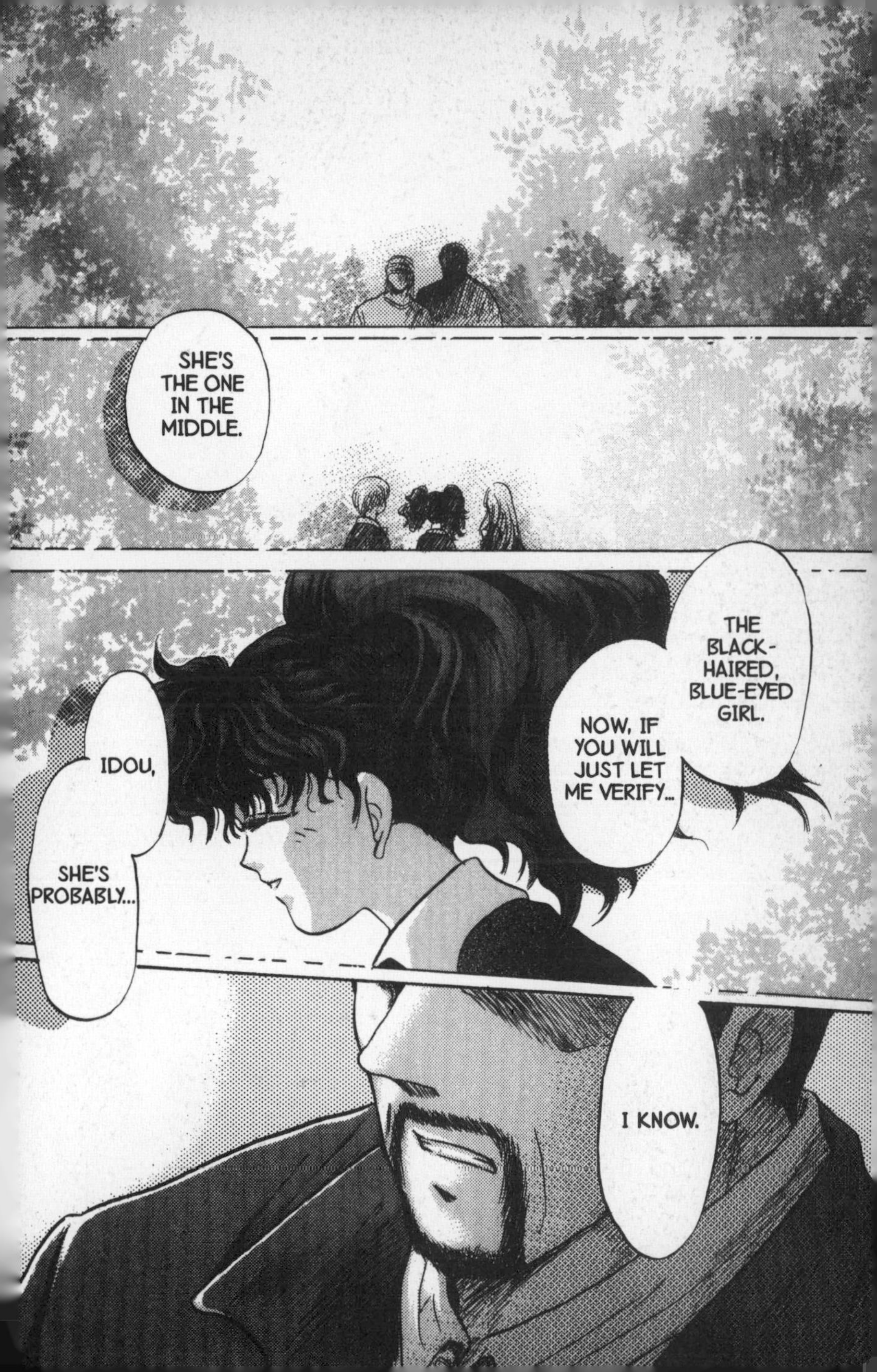
SHE'S THE ONE IN THE MIDDLE.
THE BLACK-HAIRED, BLUE-EYED GIRL.
NOW, IF YOU WILL JUST LET ME VERIFY...
IDOU, SHE'S PROBABLY...
I KNOW.

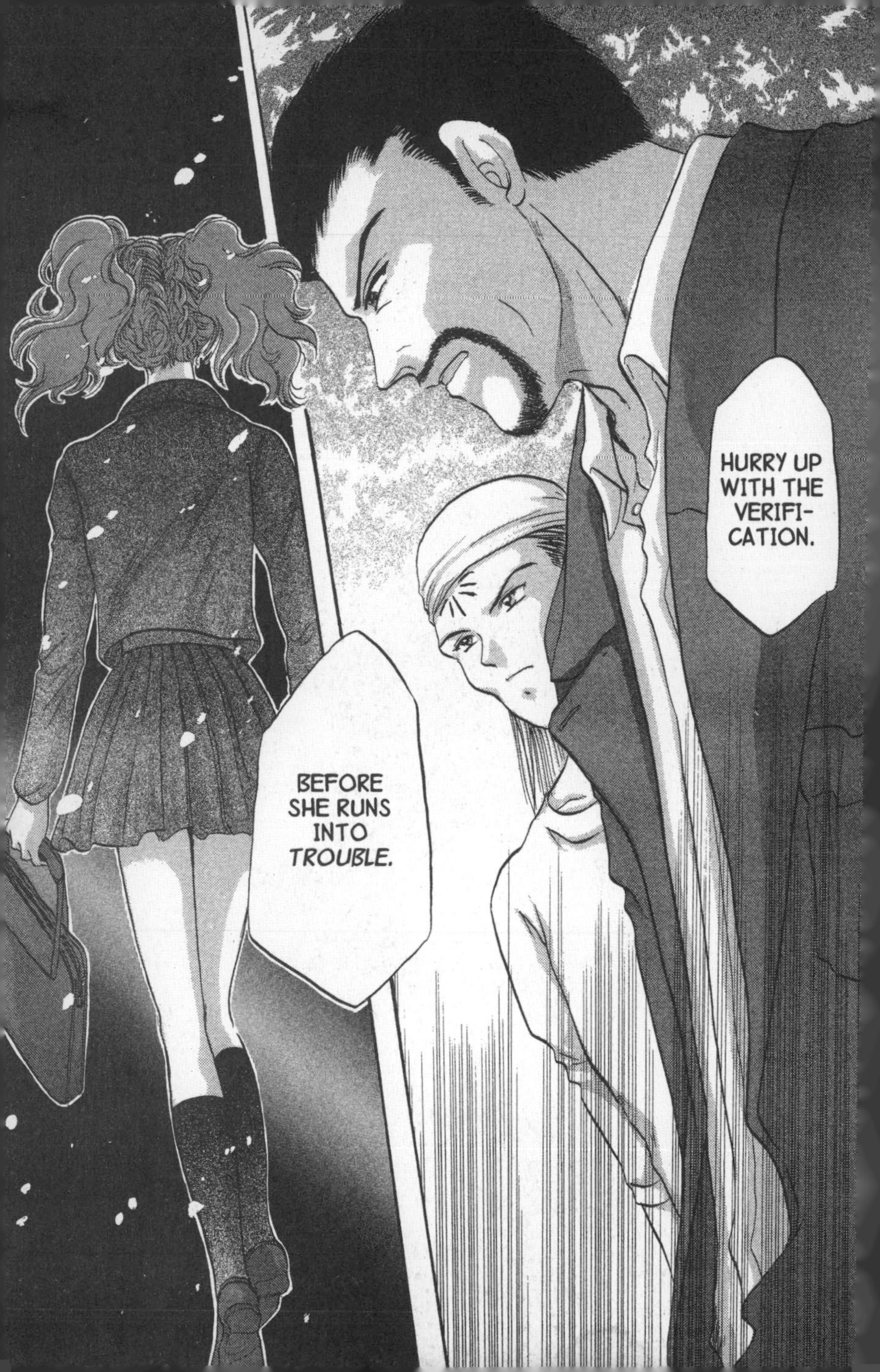
HURRY UP WITH THE VERIFI- CATION.
BEFORE SHE RUNS INTO *TROUBLE.*

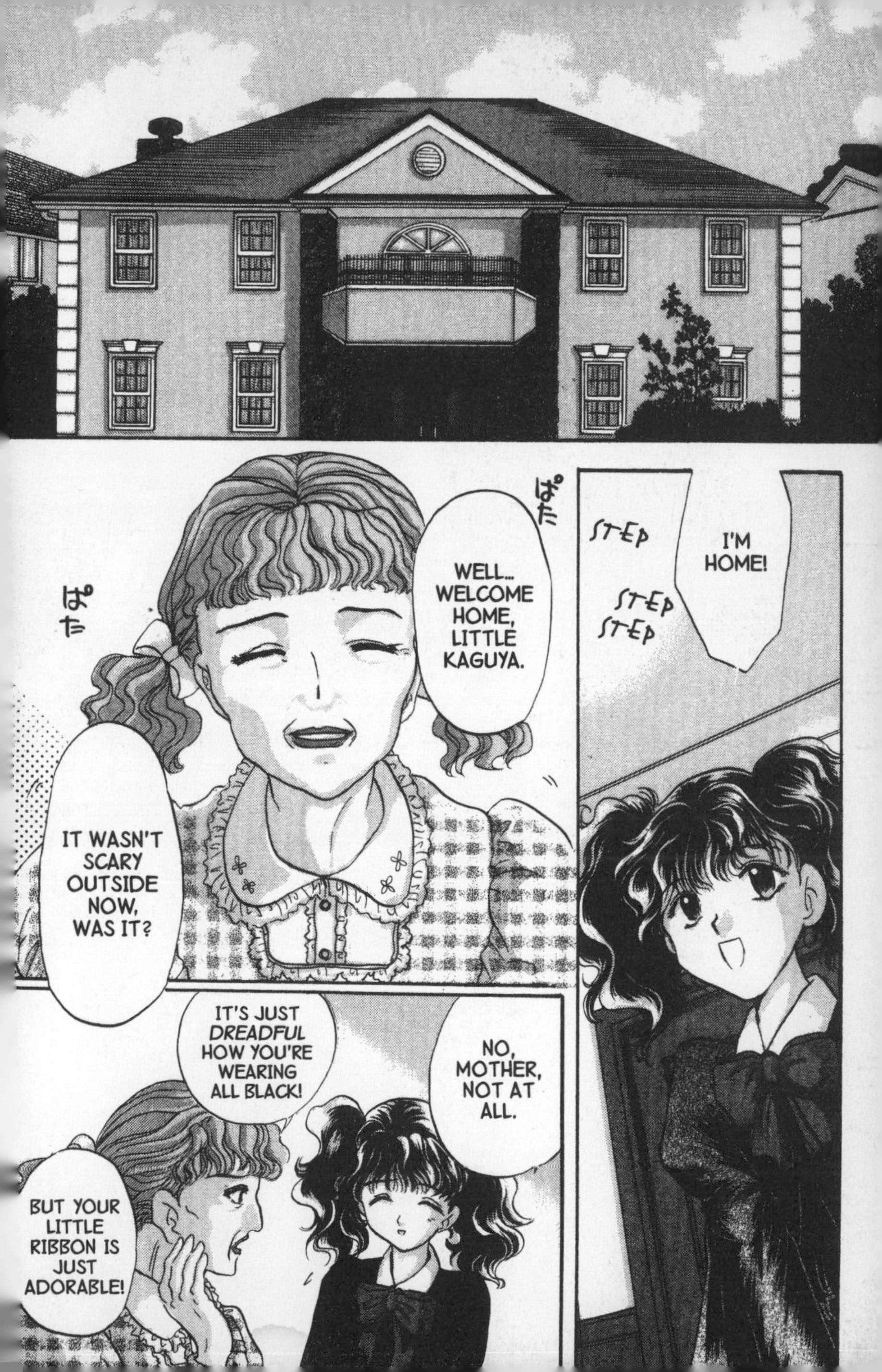
I'M HOME!
STEP
STEP
STEP
ぱた
WELL... WELCOME HOME, LITTLE KAGUYA.
ぱた
IT WASN'T SCARY OUTSIDE NOW, WAS IT?
NO, MOTHER, NOT AT ALL.
IT'S JUST *DREADFUL* HOW YOU'RE WEARING ALL BLACK!
BUT YOUR LITTLE RIBBON IS JUST ADORABLE!

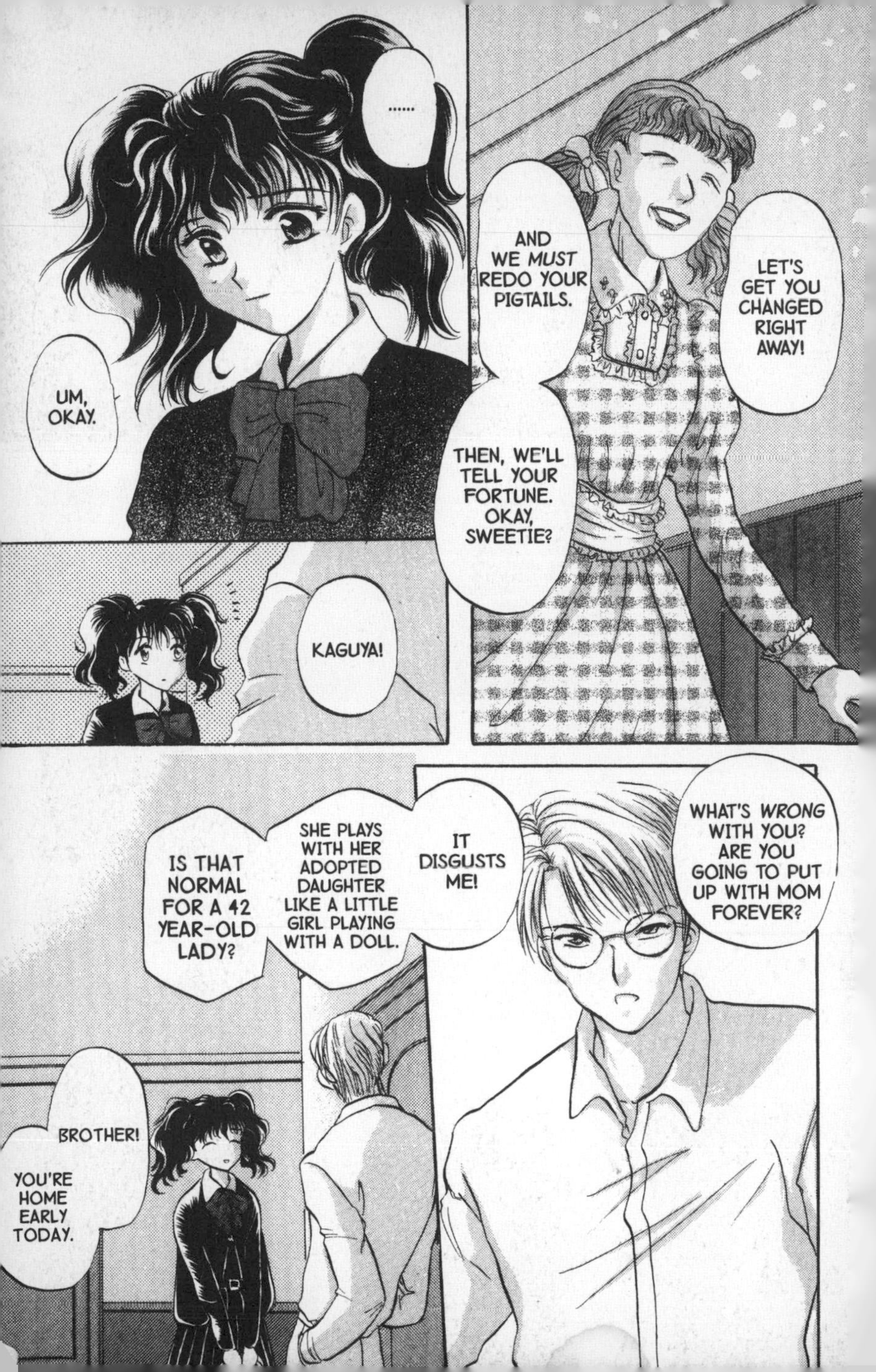
LET'S GET YOU CHANGED RIGHT AWAY!
AND WE *MUST* REDO YOUR PIGTAILS.
THEN, WE'LL TELL YOUR FORTUNE. OKAY, SWEETIE?
......
UM, OKAY.
KAGUYA!
WHAT'S *WRONG* WITH YOU? ARE YOU GOING TO PUT UP WITH MOM FOREVER?
IT DISGUSTS ME!
SHE PLAYS WITH HER ADOPTED DAUGHTER LIKE A LITTLE GIRL PLAYING WITH A DOLL.
IS THAT NORMAL FOR A 42 YEAR-OLD LADY?
BROTHER!
YOU'RE HOME EARLY TODAY.

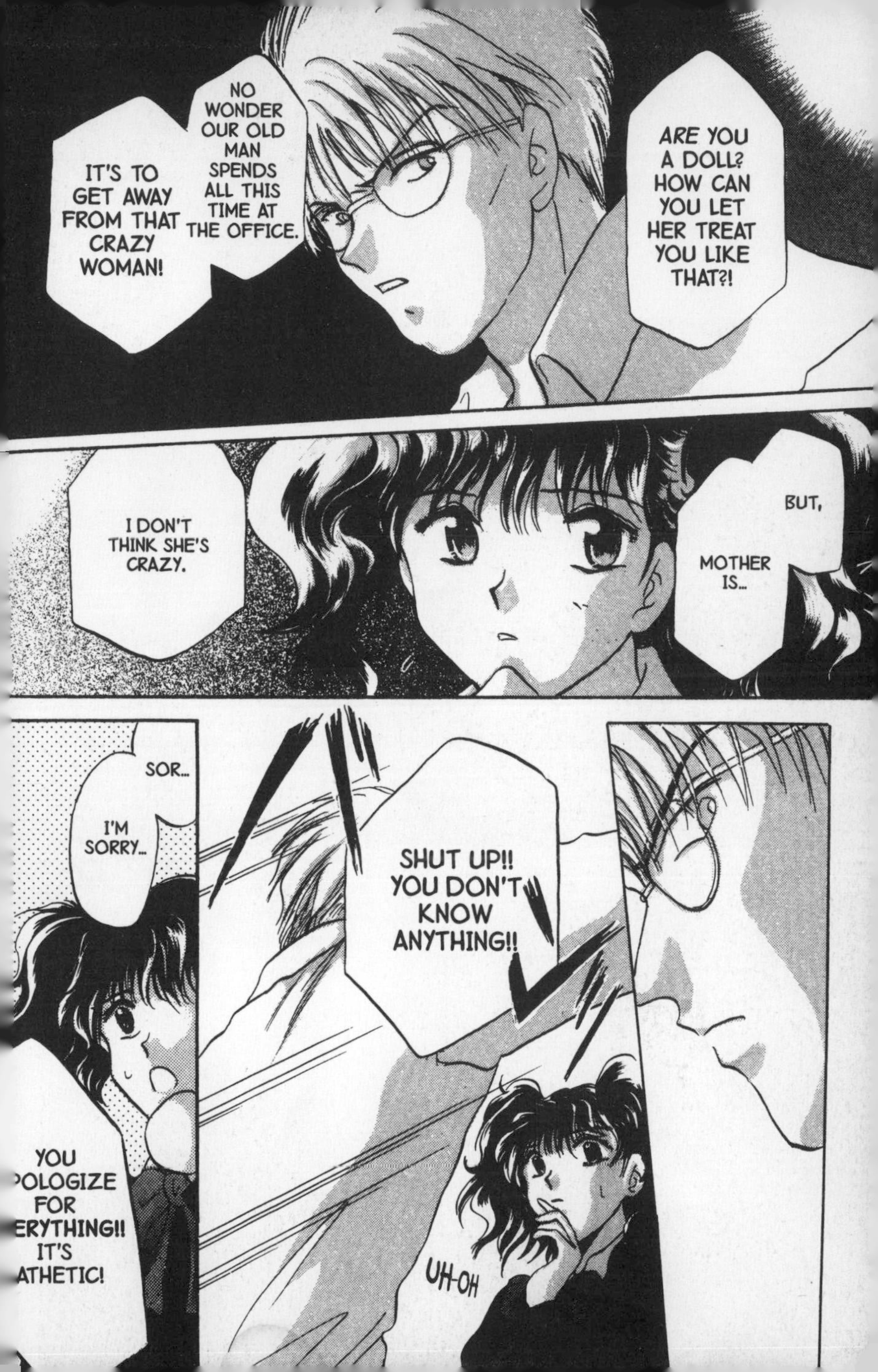
ARE YOU A DOLL? HOW CAN YOU LET HER TREAT YOU LIKE THAT?!
NO WONDER OUR OLD MAN SPENDS ALL THIS TIME AT THE OFFICE.
IT'S TO GET AWAY FROM THAT CRAZY WOMAN!
BUT,
MOTHER IS...
I DON'T THINK SHE'S CRAZY.
SHUT UP!! YOU DON'T KNOW ANYTHING!!
UH-OH
SOR...
I'M SORRY...
YOU POLOGIZE FOR ERYTHING!! IT'S ATHETIC!

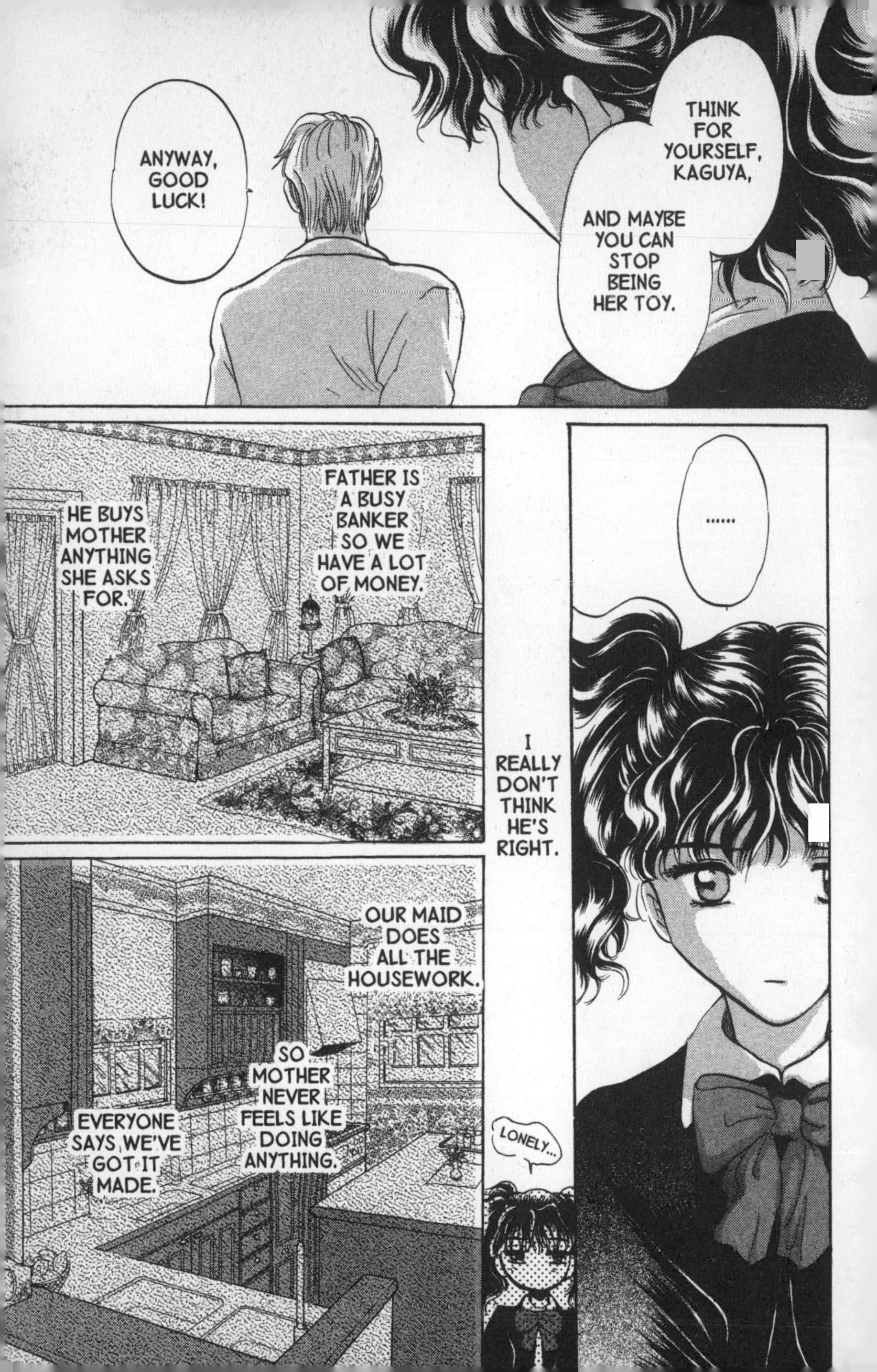
THINK FOR YOURSELF, KAGUYA,
AND MAYBE YOU CAN STOP BEING HER TOY.
ANYWAY, GOOD LUCK!
......
I REALLY DON'T THINK HE'S RIGHT.
LONELY...
FATHER IS A BUSY BANKER SO WE HAVE A LOT OF MONEY.
HE BUYS MOTHER ANYTHING SHE ASKS FOR.
OUR MAID DOES ALL THE HOUSEWORK.
SO MOTHER NEVER FEELS LIKE DOING ANYTHING.
EVERYONE SAYS WE'VE GOT IT MADE.

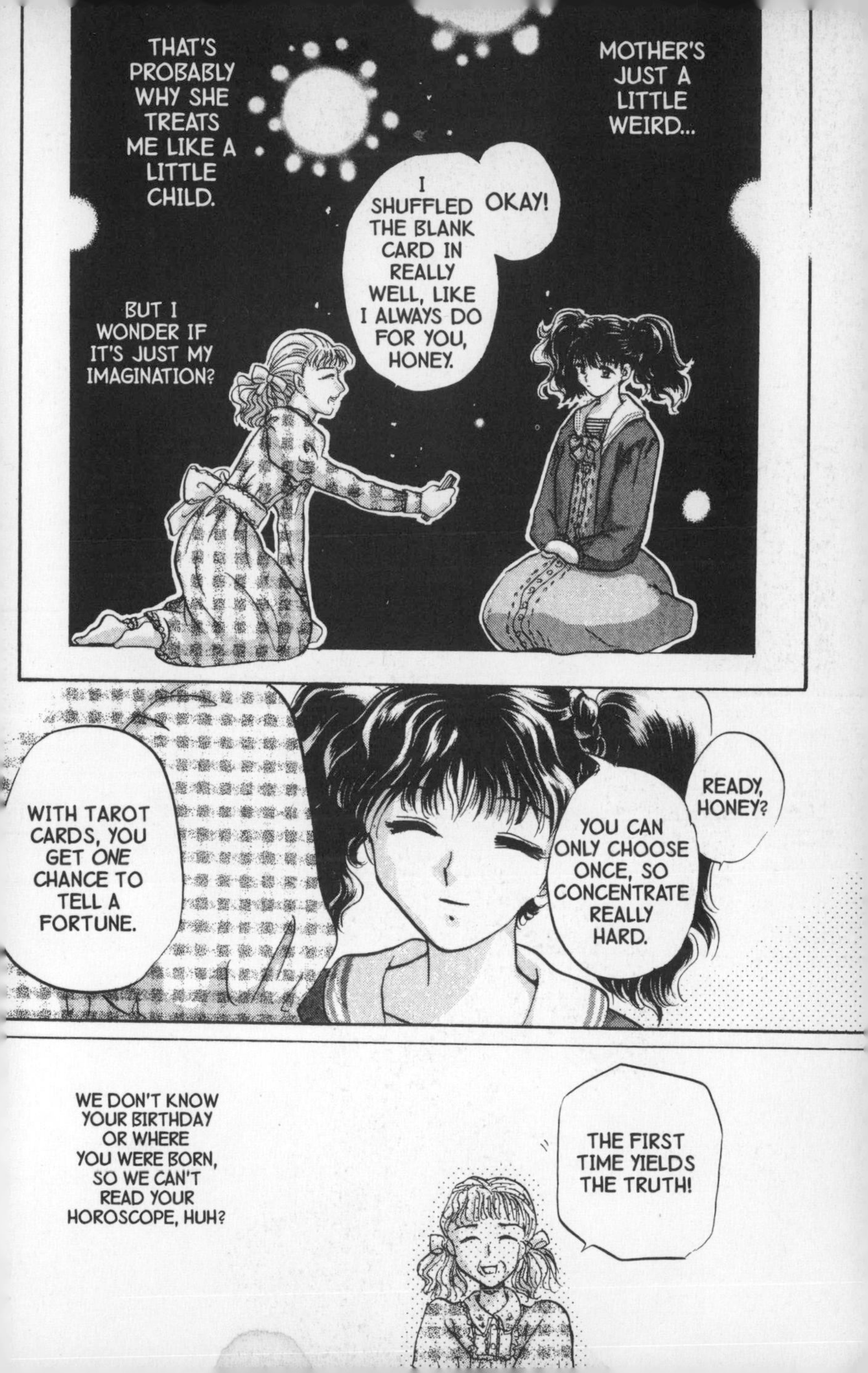
MOTHER'S JUST A LITTLE WEIRD...
THAT'S PROBABLY WHY SHE TREATS ME LIKE A LITTLE CHILD.
OKAY!
I SHUFFLED THE BLANK CARD IN REALLY WELL, LIKE I ALWAYS DO FOR YOU, HONEY.
BUT I WONDER IF IT'S JUST MY IMAGINATION?
READY, HONEY?
YOU CAN ONLY CHOOSE ONCE, SO CONCENTRATE REALLY HARD.
WITH TAROT CARDS, YOU GET *ONE* CHANCE TO TELL A FORTUNE.
THE FIRST TIME YIELDS THE TRUTH!
WE DON'T KNOW YOUR BIRTHDAY OR WHERE YOU WERE BORN, SO WE CAN'T READ YOUR HOROSCOPE, HUH?

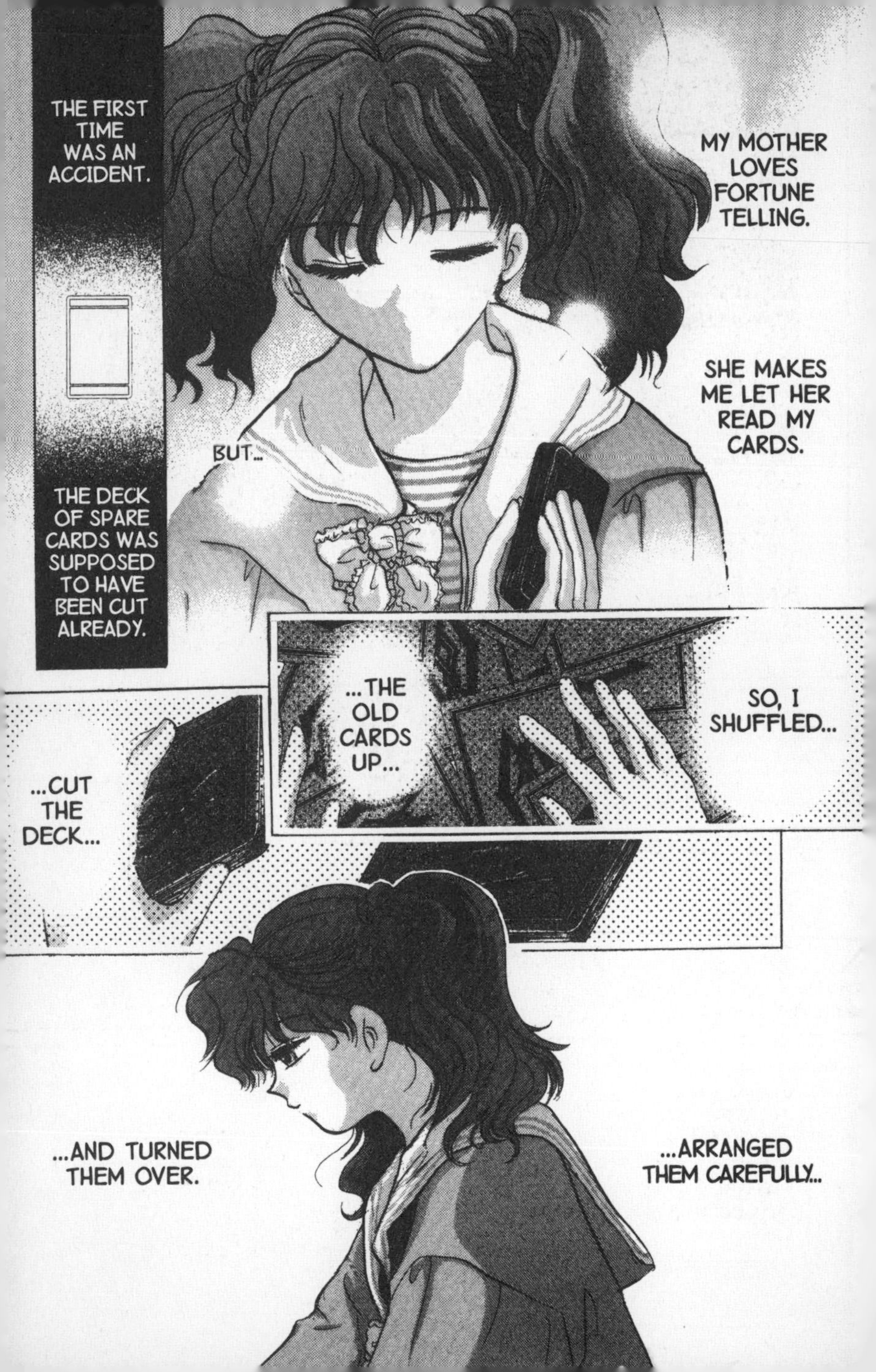
MY MOTHER LOVES FORTUNE TELLING.
SHE MAKES ME LET HER READ MY CARDS.
BUT...
THE FIRST TIME WAS AN ACCIDENT.
THE DECK OF SPARE CARDS WAS SUPPOSED TO HAVE BEEN CUT ALREADY.
SO, I SHUFFLED...
...THE OLD CARDS UP...
...CUT THE DECK...
...ARRANGED THEM CAREFULLY...
...AND TURNED THEM OVER.

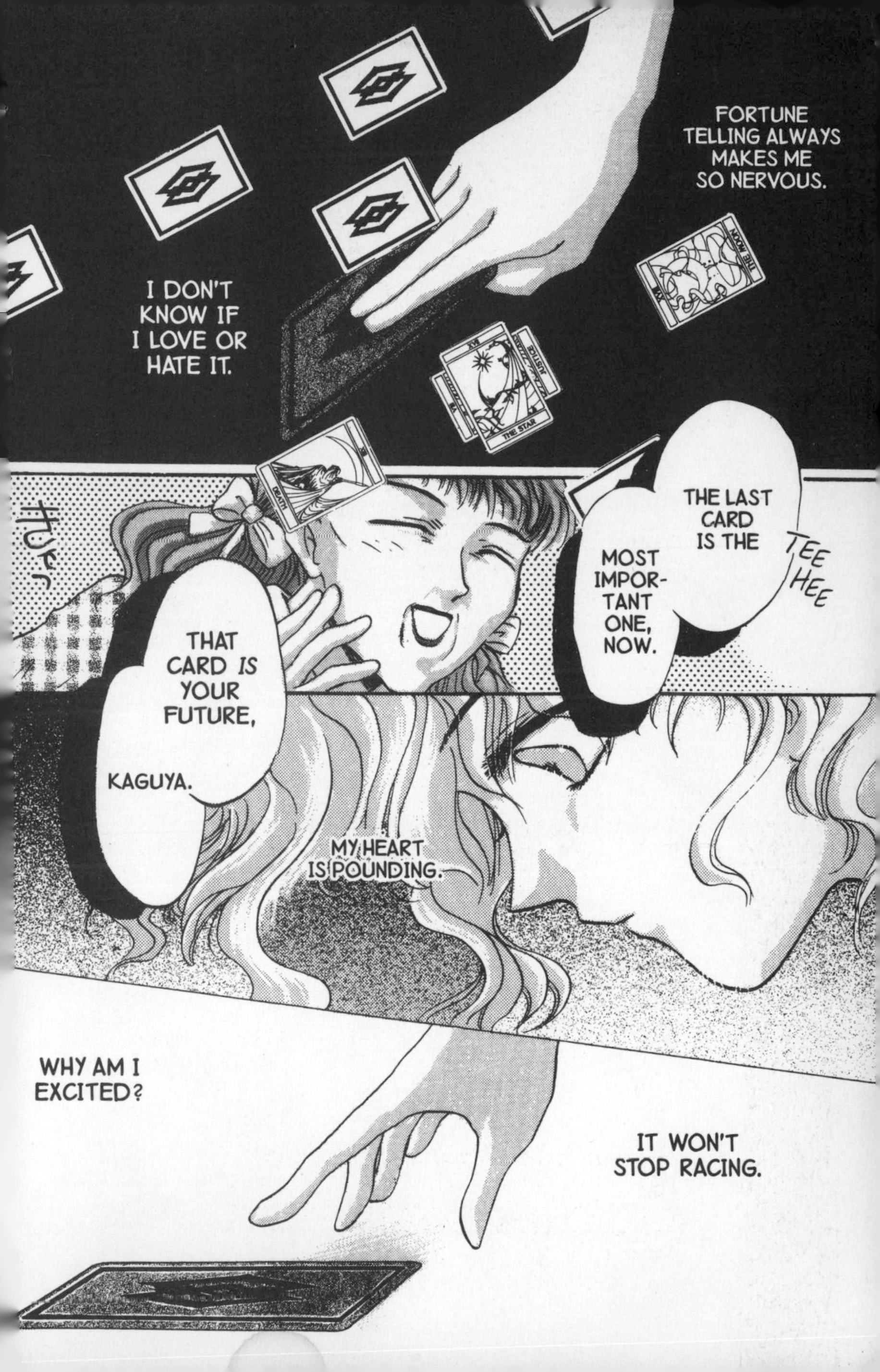
FORTUNE TELLING ALWAYS MAKES ME SO NERVOUS.
I DON'T KNOW IF I LOVE OR HATE IT.
THE MOON
THE STAR
JUSTICE
DEATH
THE LAST CARD IS THE MOST IMPORTANT ONE, NOW.
TEE HEE
THAT CARD *IS* YOUR FUTURE,
KAGUYA.
MY HEART IS POUNDING.
IT WON'T STOP RACING.
WHY AM I EXCITED?

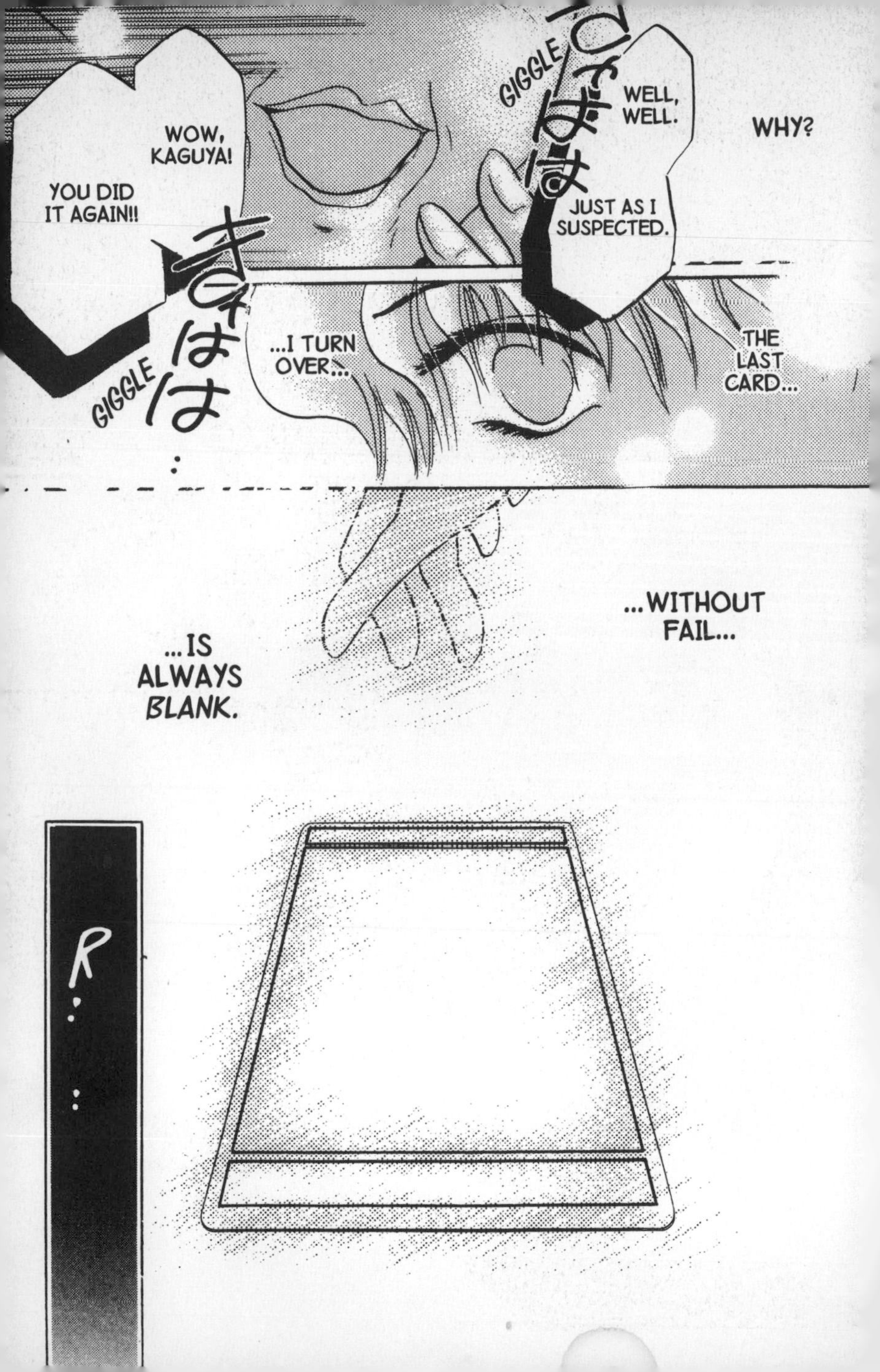
WHY?
WELL, WELL.
JUST AS I SUSPECTED.
GIGGLE
WOW, KAGUYA!
YOU DID IT AGAIN!!
GIGGLE
THE LAST CARD...
...I TURN OVER...
...WITHOUT FAIL...
...IS ALWAYS BLANK.
R...

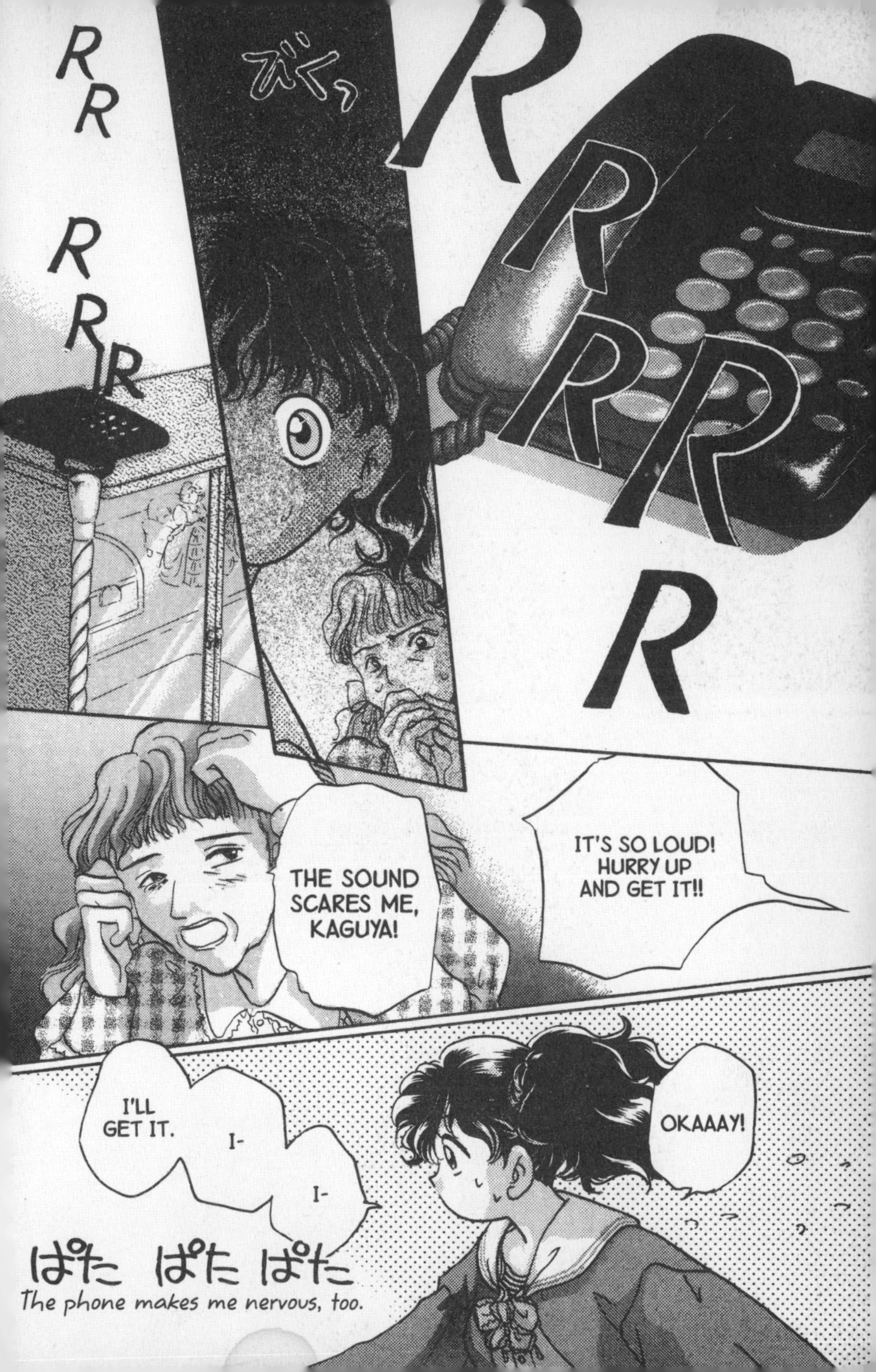
R
R
R
R
R
R
R
びくっ
R
R
R
R
R
R
R
IT'S SO LOUD! HURRY UP AND GET IT!!
THE SOUND SCARES ME, KAGUYA!
OKAAAY!
I-
I-
I'LL GET IT.
ぱた ぱた ぱた
The phone makes me nervous, too.

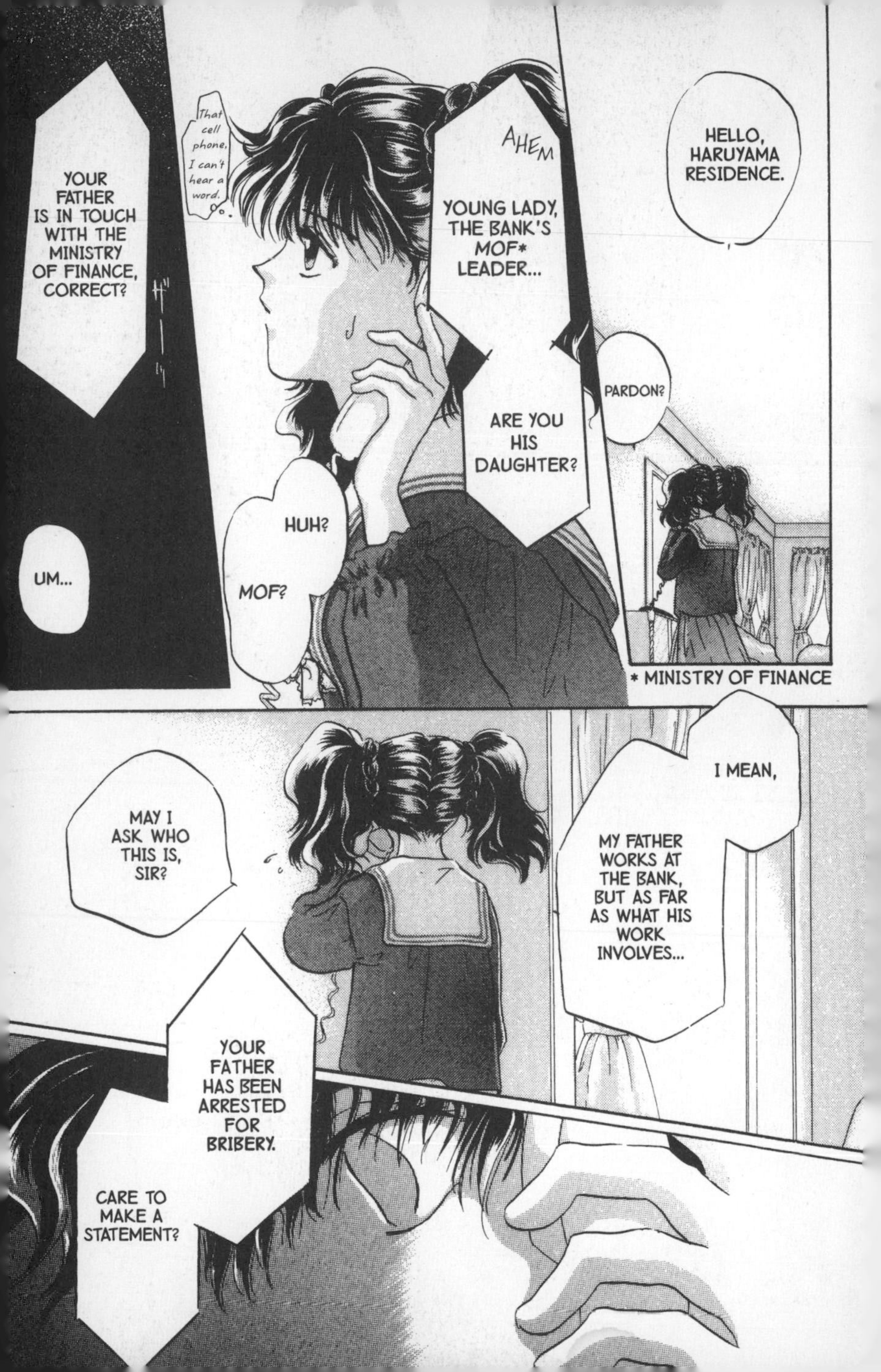
HELLO, HARUYAMA RESIDENCE.
PARDON?
AHEM
YOUNG LADY, THE BANK'S MOF* LEADER...
ARE YOU HIS DAUGHTER?
That cell phone, I can't hear a word.
HUH? MOF?
YOUR FATHER IS IN TOUCH WITH THE MINISTRY OF FINANCE, CORRECT?
UM...
* MINISTRY OF FINANCE
I MEAN,
MY FATHER WORKS AT THE BANK, BUT AS FAR AS WHAT HIS WORK INVOLVES...
MAY I ASK WHO THIS IS, SIR?
YOUR FATHER HAS BEEN ARRESTED FOR BRIBERY.
CARE TO MAKE A STATEMENT?

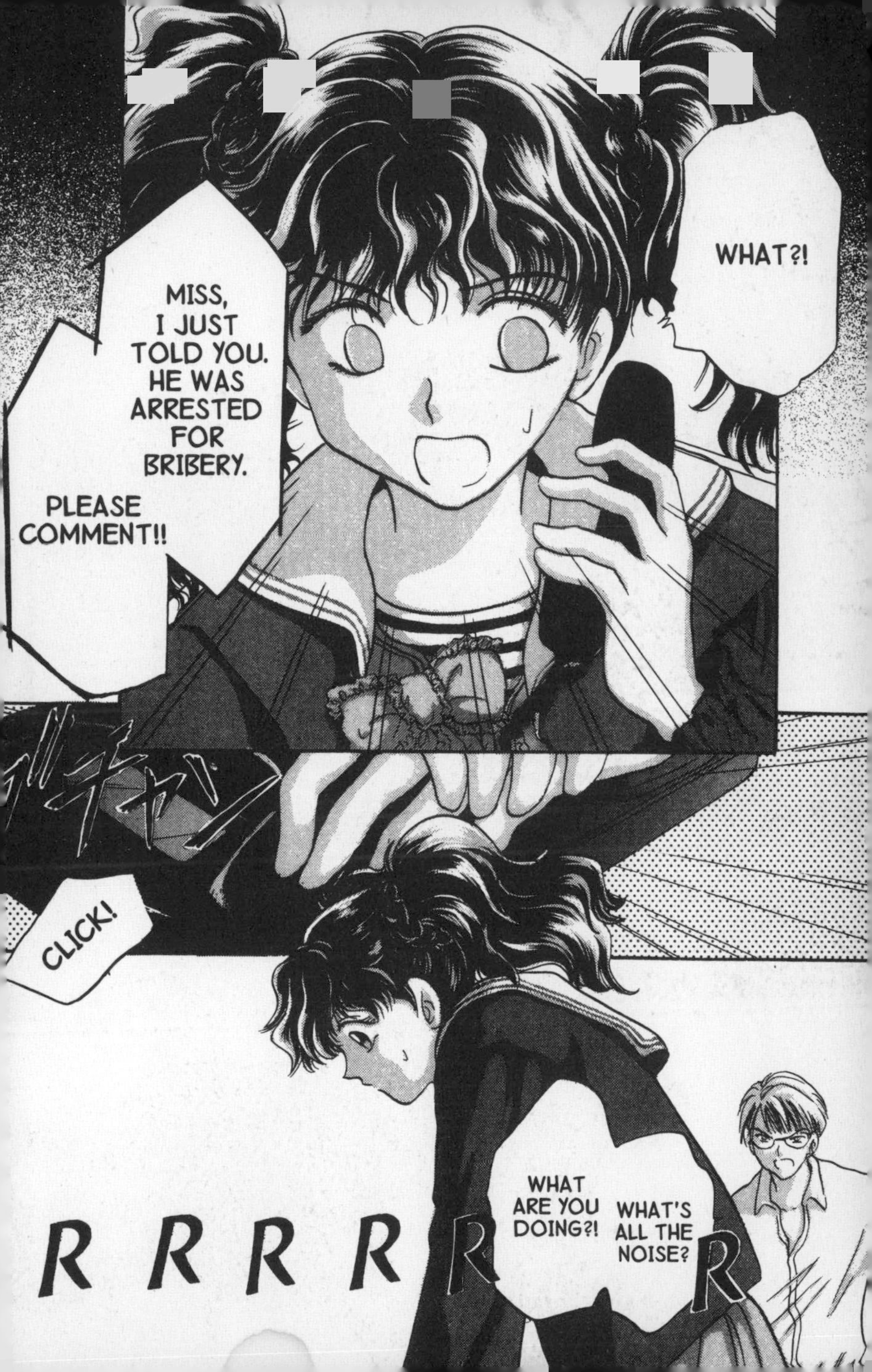
WHAT?!
MISS, I JUST TOLD YOU. HE WAS ARRESTED FOR BRIBERY.
PLEASE COMMENT!!
CLICK!
WHAT'S ALL THE NOISE?
WHAT ARE YOU DOING?!
R R R R R R

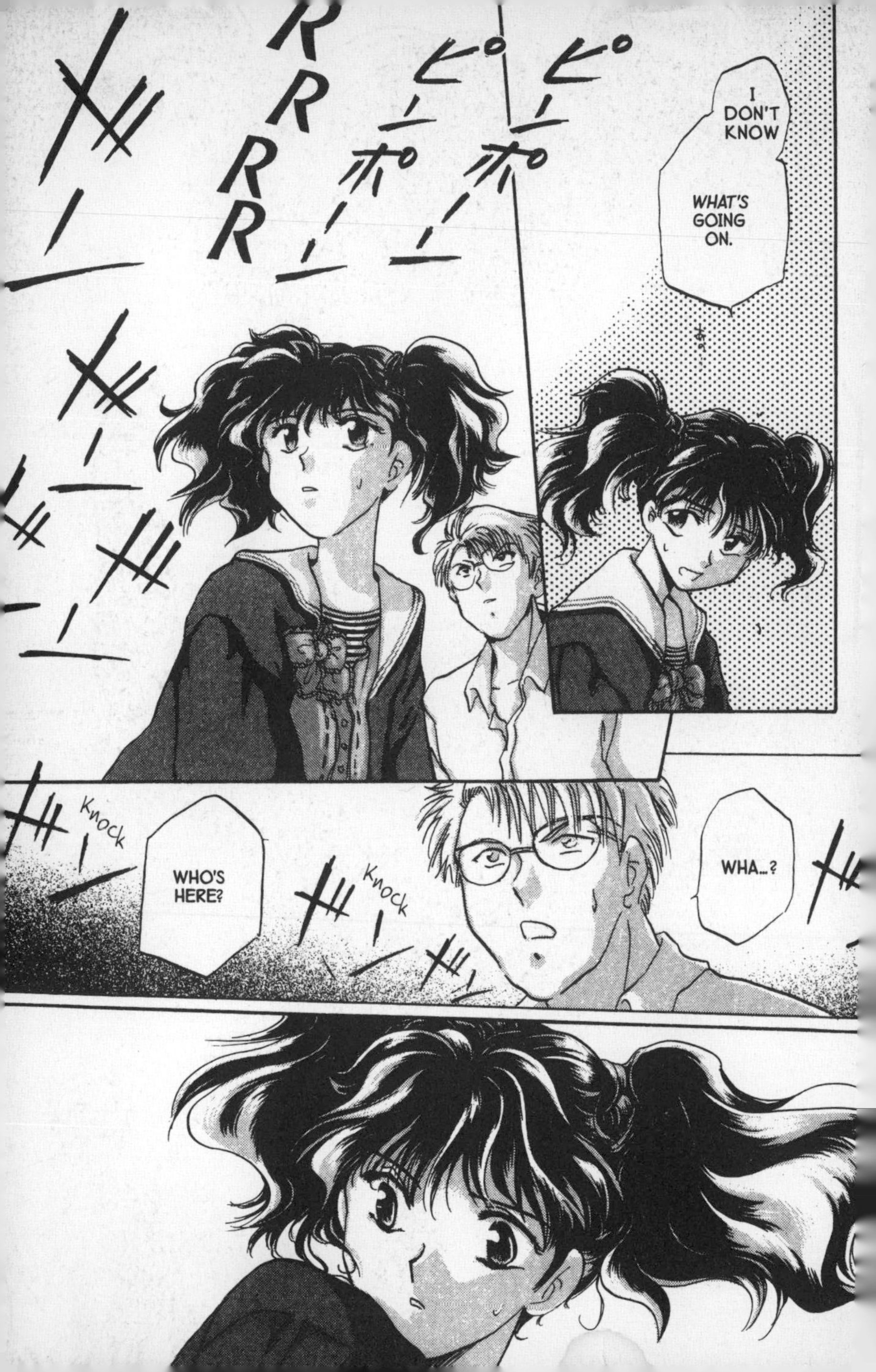
I DON'T KNOW
WHAT'S GOING ON.
ピーポーピーポー
RRRR
WHA...?
Knock
WHO'S HERE?
Knock

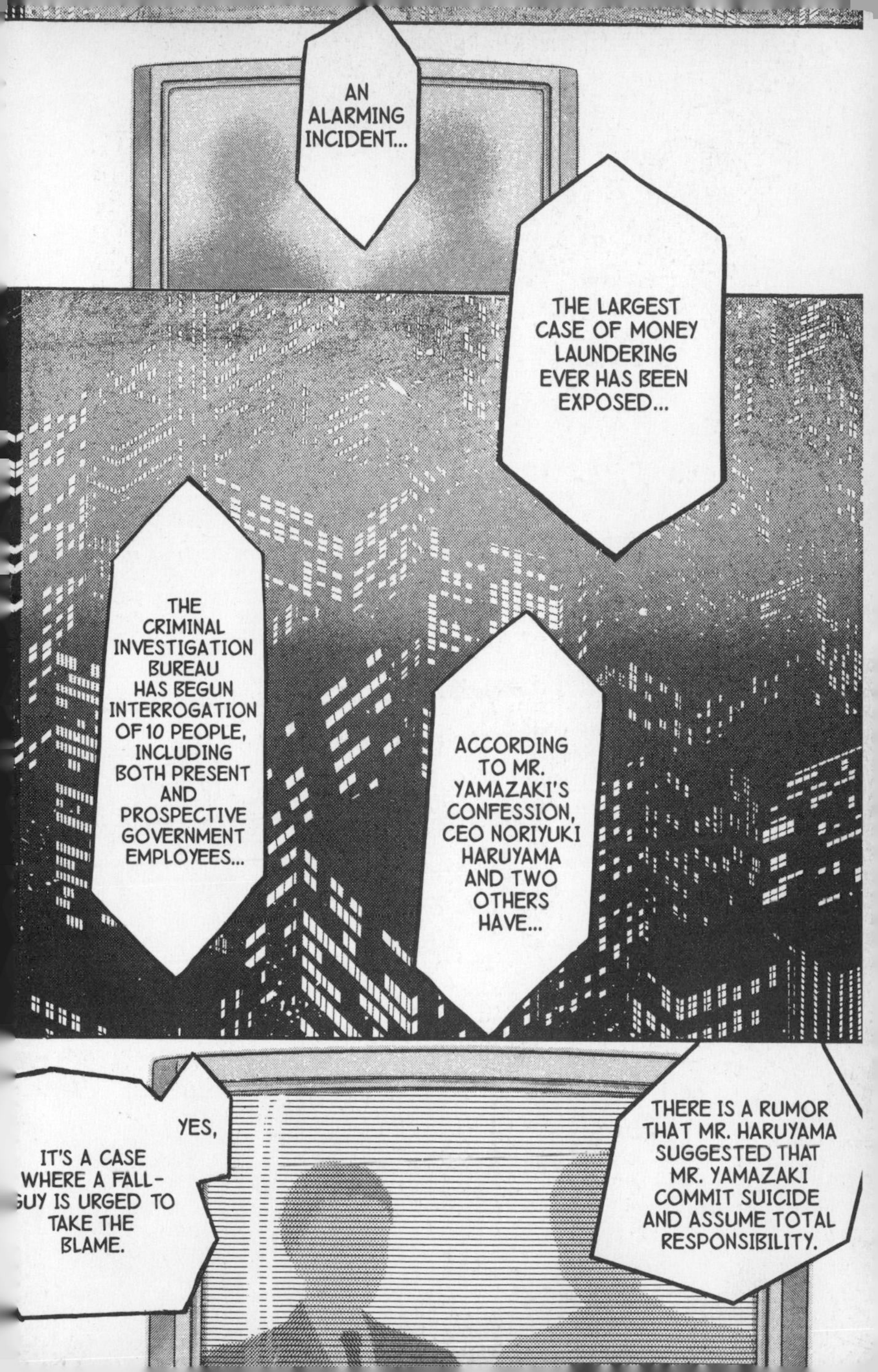

AN ALARMING INCIDENT...
THE LARGEST CASE OF MONEY LAUNDERING EVER HAS BEEN EXPOSED...
THE CRIMINAL INVESTIGATION BUREAU HAS BEGUN INTERROGATION OF 10 PEOPLE, INCLUDING BOTH PRESENT AND PROSPECTIVE GOVERNMENT EMPLOYEES...
ACCORDING TO MR. YAMAZAKI'S CONFESSION, CEO NORIYUKI HARUYAMA AND TWO OTHERS HAVE...
THERE IS A RUMOR THAT MR. HARUYAMA SUGGESTED THAT MR. YAMAZAKI COMMIT SUICIDE AND ASSUME TOTAL RESPONSIBILITY.
YES, IT'S A CASE WHERE A FALL-GUY IS URGED TO TAKE THE BLAME.

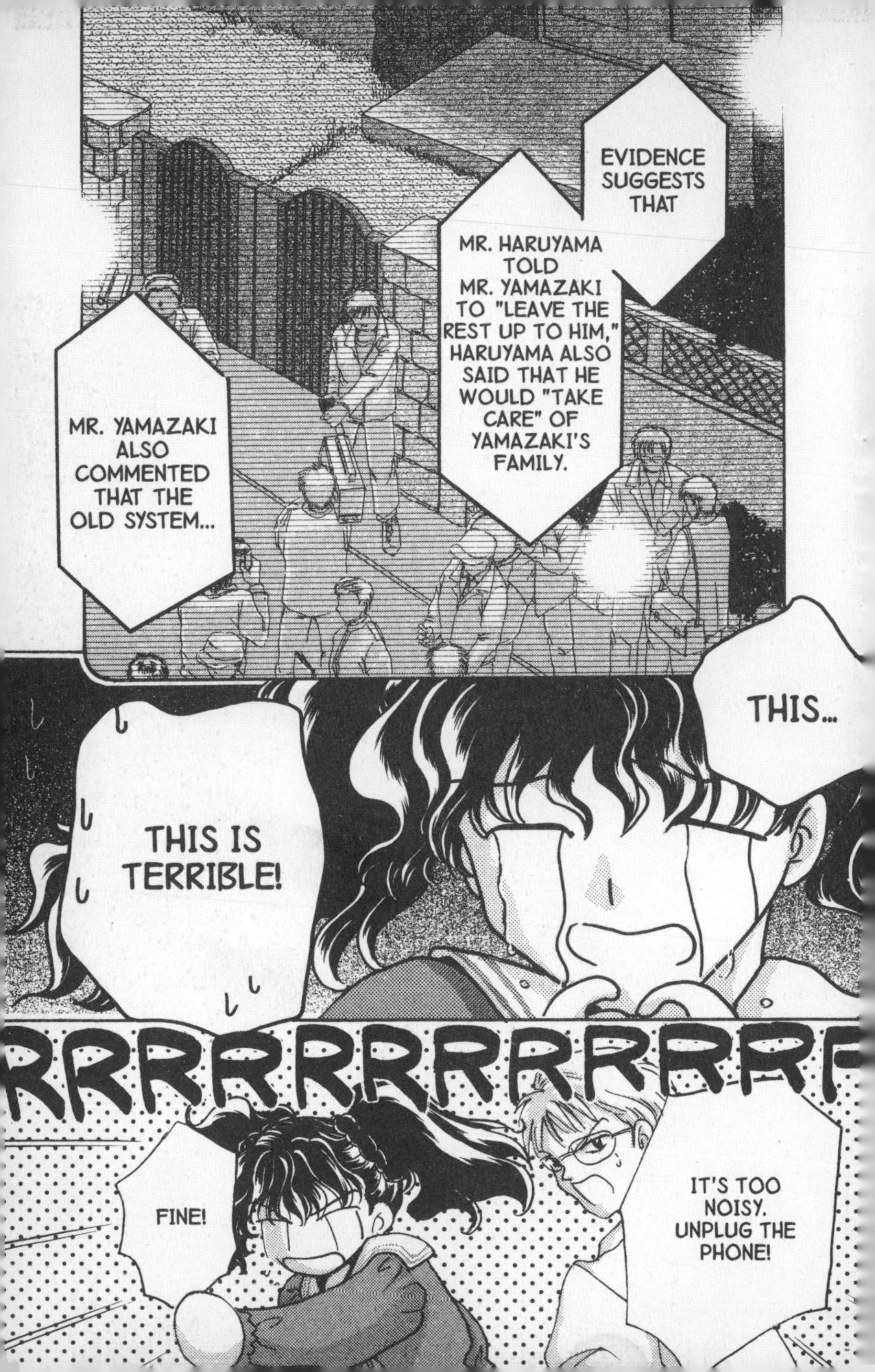
EVIDENCE SUGGESTS THAT
MR. HARUYAMA TOLD MR. YAMAZAKI TO "LEAVE THE REST UP TO HIM," HARUYAMA ALSO SAID THAT HE WOULD "TAKE CARE" OF YAMAZAKI'S FAMILY.
MR. YAMAZAKI ALSO COMMENTED THAT THE OLD SYSTEM...
THIS...
THIS IS TERRIBLE!
RRRRRRRRRRRRRR
IT'S TOO NOISY. UNPLUG THE PHONE!
FINE!

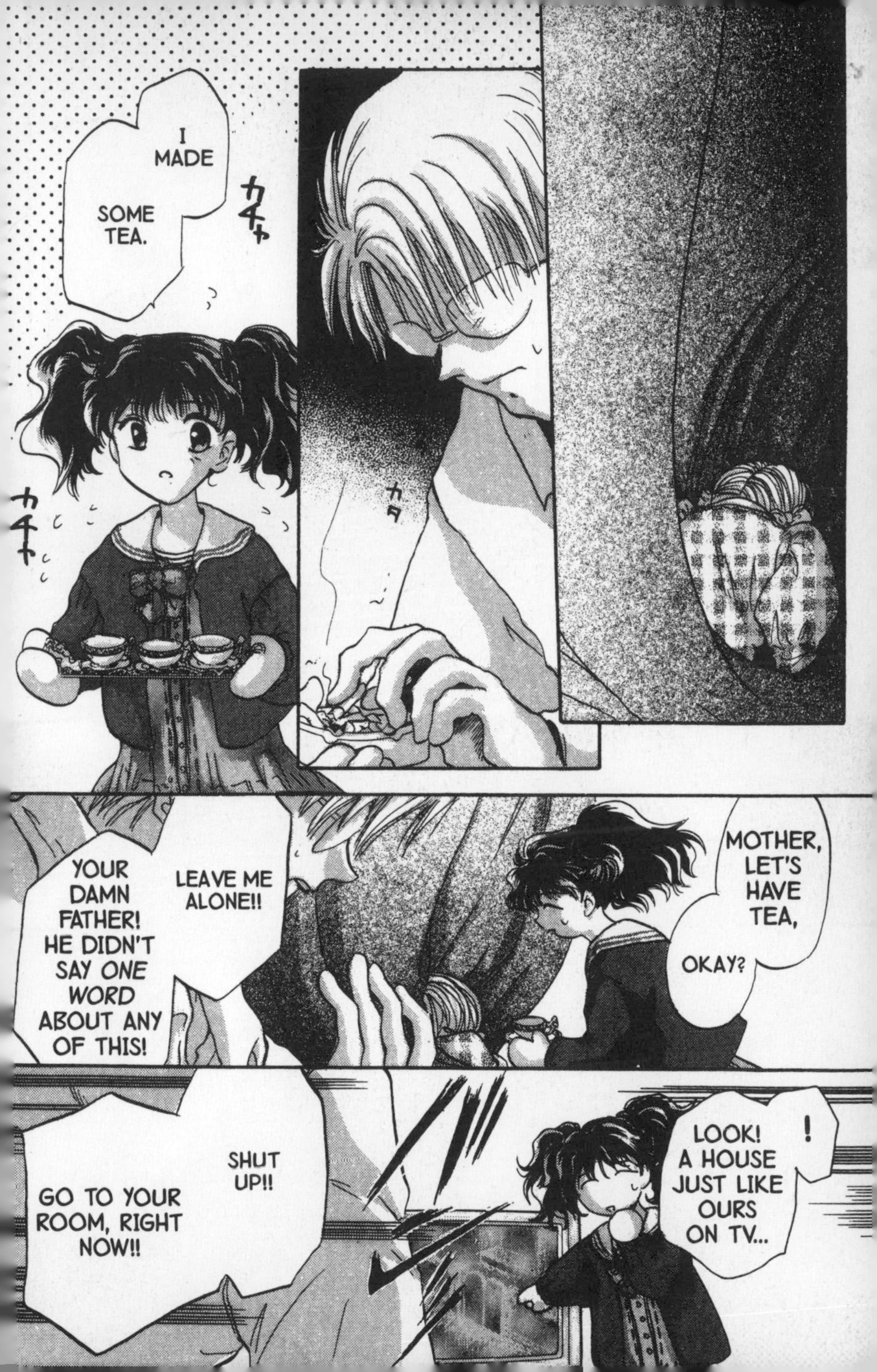
カタ
I MADE SOME TEA.
カチャ
カチャ
MOTHER, LET'S HAVE TEA, OKAY?
LEAVE ME ALONE!!
YOUR DAMN FATHER! HE DIDN'T SAY *ONE WORD* ABOUT ANY OF THIS!
!
LOOK! A HOUSE JUST LIKE OURS ON TV...
SHUT UP!!
GO TO YOUR ROOM, RIGHT NOW!!

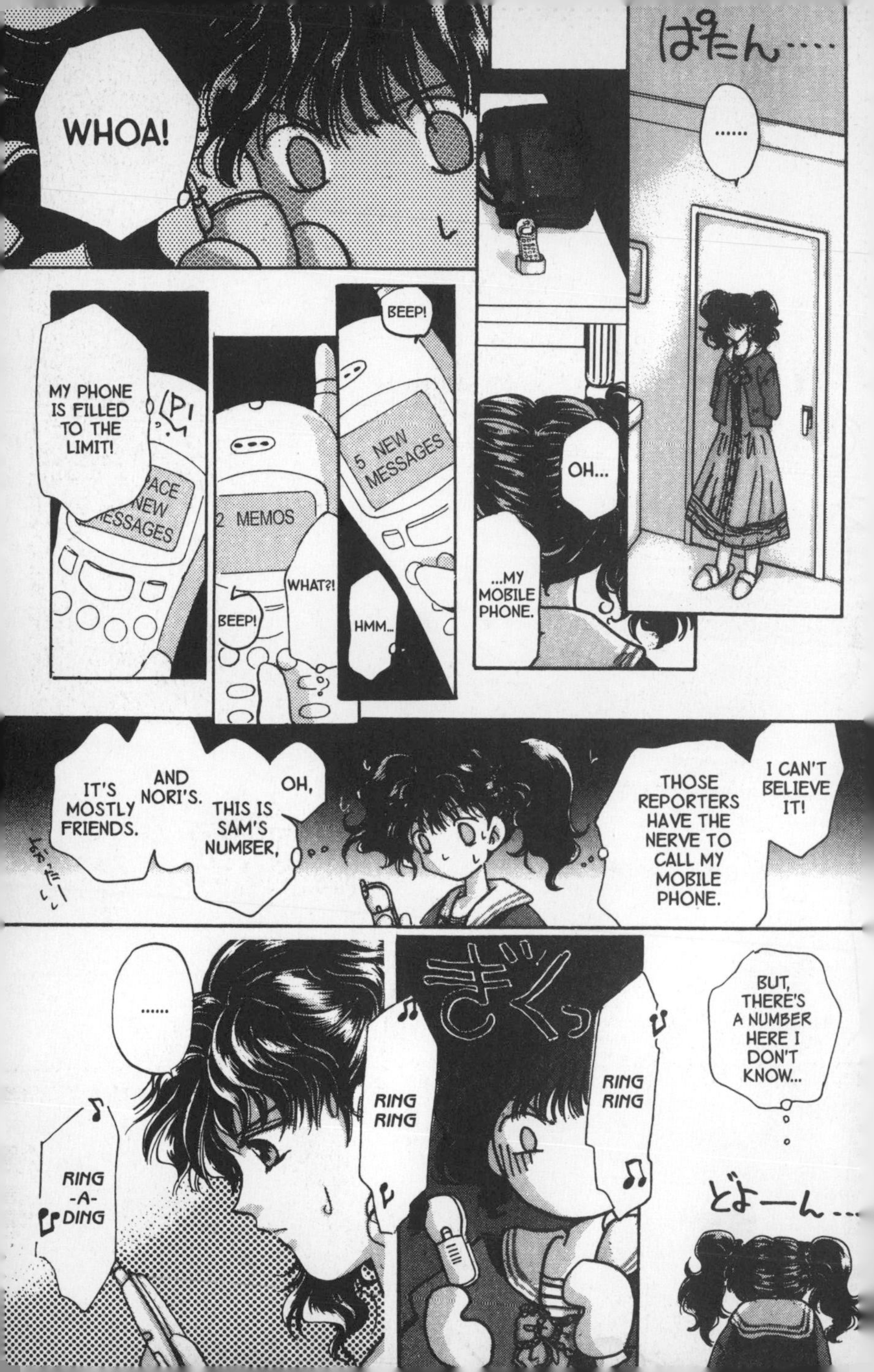
ぱたん……
......
WHOA!
OH...
...MY MOBILE PHONE.
BEEP!
5 NEW MESSAGES
HMM...
WHAT?!
2 MEMOS
BEEP!
MY PHONE IS FILLED TO THE LIMIT!
I CAN'T BELIEVE IT!
THOSE REPORTERS HAVE THE NERVE TO CALL MY MOBILE PHONE.
OH, THIS IS SAM'S NUMBER,
AND NORI'S.
IT'S MOSTLY FRIENDS.
BUT, THERE'S A NUMBER HERE I DON'T KNOW...
どよーん…
ぎくっ
RING RING
RING RING
......
RING -A- DING

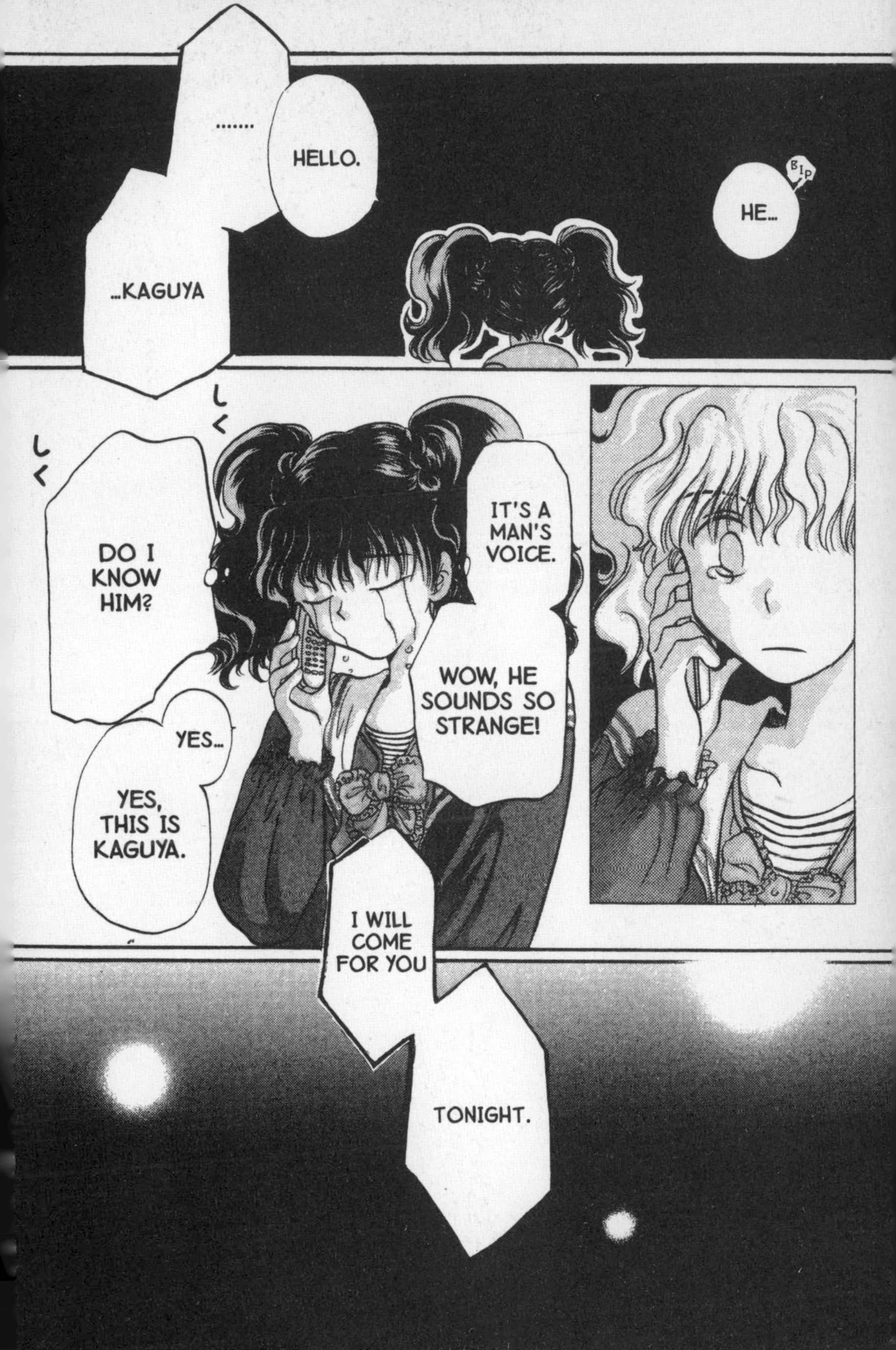
BIP
HE...
HELLO.
....
...KAGUYA
しく
しく
IT'S A MAN'S VOICE.
WOW, HE SOUNDS SO STRANGE!
DO I KNOW HIM?
YES...
YES, THIS IS KAGUYA.
I WILL COME FOR YOU
TONIGHT.

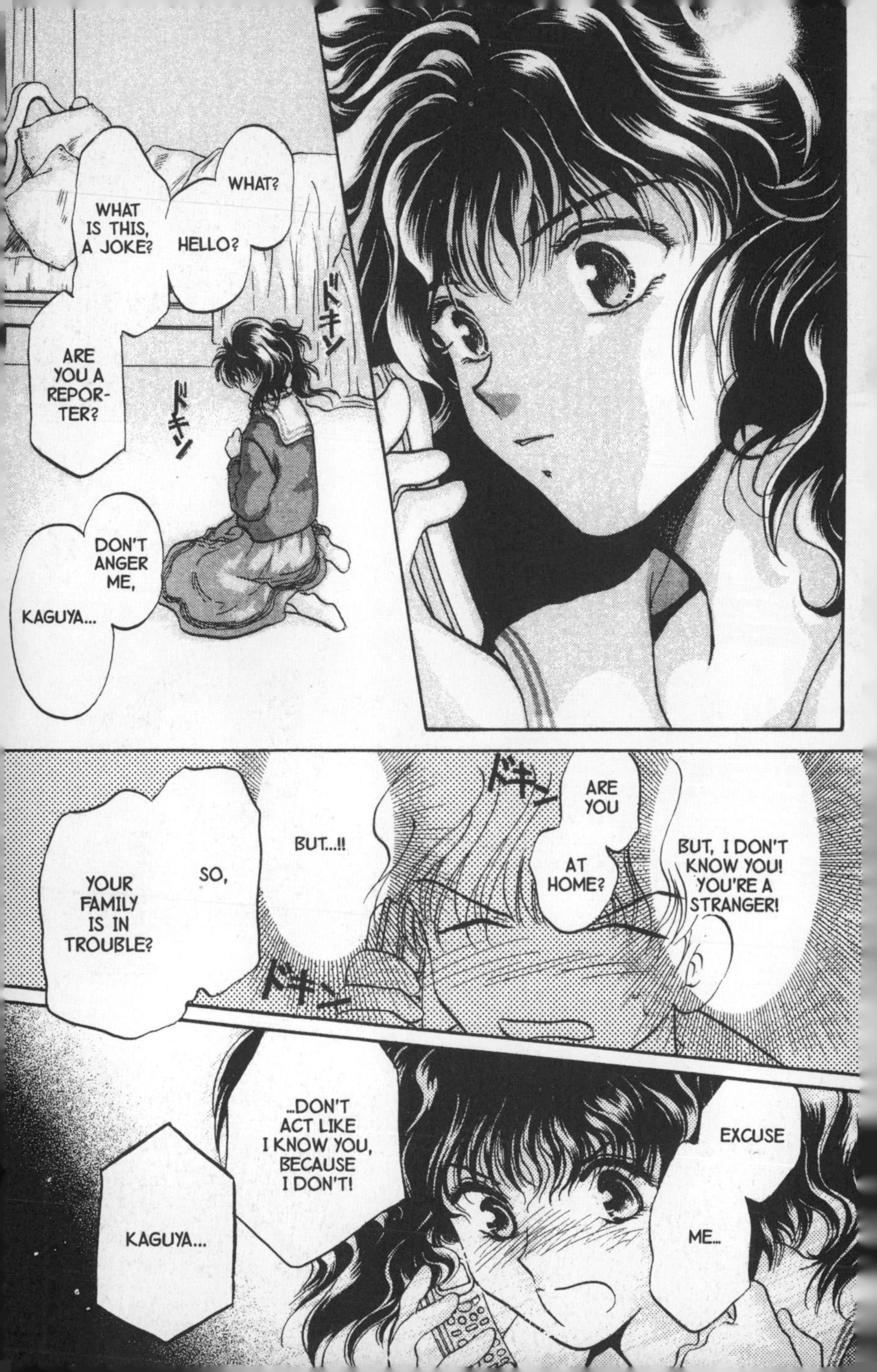
WHAT?
HELLO?
WHAT IS THIS, A JOKE?
ドキン
ドキン
ARE YOU A REPORTER?
DON'T ANGER ME, KAGUYA...
BUT, I DON'T KNOW YOU! YOU'RE A STRANGER!
ARE YOU AT HOME?
ドキン
BUT...!!
SO, YOUR FAMILY IS IN TROUBLE?
ドキン
EXCUSE ME..
...DON'T ACT LIKE I KNOW YOU, BECAUSE I DON'T!
KAGUYA...

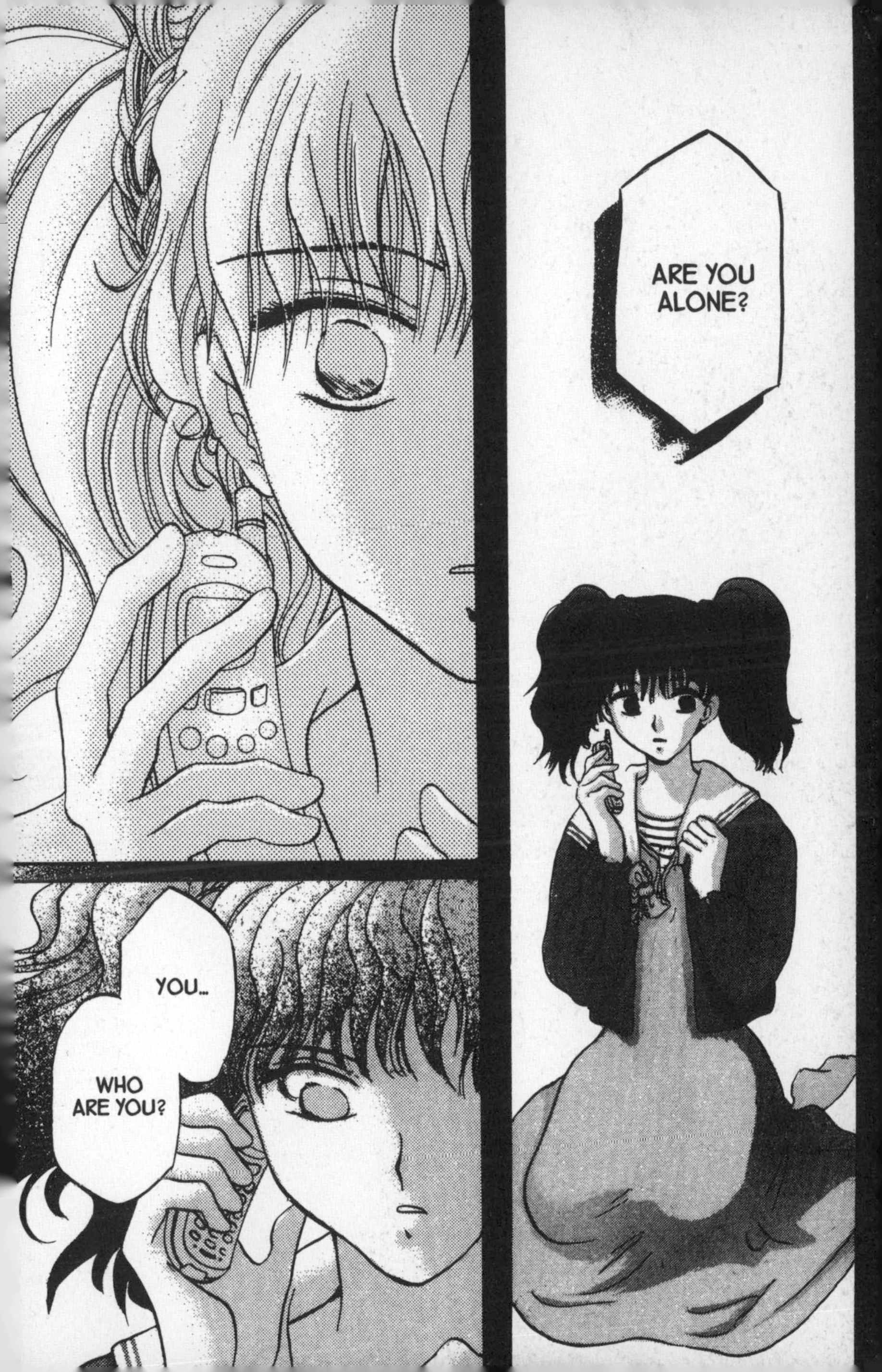
ARE YOU ALONE?
YOU...
WHO ARE YOU?

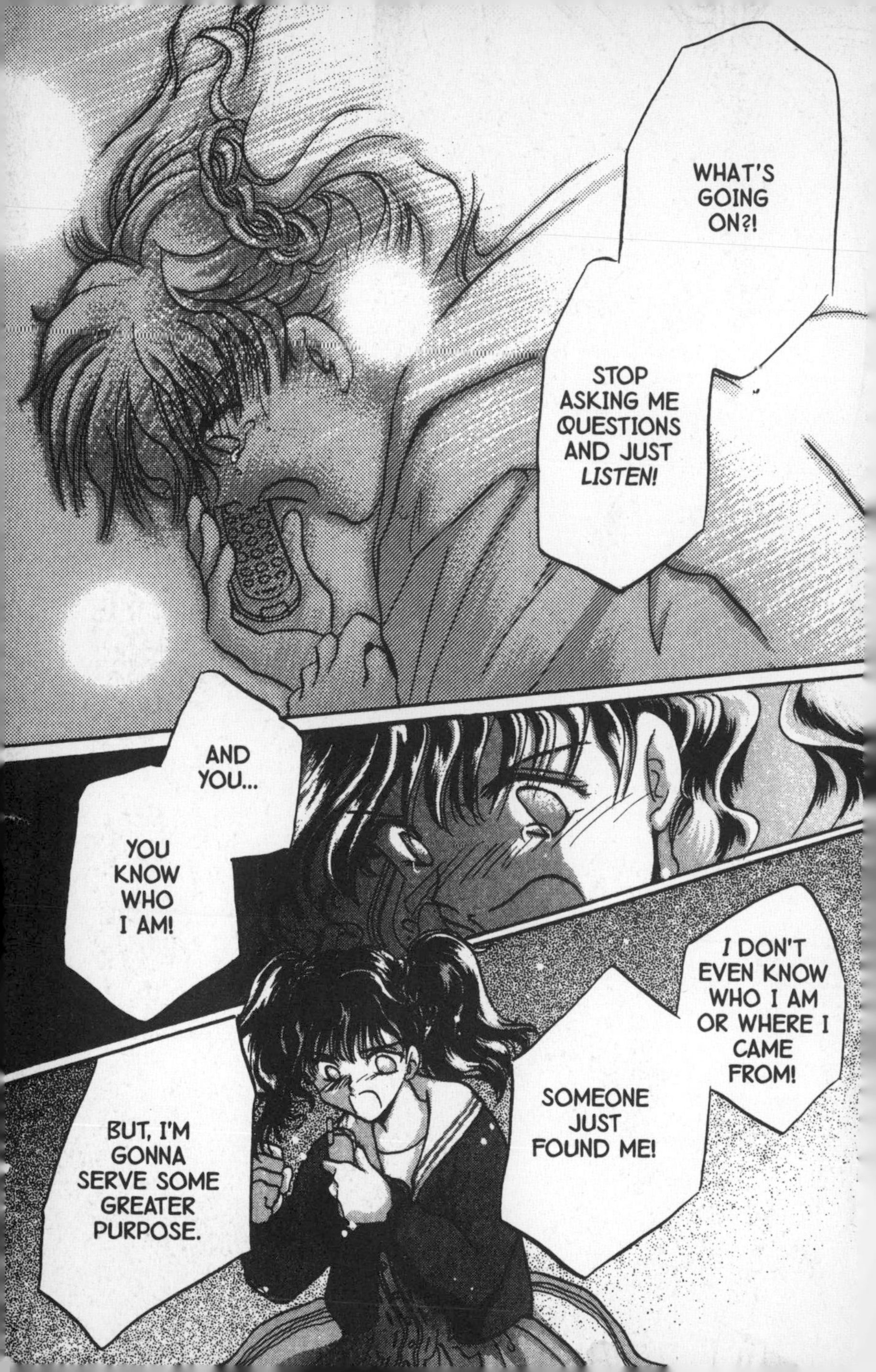
WHAT'S GOING ON?!
STOP ASKING ME QUESTIONS AND JUST *LISTEN!*
AND YOU...
YOU KNOW WHO I AM!
I DON'T EVEN KNOW WHO I AM OR WHERE I CAME FROM!
SOMEONE JUST FOUND ME!
BUT, I'M GONNA SERVE SOME GREATER PURPOSE.

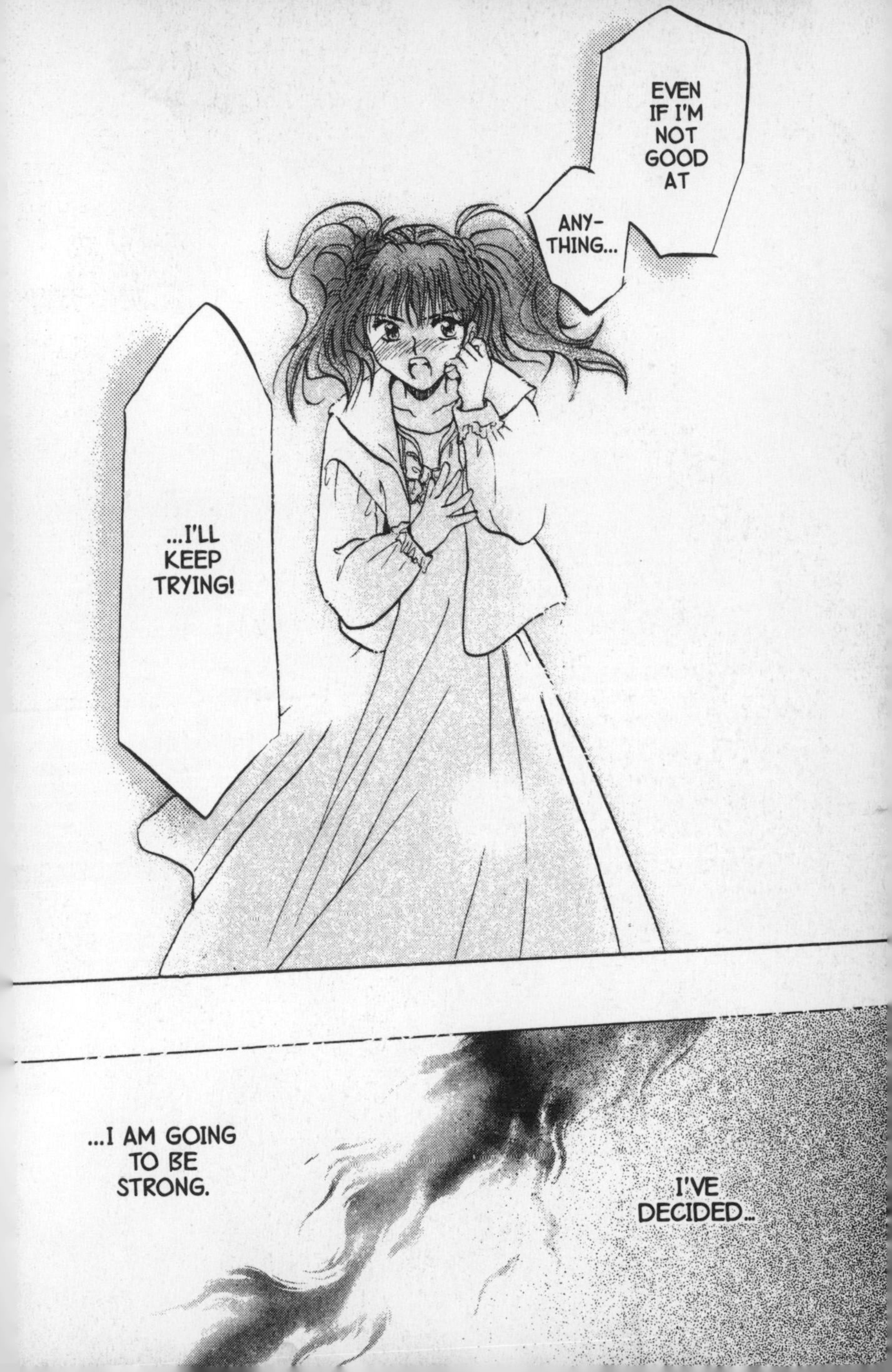
EVEN IF I'M NOT GOOD AT ANY-THING...
...I'LL KEEP TRYING!
I'VE DECIDED...
...I AM GOING TO BE STRONG.

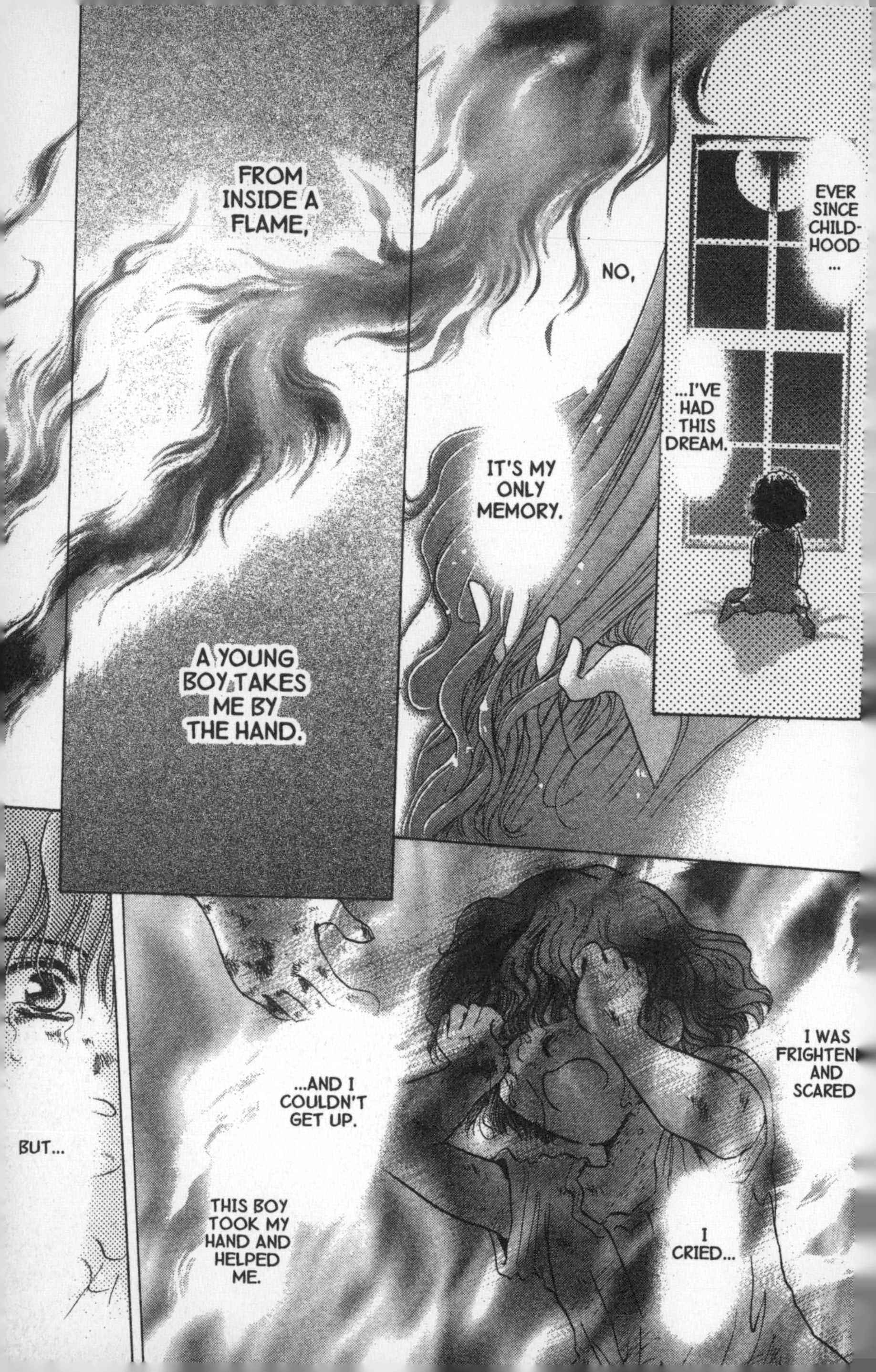
EVER SINCE CHILDHOOD...
...I'VE HAD THIS DREAM.
NO,
IT'S MY ONLY MEMORY.
FROM INSIDE A FLAME,
A YOUNG BOY TAKES ME BY THE HAND.
I WAS FRIGHTEN AND SCARED
I CRIED...
...AND I COULDN'T GET UP.
THIS BOY TOOK MY HAND AND HELPED ME.
BUT...

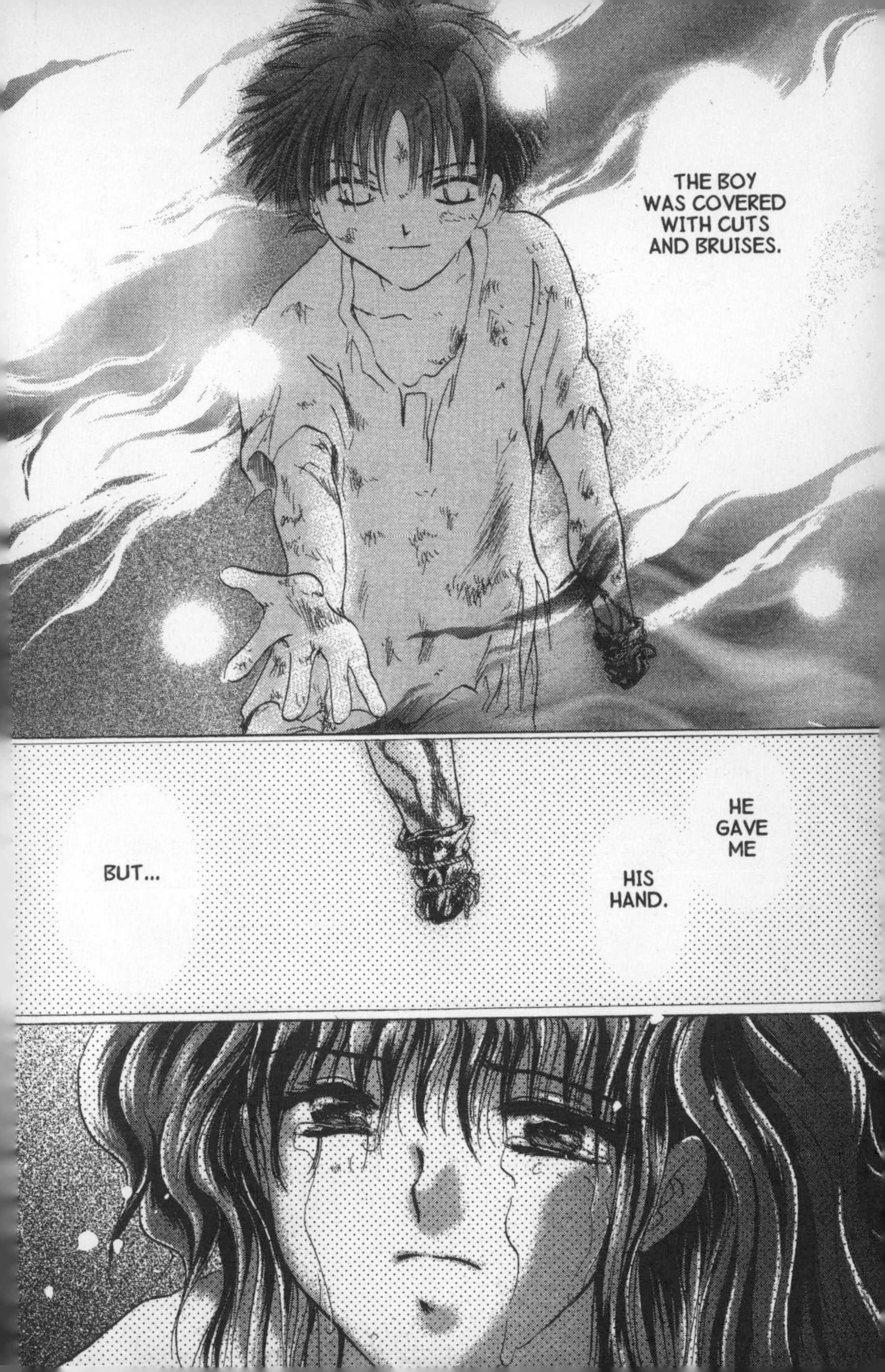
THE BOY WAS COVERED WITH CUTS AND BRUISES.
HE GAVE ME
HIS HAND.
BUT...

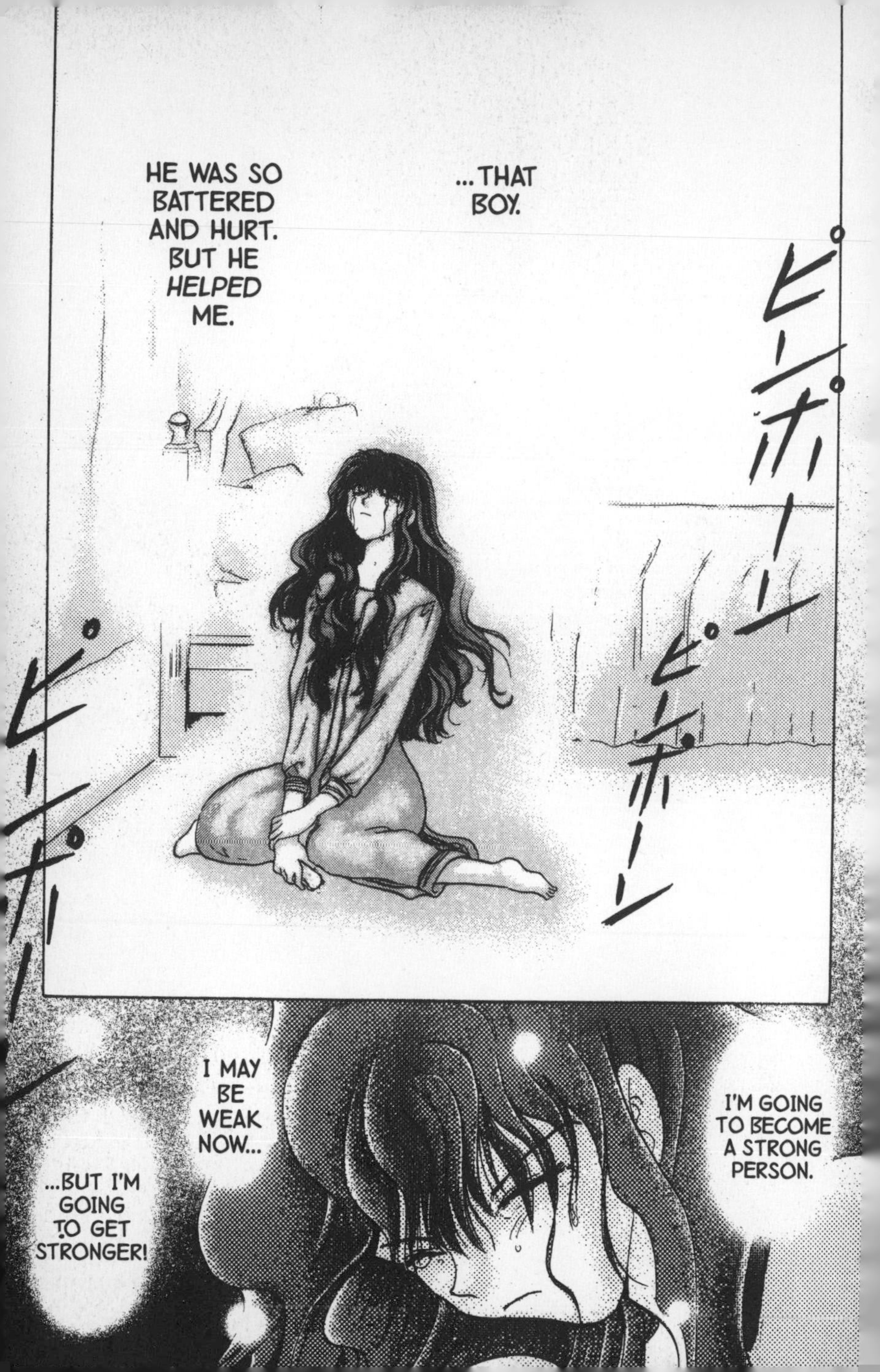
ピーポーン
ピーポーン
HE WAS SO BATTERED AND HURT. BUT HE *HELPED* ME.
...THAT BOY.
ピーポー
I'M GOING TO BECOME A STRONG PERSON.
I MAY BE WEAK NOW...
...BUT I'M GOING TO GET STRONGER!

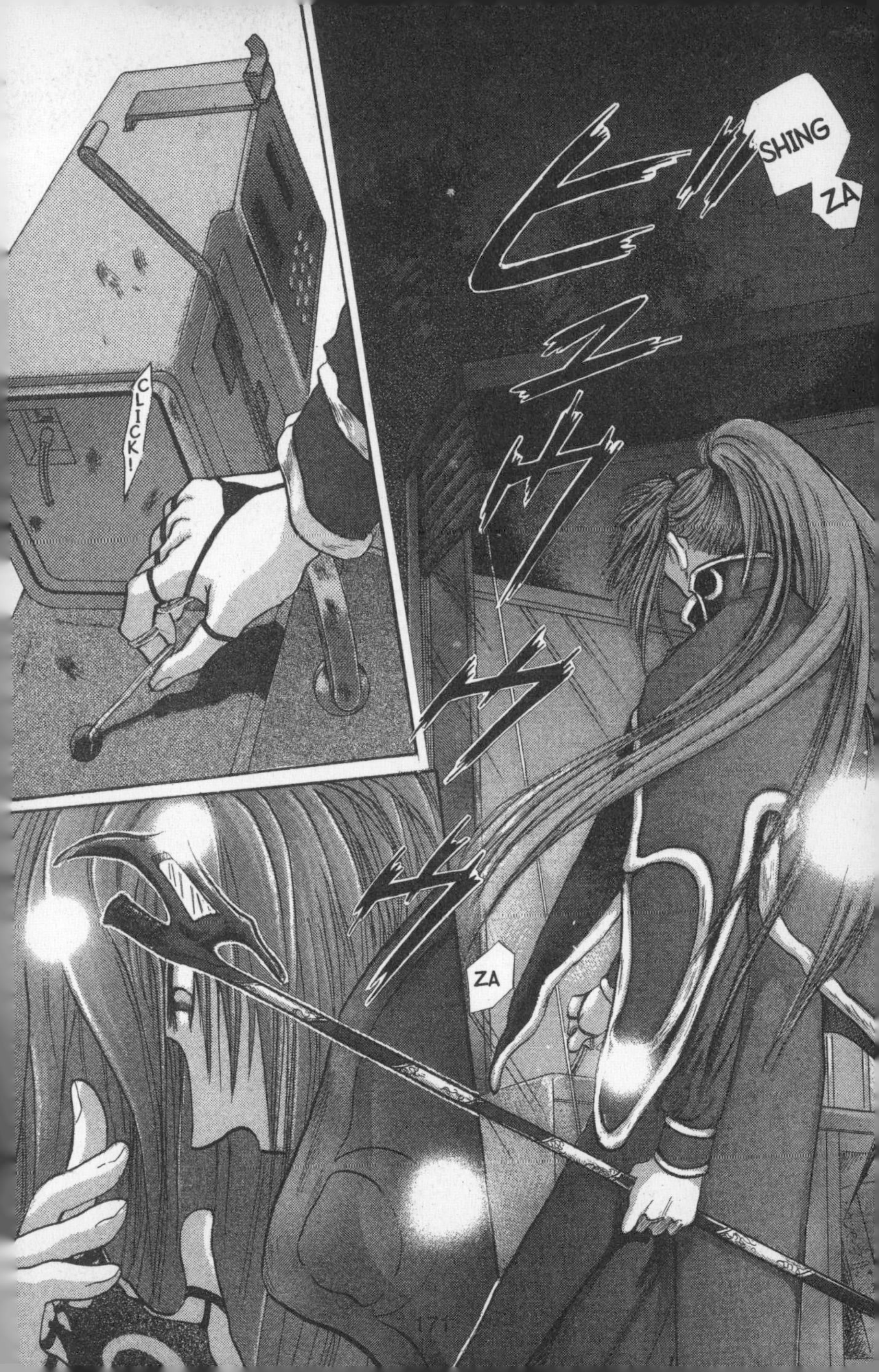
SHING
ZA
ZA
CLICK!

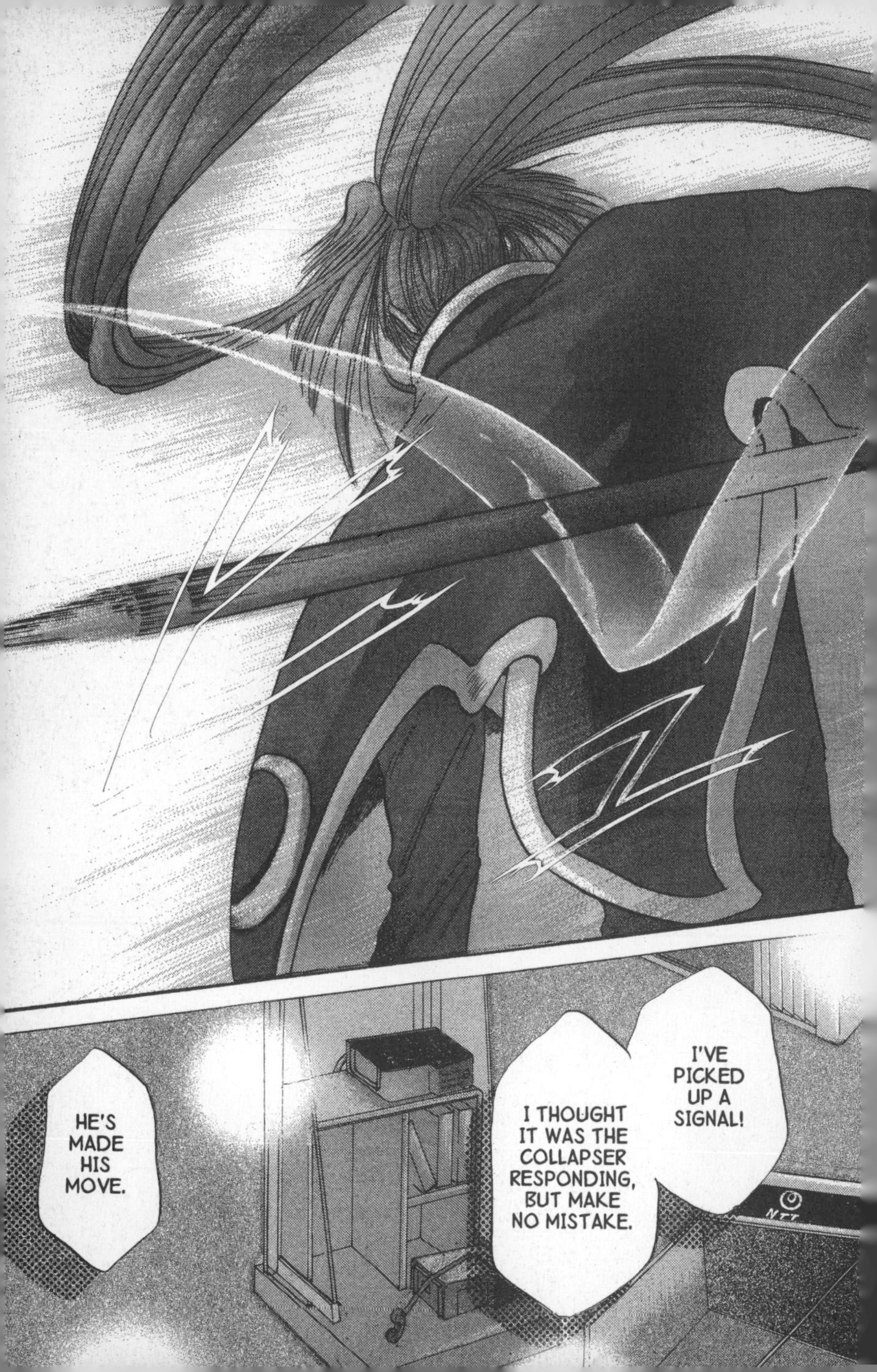
I'VE PICKED UP A SIGNAL!
I THOUGHT IT WAS THE COLLAPSER RESPONDING, BUT MAKE NO MISTAKE.
HE'S MADE HIS MOVE.

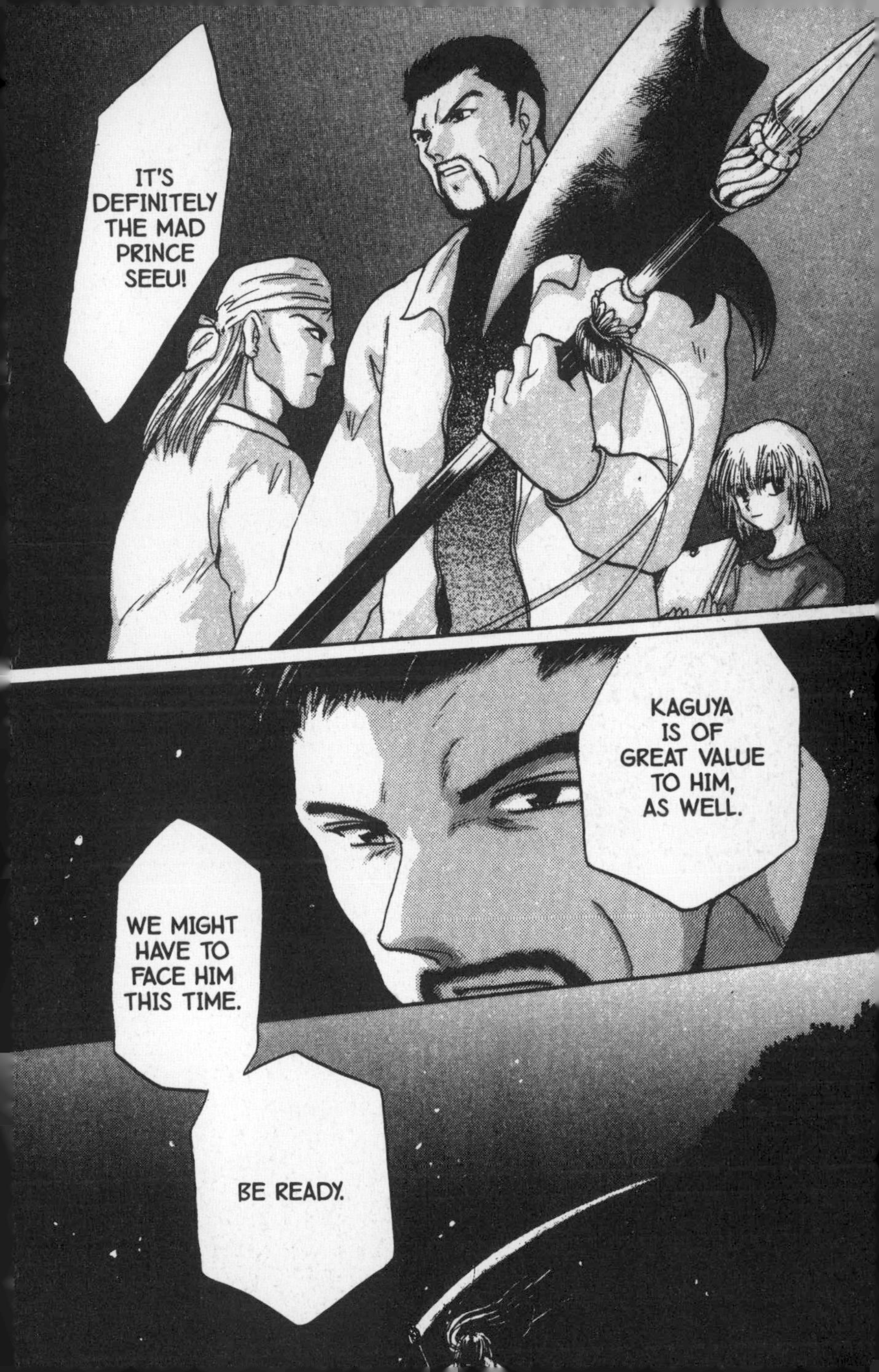
IT'S DEFINITELY THE MAD PRINCE SEEU!
KAGUYA IS OF GREAT VALUE TO HIM, AS WELL.
WE MIGHT HAVE TO FACE HIM THIS TIME.
BE READY.

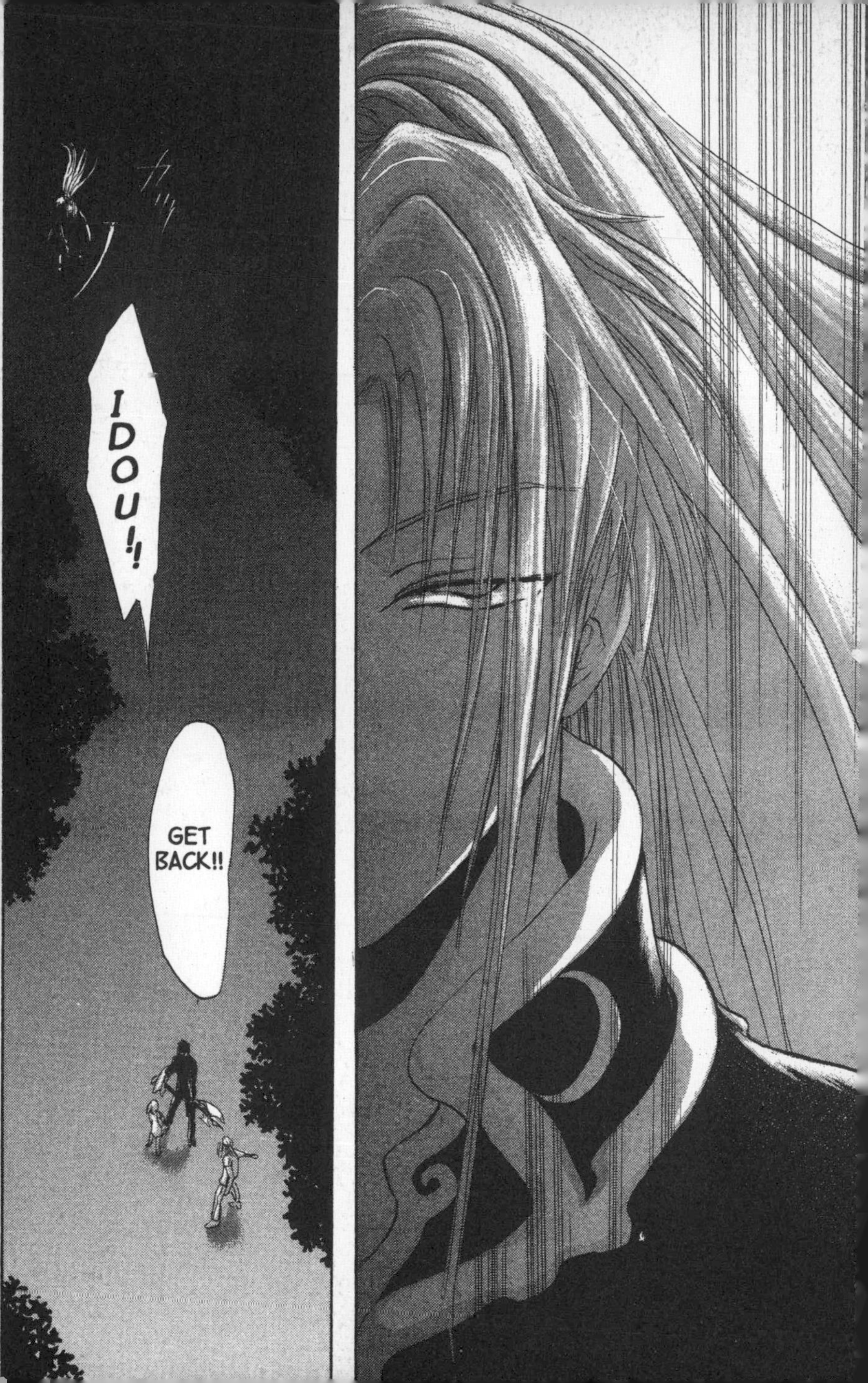
IDOU!!
GET BACK!!

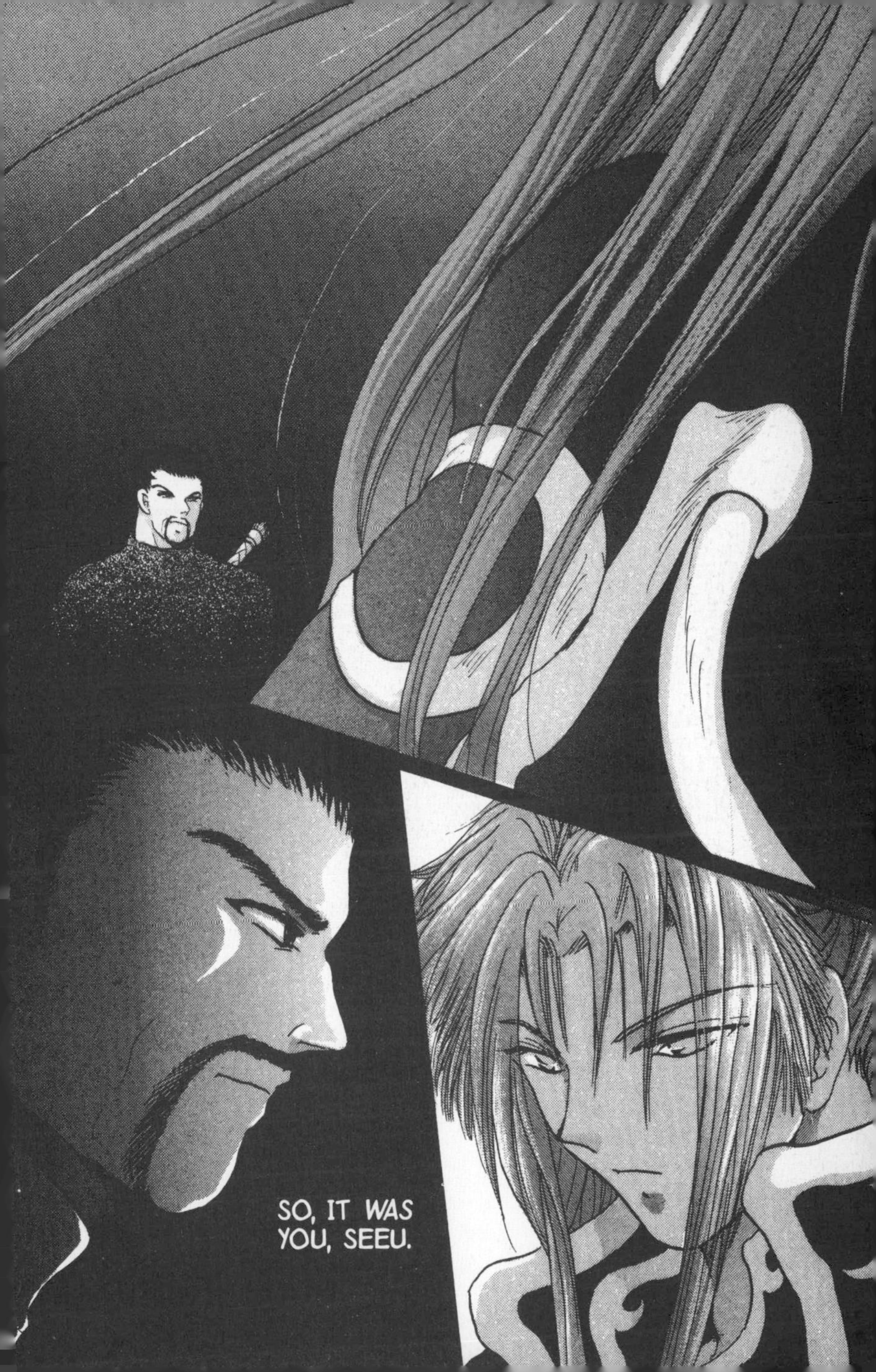
SO, IT WAS
YOU, SEEU.

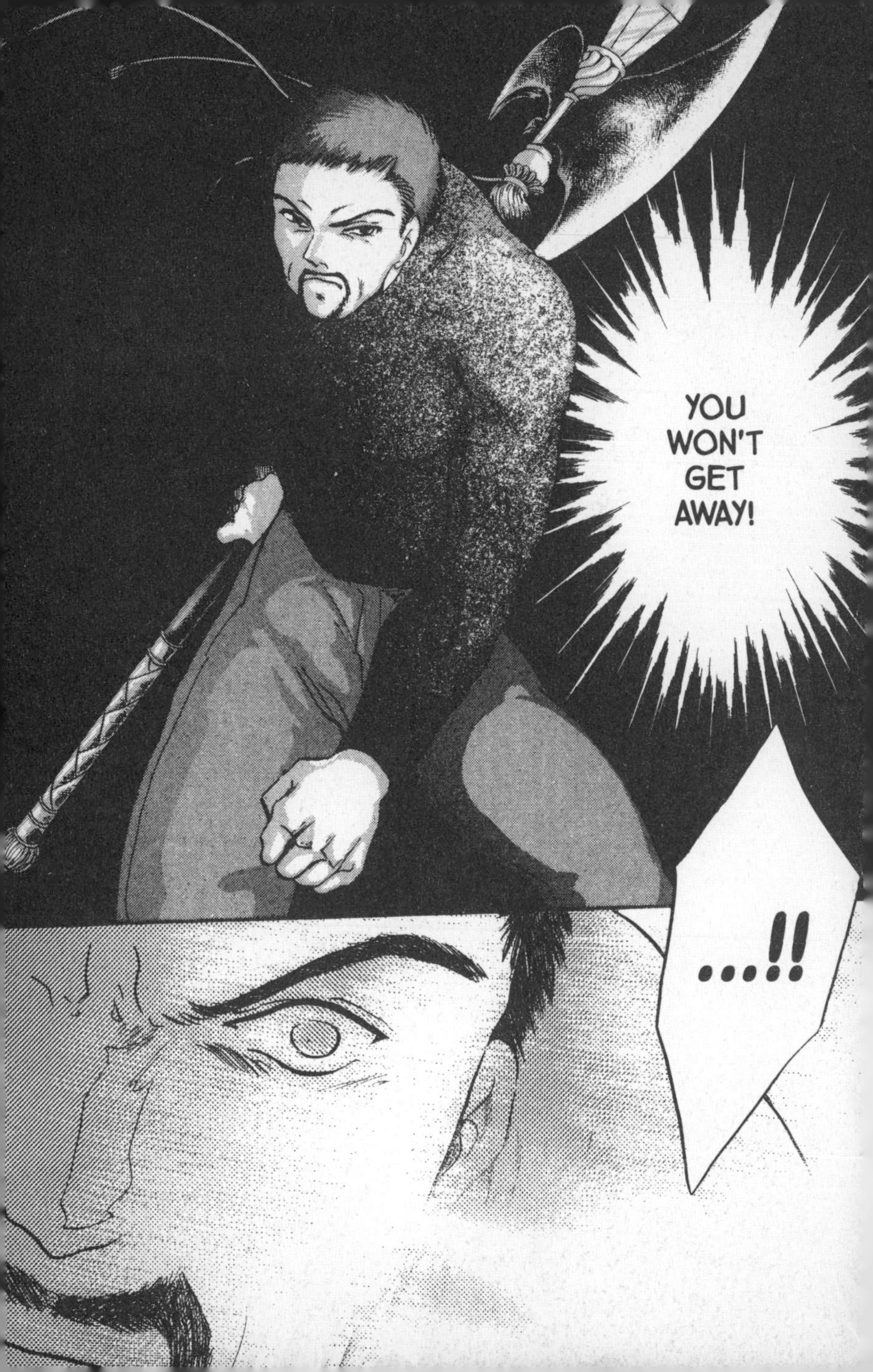
YOU WON'T GET AWAY!
...!!

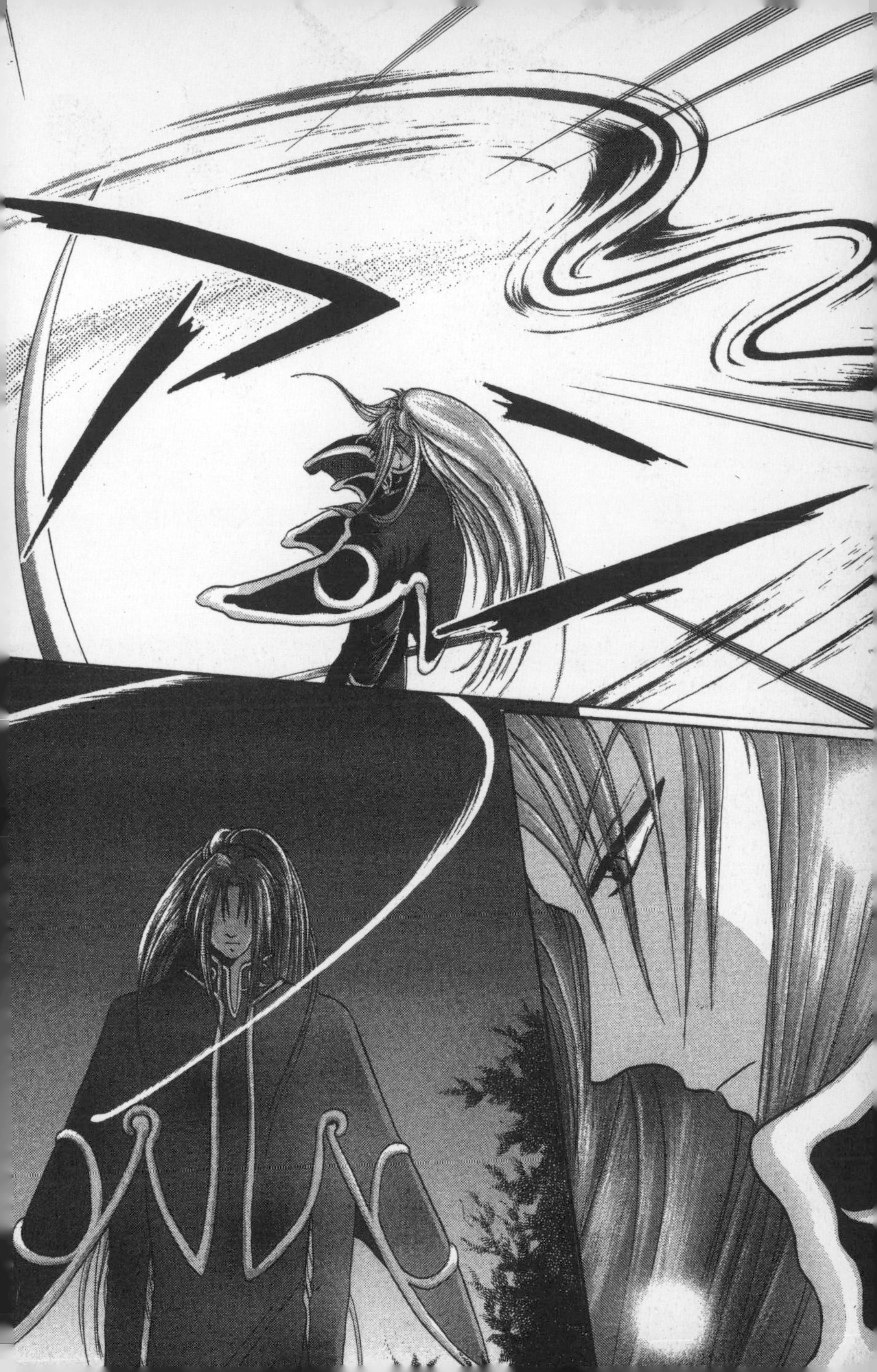

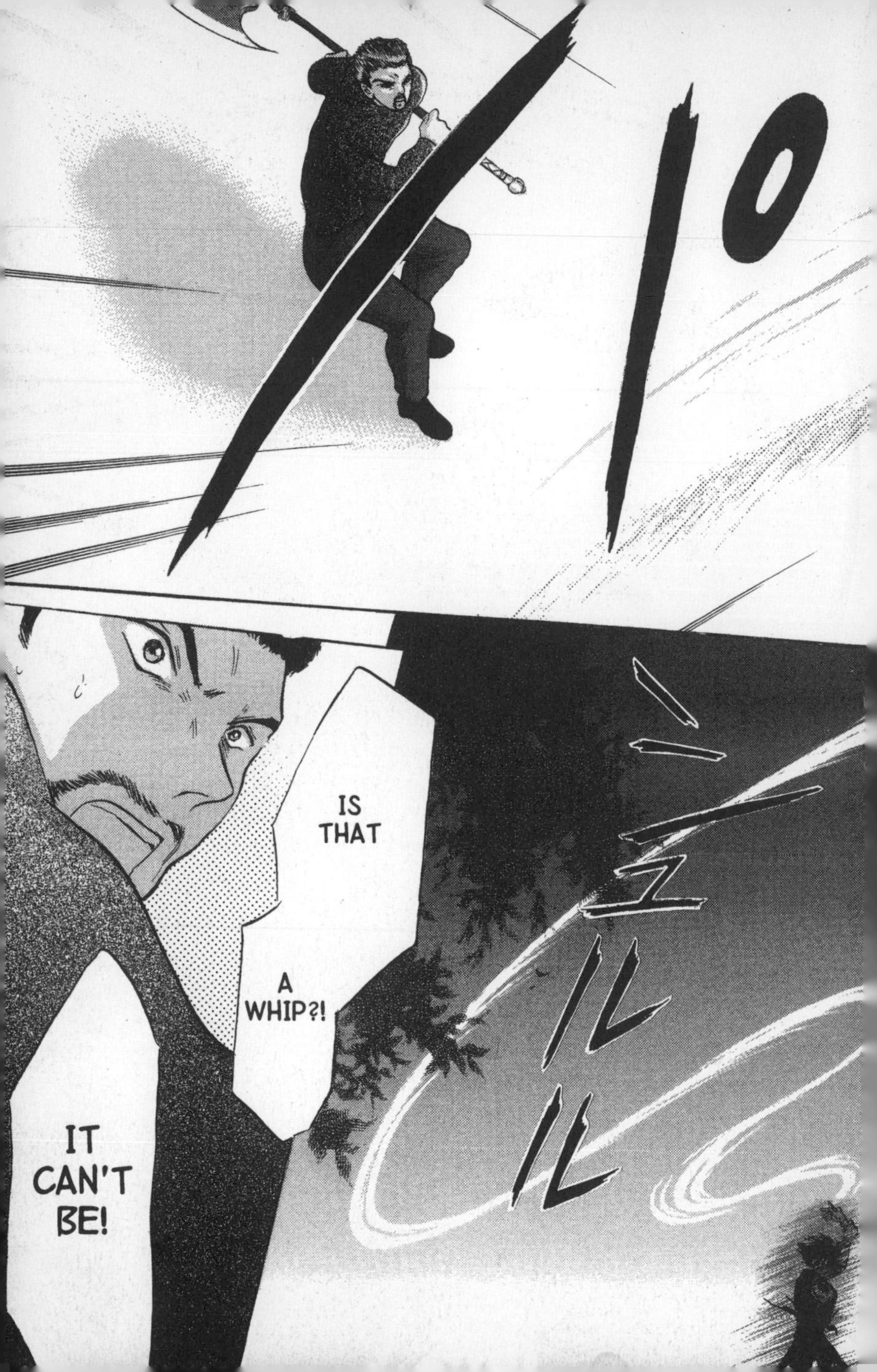
IS THAT
A WHIP?!
IT CAN'T BE!

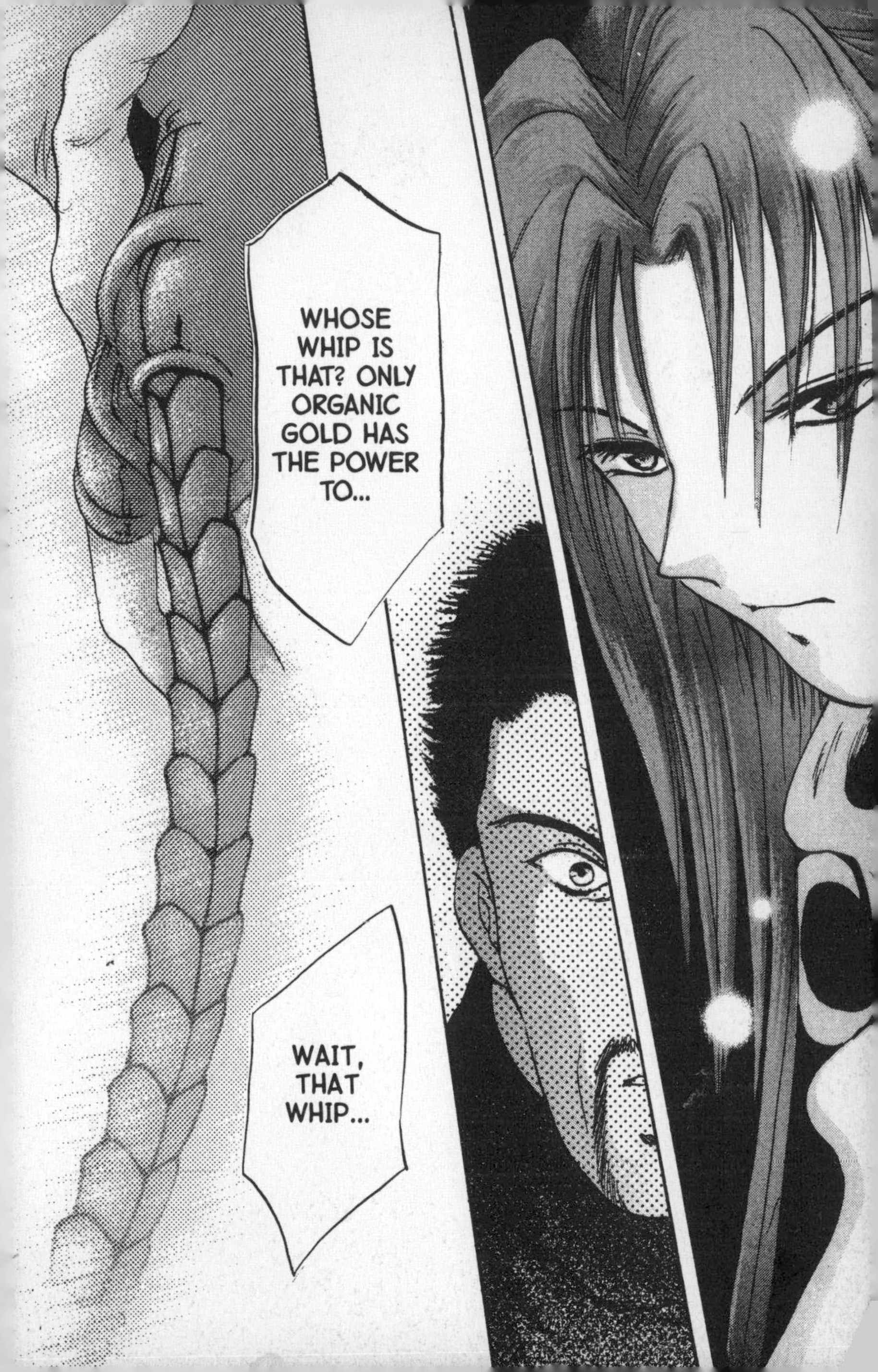
WHOSE WHIP IS THAT? ONLY ORGANIC GOLD HAS THE POWER TO...
WAIT, THAT WHIP...

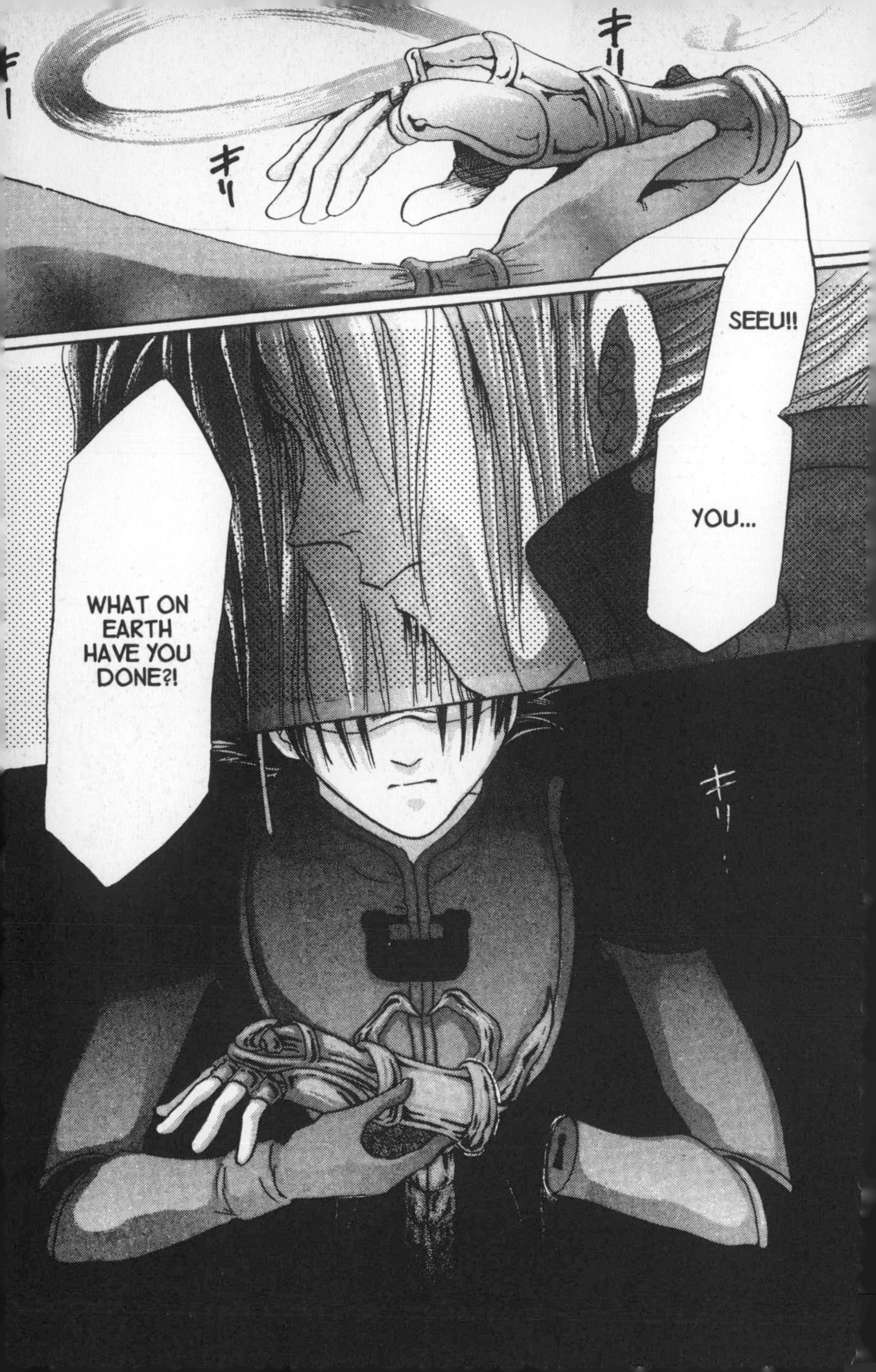
キリ
キリ
SEEU!!
YOU...
WHAT ON EARTH HAVE YOU DONE?!
キリ

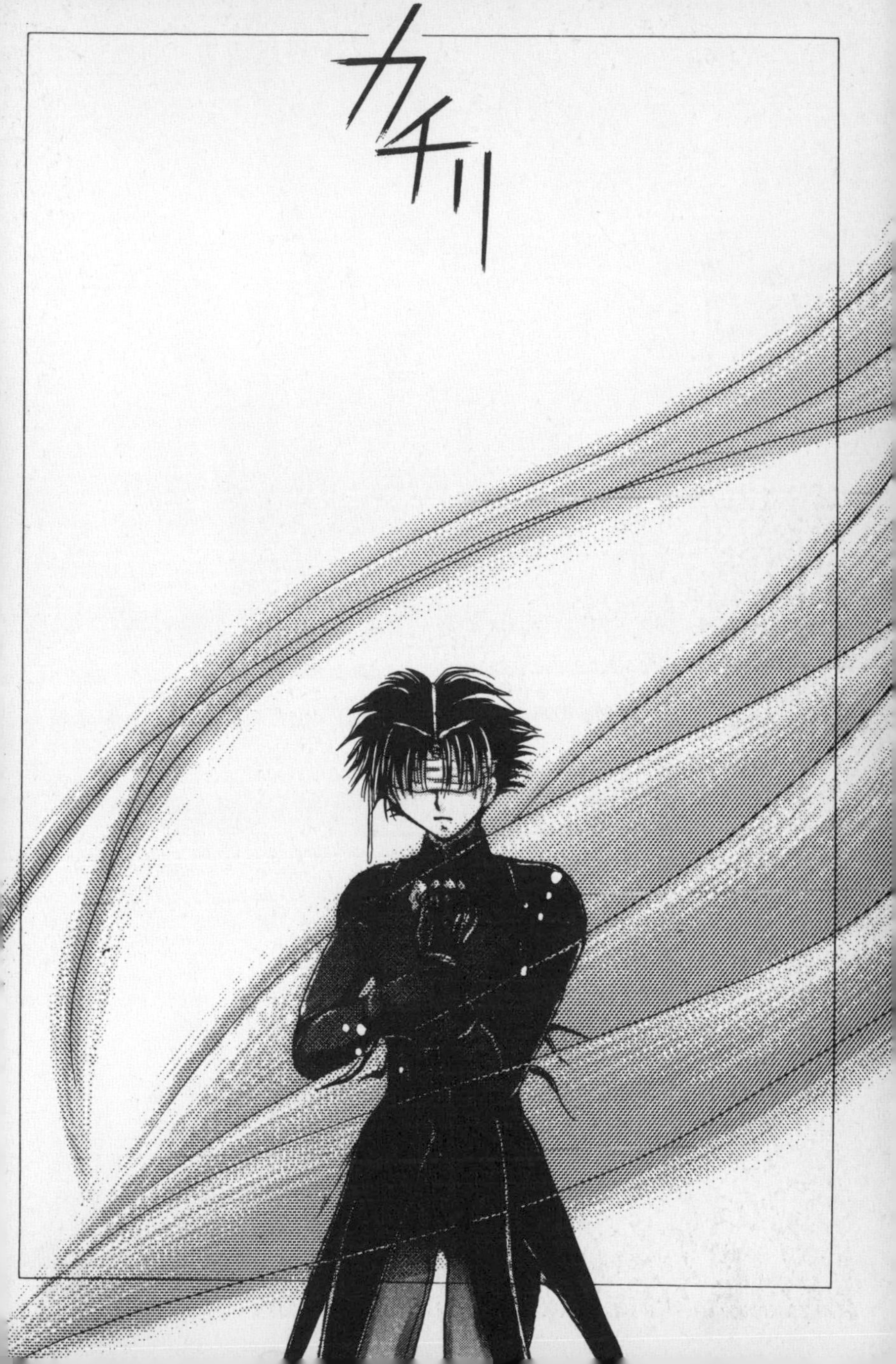
カチリ

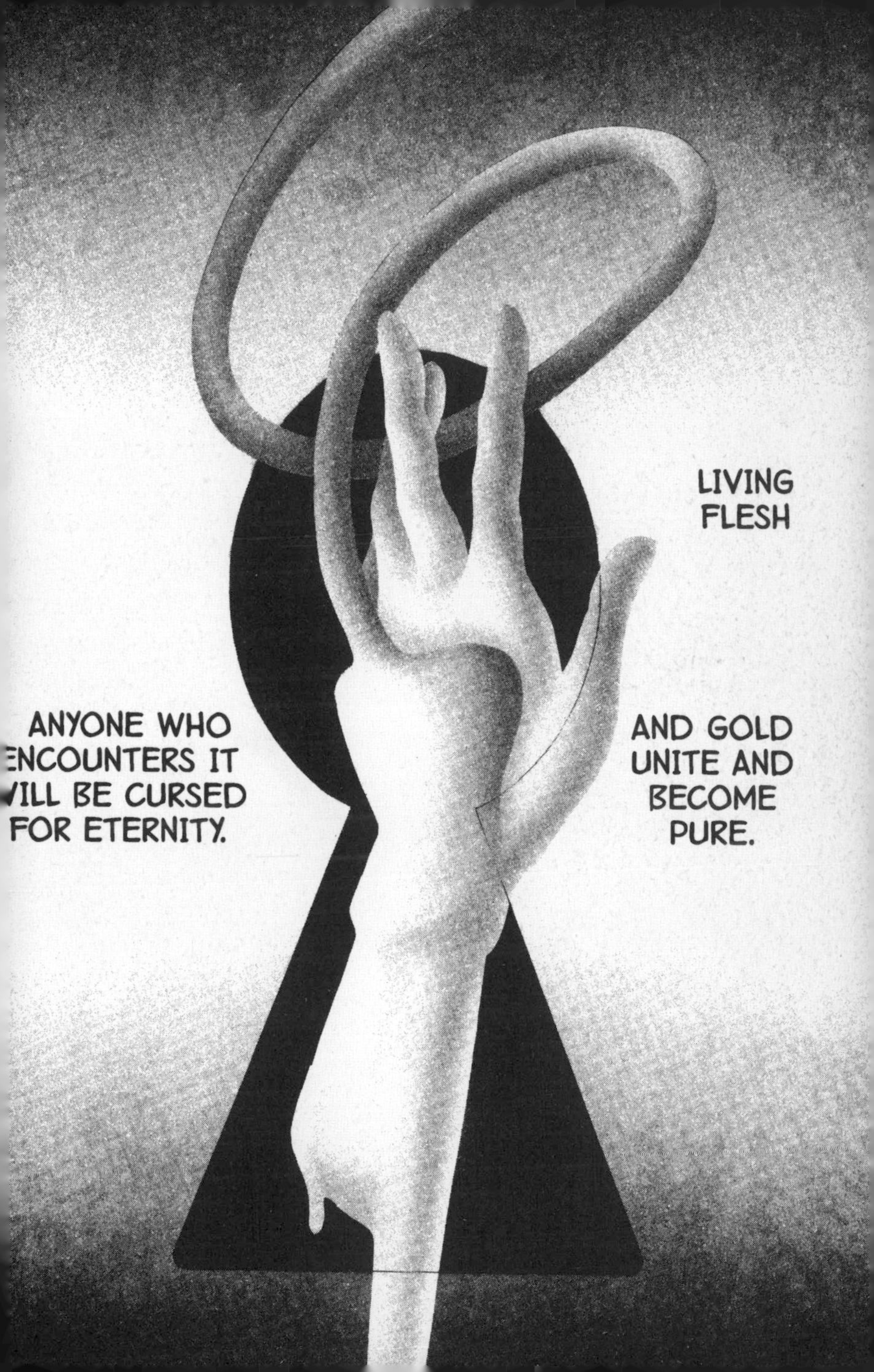
LIVING FLESH
AND GOLD UNITE AND BECOME PURE.
ANYONE WHO ENCOUNTERS IT WILL BE CURSED FOR ETERNITY.

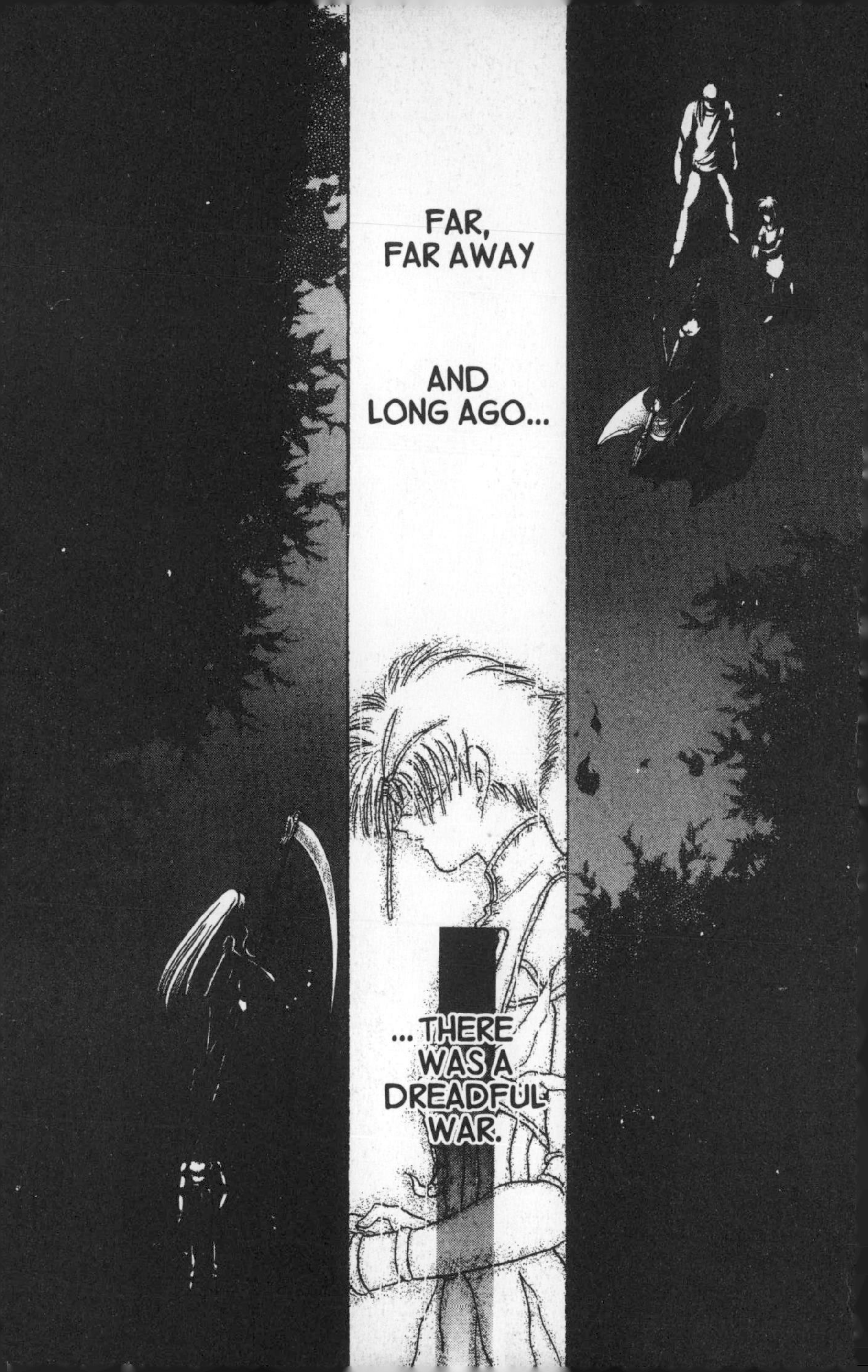
FAR, FAR AWAY
AND LONG AGO...
... THERE WAS A DREADFUL WAR.

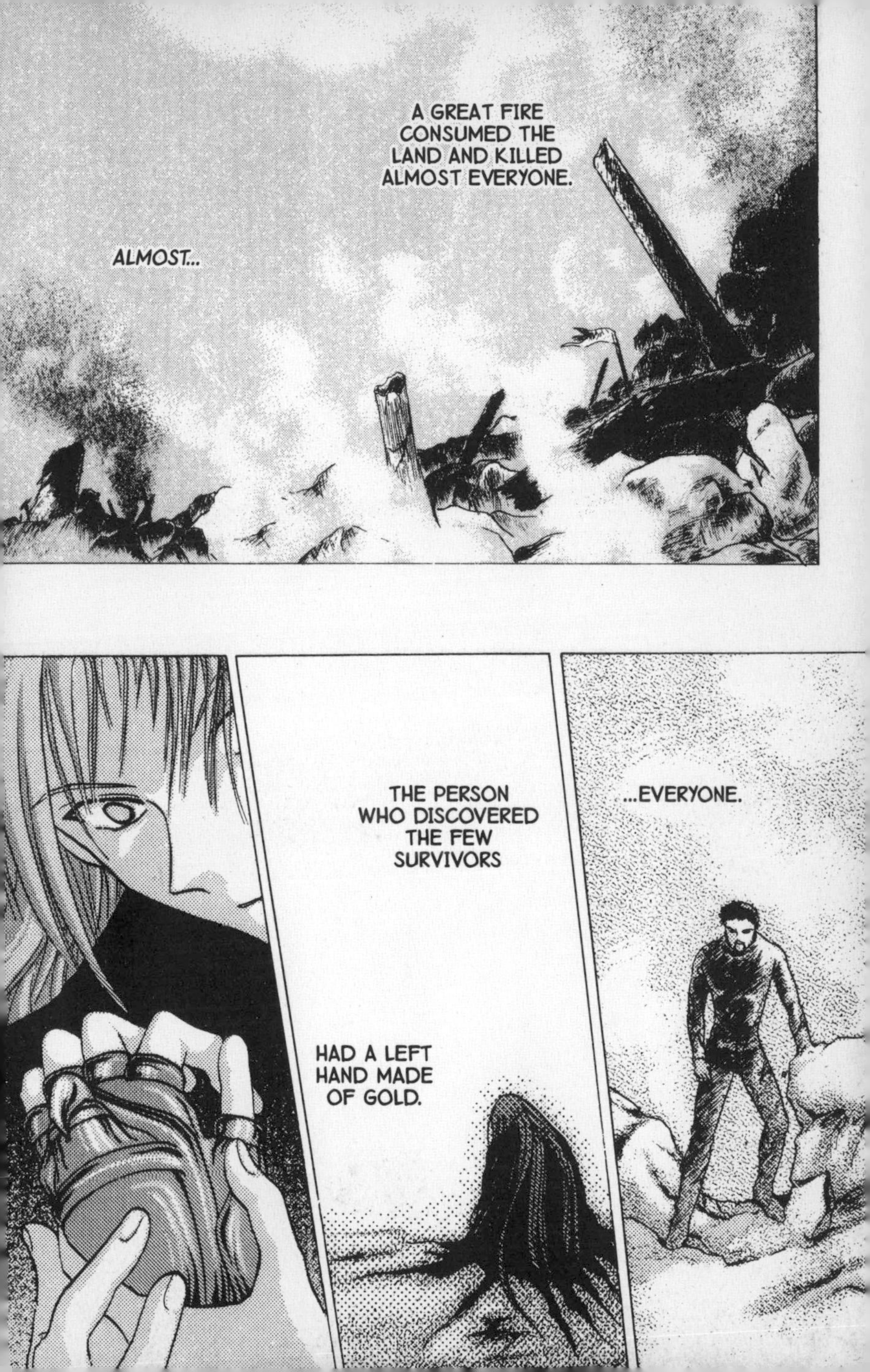
A GREAT FIRE CONSUMED THE LAND AND KILLED ALMOST EVERYONE.
ALMOST...
...EVERYONE.
THE PERSON WHO DISCOVERED THE FEW SURVIVORS
HAD A LEFT HAND MADE OF GOLD.

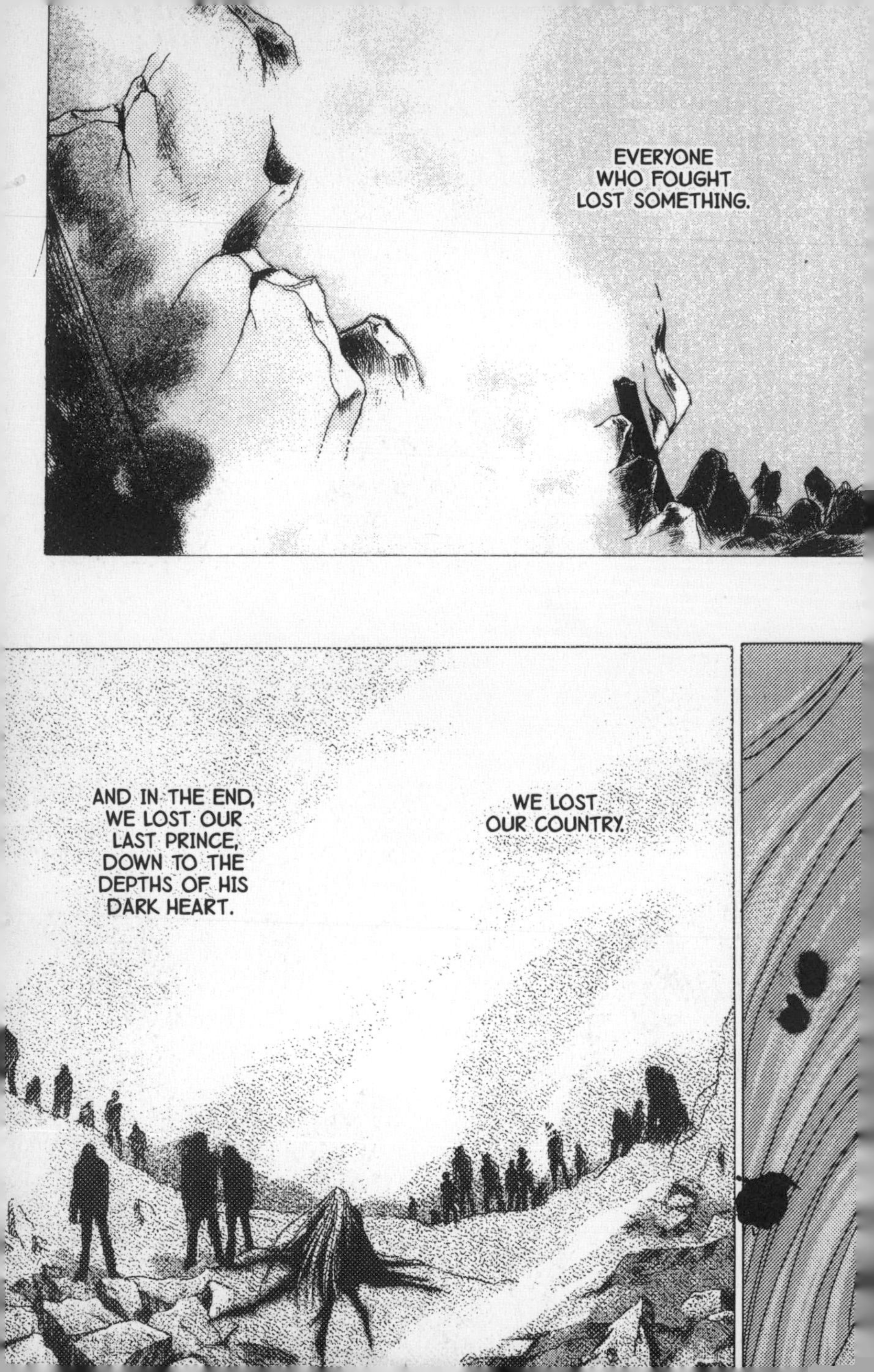
EVERYONE WHO FOUGHT LOST SOMETHING.
WE LOST OUR COUNTRY.
AND IN THE END, WE LOST OUR LAST PRINCE, DOWN TO THE DEPTHS OF HIS DARK HEART.

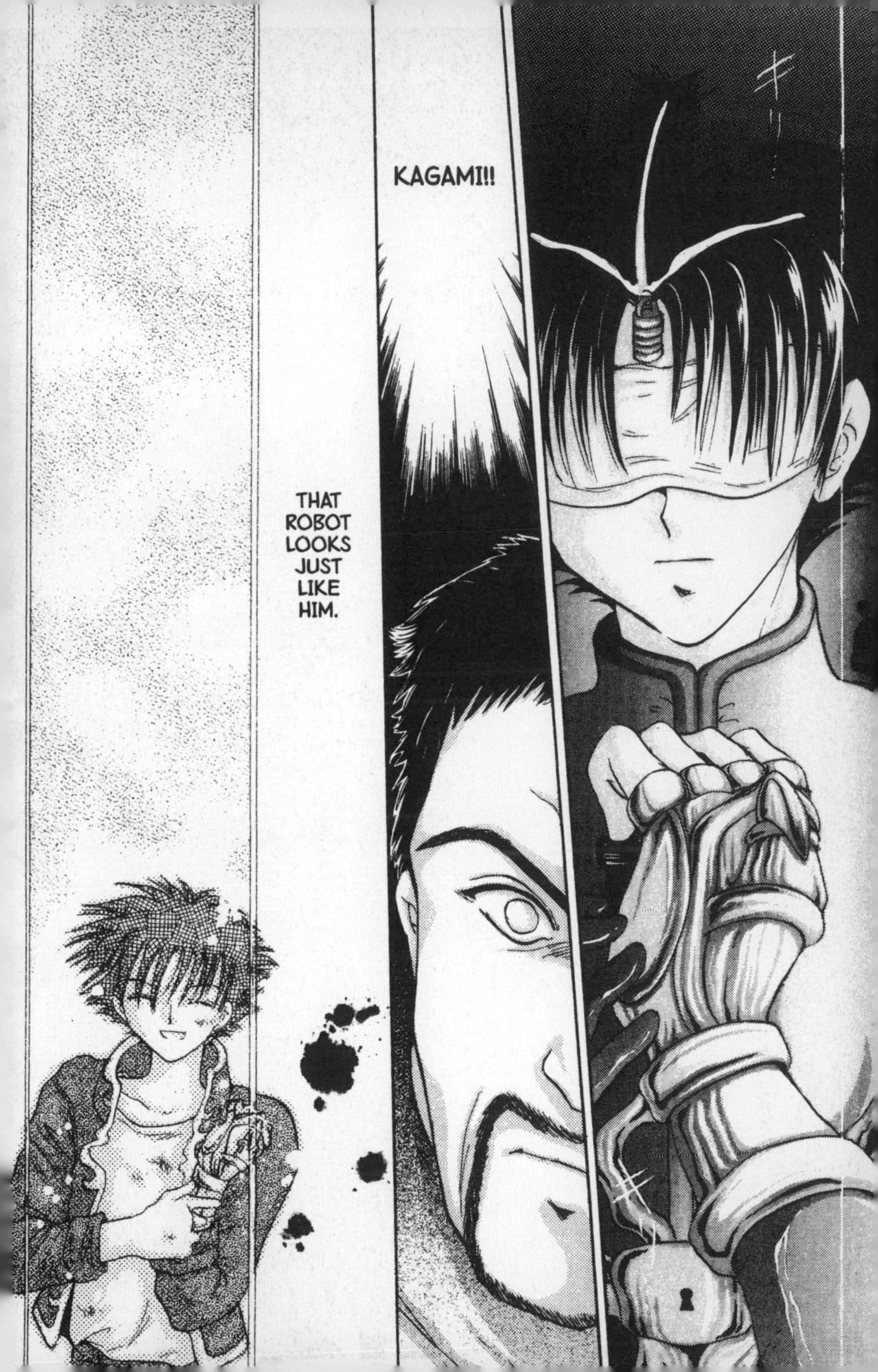
KAGAMI!!
THAT ROBOT LOOKS JUST LIKE HIM.

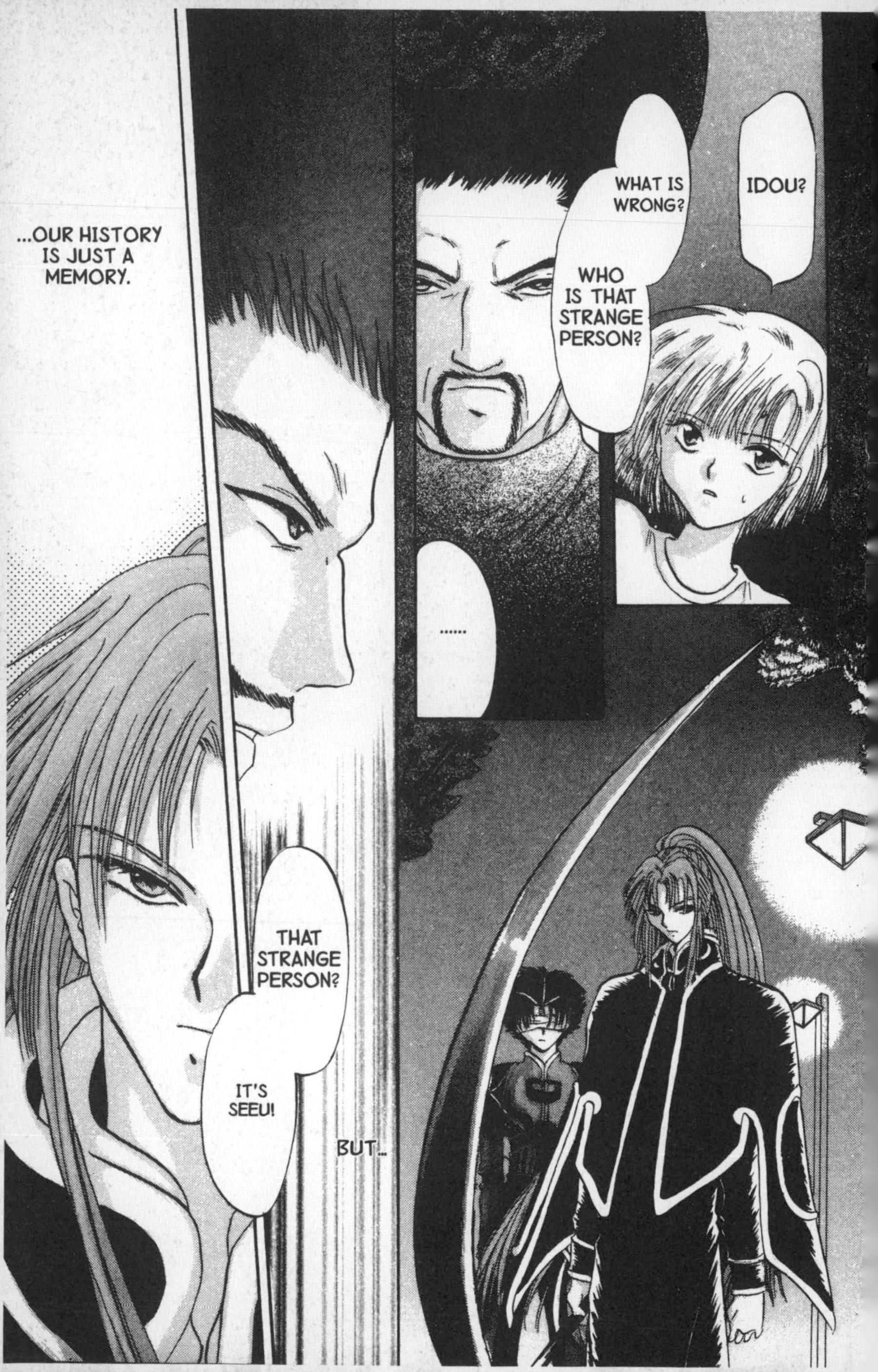
IDOU?
WHAT IS WRONG?
WHO IS THAT STRANGE PERSON?
......
THAT STRANGE PERSON?
IT'S SEEU!
BUT...
...OUR HISTORY IS JUST A MEMORY.

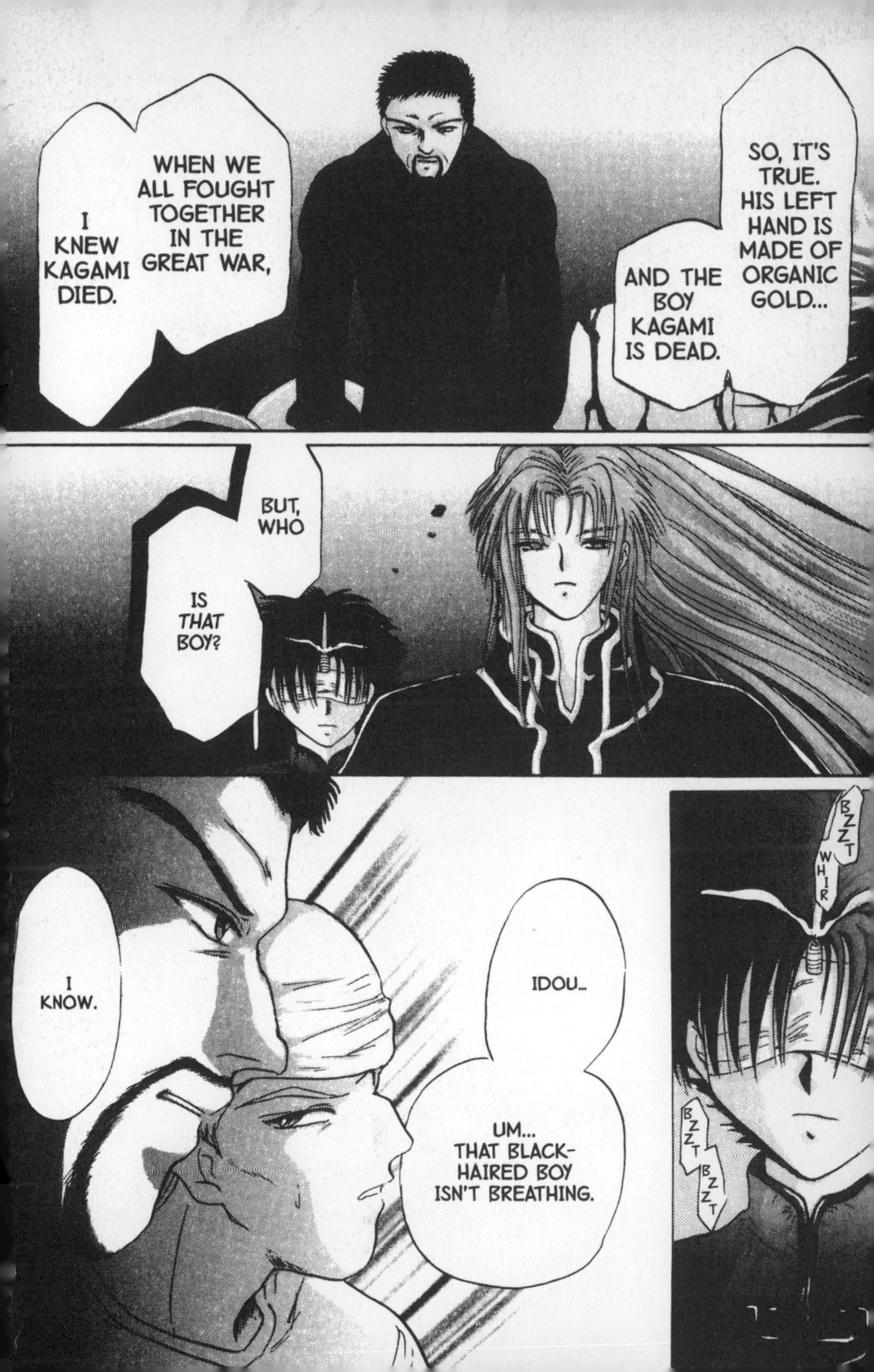
SO, IT'S TRUE. HIS LEFT HAND IS MADE OF ORGANIC GOLD...
AND THE BOY KAGAMI IS DEAD.
WHEN WE ALL FOUGHT TOGETHER IN THE GREAT WAR,
I KNEW KAGAMI DIED.
BUT, WHO
IS THAT BOY?
BZZT
WHIR
BZZT
BZZT
IDOU...
UM... THAT BLACK-HAIRED BOY ISN'T BREATHING.
I KNOW.

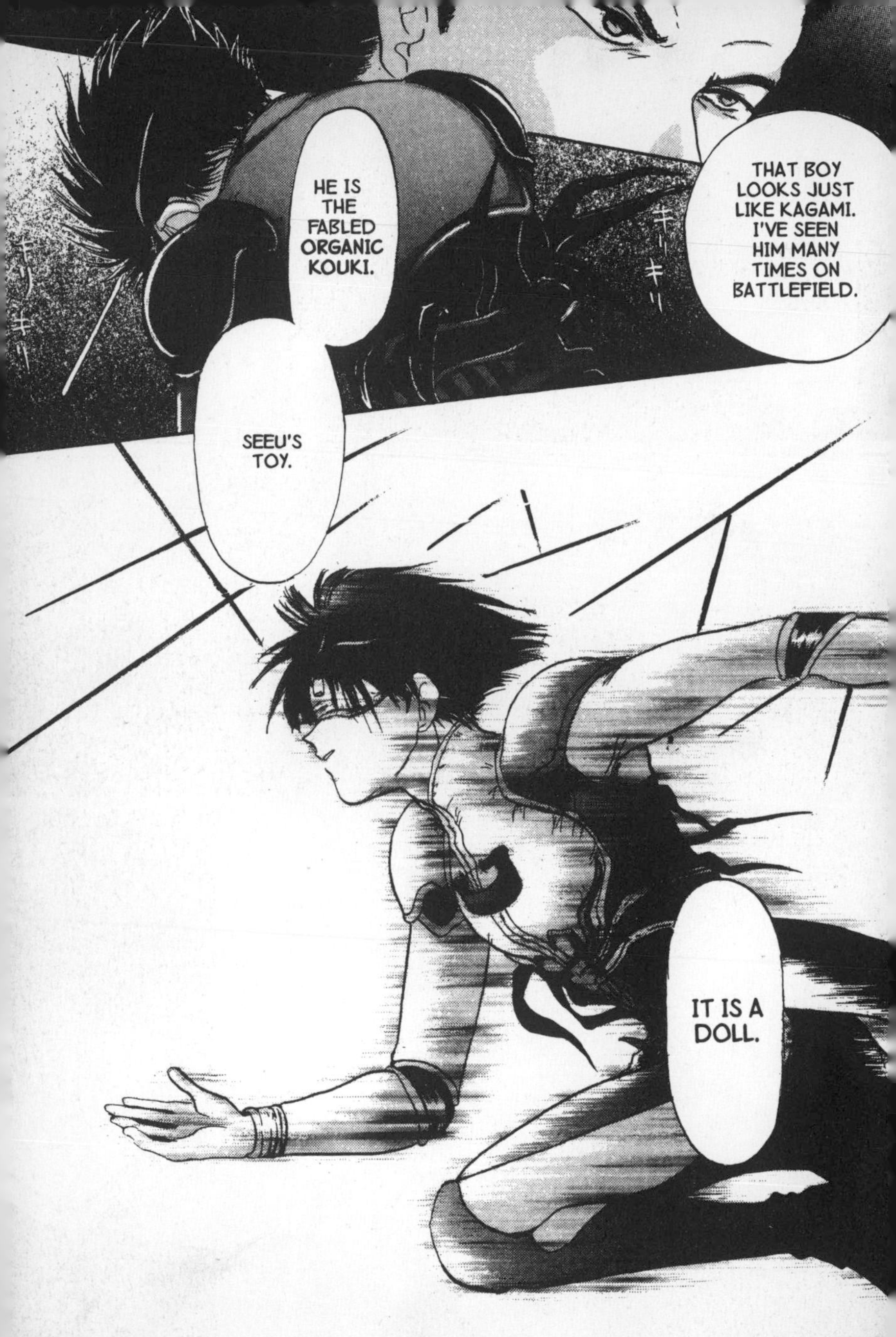
THAT BOY LOOKS JUST LIKE KAGAMI. I'VE SEEN HIM MANY TIMES ON BATTLEFIELD.
HE IS THE FABLED ORGANIC KOUKI.
SEEU'S TOY.
IT IS A DOLL.

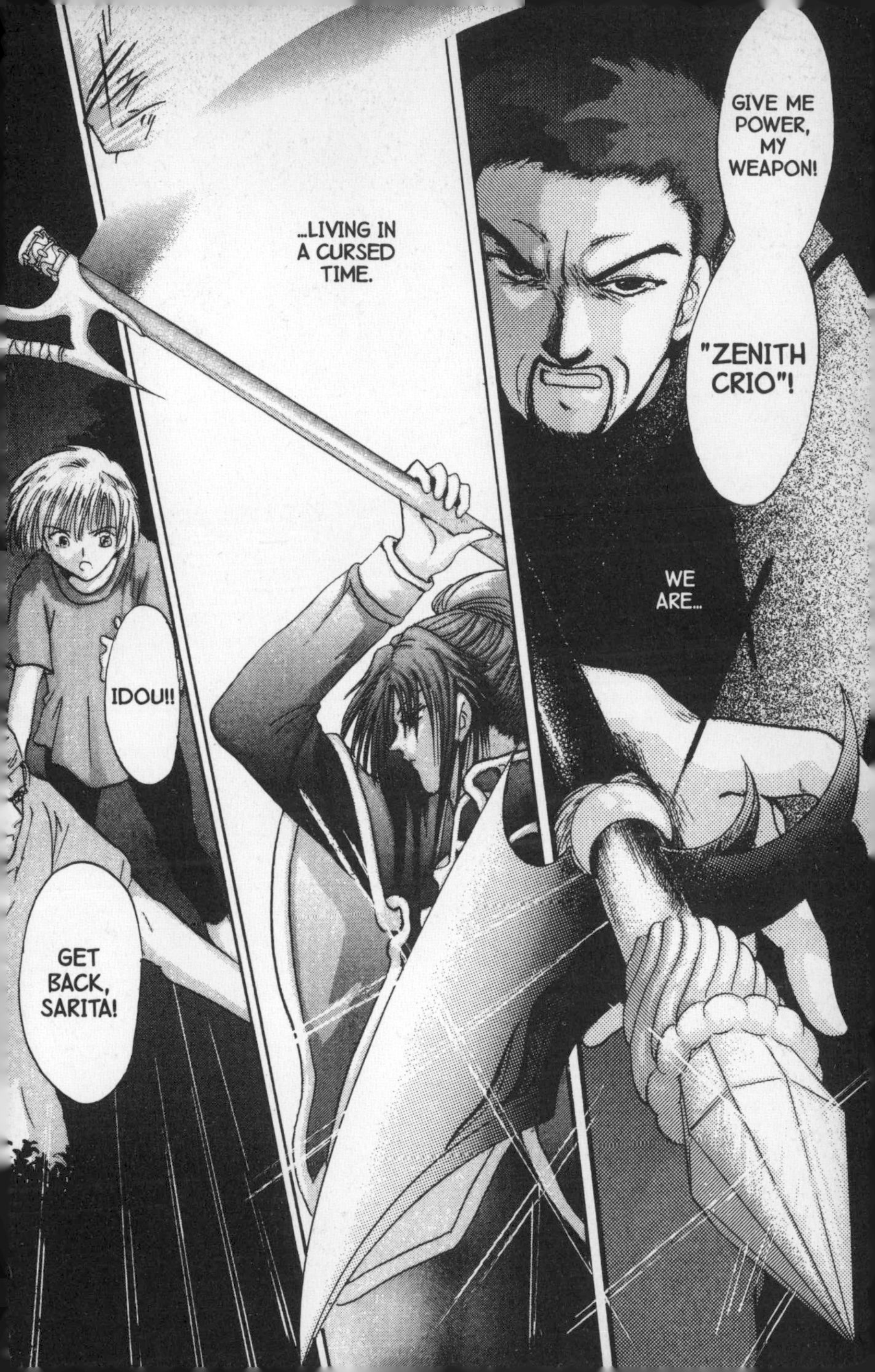
GIVE ME POWER, MY WEAPON!
"ZENITH CRIO"!
WE ARE...
...LIVING IN A CURSED TIME.
IDOU!!
GET BACK, SARITA!

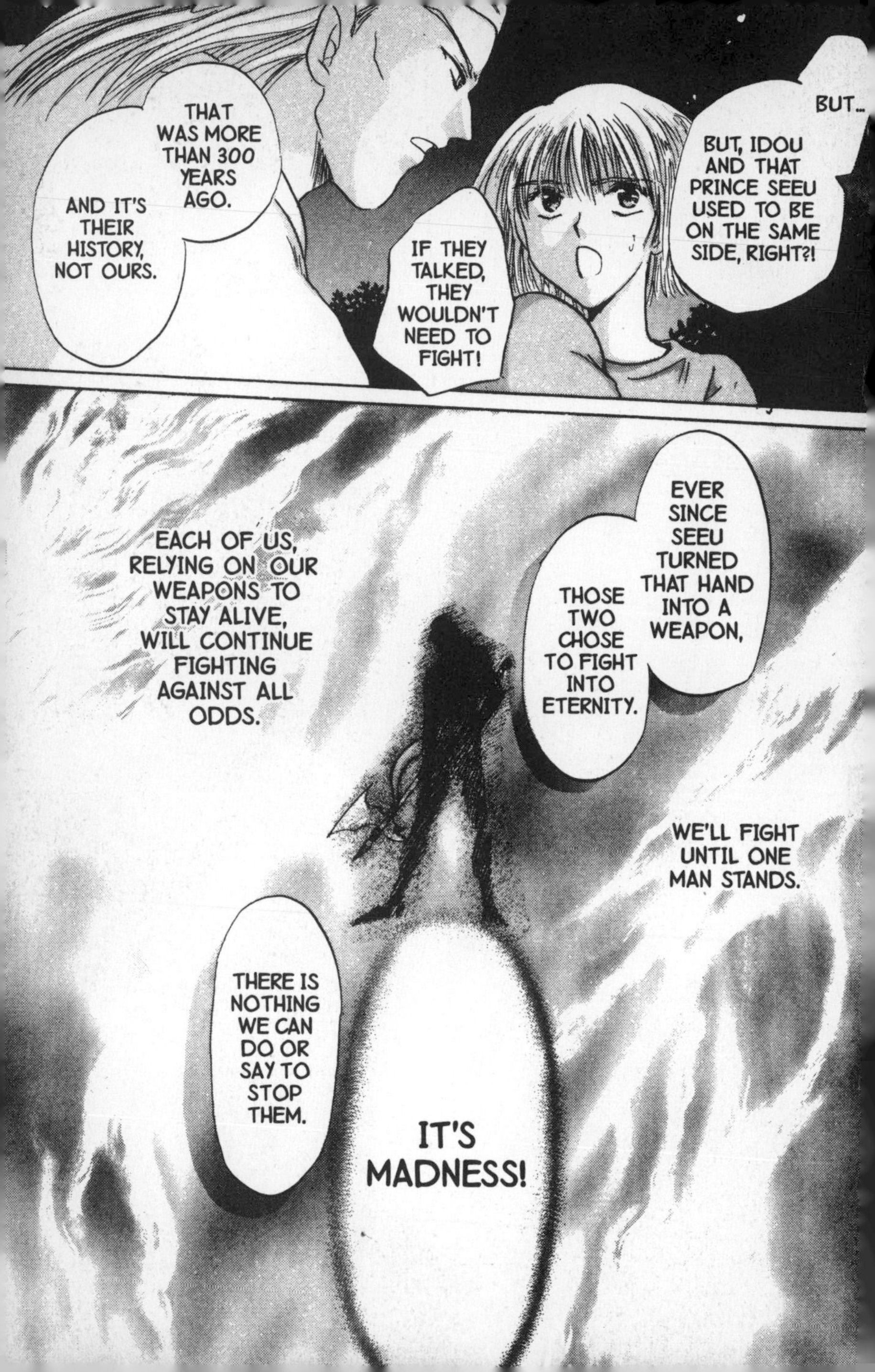
BUT...
BUT, IDOU AND THAT PRINCE SEEU USED TO BE ON THE SAME SIDE, RIGHT?!
IF THEY TALKED, THEY WOULDN'T NEED TO FIGHT!
THAT WAS MORE THAN 300 YEARS AGO.
AND IT'S THEIR HISTORY, NOT OURS.
EVER SINCE SEEU TURNED THAT HAND INTO A WEAPON,
THOSE TWO CHOSE TO FIGHT INTO ETERNITY.
EACH OF US, RELYING ON OUR WEAPONS TO STAY ALIVE, WILL CONTINUE FIGHTING AGAINST ALL ODDS.
WE'LL FIGHT UNTIL ONE MAN STANDS.
IT'S MADNESS!
THERE IS NOTHING WE CAN DO OR SAY TO STOP THEM.

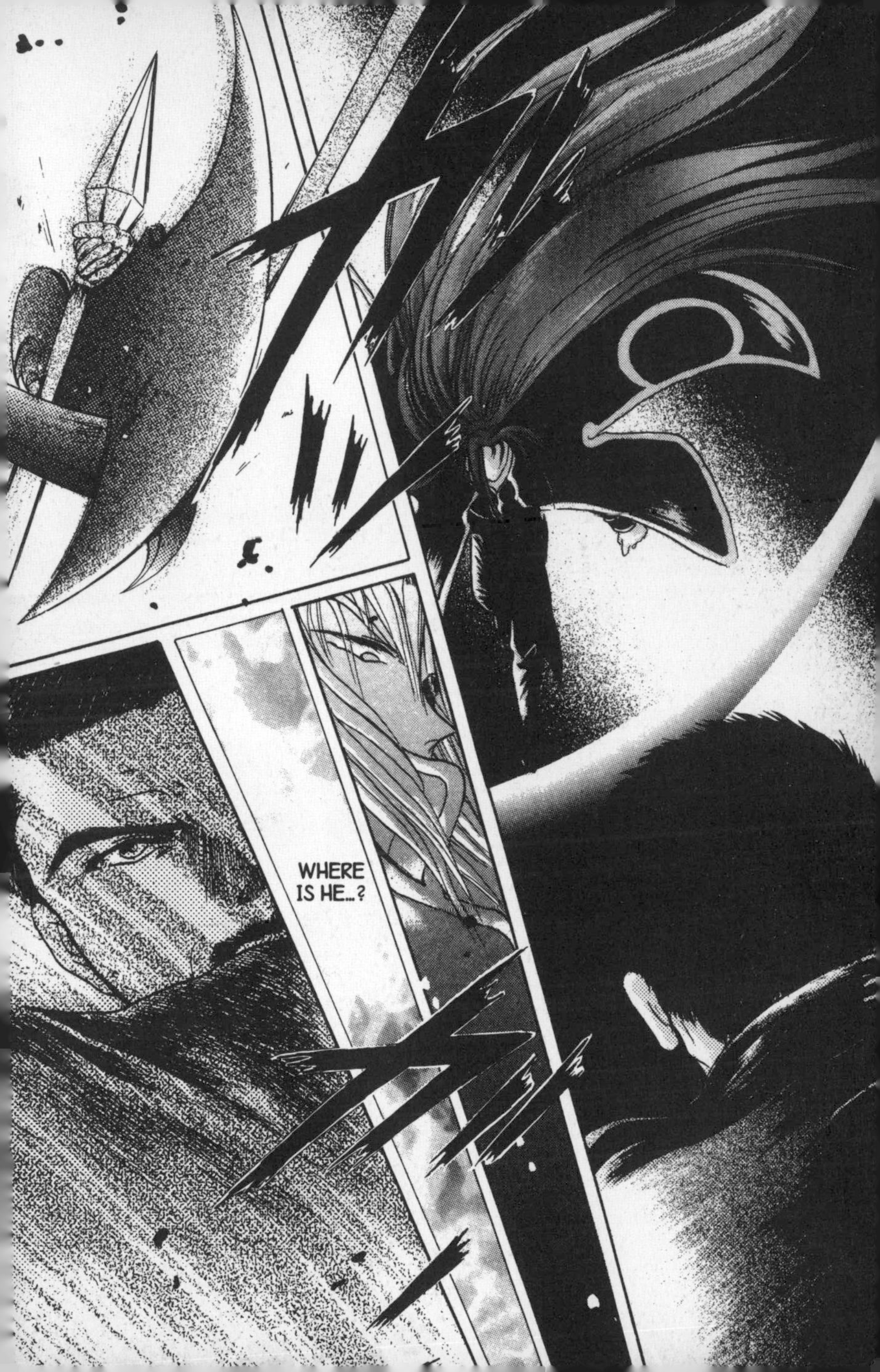
WHERE IS HE...?

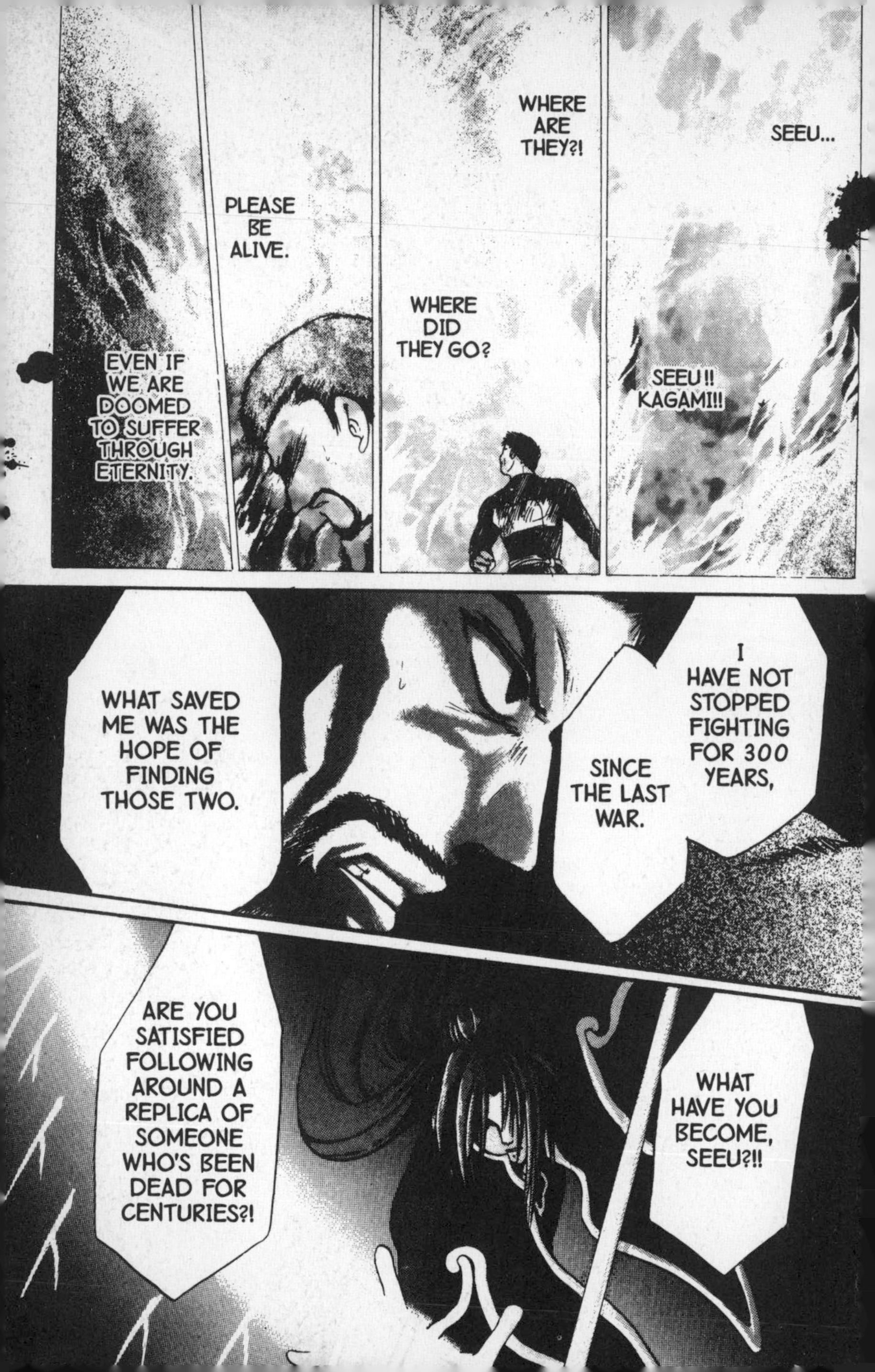
SEEU...
SEEU!! KAGAMI!!
WHERE ARE THEY?!
WHERE DID THEY GO?
PLEASE BE ALIVE.
EVEN IF WE ARE DOOMED TO SUFFER THROUGH ETERNITY.
I HAVE NOT STOPPED FIGHTING FOR 300 YEARS,
SINCE THE LAST WAR.
WHAT SAVED ME WAS THE HOPE OF FINDING THOSE TWO.
WHAT HAVE YOU BECOME, SEEU?!!
ARE YOU SATISFIED FOLLOWING AROUND A REPLICA OF SOMEONE WHO'S BEEN DEAD FOR CENTURIES?!

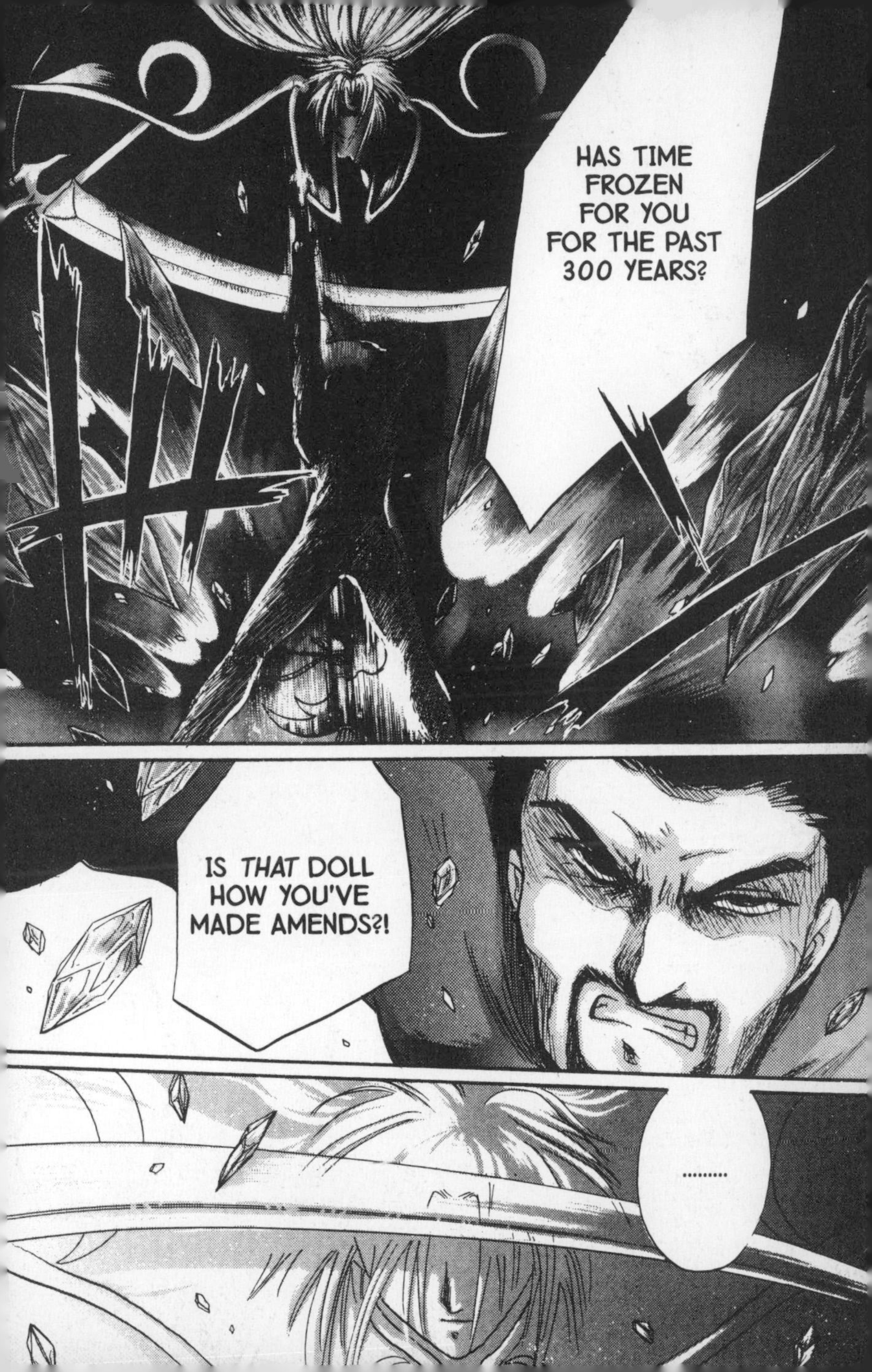
HAS TIME FROZEN FOR YOU FOR THE PAST 300 YEARS?
IS *THAT* DOLL HOW YOU'VE MADE AMENDS?!
....

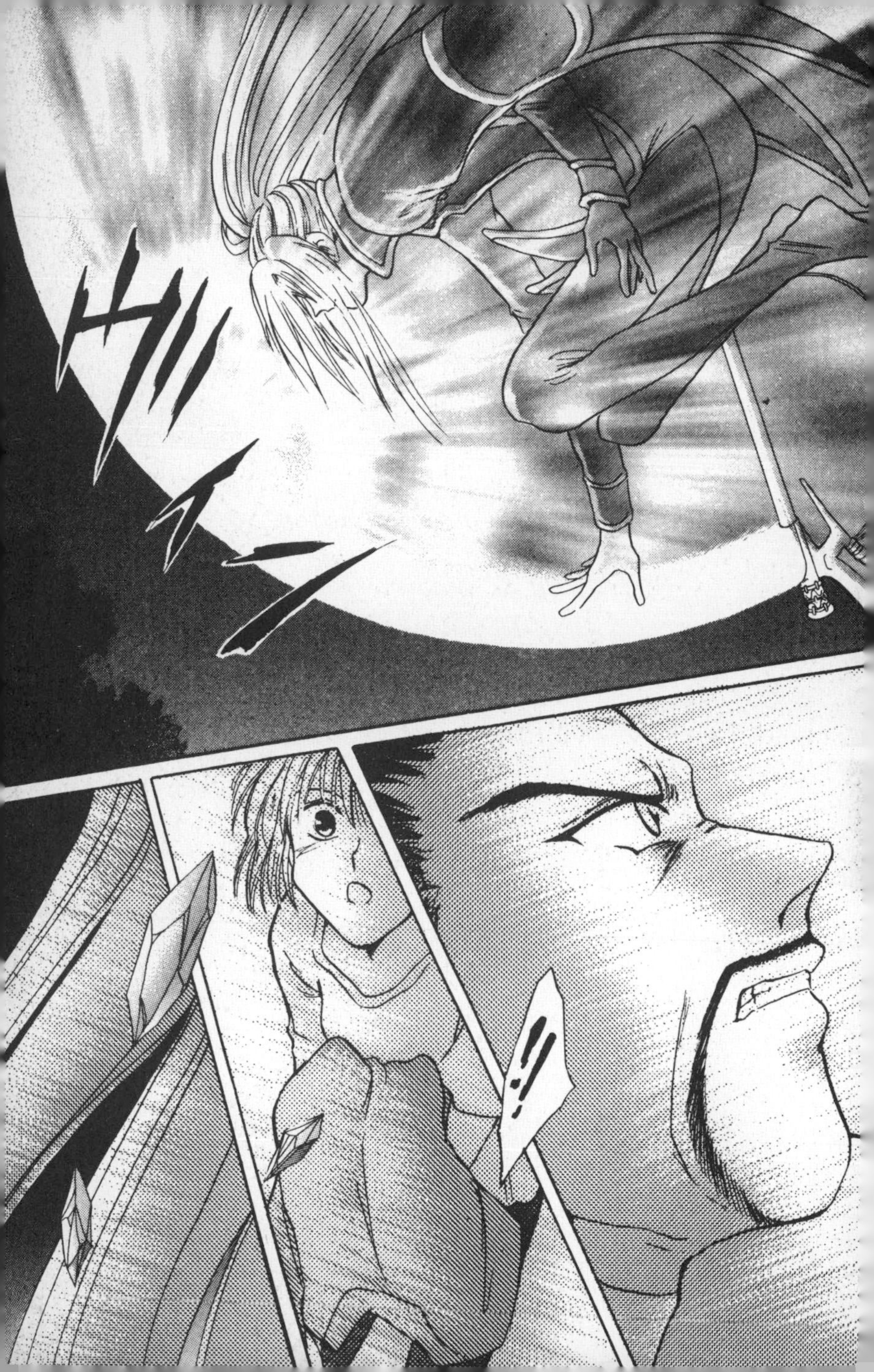
サリイーン
!!

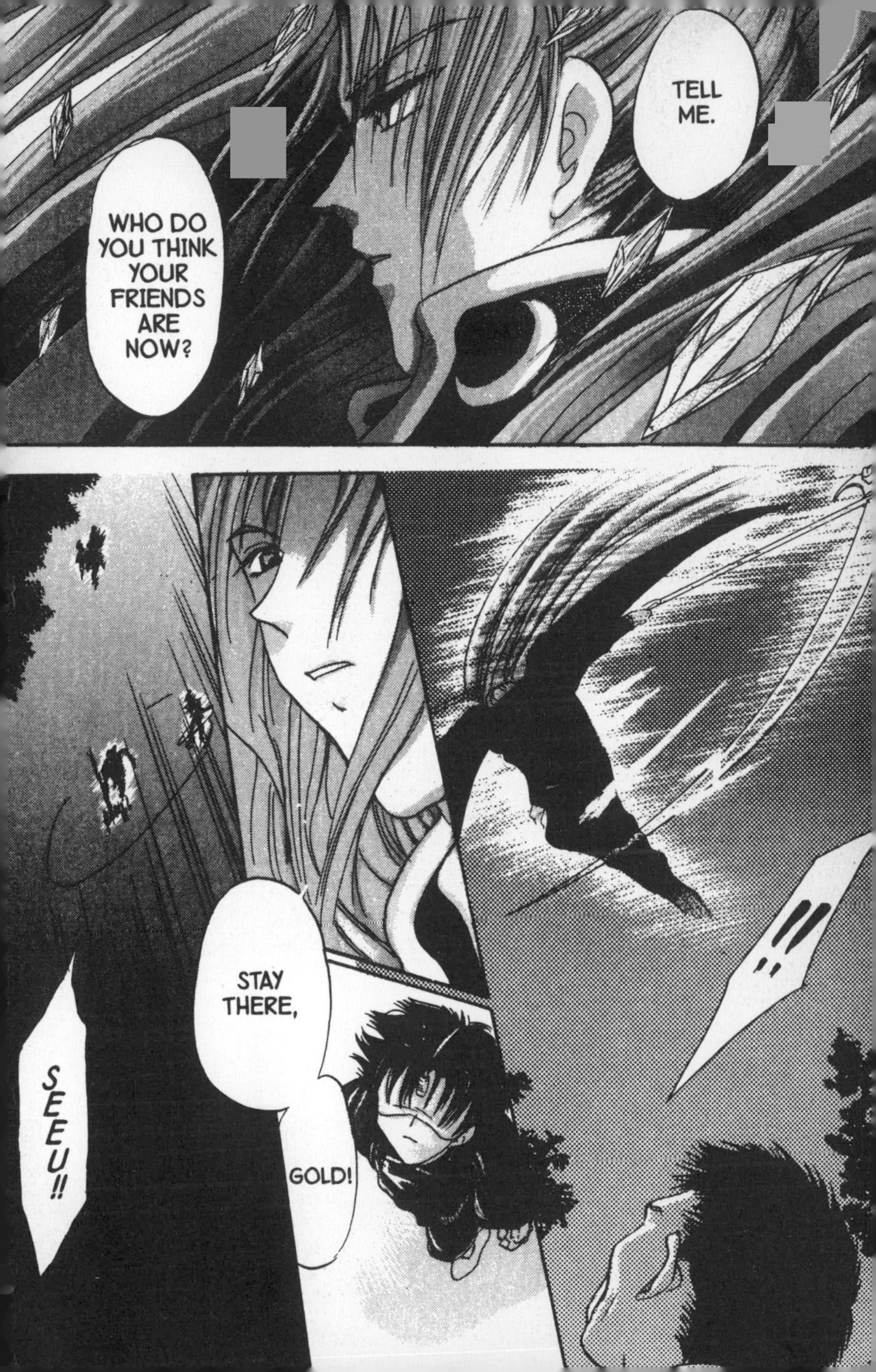
TELL ME.
WHO DO YOU THINK YOUR FRIENDS ARE NOW?
!!
STAY THERE,
GOLD!
SEEU!!

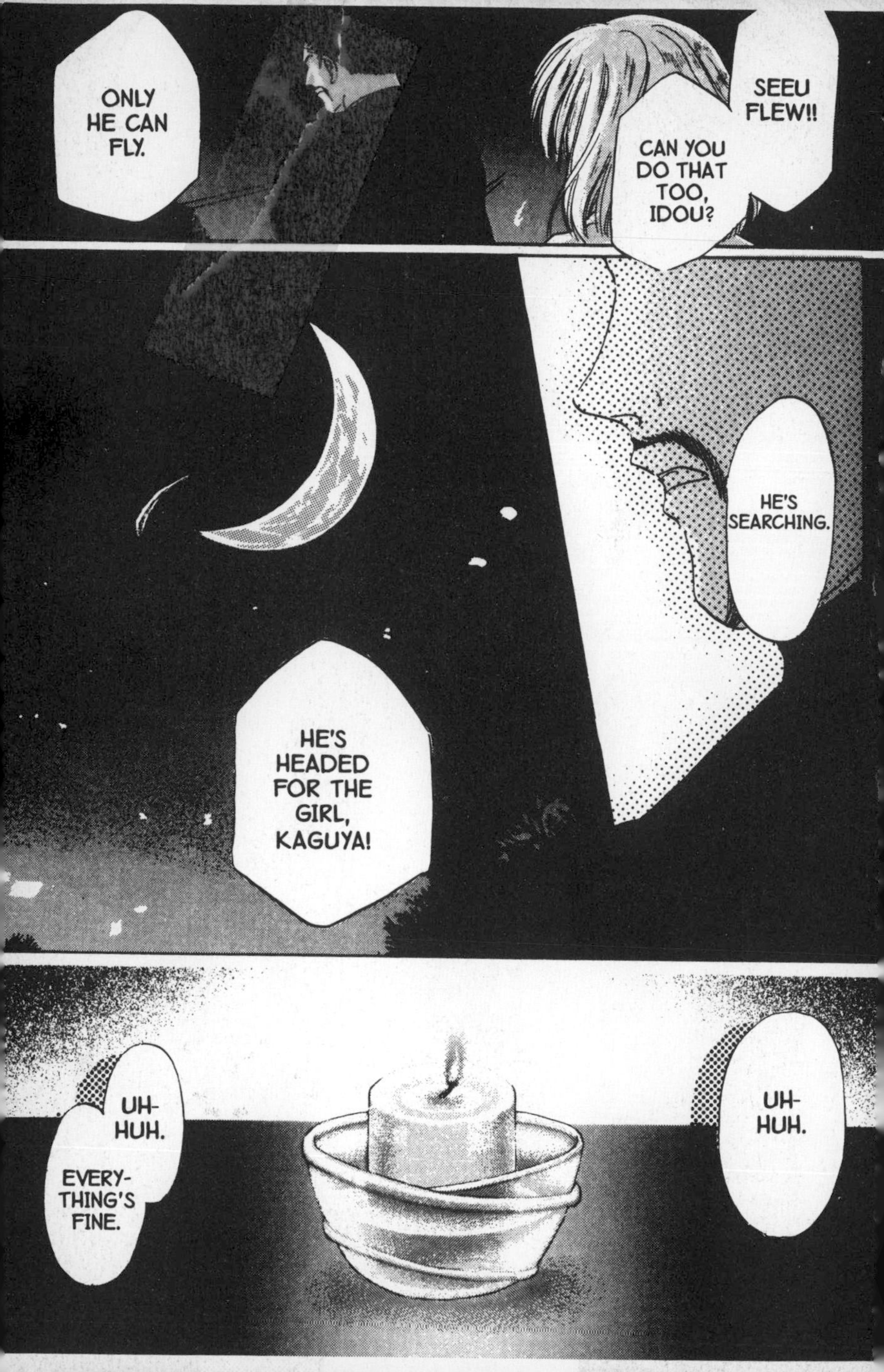
SEEU FLEW!!
CAN YOU DO THAT TOO, IDOU?
ONLY HE CAN FLY.
HE'S SEARCHING.
HE'S HEADED FOR THE GIRL, KAGUYA!
UH-HUH.
UH-HUH.
EVERY-THING'S FINE.

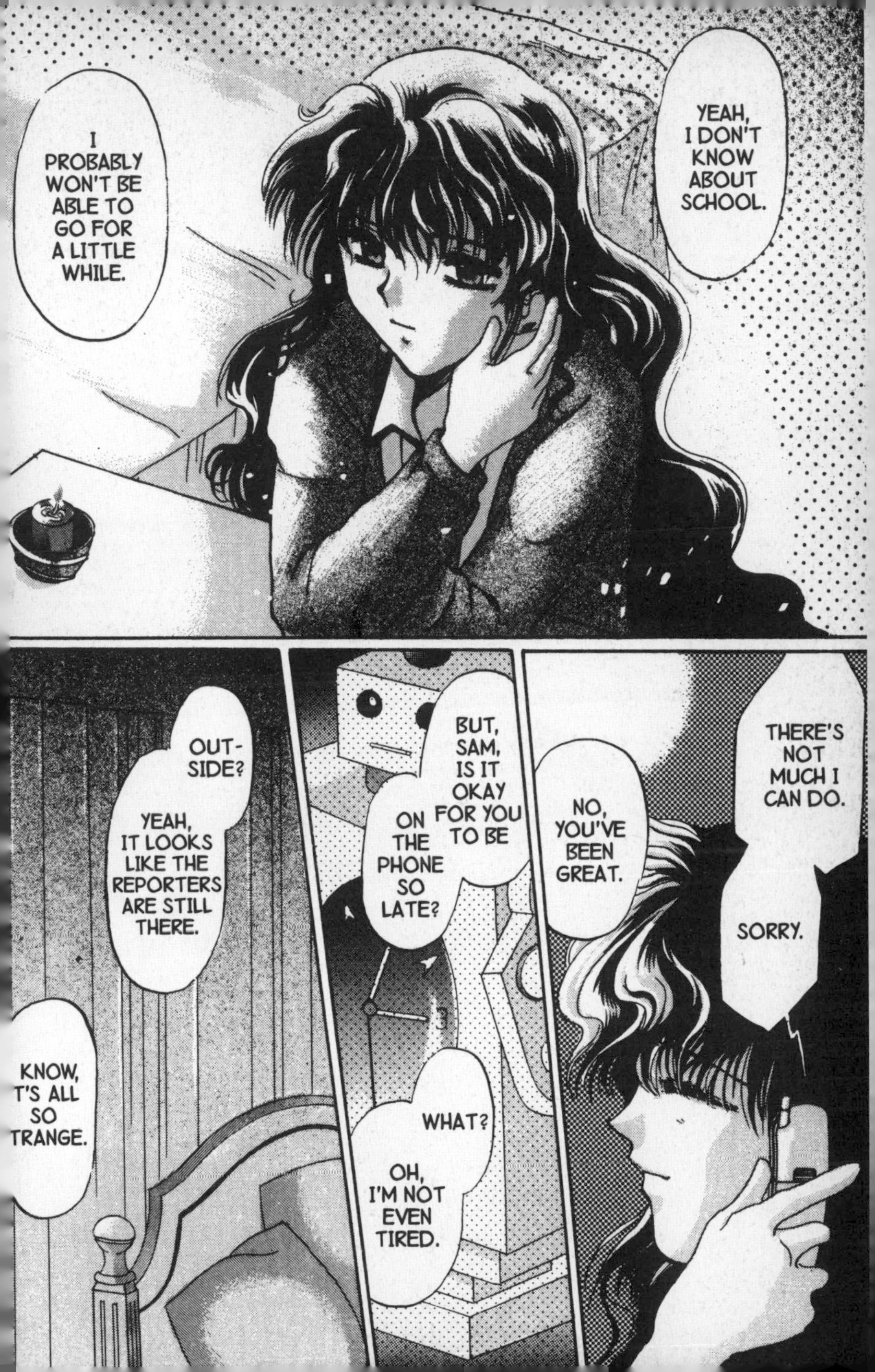
YEAH, I DON'T KNOW ABOUT SCHOOL.
I PROBABLY WON'T BE ABLE TO GO FOR A LITTLE WHILE.
THERE'S NOT MUCH I CAN DO.
SORRY.
NO, YOU'VE BEEN GREAT.
BUT, SAM, IS IT OKAY FOR YOU TO BE
ON THE PHONE SO LATE?
WHAT?
OH, I'M NOT EVEN TIRED.
OUT-SIDE?
YEAH, IT LOOKS LIKE THE REPORTERS ARE STILL THERE.
KNOW, T'S ALL SO TRANGE.

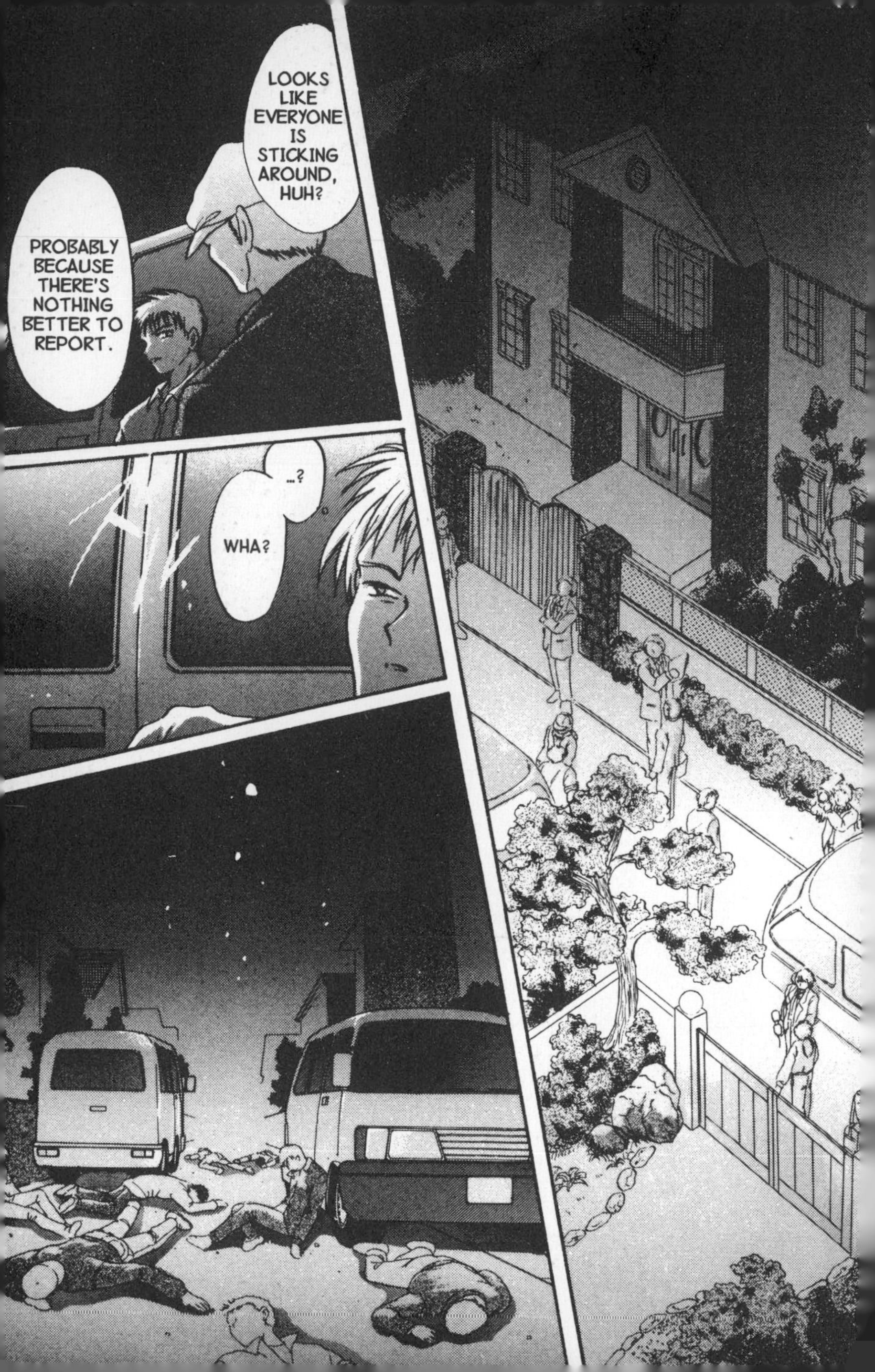
LOOKS LIKE EVERYONE IS STICKING AROUND, HUH?
PROBABLY BECAUSE THERE'S NOTHING BETTER TO REPORT.
...?
WHA?

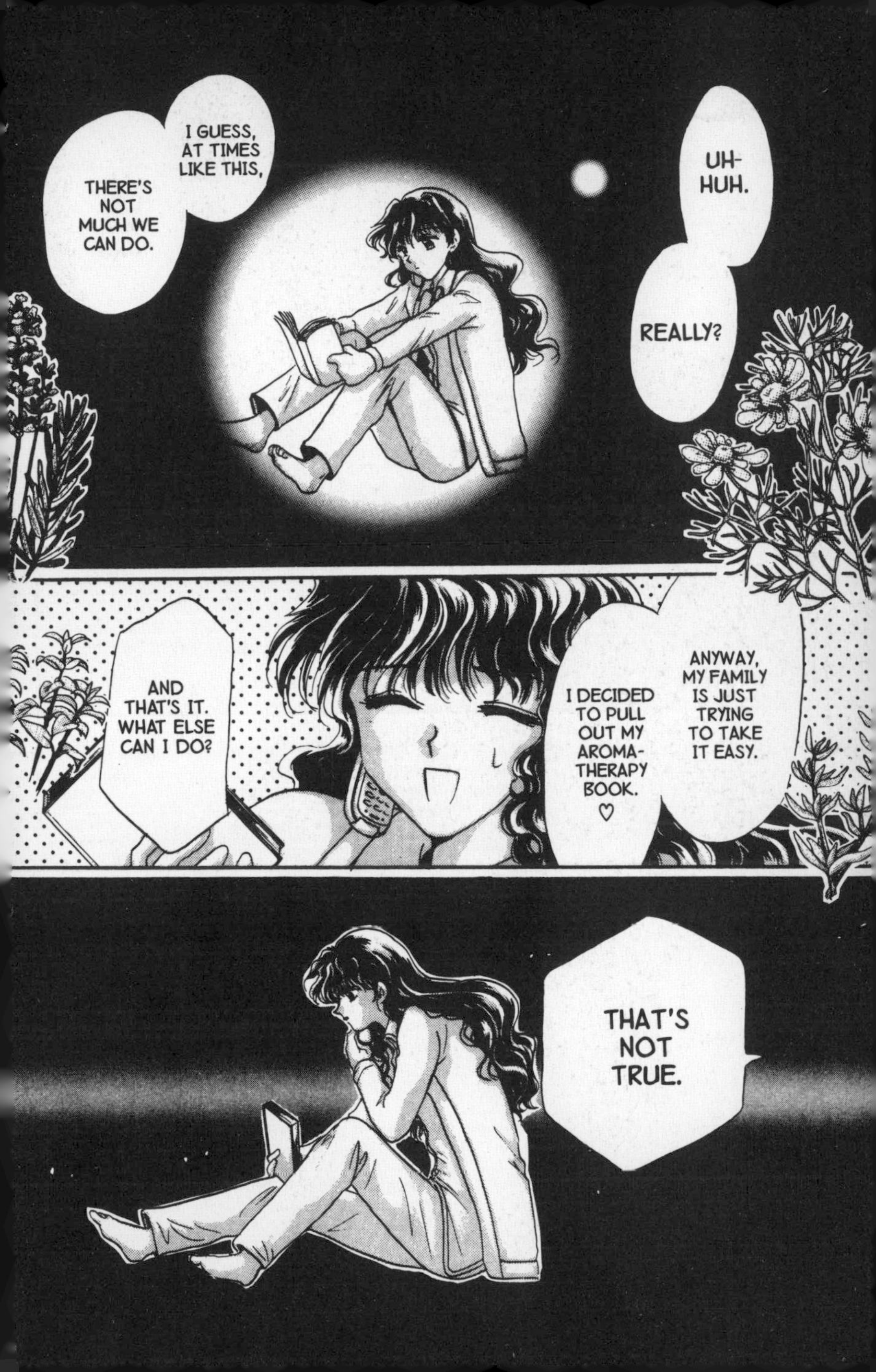
UH-HUH.
REALLY?
I GUESS, AT TIMES LIKE THIS,
THERE'S NOT MUCH WE CAN DO.
ANYWAY, MY FAMILY IS JUST TRYING TO TAKE IT EASY.
I DECIDED TO PULL OUT MY AROMA-THERAPY BOOK. ♡
AND THAT'S IT. WHAT ELSE CAN I DO?
THAT'S NOT TRUE.

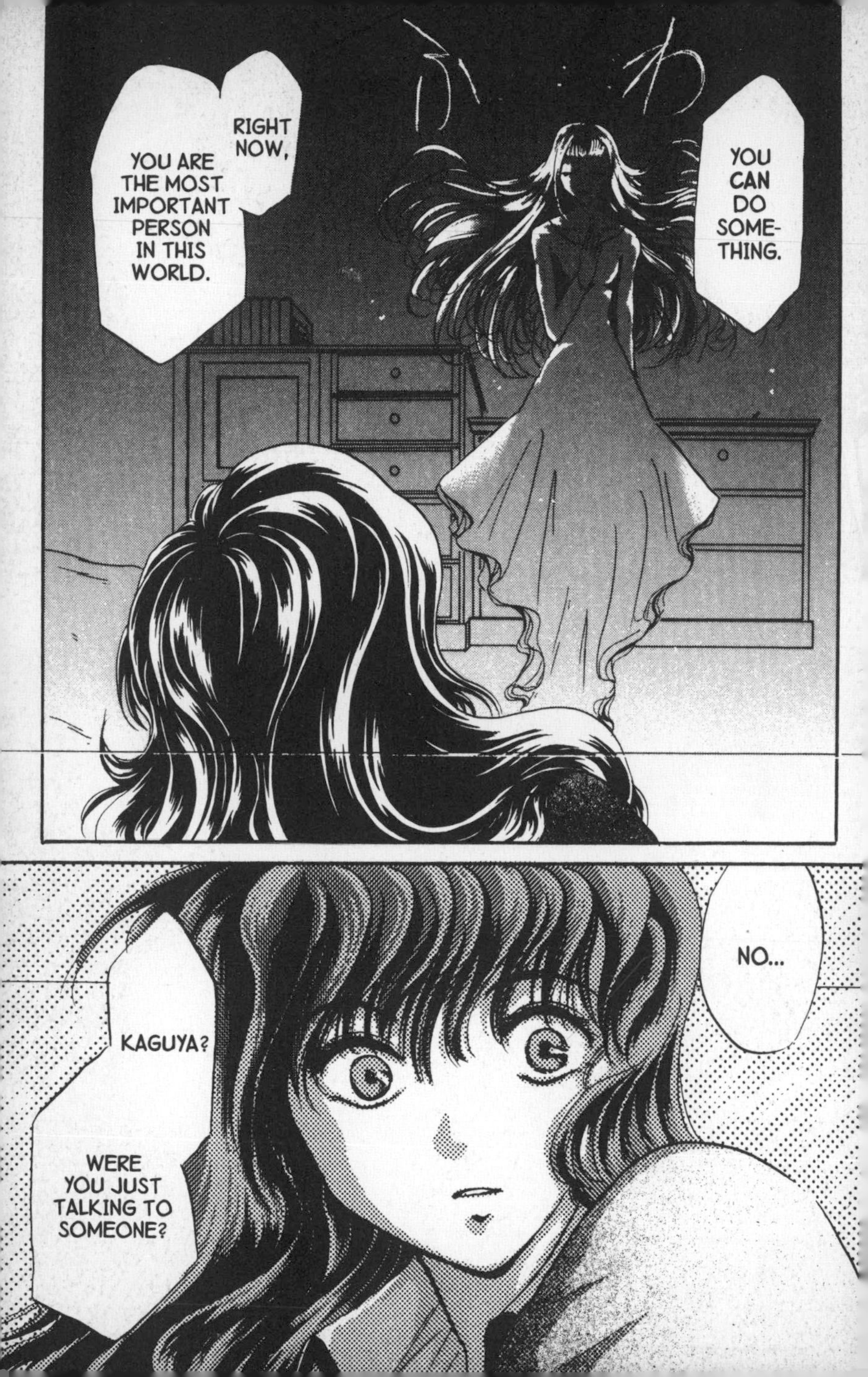
YOU CAN DO SOME-THING.
RIGHT NOW, YOU ARE THE MOST IMPORTANT PERSON IN THIS WORLD.
NO...
KAGUYA?
WERE YOU JUST TALKING TO SOMEONE?

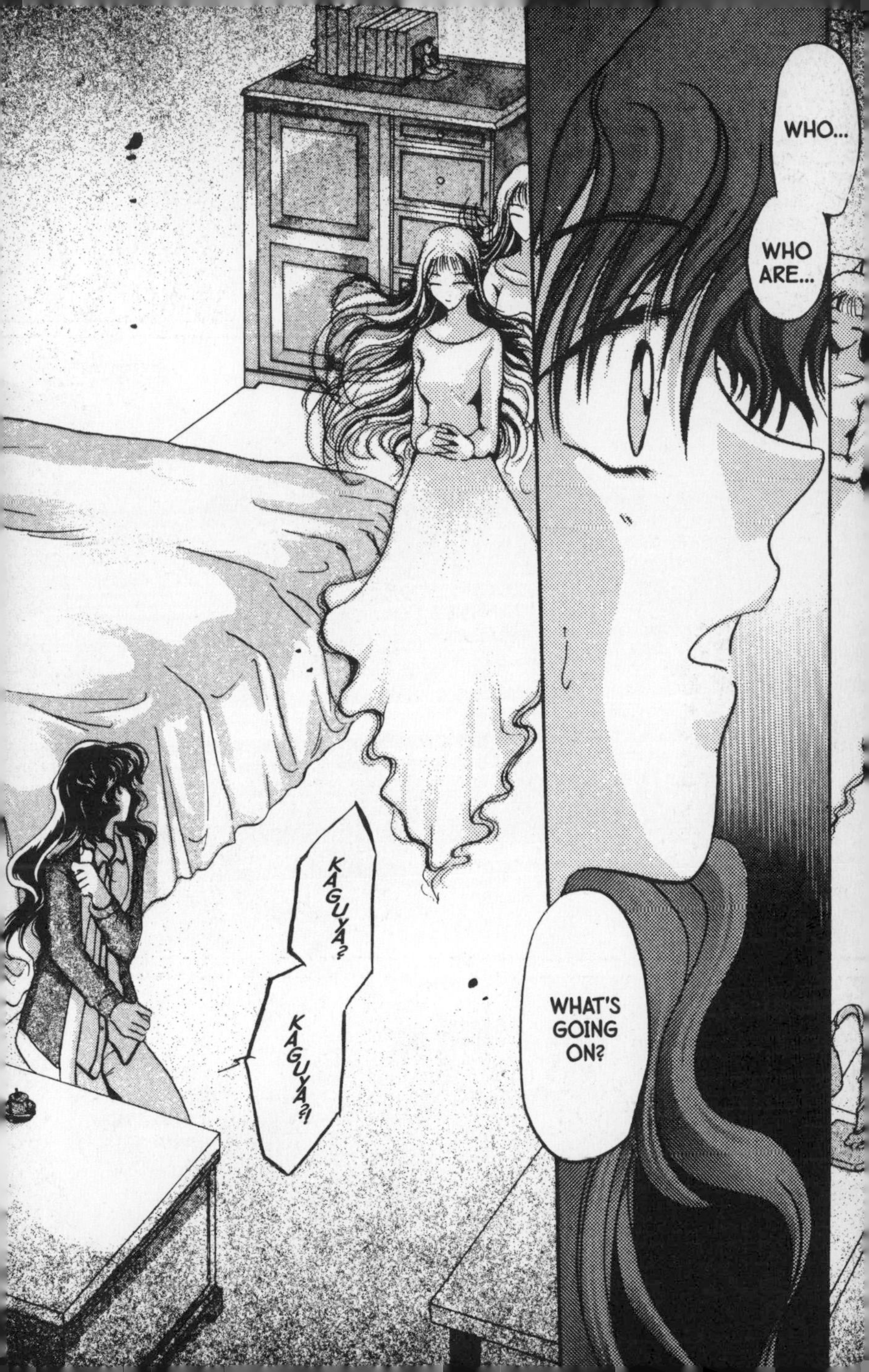
WHO...
WHO ARE...
WHAT'S GOING ON?
KAGUYA?
KAGUYA?!

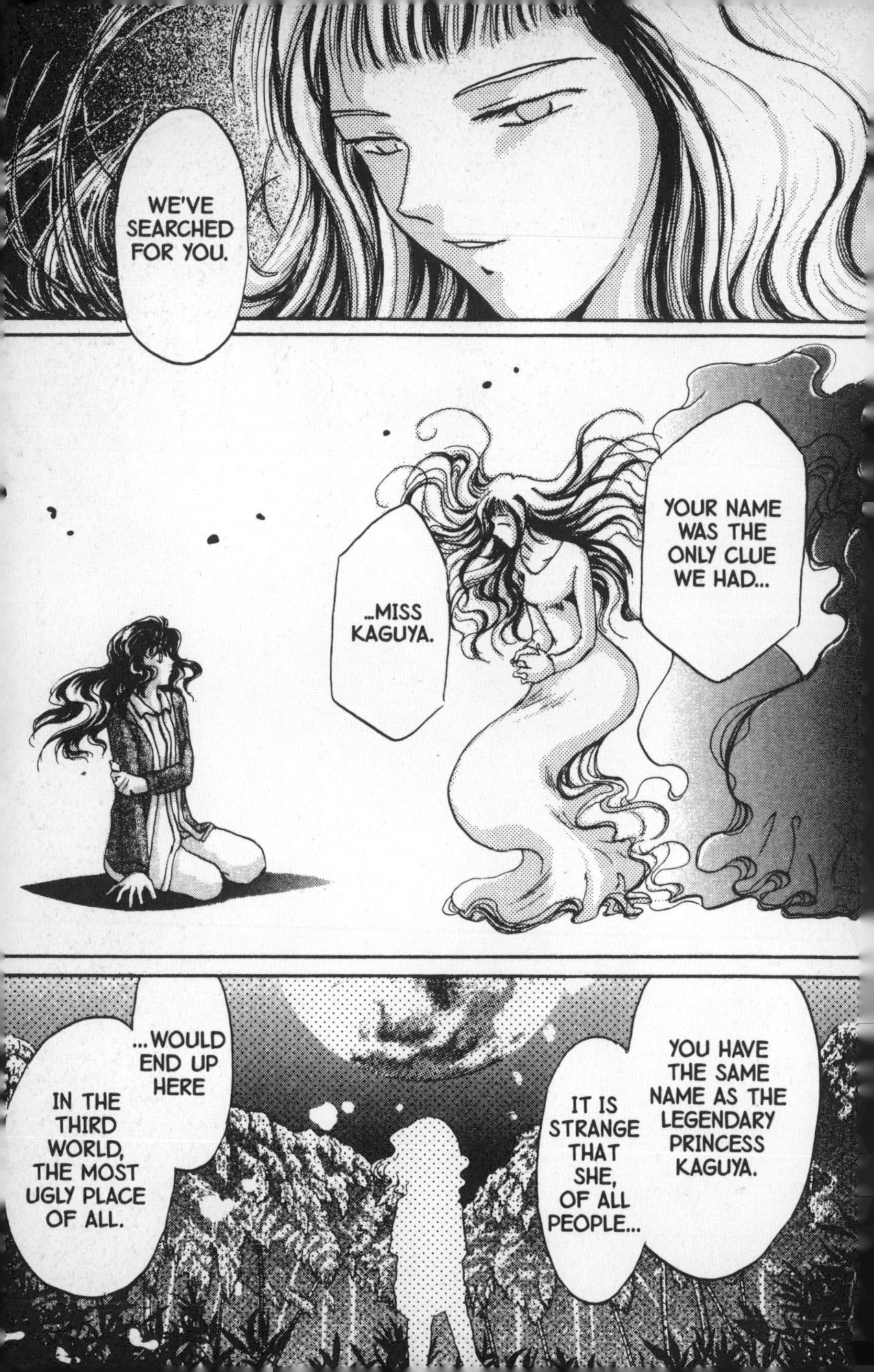
WE'VE SEARCHED FOR YOU.
YOUR NAME WAS THE ONLY CLUE WE HAD...
...MISS KAGUYA.
YOU HAVE THE SAME NAME AS THE LEGENDARY PRINCESS KAGUYA.
IT IS STRANGE THAT SHE, OF ALL PEOPLE...
...WOULD END UP HERE
IN THE THIRD WORLD, THE MOST UGLY PLACE OF ALL.

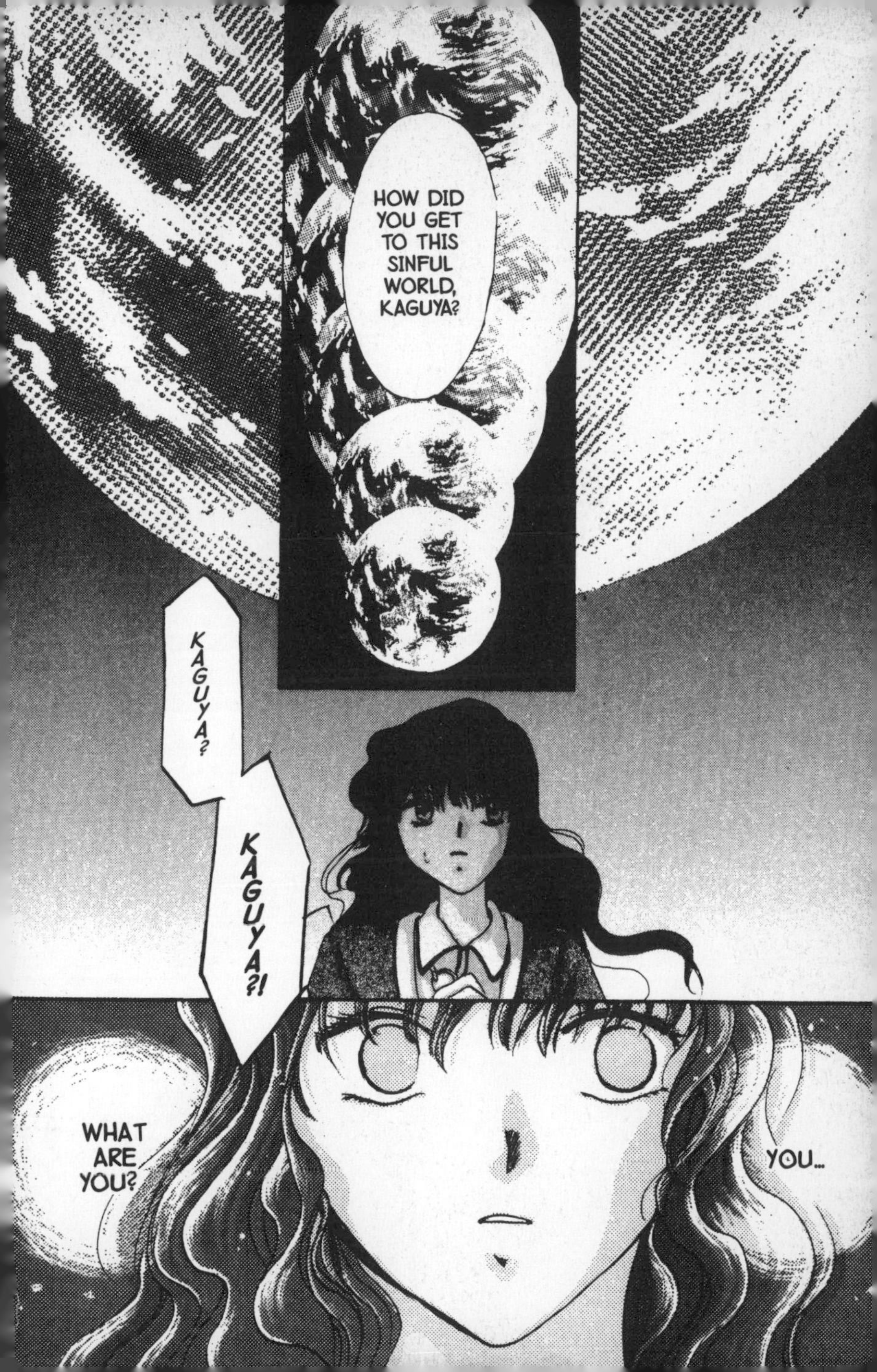
HOW DID YOU GET TO THIS SINFUL WORLD, KAGUYA?
KAGUYA?
KAGUYA?!
YOU...
WHAT ARE YOU?

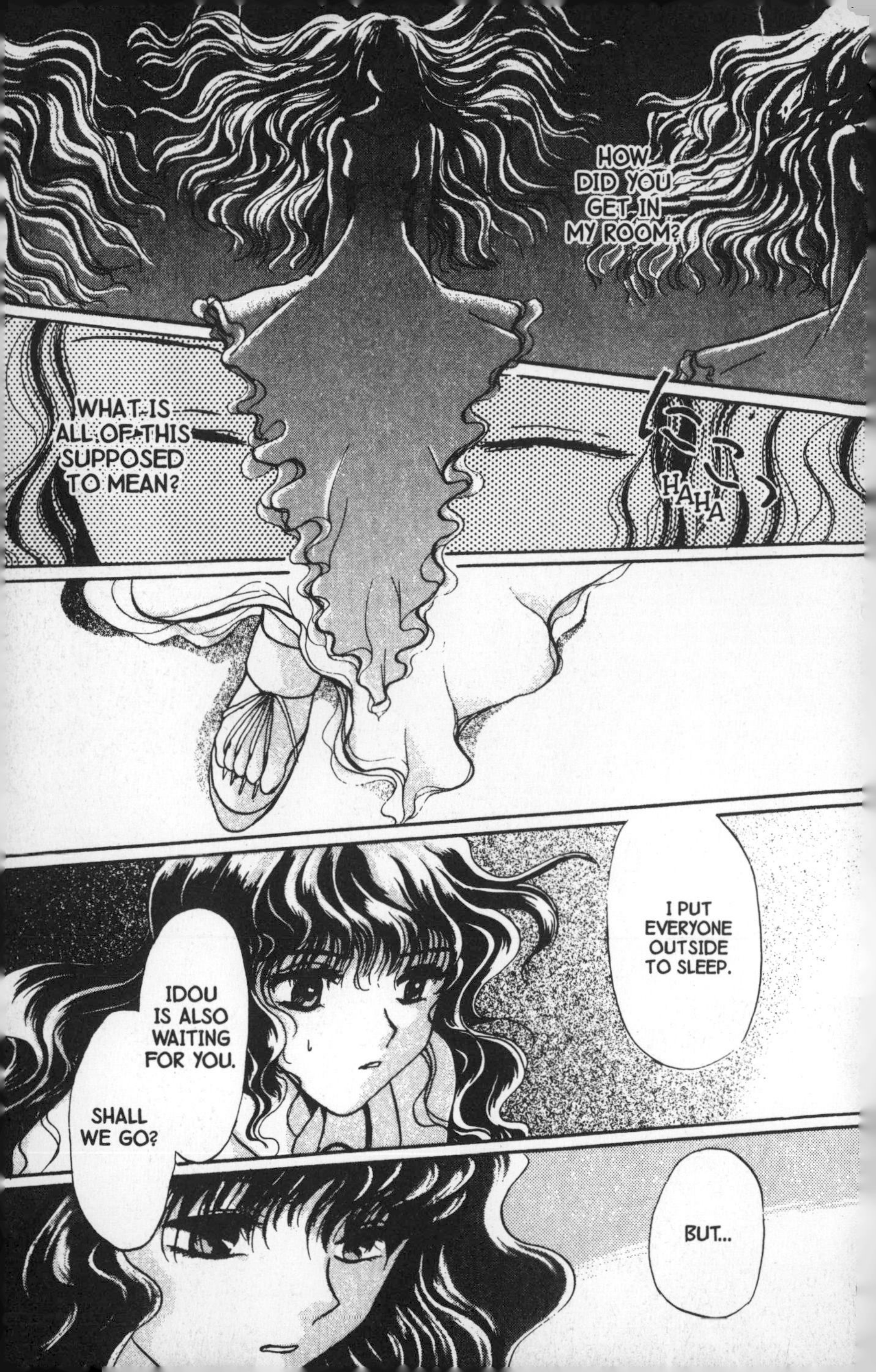
HOW DID YOU GET IN MY ROOM?
HAHA
WHAT IS ALL OF THIS SUPPOSED TO MEAN?
I PUT EVERYONE OUTSIDE TO SLEEP.
IDOU IS ALSO WAITING FOR YOU.
SHALL WE GO?
BUT...

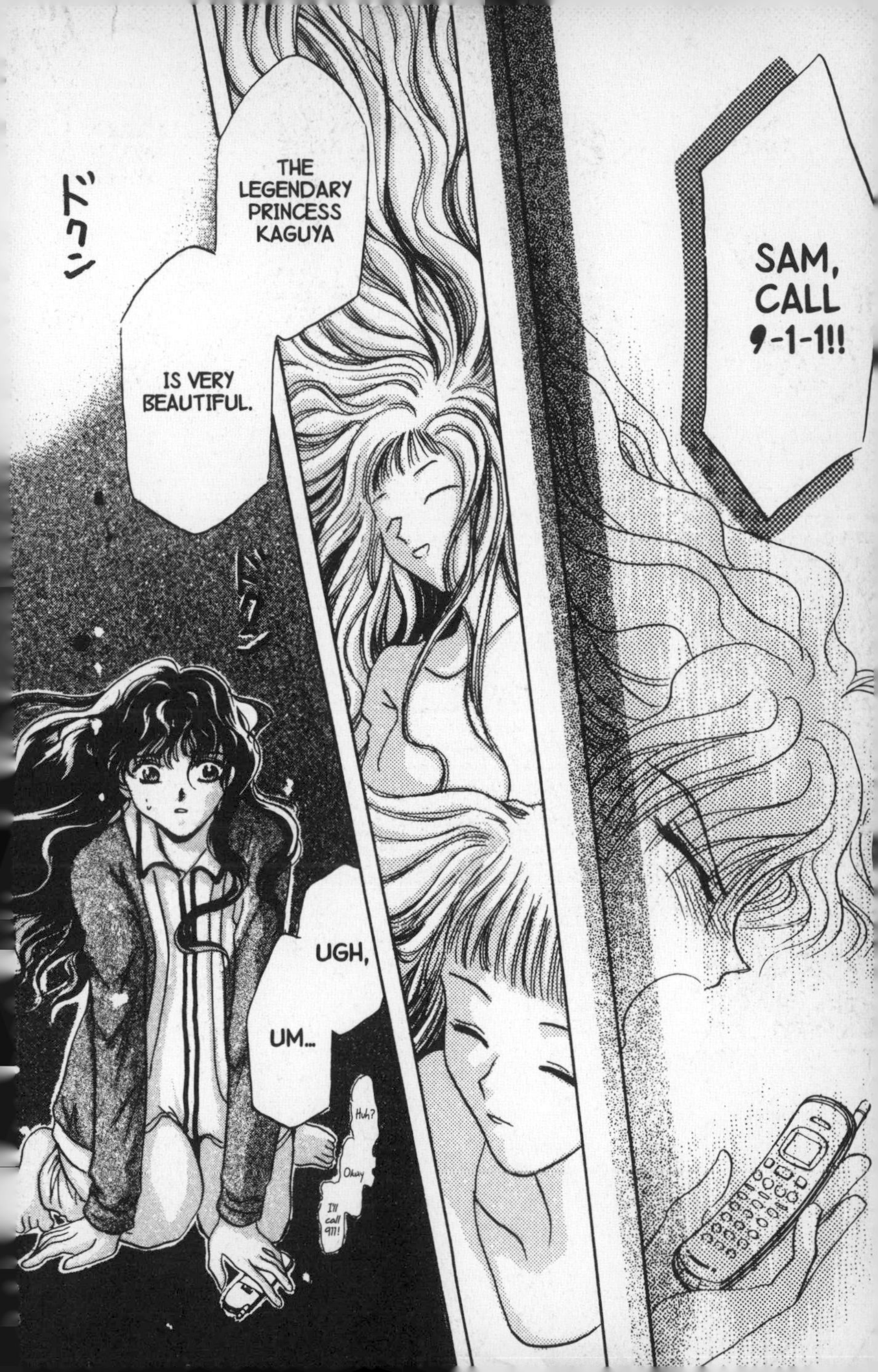
SAM, CALL 9-1-1!!
THE LEGENDARY PRINCESS KAGUYA
IS VERY BEAUTIFUL.
ドクン
ドクン
UGH,
UM...
Huh?
Okay
I'll call 911!

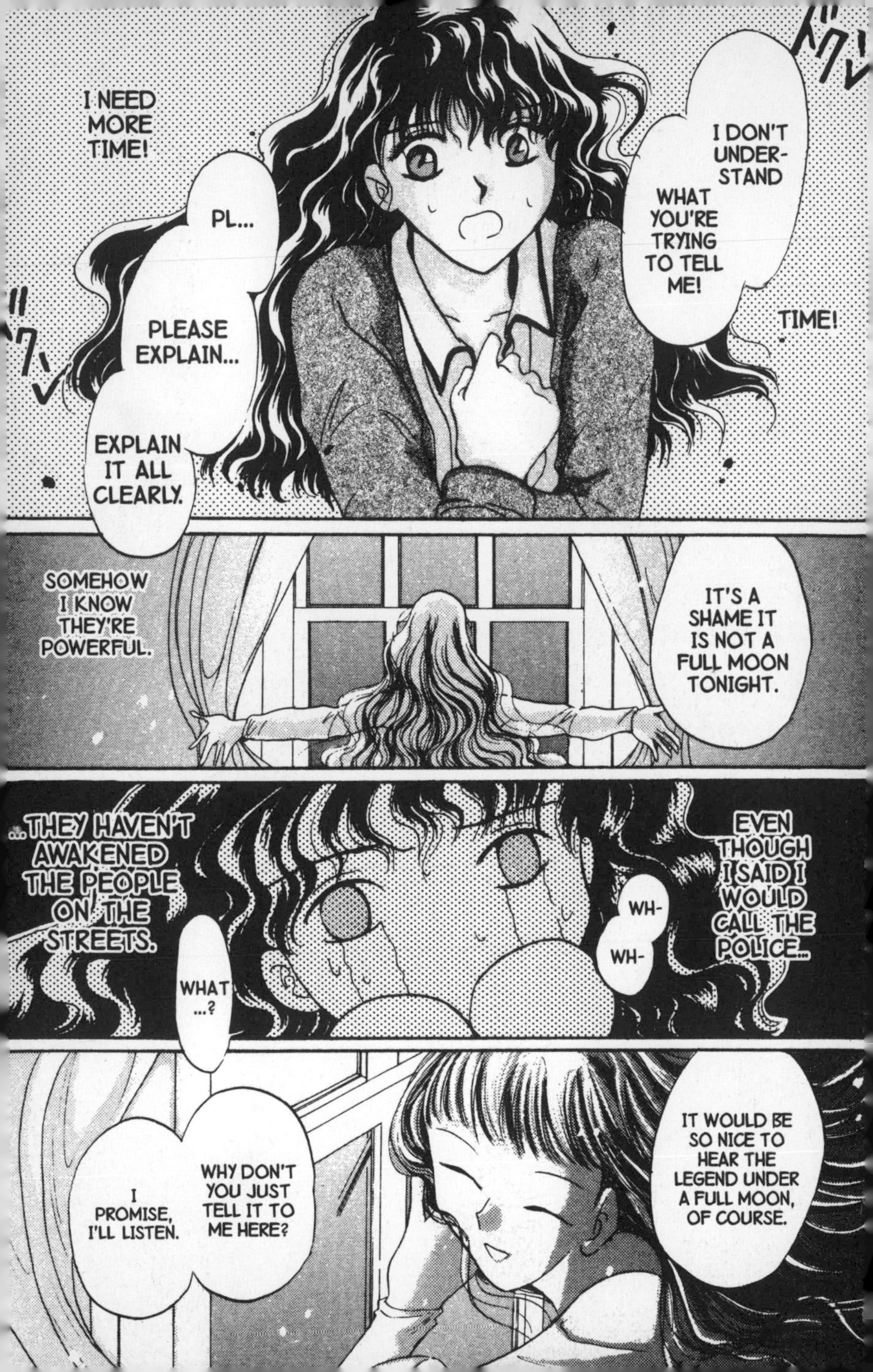
I DON'T UNDER-STAND WHAT YOU'RE TRYING TO TELL ME!
TIME!
I NEED MORE TIME!
PL...
PLEASE EXPLAIN...
EXPLAIN IT ALL CLEARLY.
IT'S A SHAME IT IS NOT A FULL MOON TONIGHT.
SOMEHOW I KNOW THEY'RE POWERFUL.
EVEN THOUGH I SAID I WOULD CALL THE POLICE...
WH-
WH-
...THEY HAVEN'T AWAKENED THE PEOPLE ON THE STREETS.
WHAT ...?
IT WOULD BE SO NICE TO HEAR THE LEGEND UNDER A FULL MOON, OF COURSE.
WHY DON'T YOU JUST TELL IT TO ME HERE?
I PROMISE, I'LL LISTEN.

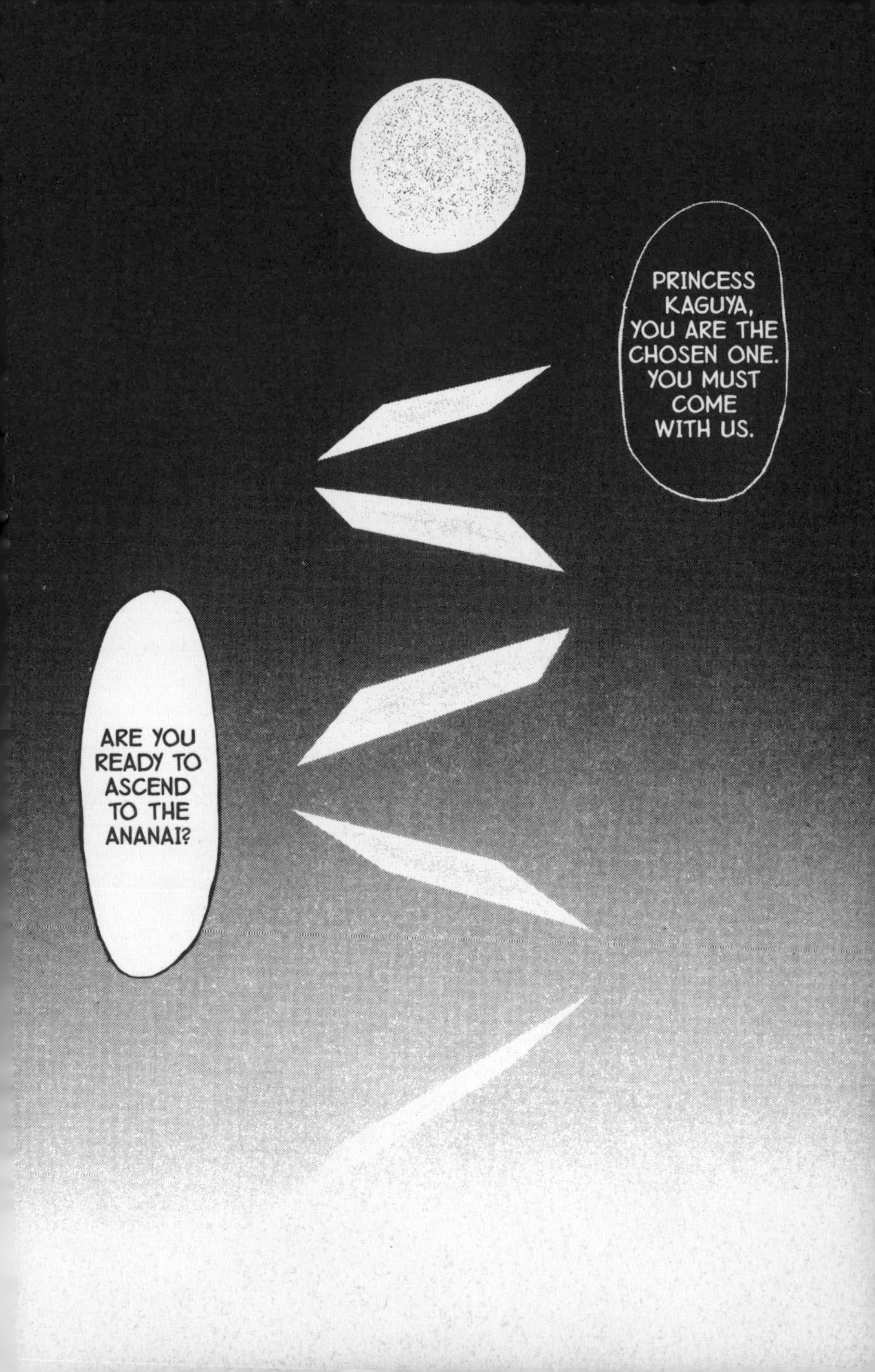
PRINCESS KAGUYA, YOU ARE THE CHOSEN ONE. YOU MUST COME WITH US.
ARE YOU READY TO ASCEND TO THE ANANAI?

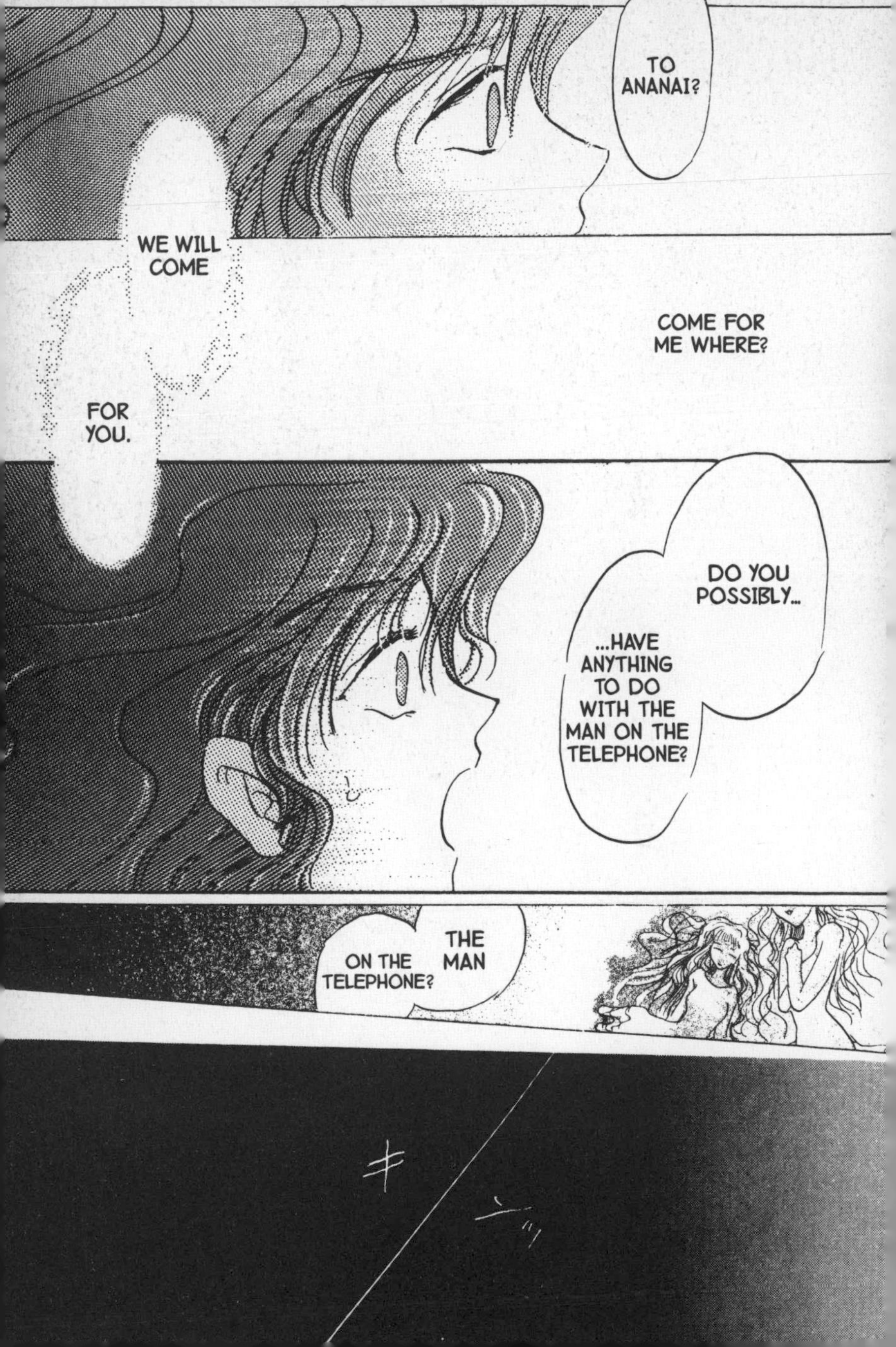
TO ANANAI?
WE WILL COME FOR YOU.
COME FOR ME WHERE?
DO YOU POSSIBLY...
...HAVE ANYTHING TO DO WITH THE MAN ON THE TELEPHONE?
THE MAN ON THE TELEPHONE?

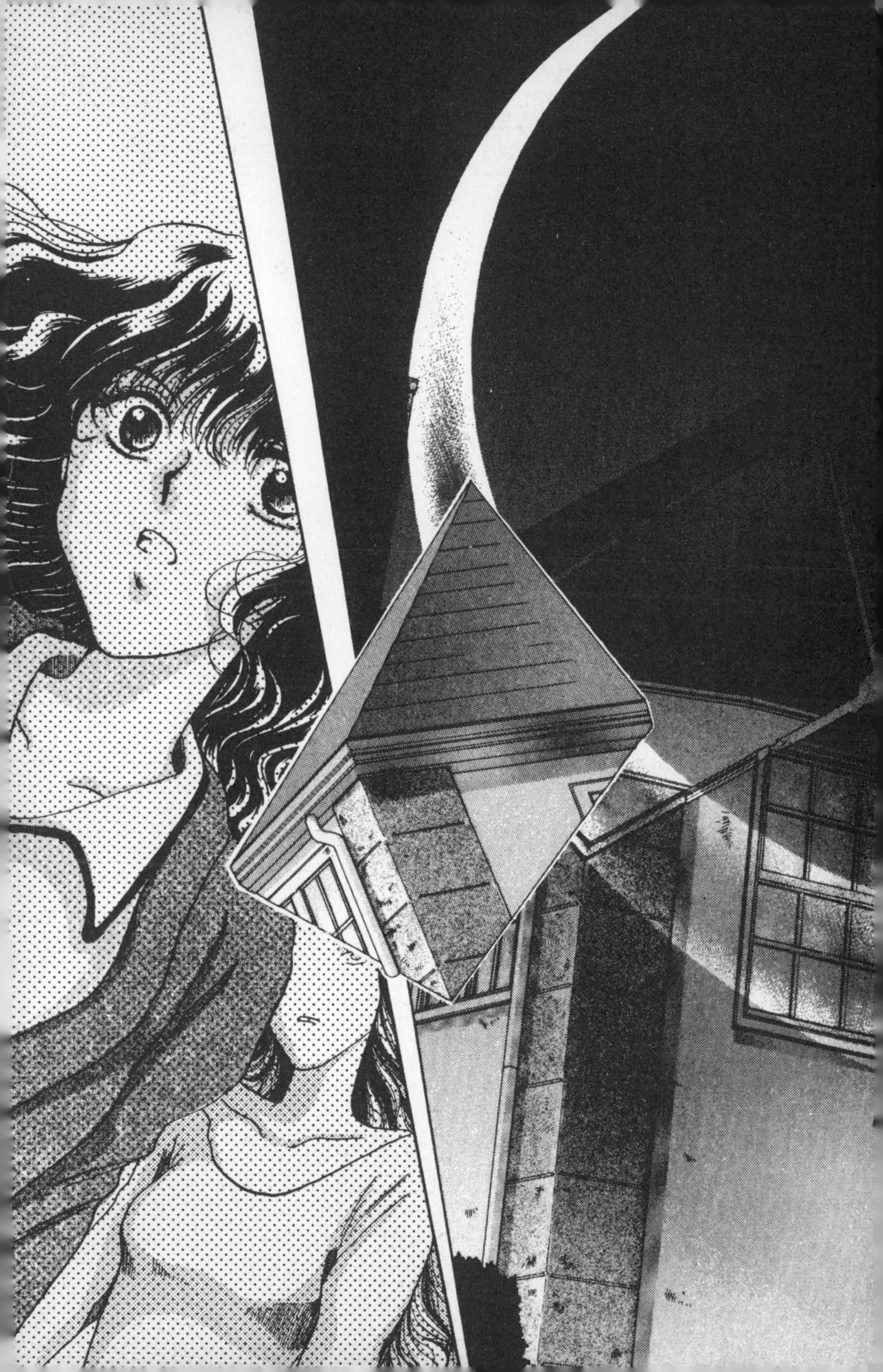

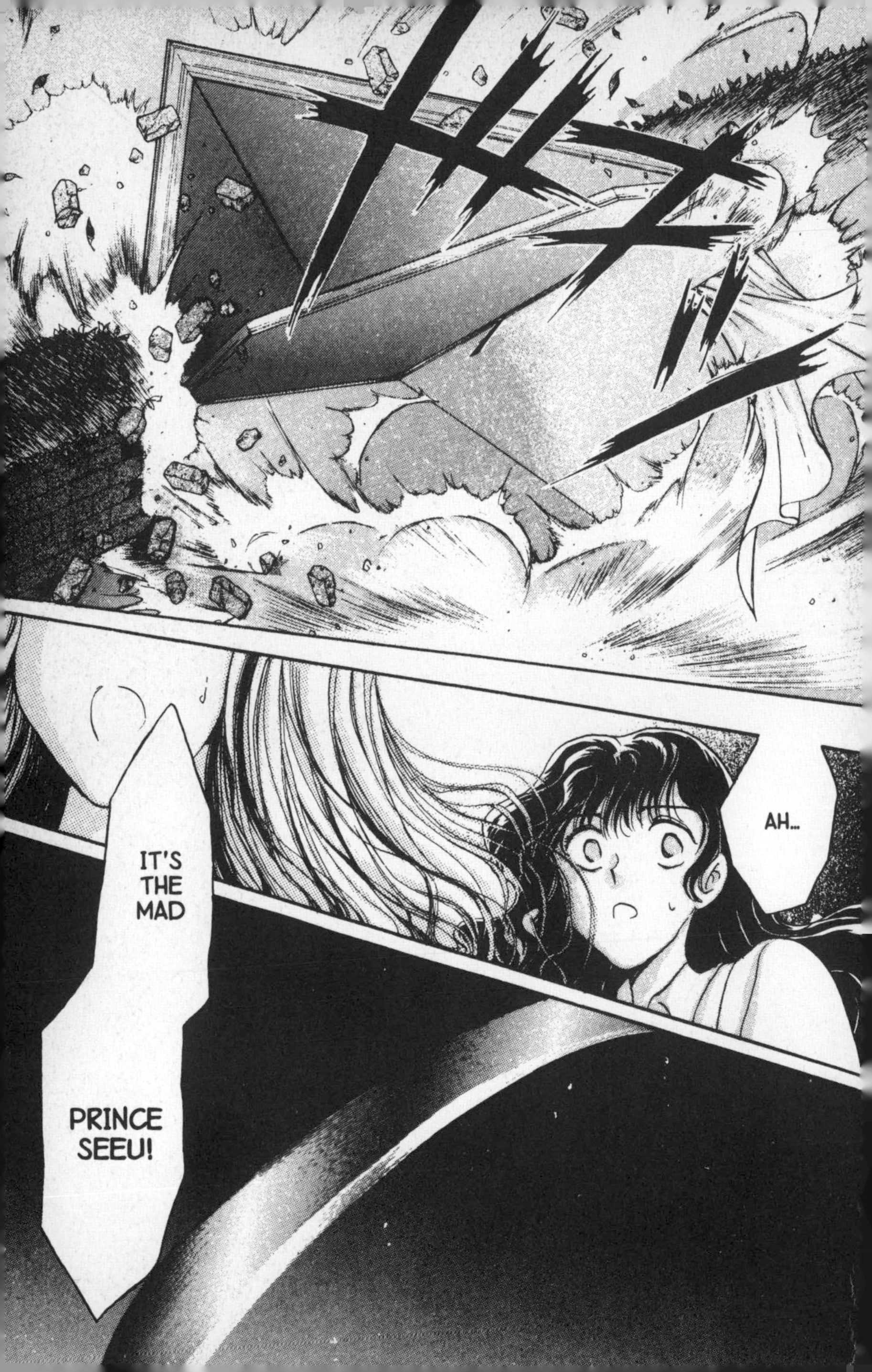
AH...
IT'S THE MAD
PRINCE SEEU!

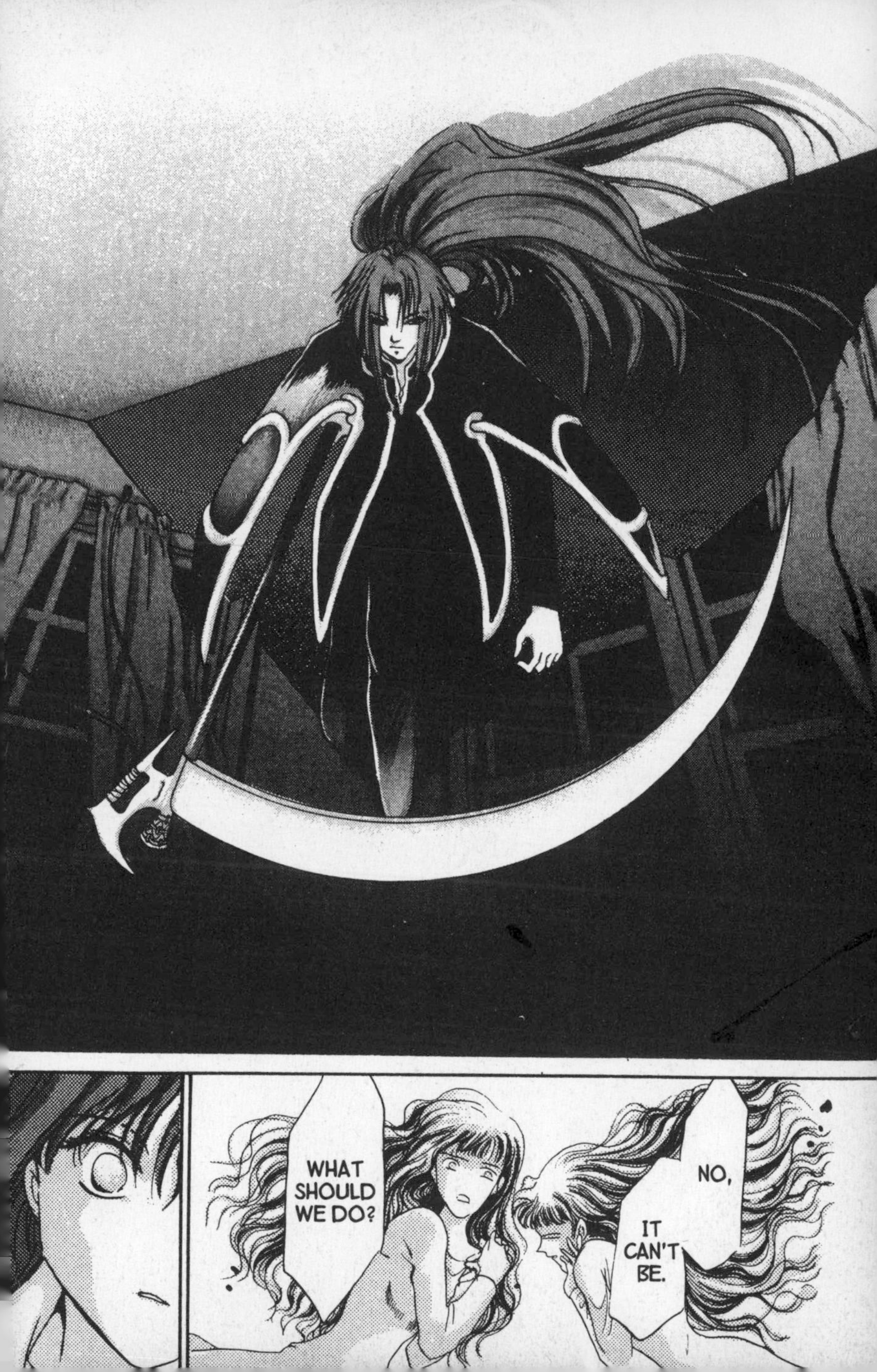
NO,
IT CAN'T BE.
WHAT SHOULD WE DO?

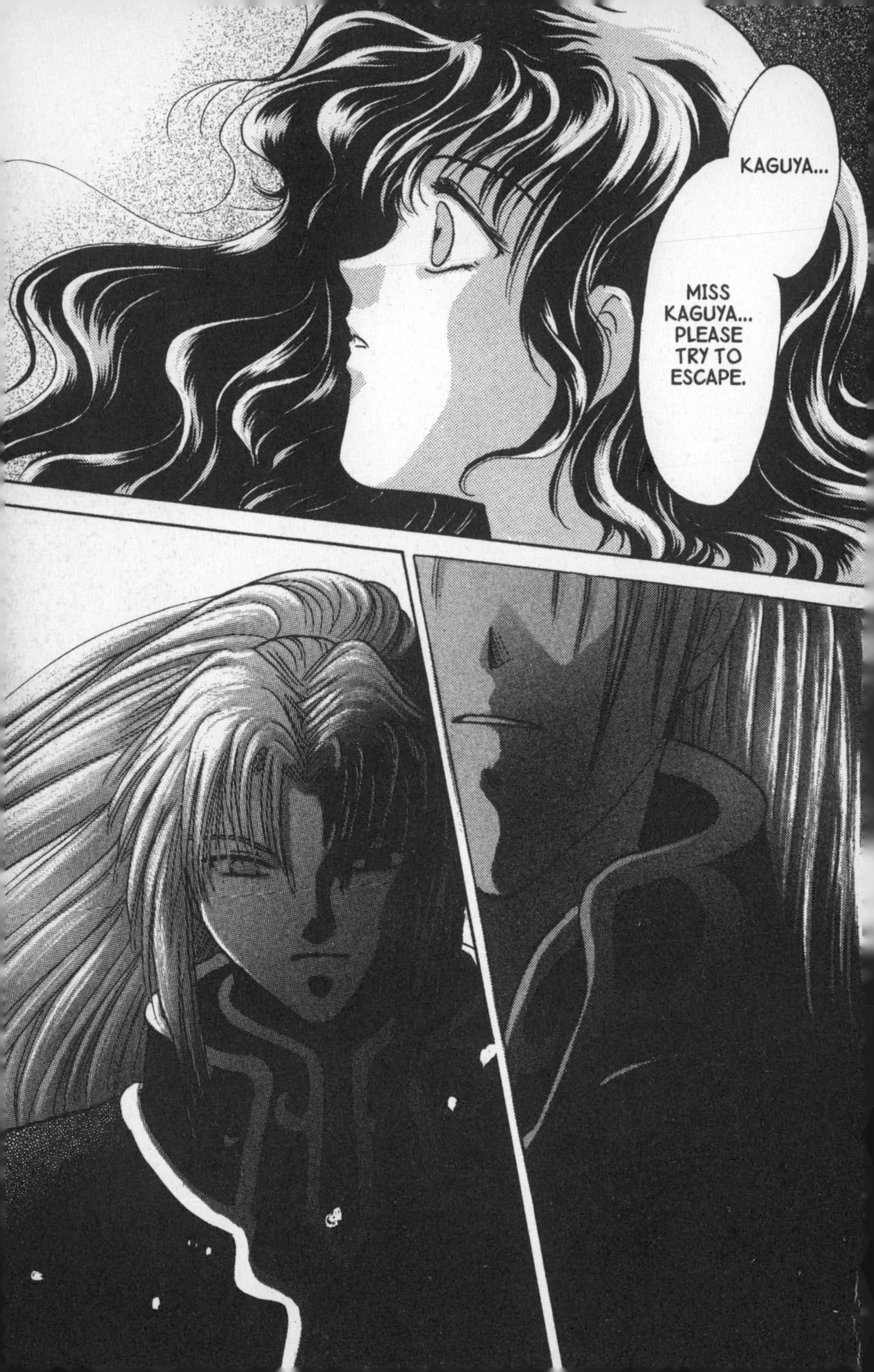
KAGUYA...
MISS KAGUYA... PLEASE TRY TO ESCAPE.

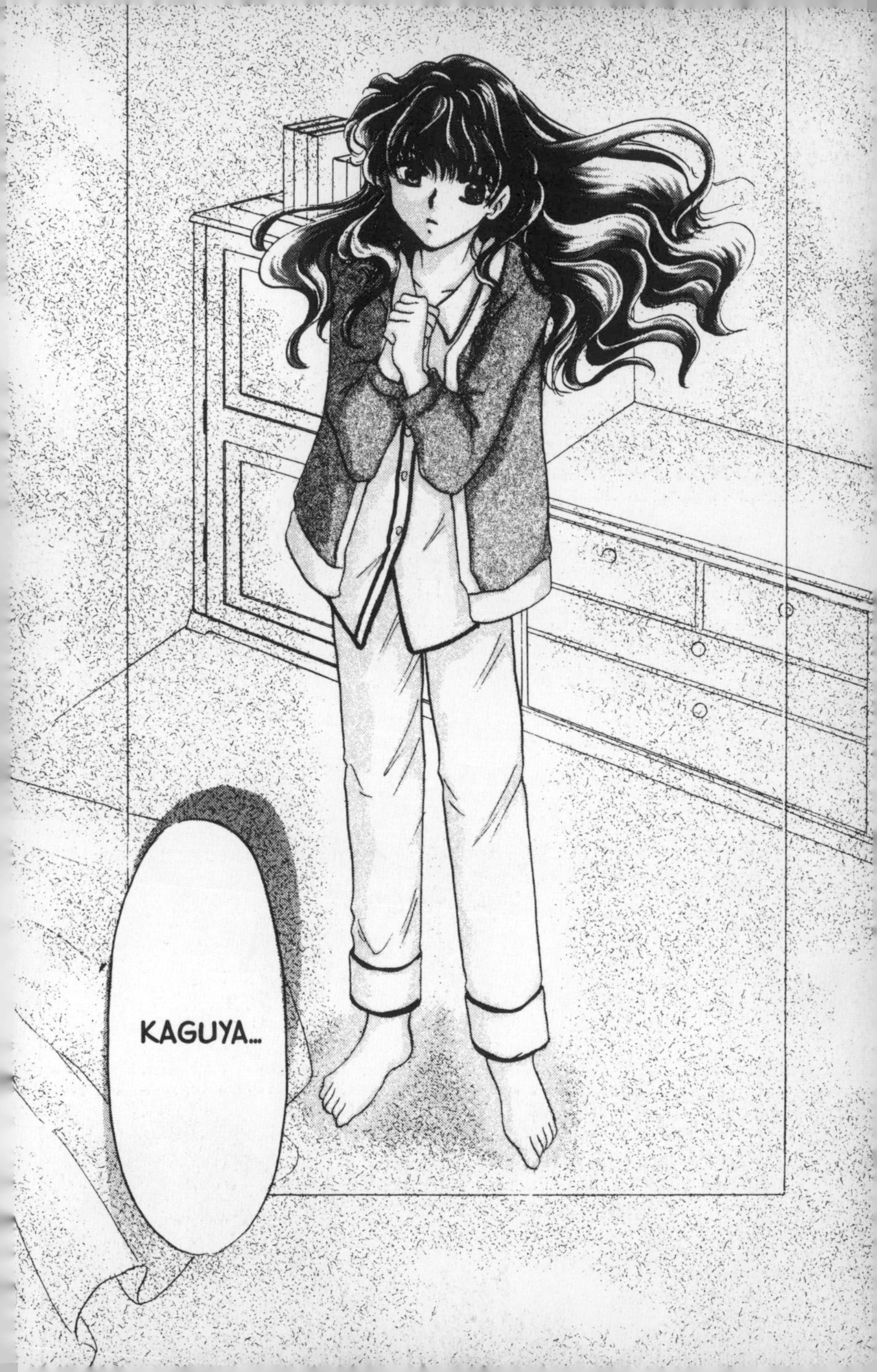
KAGUYA...

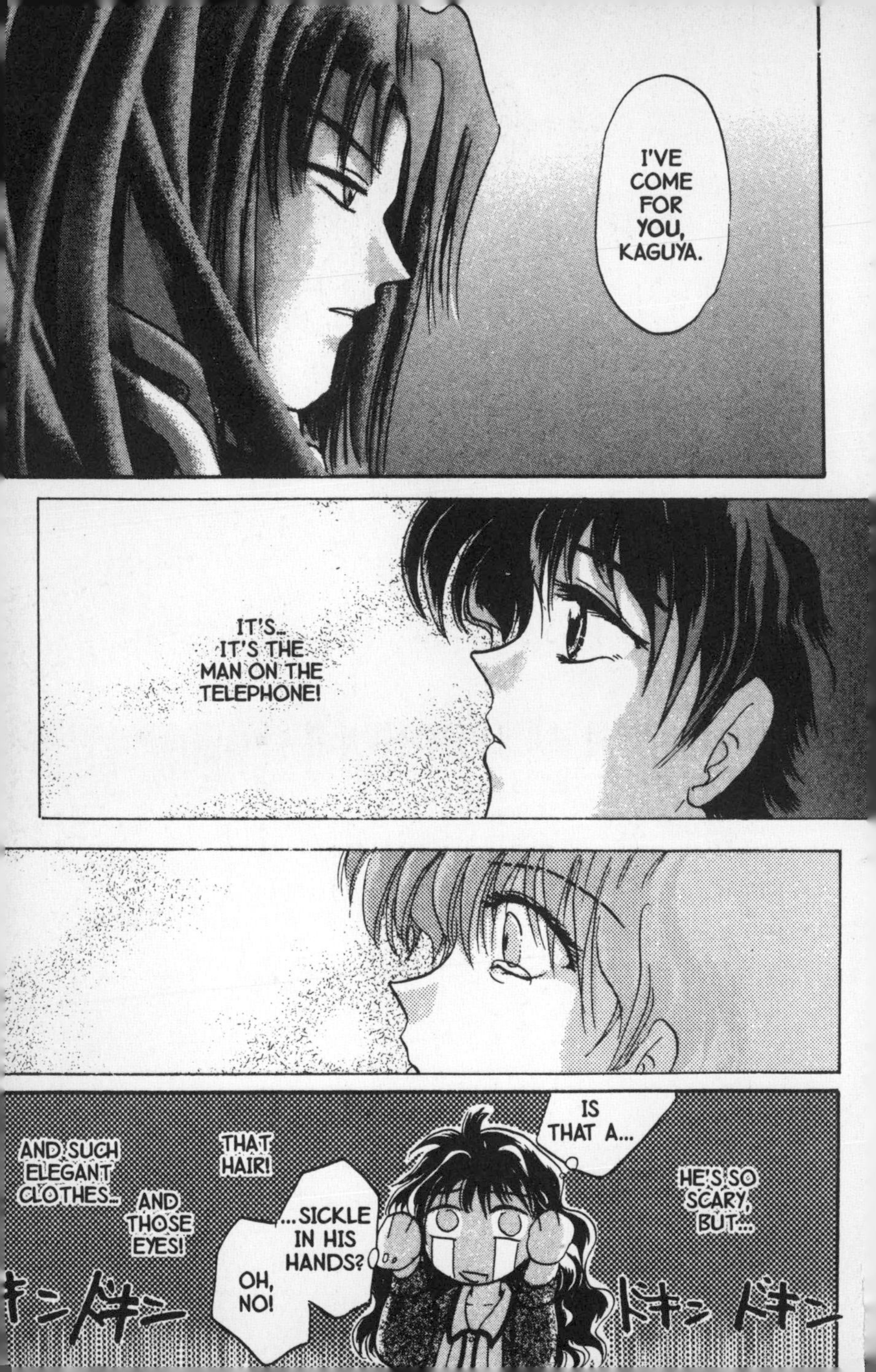
I'VE COME FOR YOU, KAGUYA.
IT'S.. IT'S THE MAN ON THE TELEPHONE!
ドキン ドキン
HE'S SO SCARY, BUT...
IS THAT A...
...SICKLE IN HIS HANDS?
OH, NO!
THAT HAIR!
AND THOSE EYES!
AND SUCH ELEGANT CLOTHES..
キン ドキン

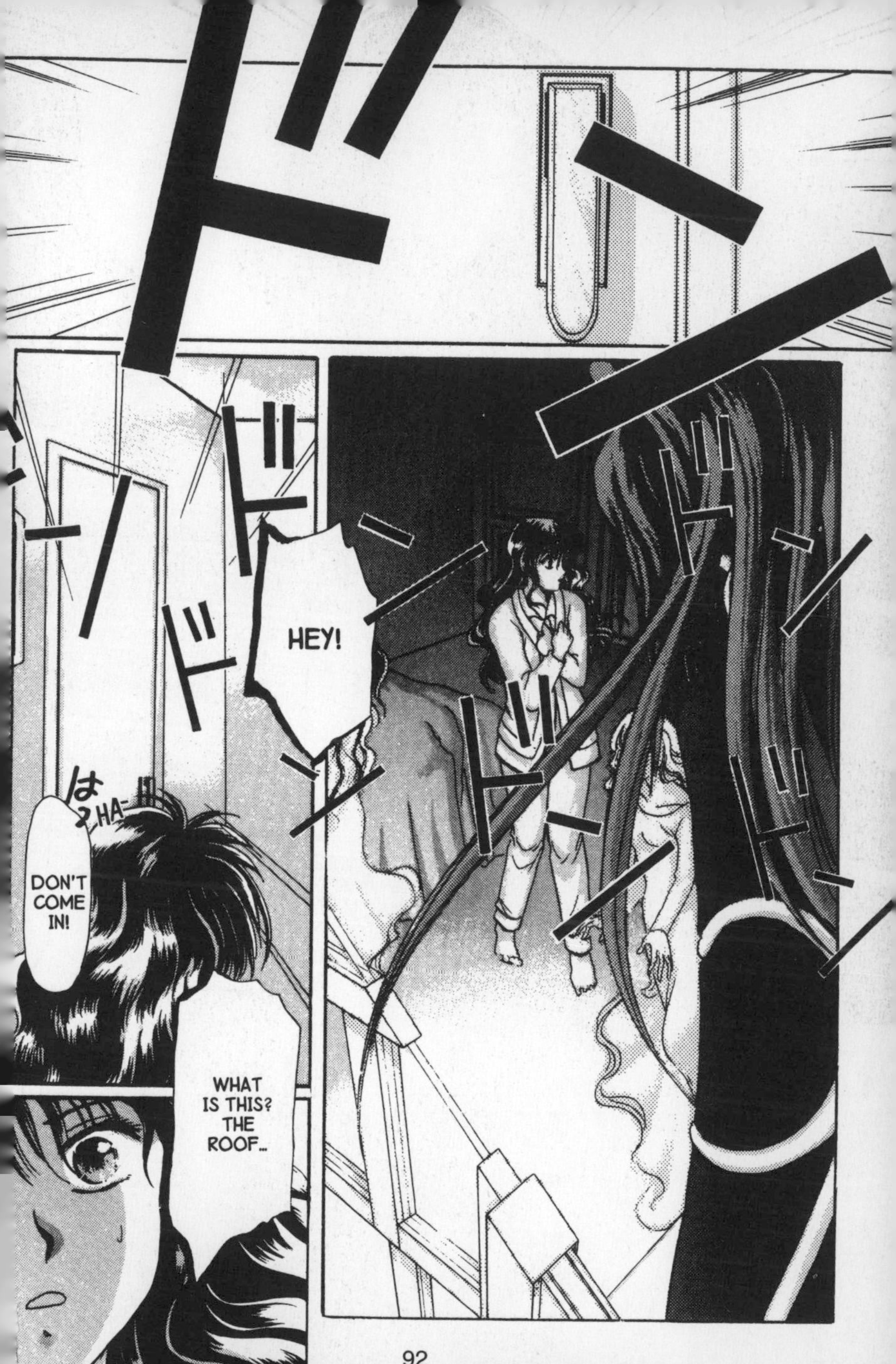
ドー
HEY!
は
HA-
DON'T COME IN!
WHAT IS THIS? THE ROOF...

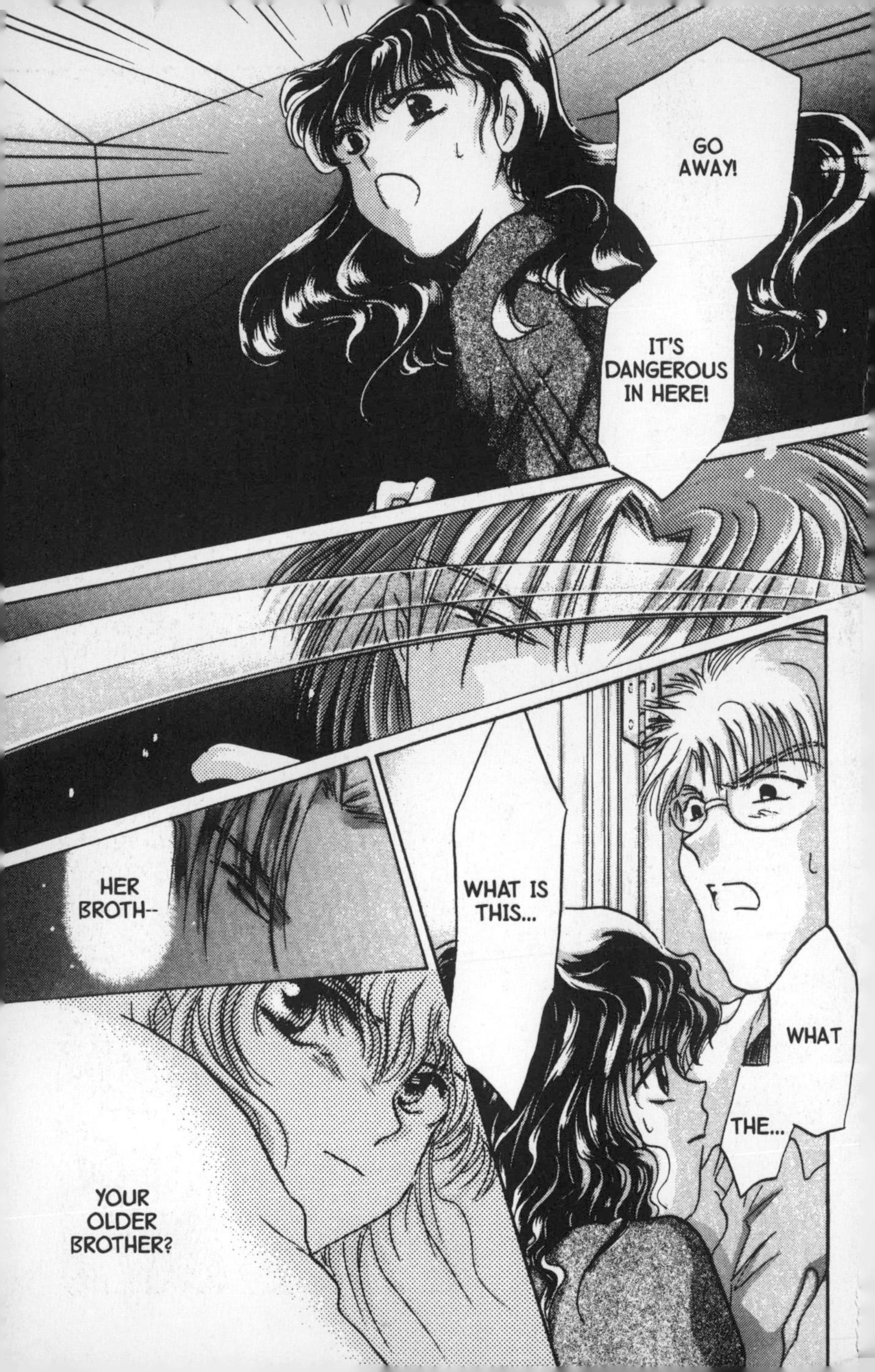
GO AWAY!
IT'S DANGEROUS IN HERE!
WHAT THE...
WHAT IS THIS...
HER BROTH--
YOUR OLDER BROTHER?

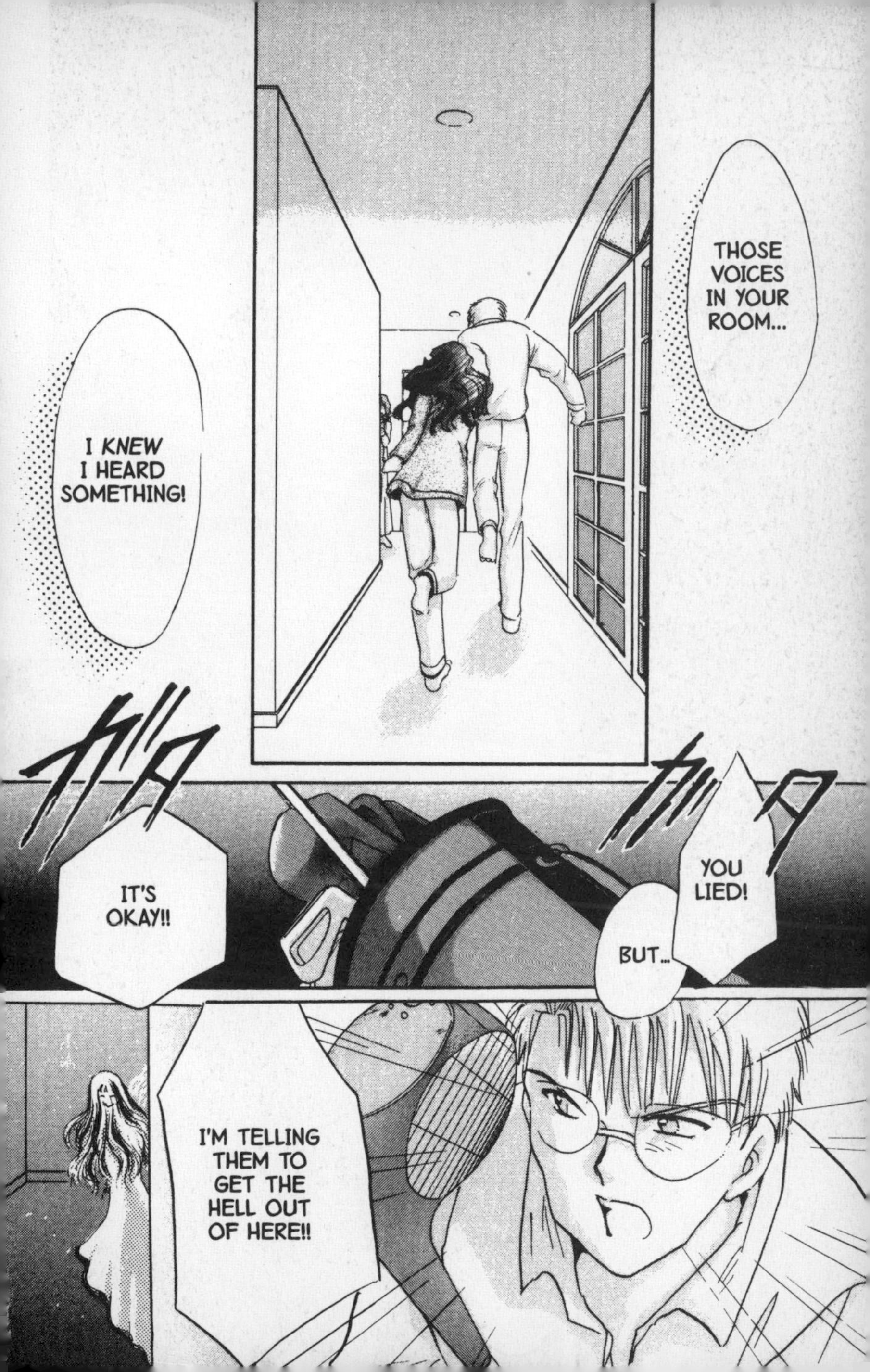
THOSE VOICES IN YOUR ROOM...
I KNEW I HEARD SOMETHING!
ガタ
ガタ
YOU LIED!
BUT...
IT'S OKAY!!
I'M TELLING THEM TO GET THE HELL OUT OF HERE!!

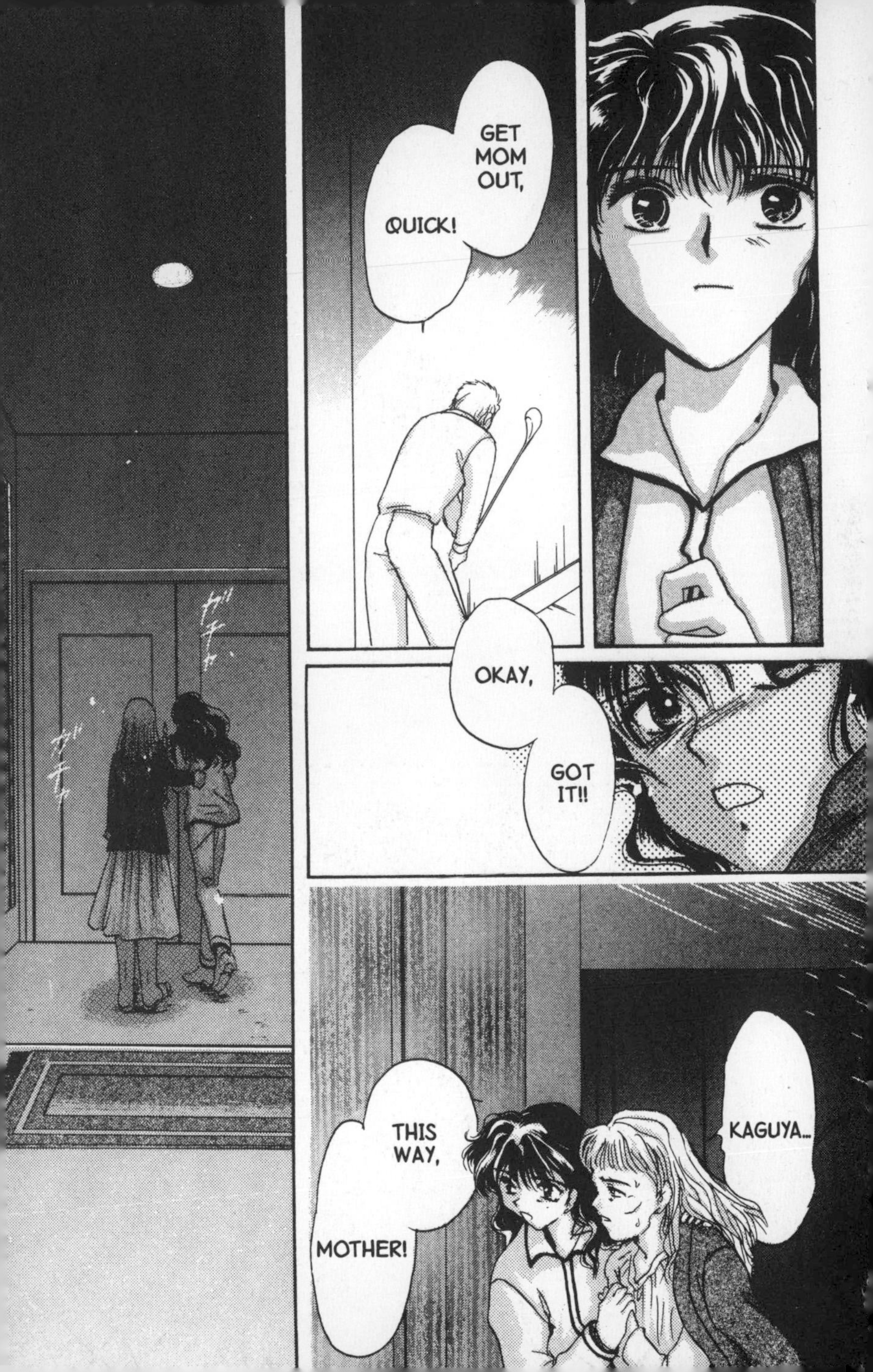
GET MOM OUT,
QUICK!
OKAY,
GOT IT!!
KAGUYA...
THIS WAY,
MOTHER!

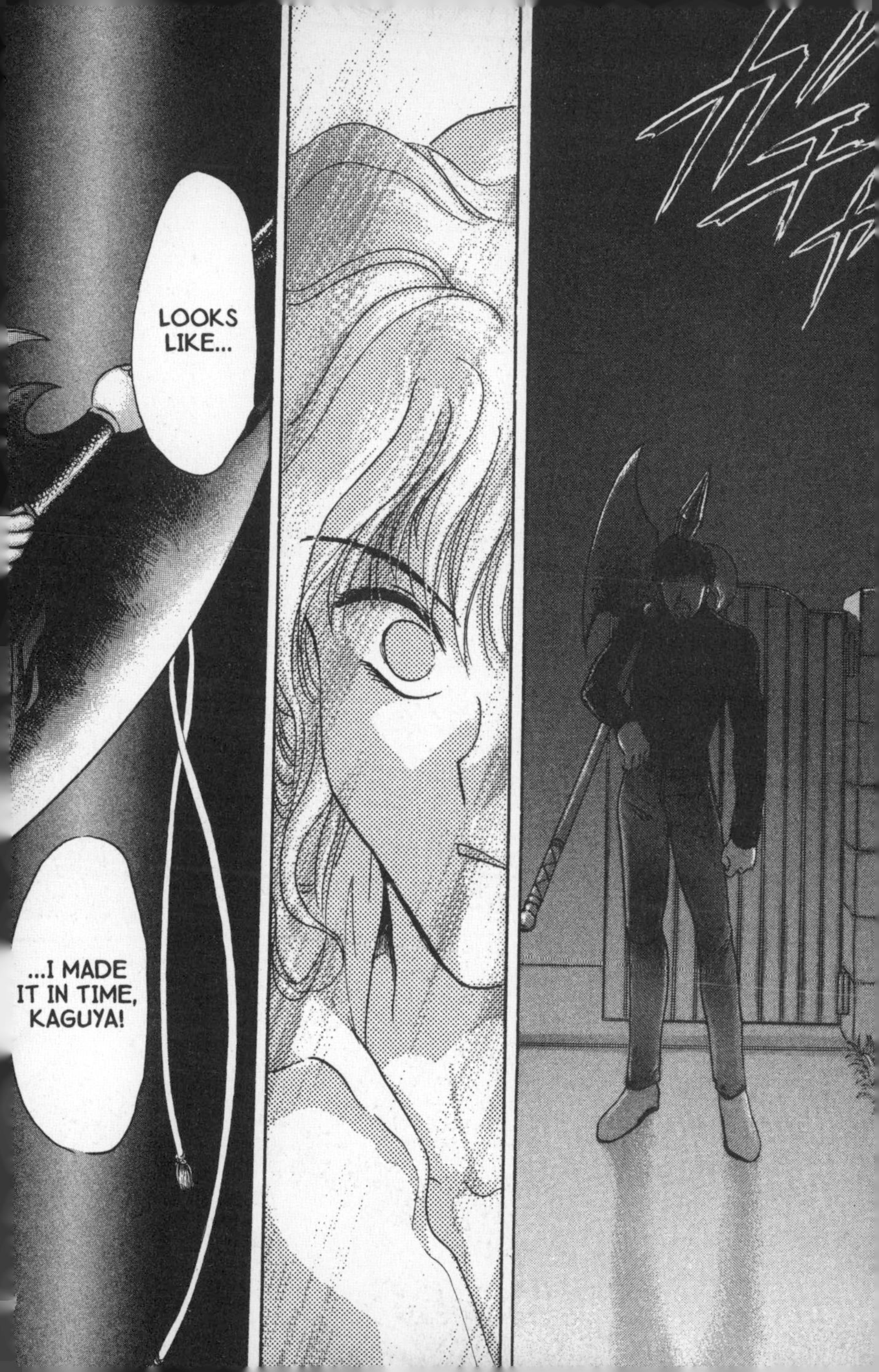
LOOKS LIKE...
...I MADE IT IN TIME, KAGUYA!

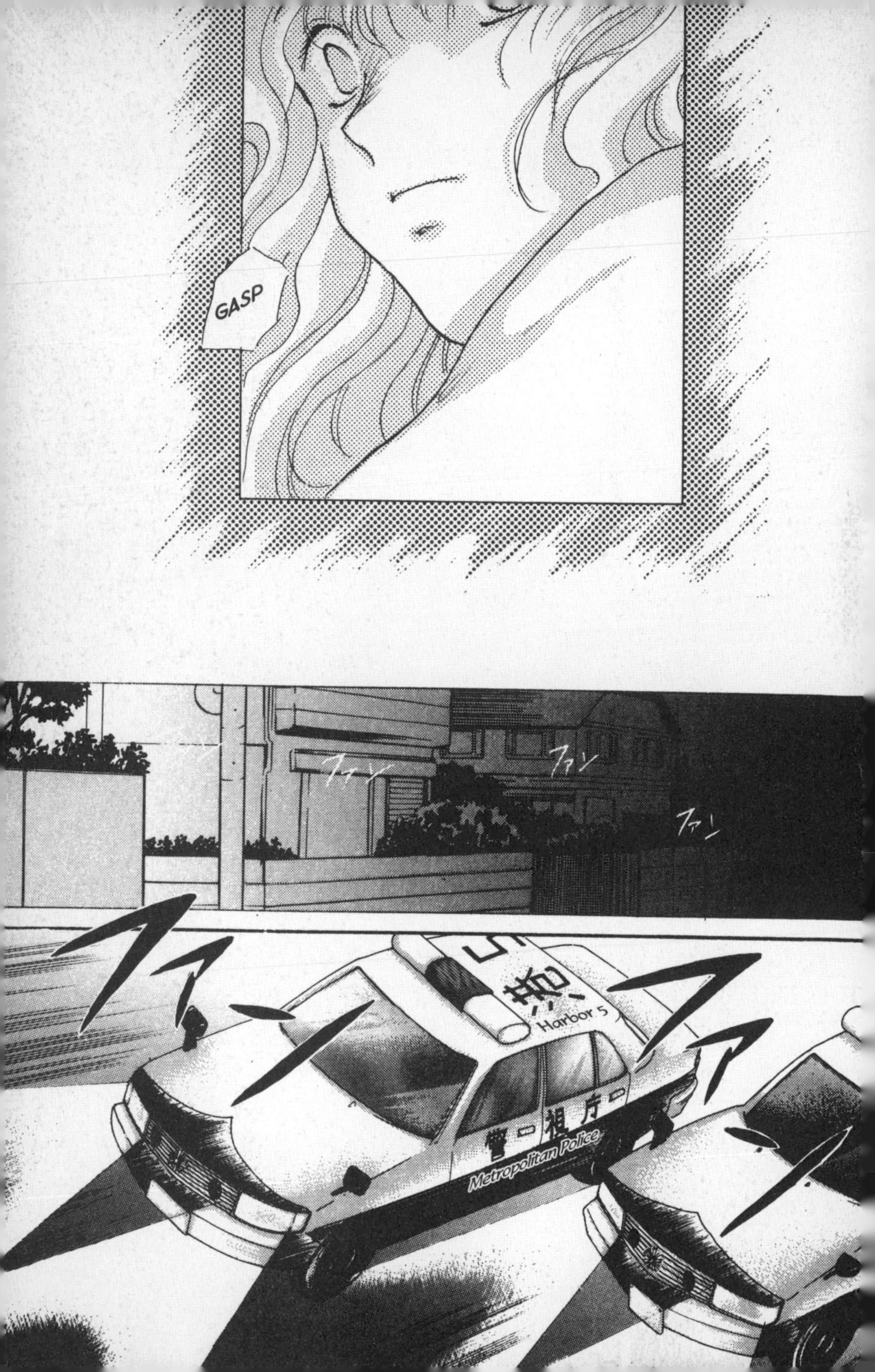
GASP
ファン
ファン
ファン
ファー
Harbor 5
警視庁
Metropolitan Police
ファーン

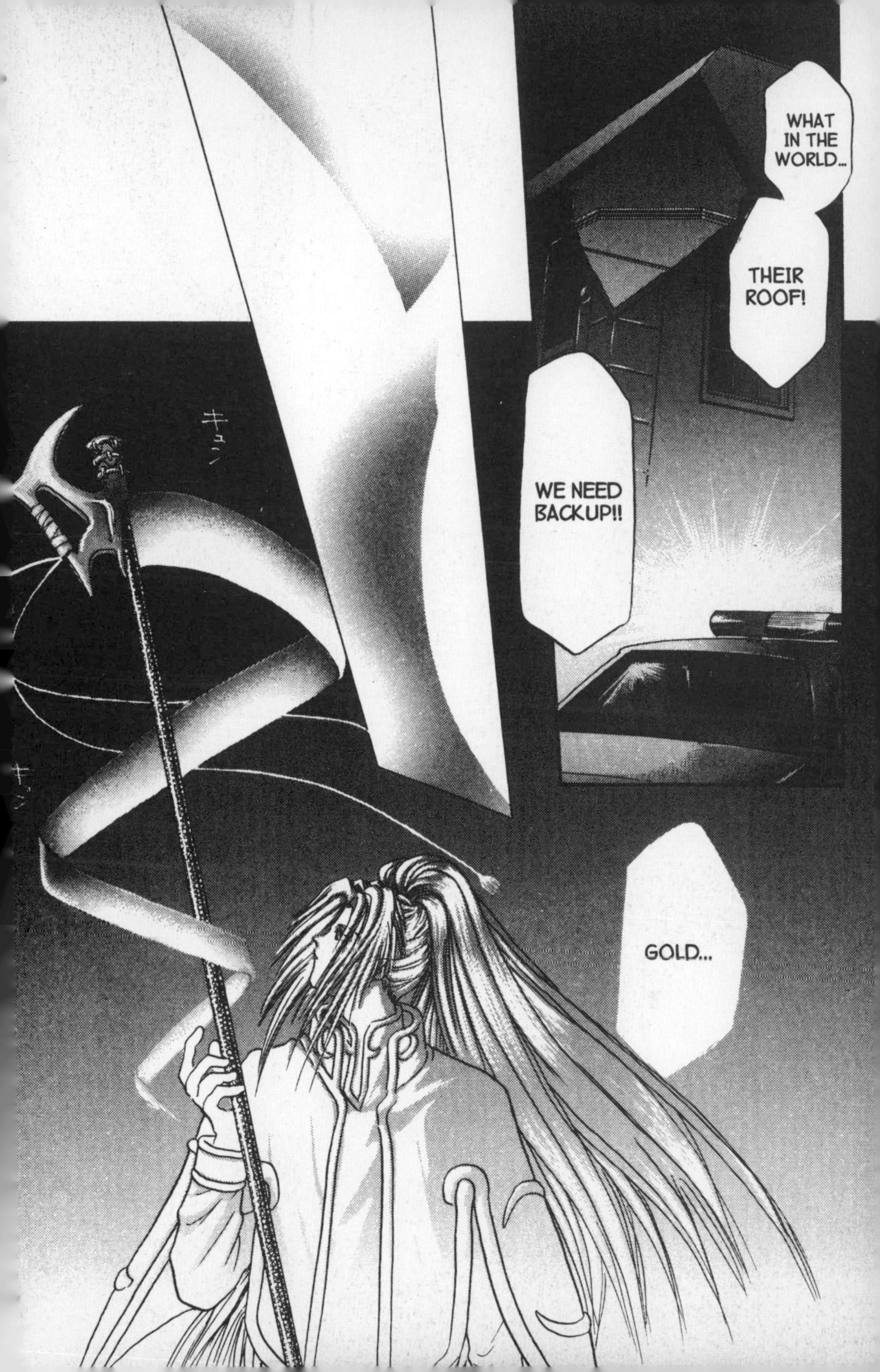
WHAT IN THE WORLD...
THEIR ROOF!
WE NEED BACKUP!!
キュン
GOLD...

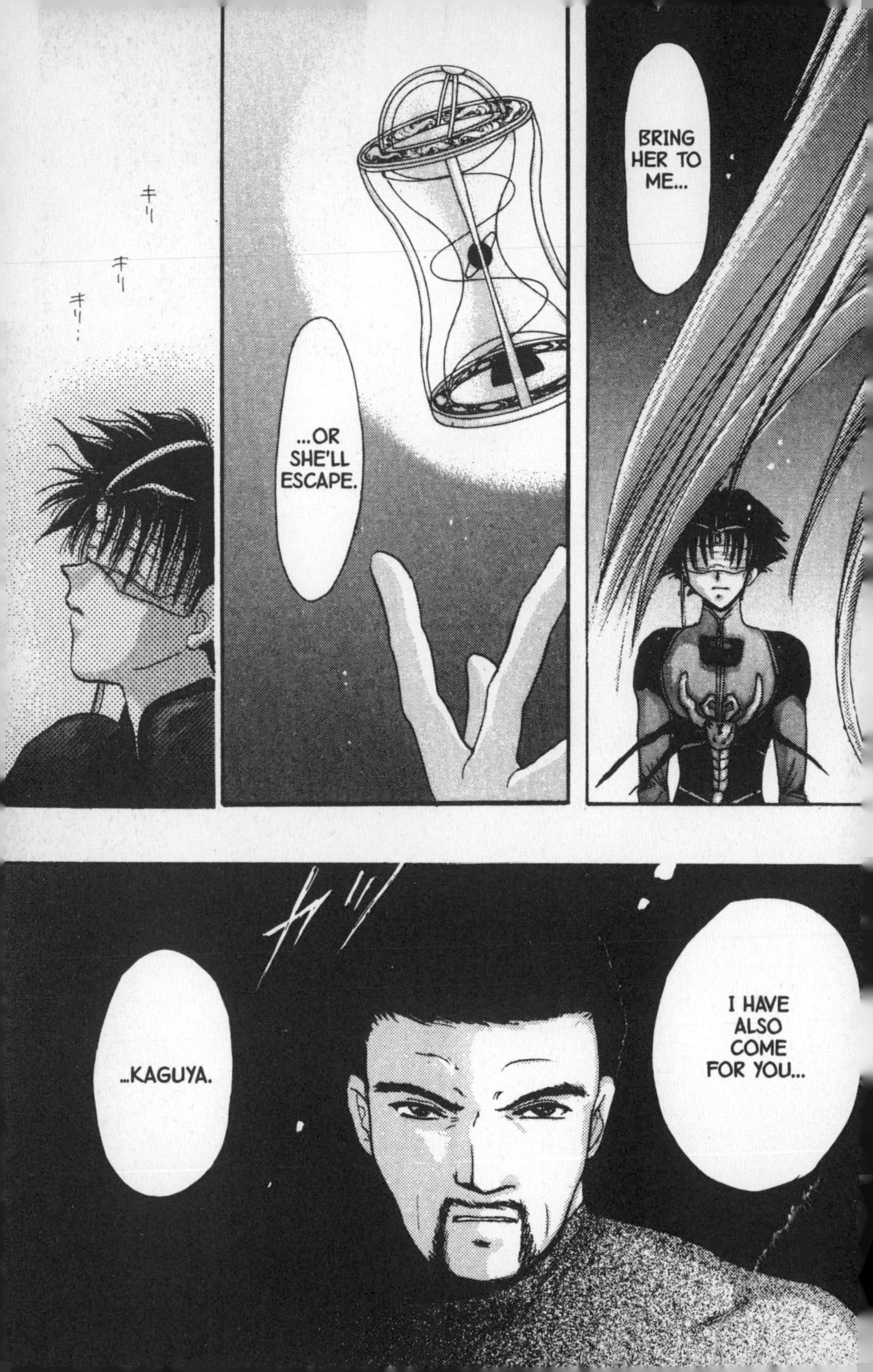
BRING HER TO ME...
...OR SHE'LL ESCAPE.
キリ
キリ
キリ...
I HAVE ALSO COME FOR YOU...
...KAGUYA.

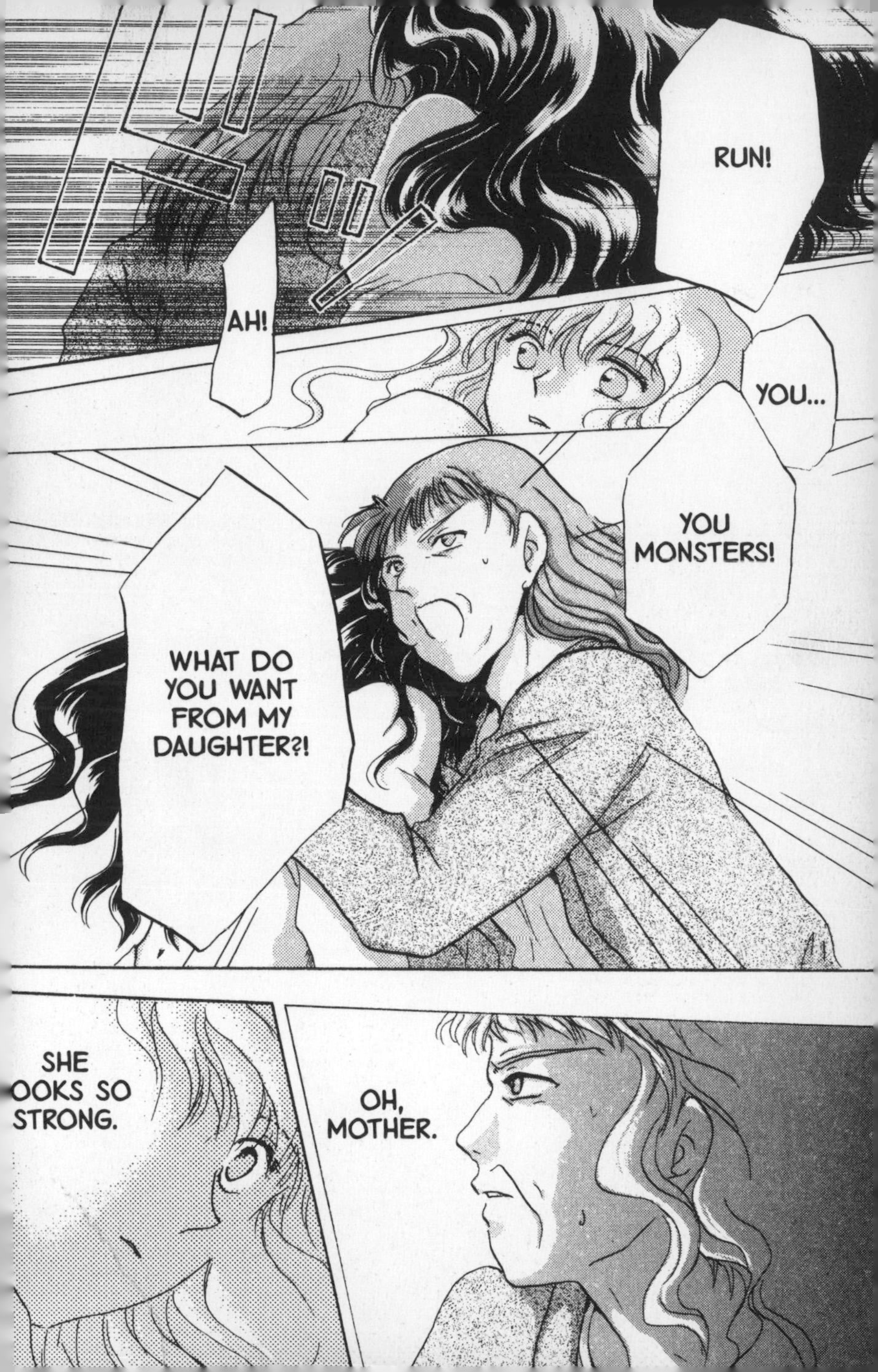
RUN!
AH!
YOU...
YOU MONSTERS!
WHAT DO YOU WANT FROM MY DAUGHTER?!
OH, MOTHER.
SHE OOKS SO STRONG.

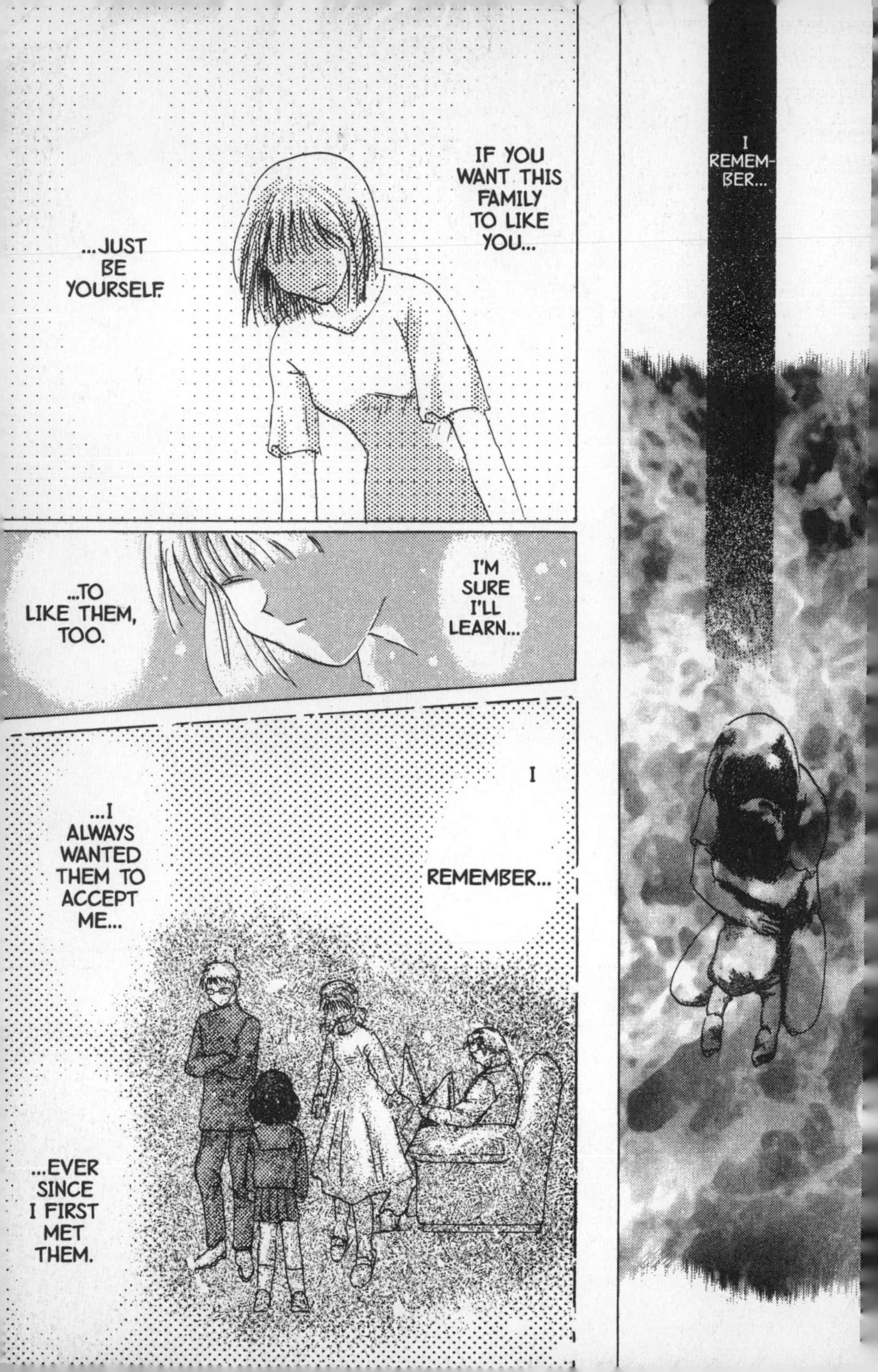
I REMEMBER...
IF YOU WANT THIS FAMILY TO LIKE YOU...
...JUST BE YOURSELF.
I'M SURE I'LL LEARN...
...TO LIKE THEM, TOO.
I
REMEMBER...
...I ALWAYS WANTED THEM TO ACCEPT ME...
...EVER SINCE I FIRST MET THEM.

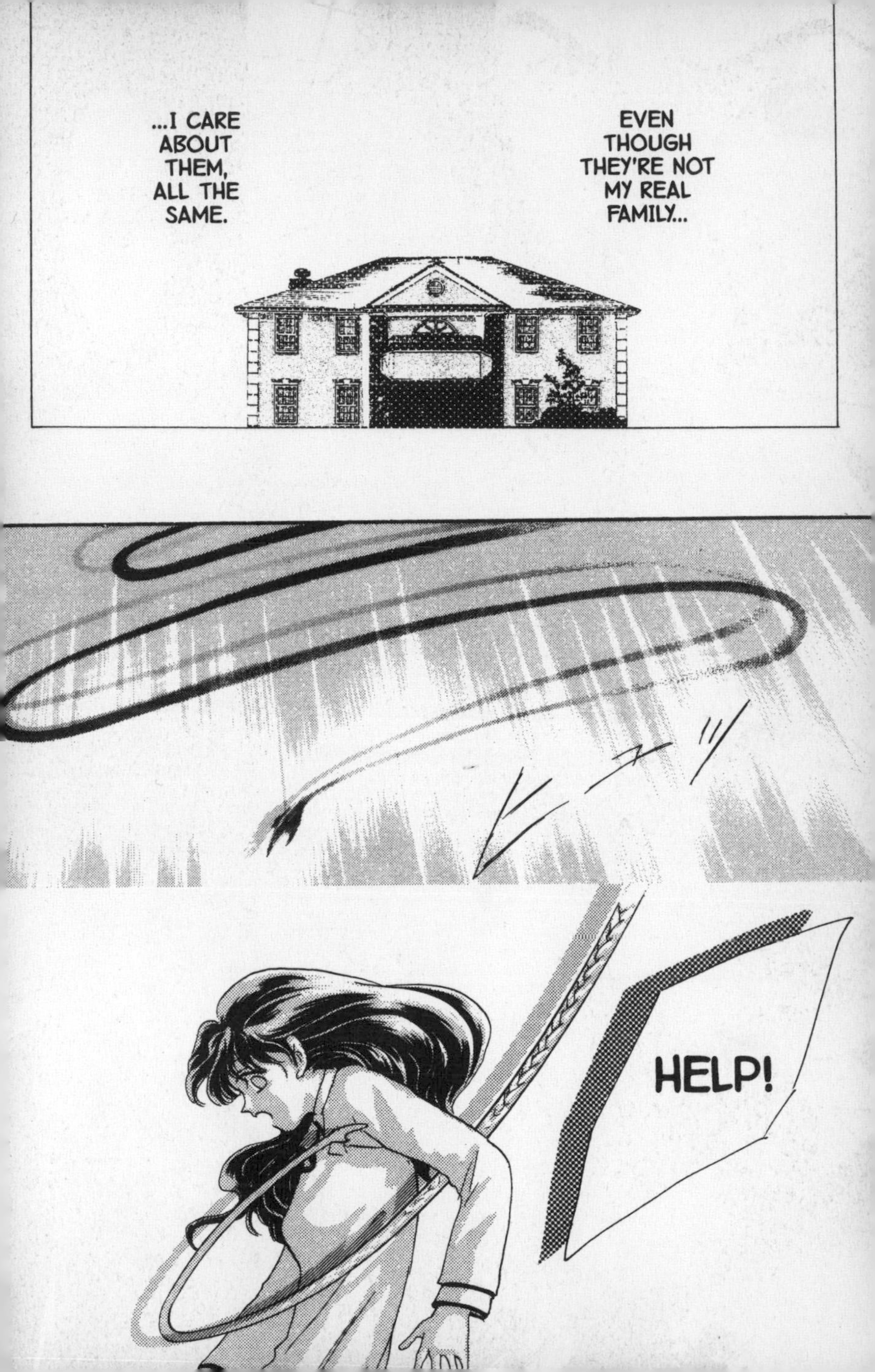
EVEN THOUGH THEY'RE NOT MY REAL FAMILY...
...I CARE ABOUT THEM, ALL THE SAME.
HELP!

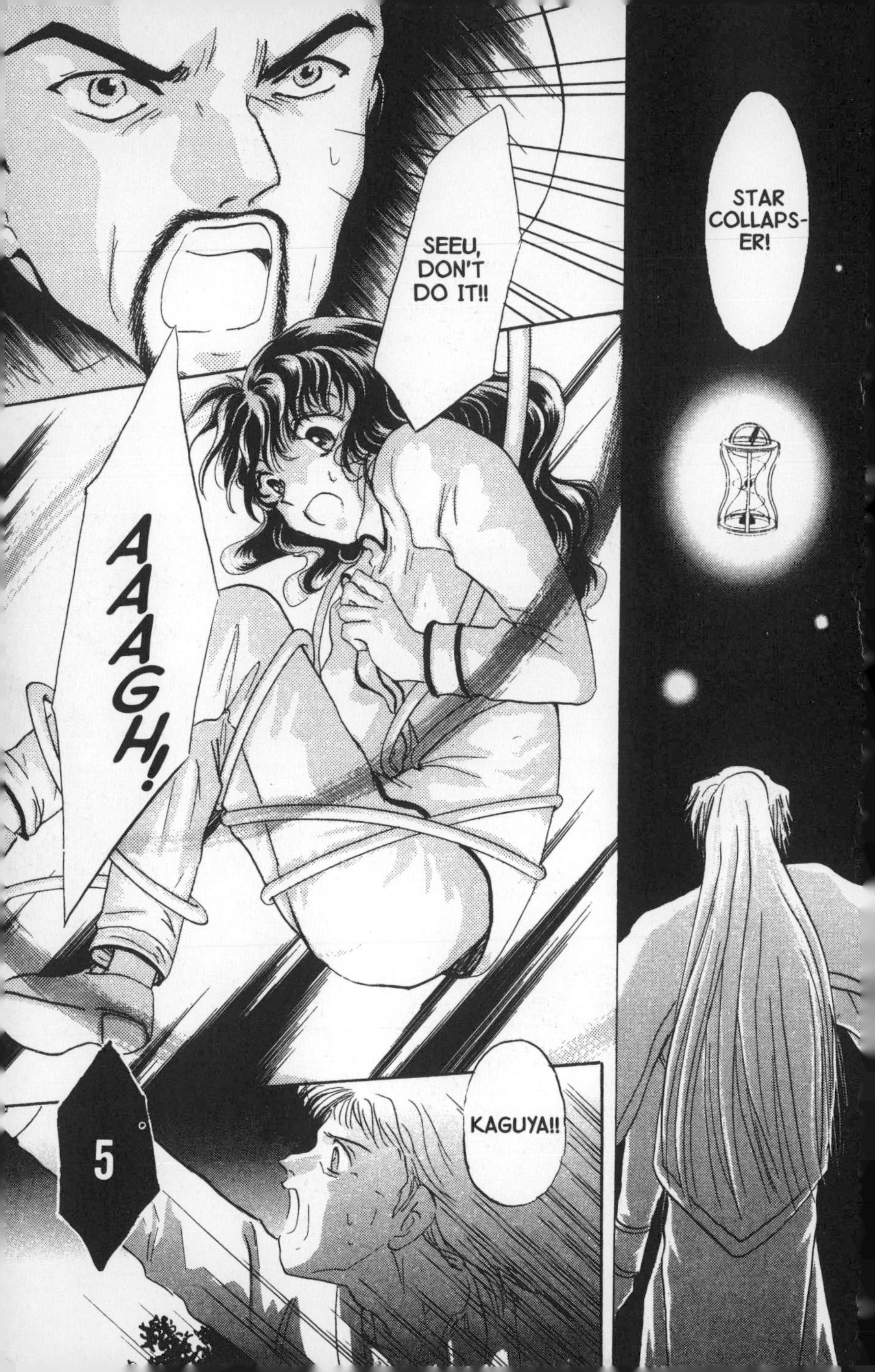
STAR COLLAPS-ER!
SEEU, DON'T DO IT!!
AAAAGH!
KAGUYA!!
5

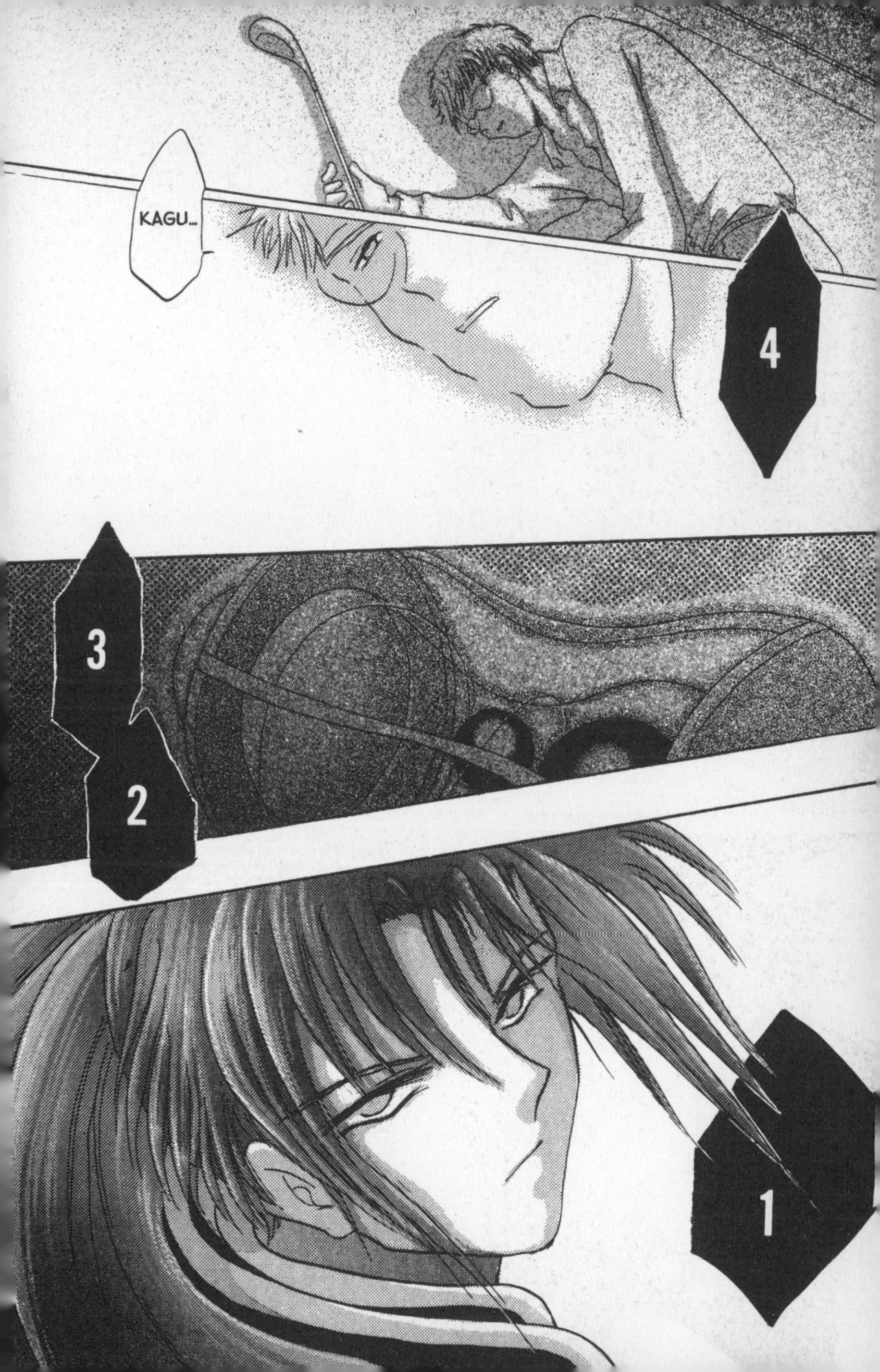
1
2
3
4
KAGU...

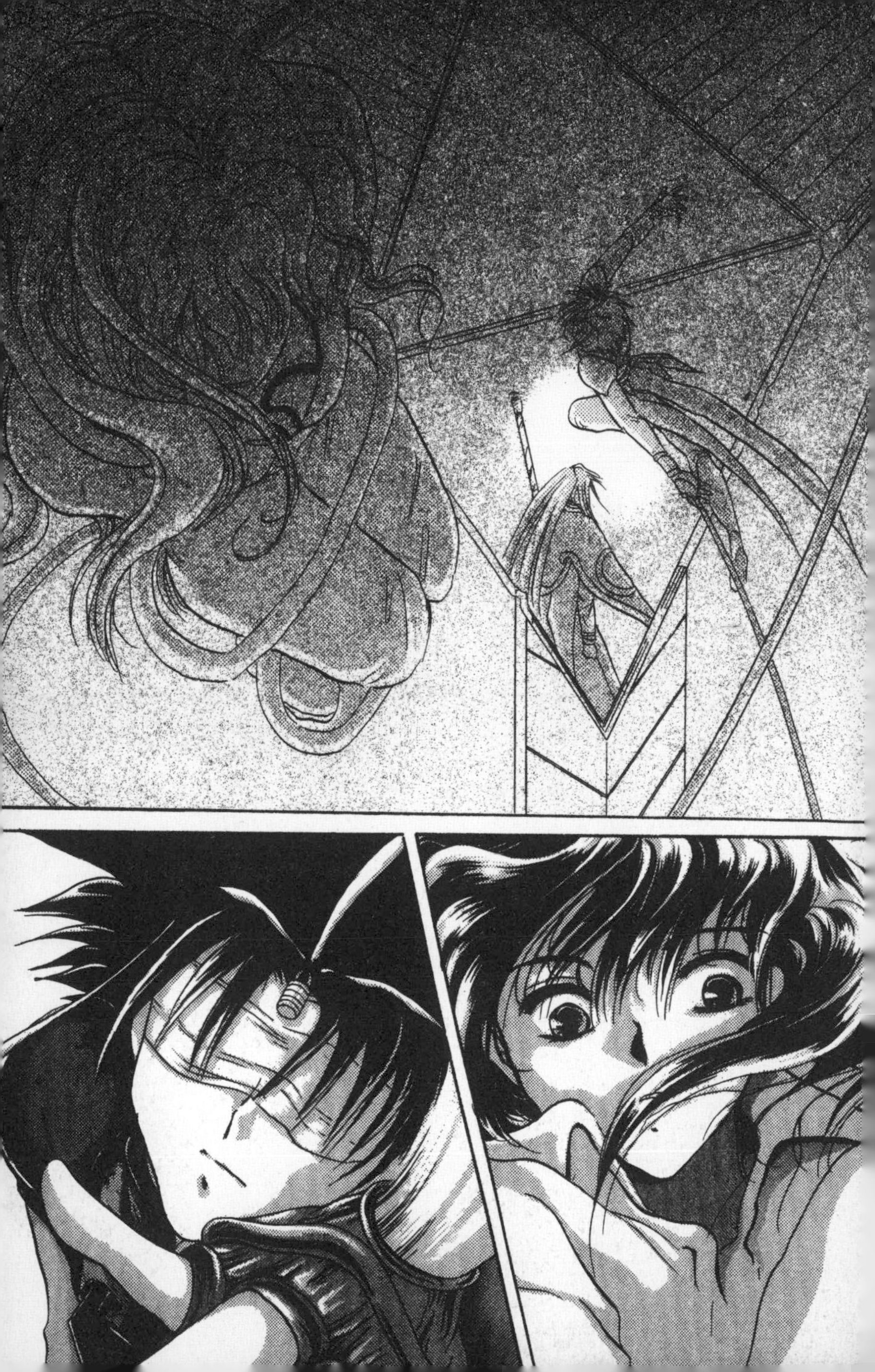

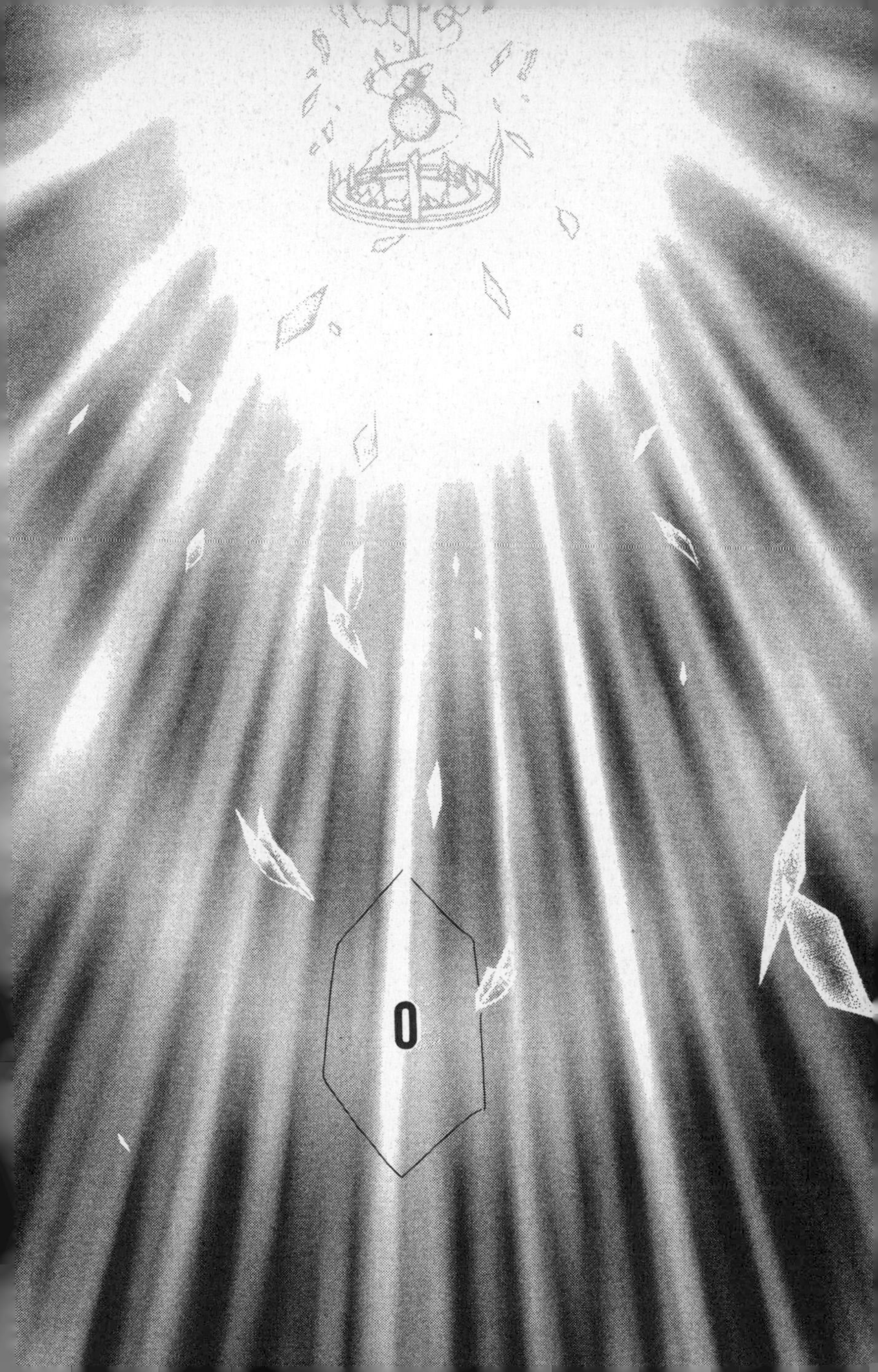

0

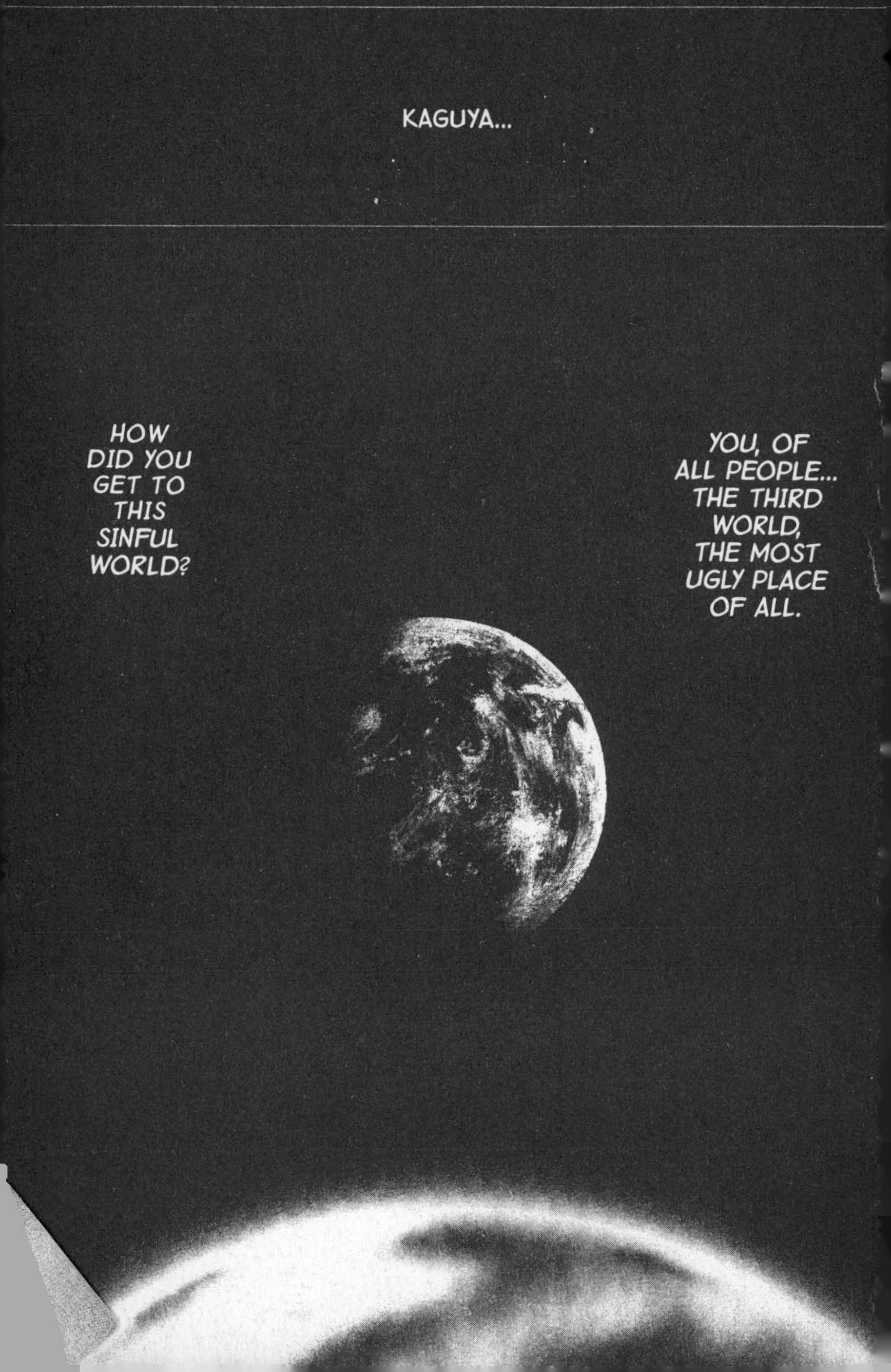
KAGUYA...
YOU, OF ALL PEOPLE... THE THIRD WORLD, THE MOST UGLY PLACE OF ALL.
HOW DID YOU GET TO THIS SINFUL WORLD?

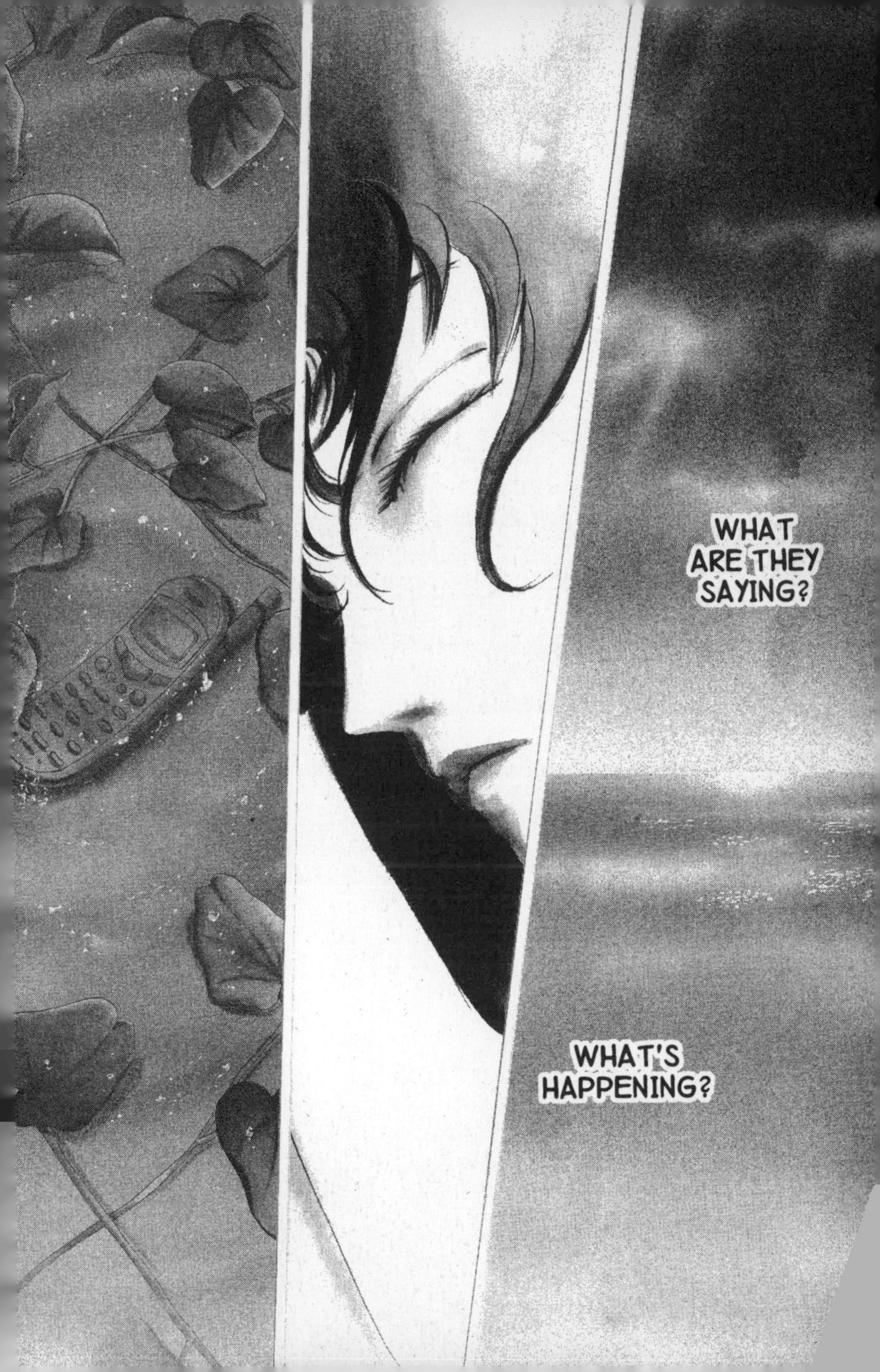
WHAT ARE THEY SAYING?
WHAT'S HAPPENING?

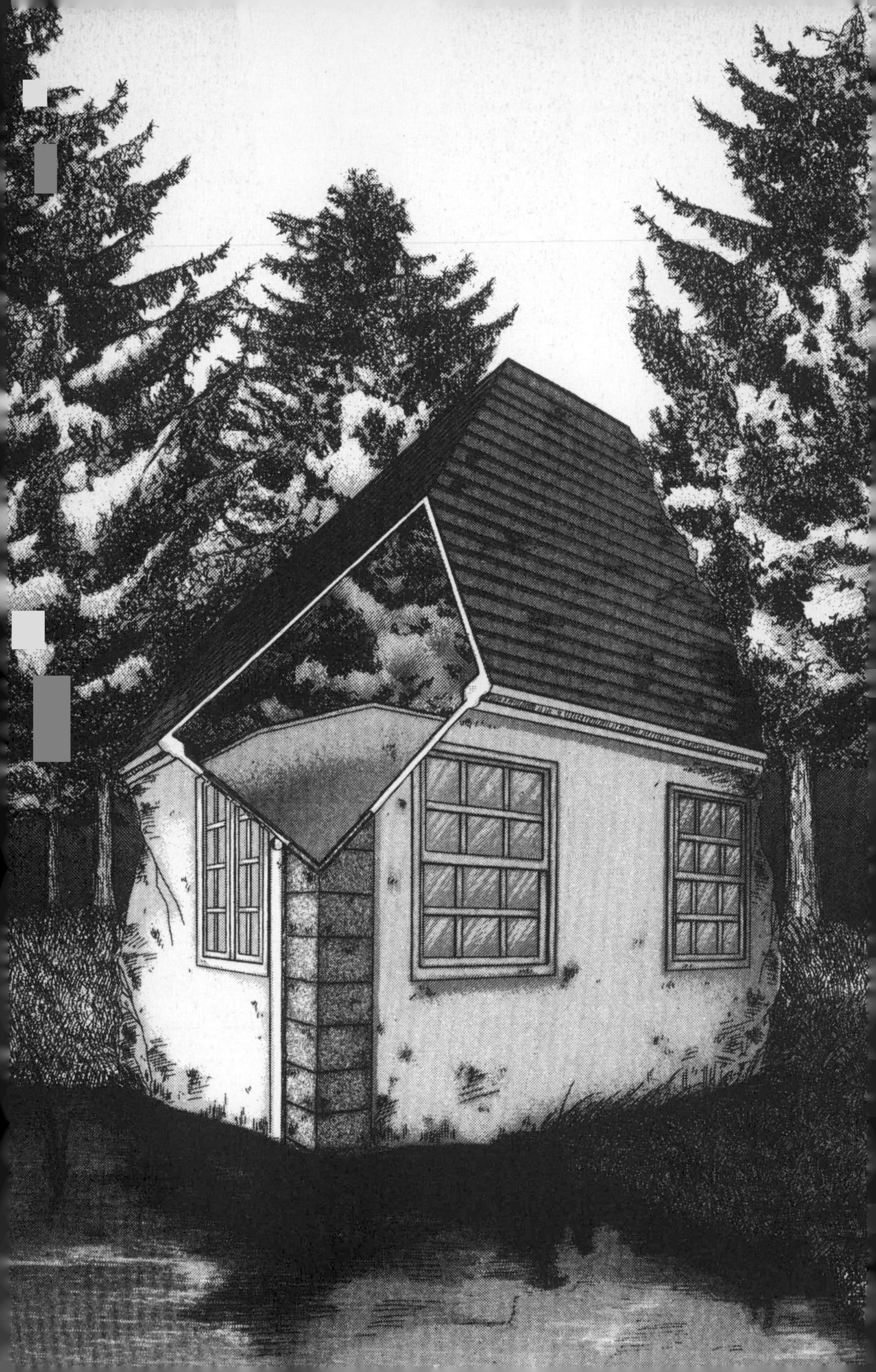

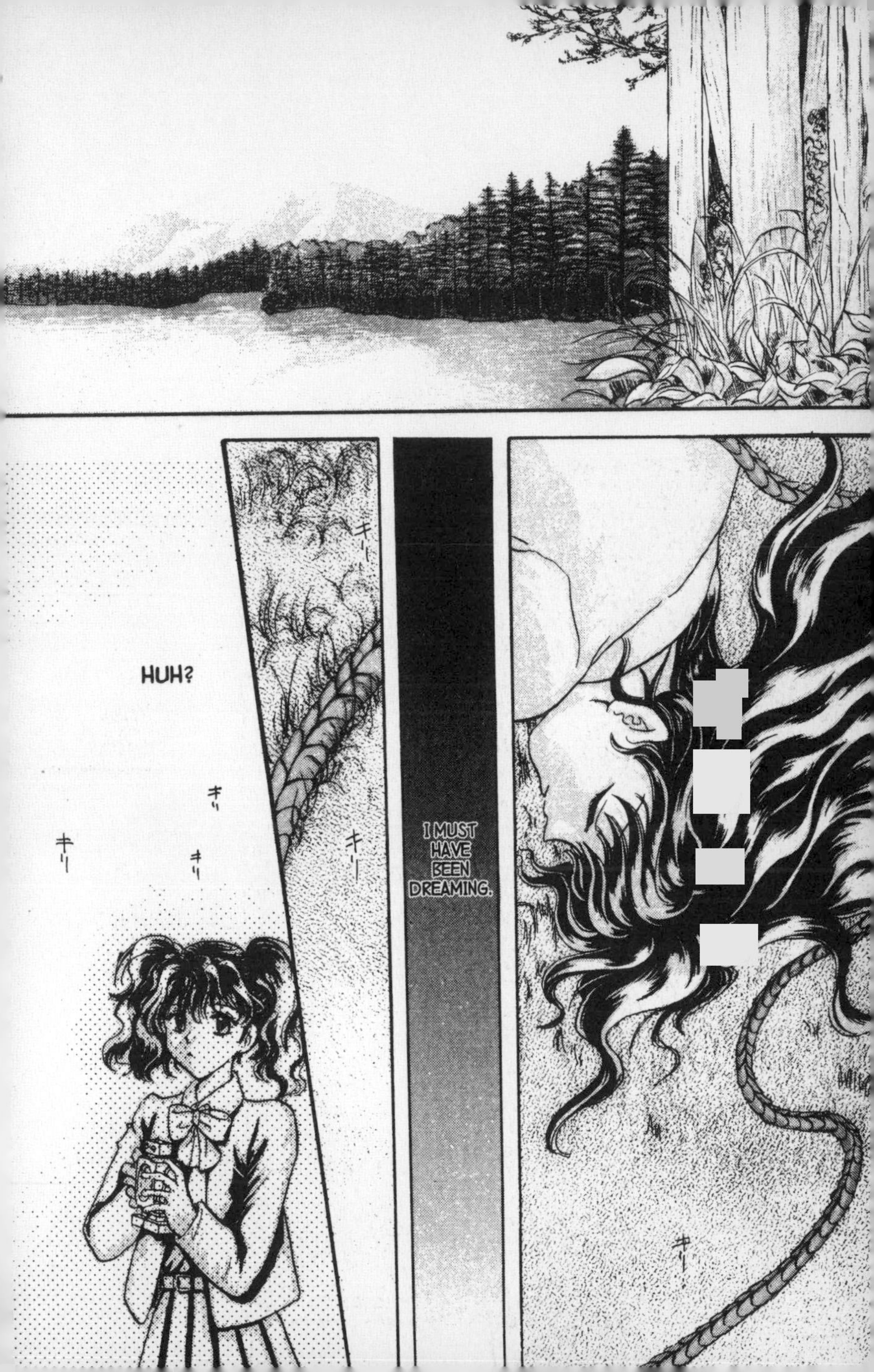
I MUST HAVE BEEN DREAMING.
HUH?

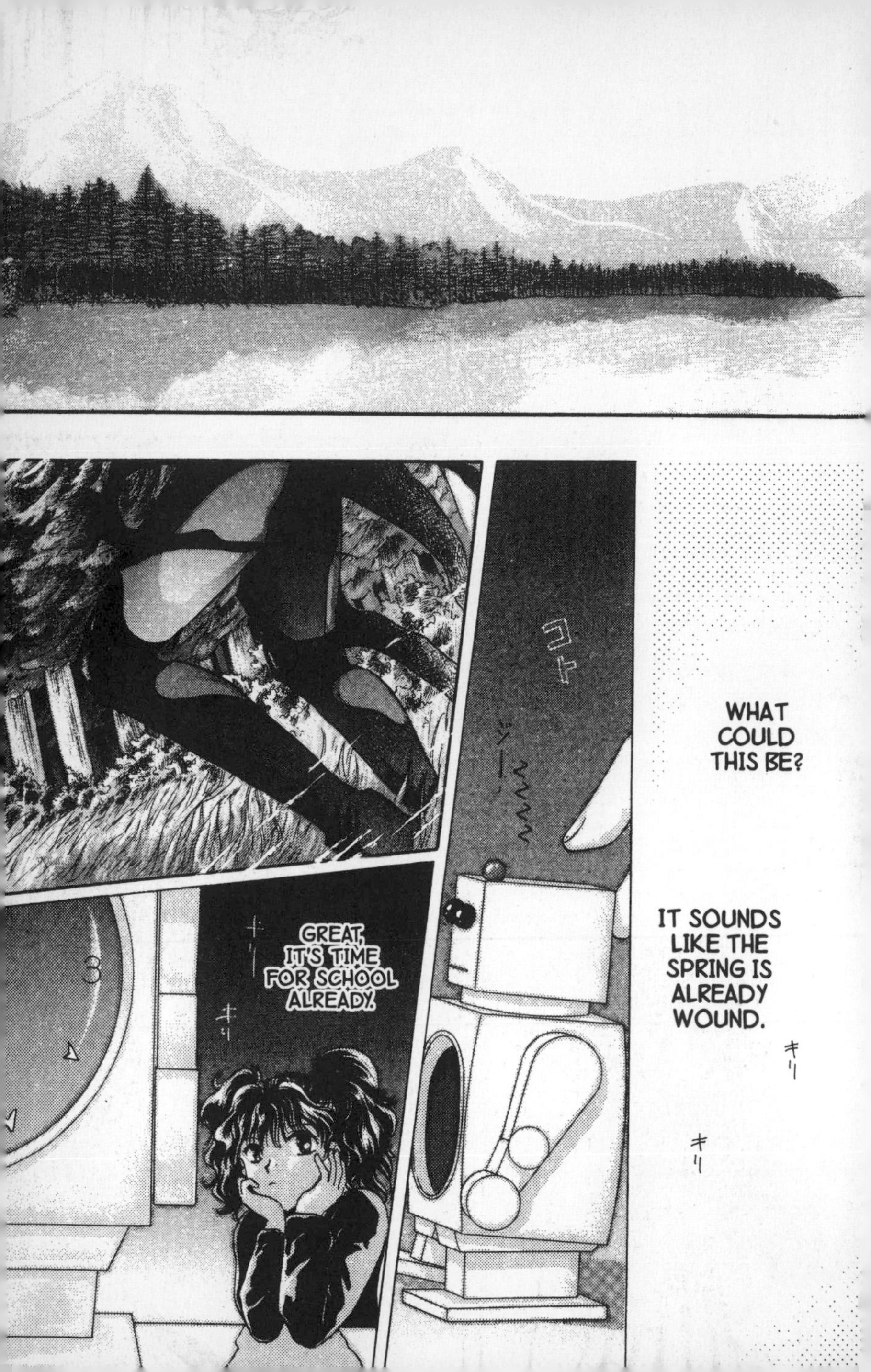
WHAT COULD THIS BE?
IT SOUNDS LIKE THE SPRING IS ALREADY WOUND.
キリ
キリ
コト
GREAT, IT'S TIME FOR SCHOOL ALREADY.

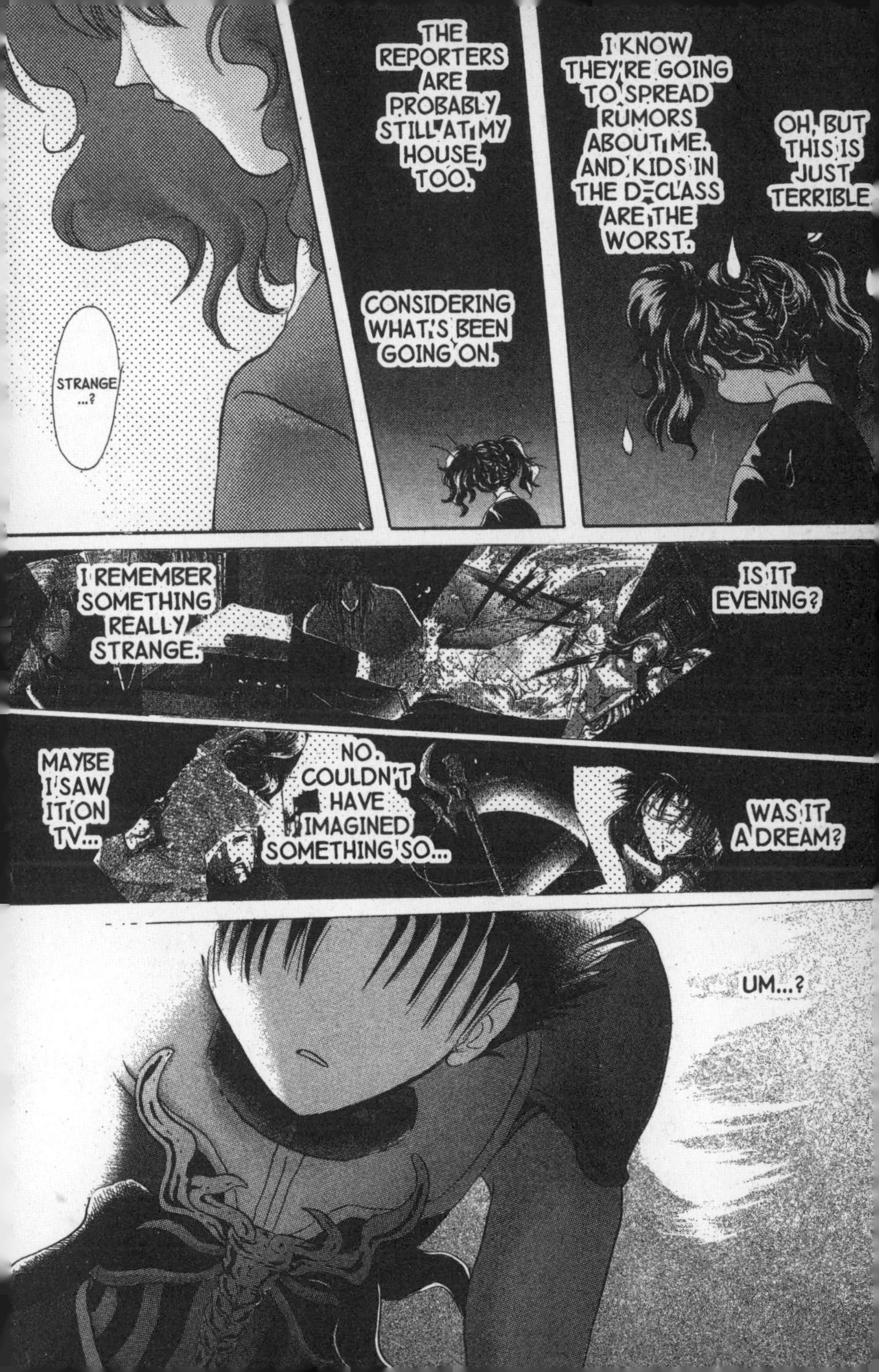
OH, BUT THIS IS JUST TERRIBLE.
I KNOW THEY'RE GOING TO SPREAD RUMORS ABOUT ME. AND KIDS IN THE D-CLASS ARE THE WORST.
THE REPORTERS ARE PROBABLY STILL AT MY HOUSE, TOO.
CONSIDERING WHAT'S BEEN GOING ON.
STRANGE ...?
IS IT EVENING?
I REMEMBER SOMETHING REALLY STRANGE.
WAS IT A DREAM?
NO. COULDN'T HAVE IMAGINED SOMETHING SO...
MAYBE I SAW IT ON TV...
UM...?

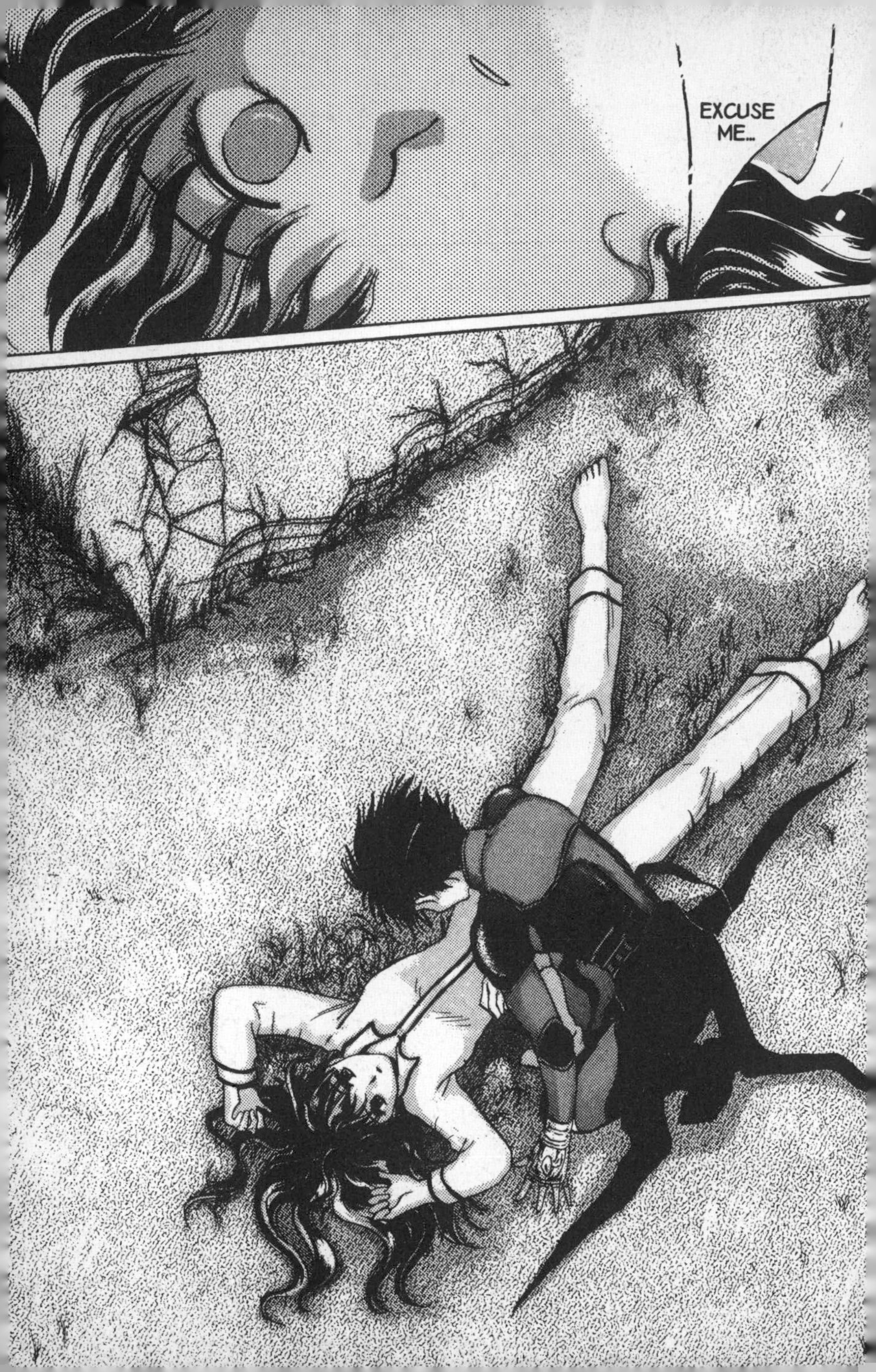
EXCUSE ME...

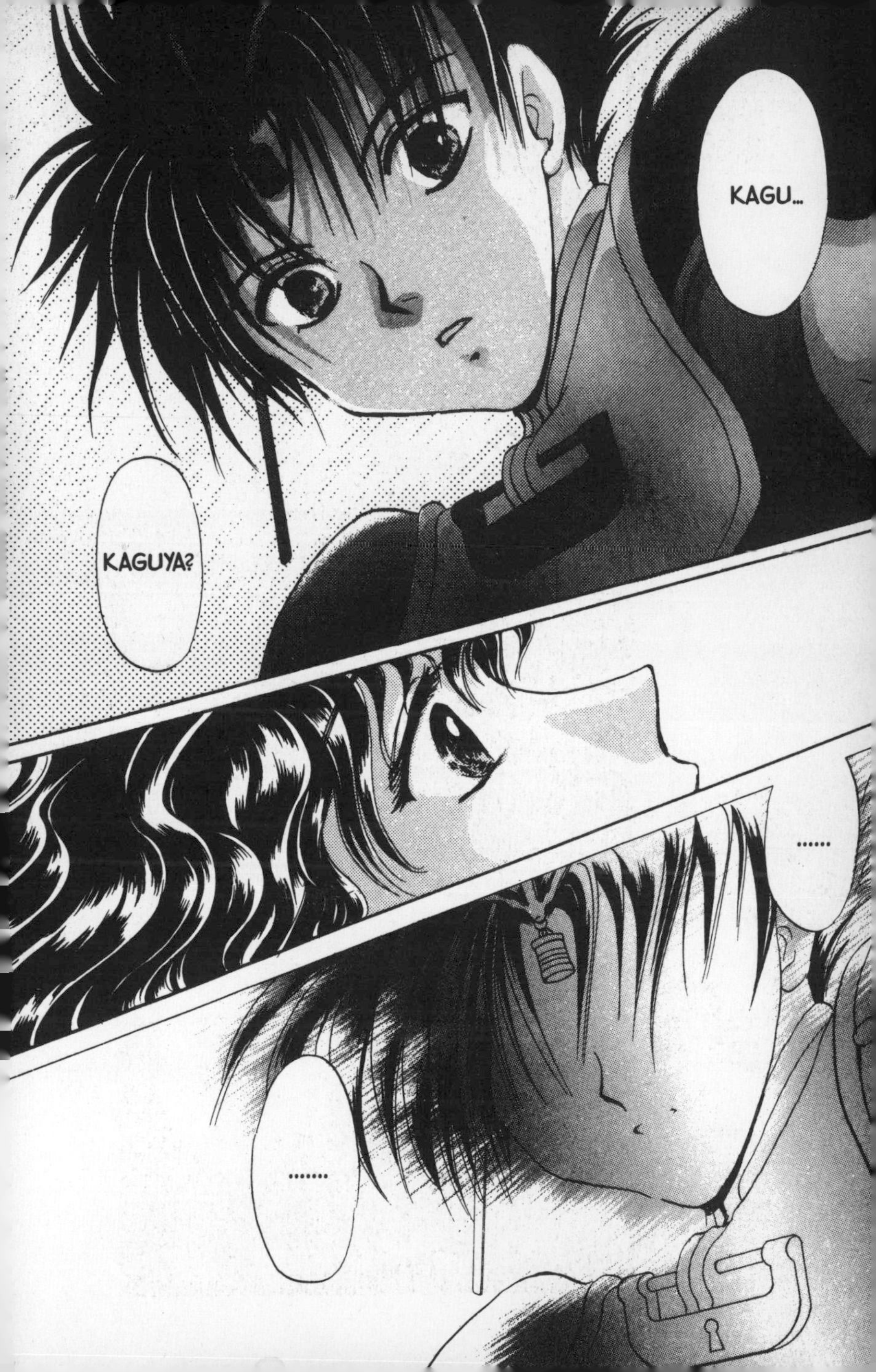
KAGU...
KAGUYA?
......
....

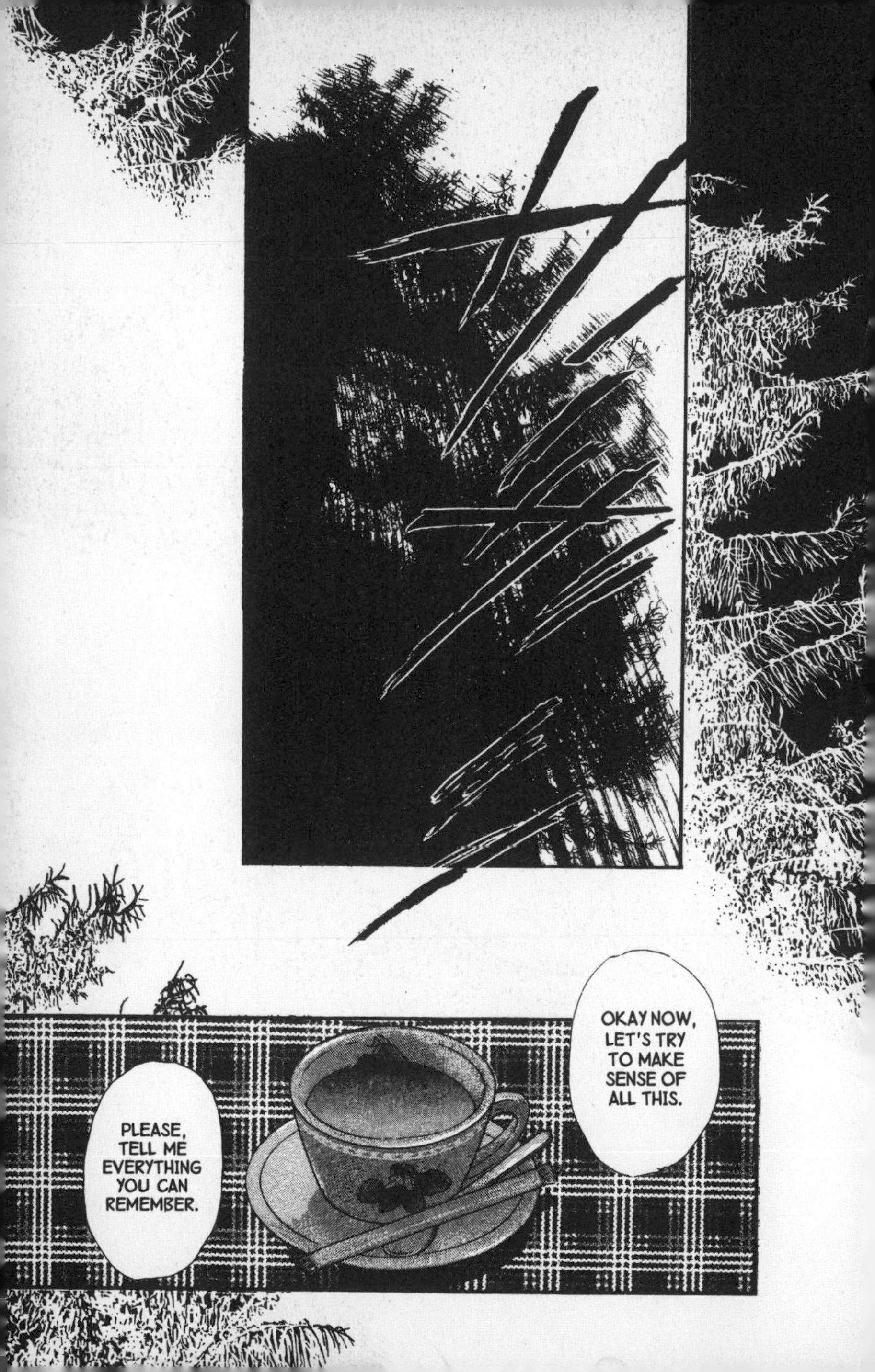
OKAY NOW, LET'S TRY TO MAKE SENSE OF ALL THIS.
PLEASE, TELL ME EVERYTHING YOU CAN REMEMBER.

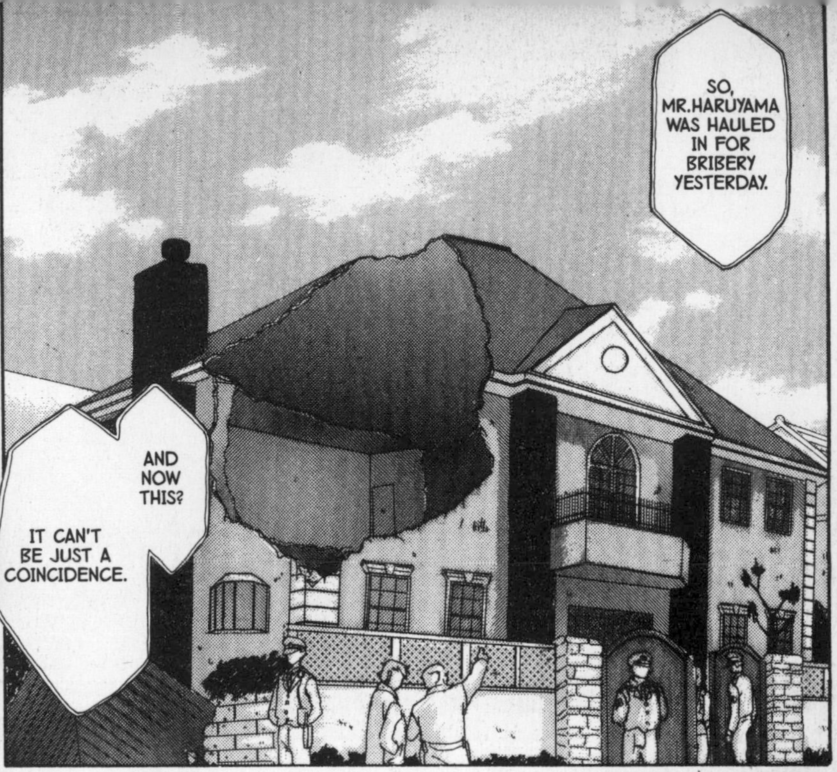
SO, MR.HARUYAMA WAS HAULED IN FOR BRIBERY YESTERDAY.
AND NOW THIS?
IT CAN'T BE JUST A COINCIDENCE.

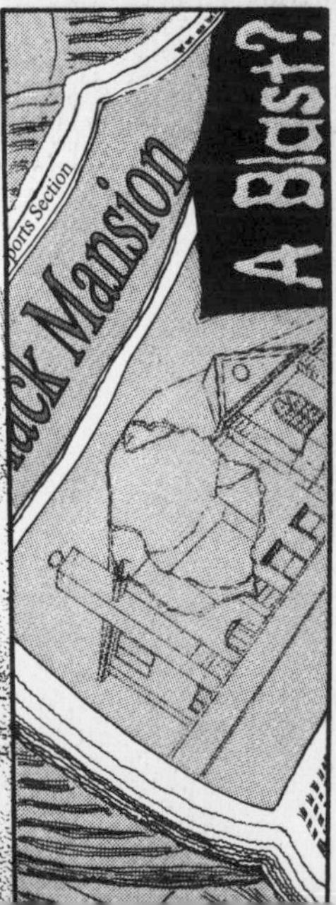
A Blast?

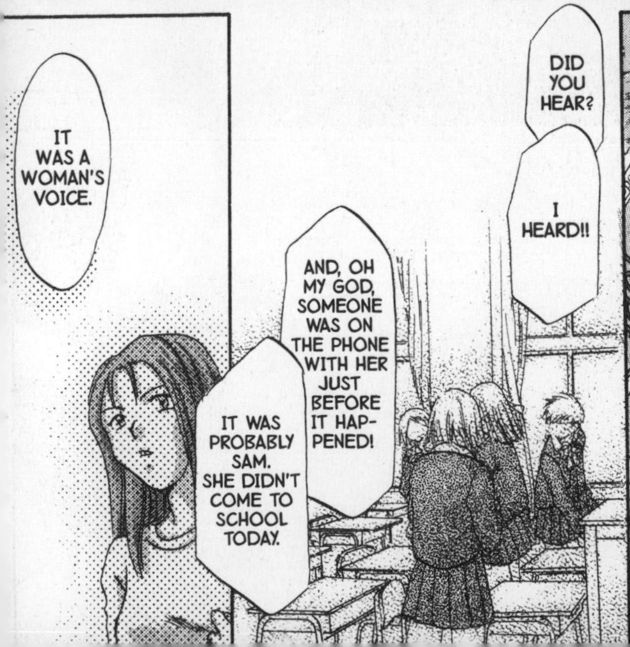
DID YOU HEAR?
I HEARD!!
AND, OH MY GOD, SOMEONE WAS ON THE PHONE WITH HER JUST BEFORE IT HAP-PENED!
IT WAS PROBABLY SAM. SHE DIDN'T COME TO SCHOOL TODAY.
IT WAS A WOMAN'S VOICE.

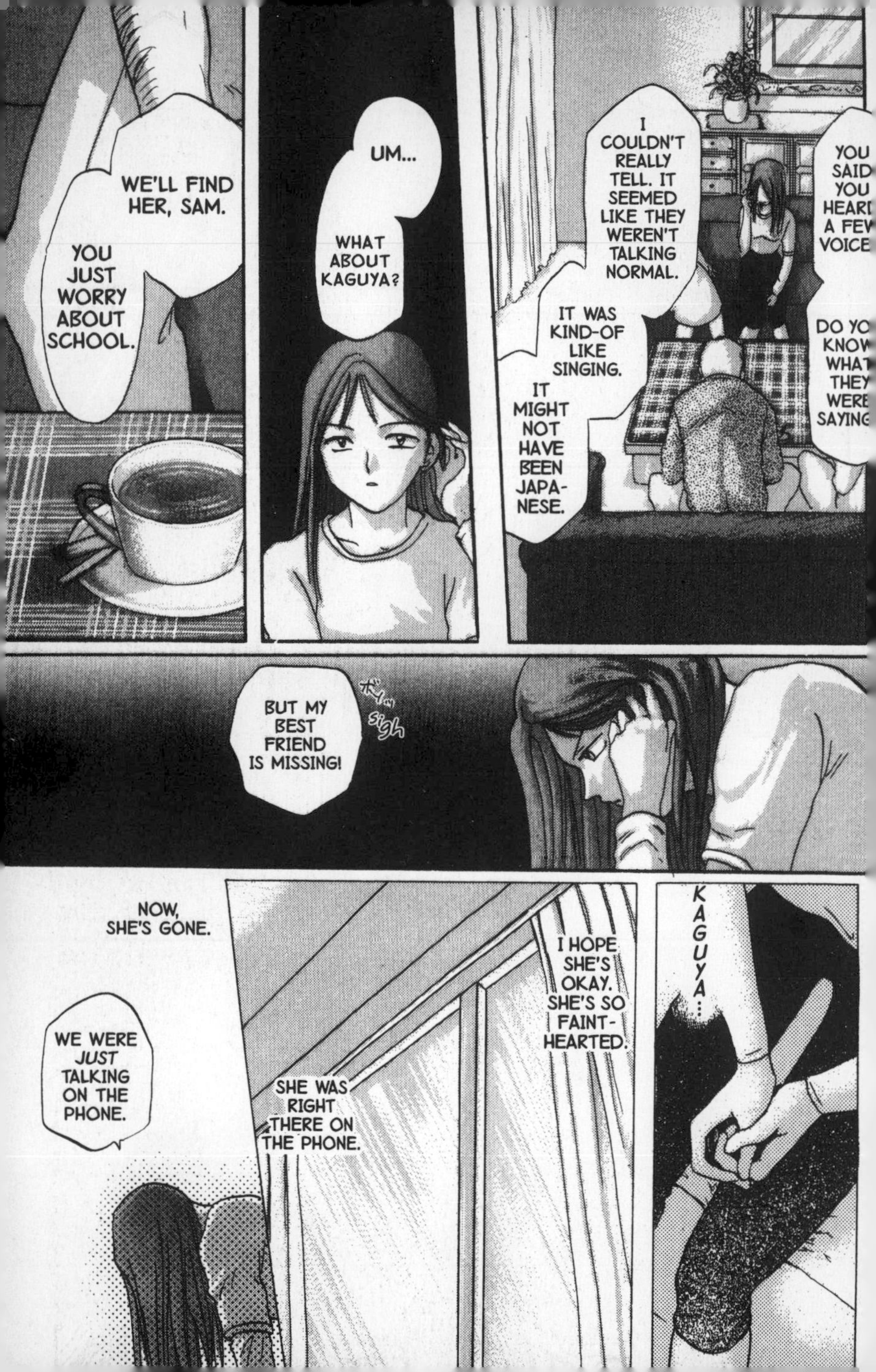
YOU SAID YOU HEARD A FEW VOICE
DO YO KNOW WHAT THEY WERE SAYING
I COULDN'T REALLY TELL. IT SEEMED LIKE THEY WEREN'T TALKING NORMAL.
IT WAS KIND-OF LIKE SINGING.
IT MIGHT NOT HAVE BEEN JAPA-NESE.
UM...
WHAT ABOUT KAGUYA?
WE'LL FIND HER, SAM.
YOU JUST WORRY ABOUT SCHOOL.
sigh
BUT MY BEST FRIEND IS MISSING!
KAGUYA...
I HOPE SHE'S OKAY. SHE'S SO FAINT-HEARTED.
SHE WAS RIGHT THERE ON THE PHONE.
NOW, SHE'S GONE.
WE WERE *JUST* TALKING ON THE PHONE.

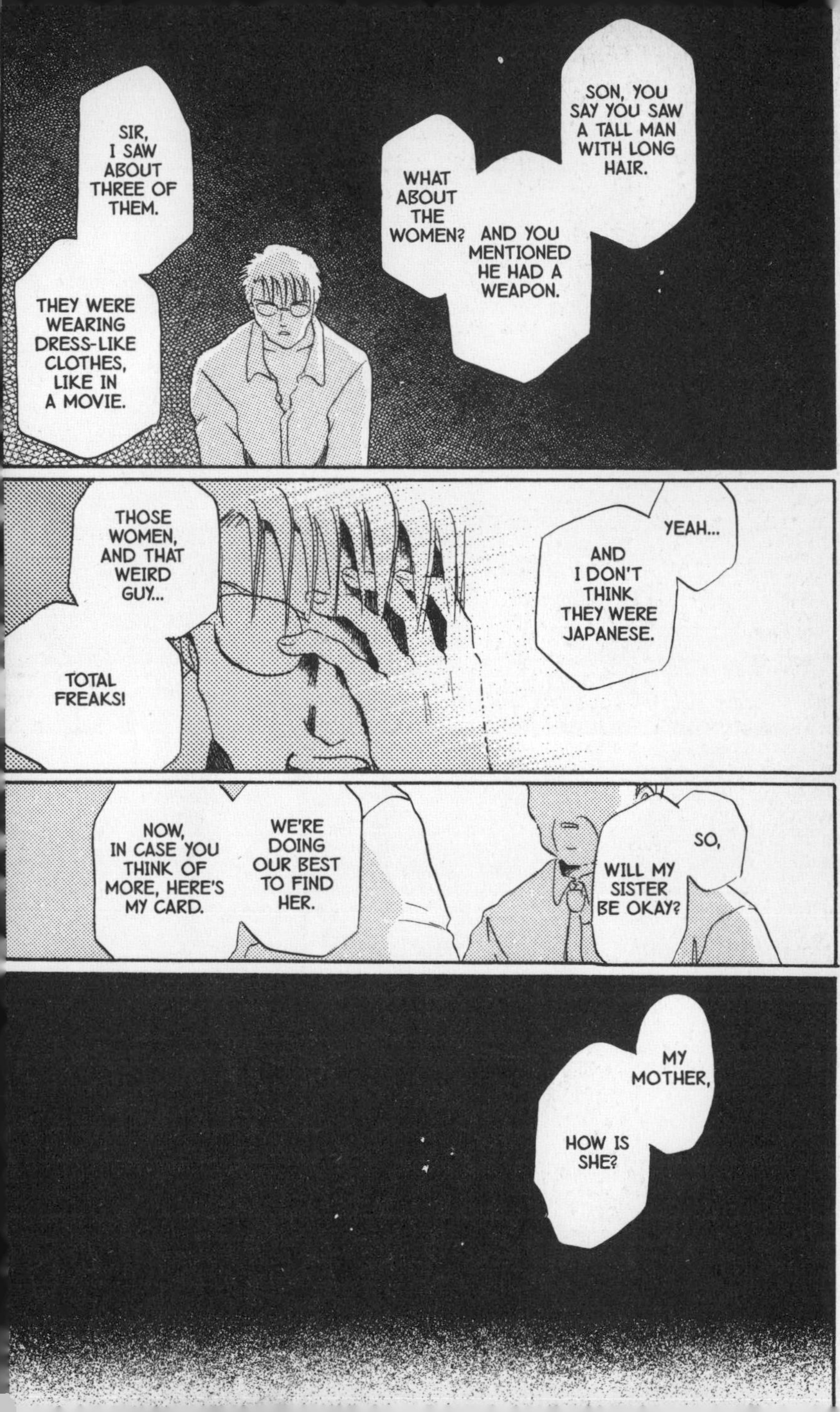
SON, YOU SAY YOU SAW A TALL MAN WITH LONG HAIR.
AND YOU MENTIONED HE HAD A WEAPON.
WHAT ABOUT THE WOMEN?
SIR, I SAW ABOUT THREE OF THEM.
THEY WERE WEARING DRESS-LIKE CLOTHES, LIKE IN A MOVIE.
YEAH...
AND I DON'T THINK THEY WERE JAPANESE.
THOSE WOMEN, AND THAT WEIRD GUY...
TOTAL FREAKS!
SO,
WILL MY SISTER BE OKAY?
WE'RE DOING OUR BEST TO FIND HER.
NOW, IN CASE YOU THINK OF MORE, HERE'S MY CARD.
MY MOTHER,
HOW IS SHE?

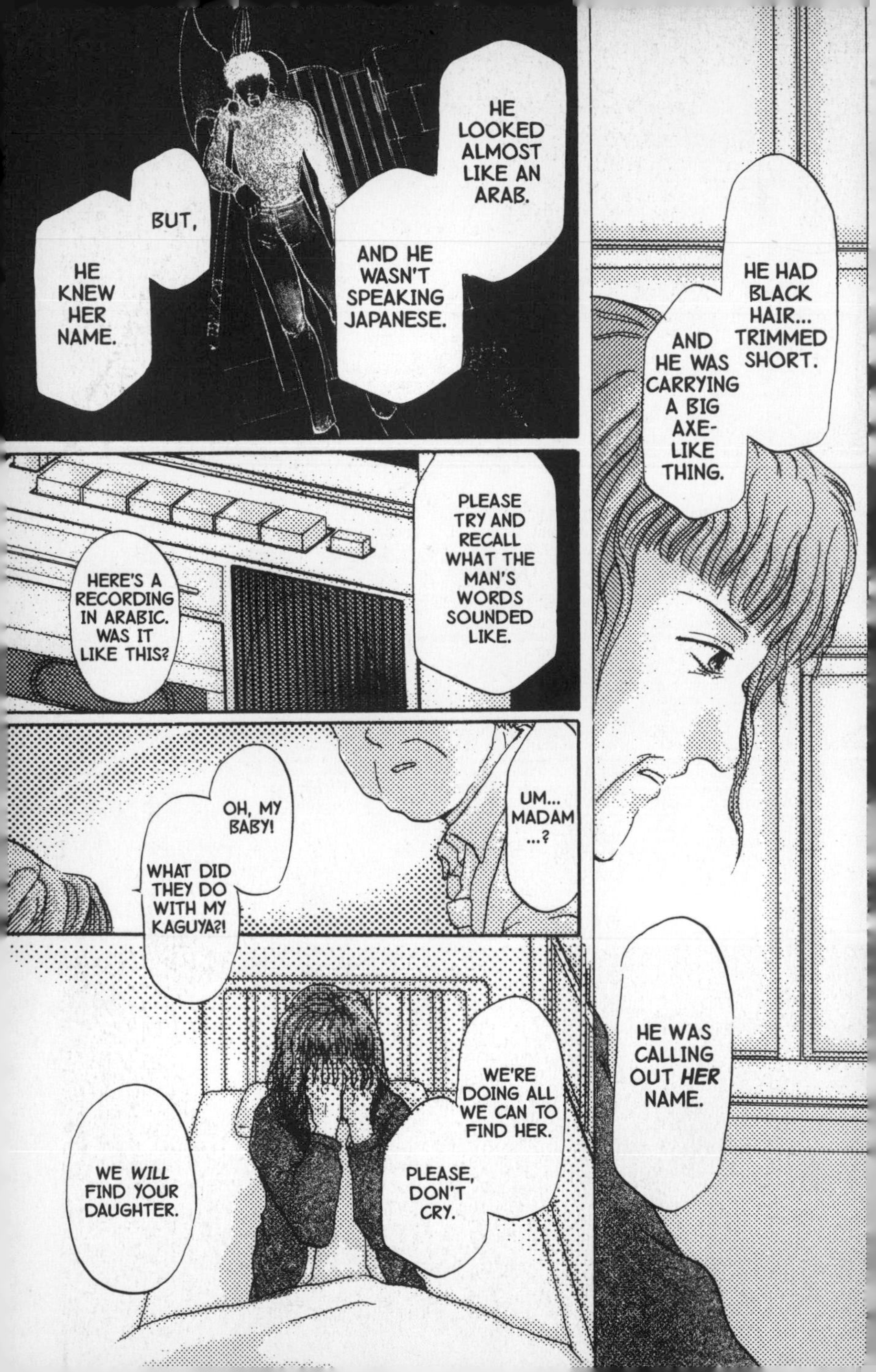
HE HAD BLACK HAIR... TRIMMED SHORT.
AND HE WAS CARRYING A BIG AXE-LIKE THING.
HE WAS CALLING OUT *HER* NAME.
HE LOOKED ALMOST LIKE AN ARAB.
AND HE WASN'T SPEAKING JAPANESE.
BUT,
HE KNEW HER NAME.
PLEASE TRY AND RECALL WHAT THE MAN'S WORDS SOUNDED LIKE.
HERE'S A RECORDING IN ARABIC. WAS IT LIKE THIS?
UM... MADAM ...?
OH, MY BABY!
WHAT DID THEY DO WITH MY KAGUYA?!
WE'RE DOING ALL WE CAN TO FIND HER.
PLEASE, DON'T CRY.
WE *WILL* FIND YOUR DAUGHTER.

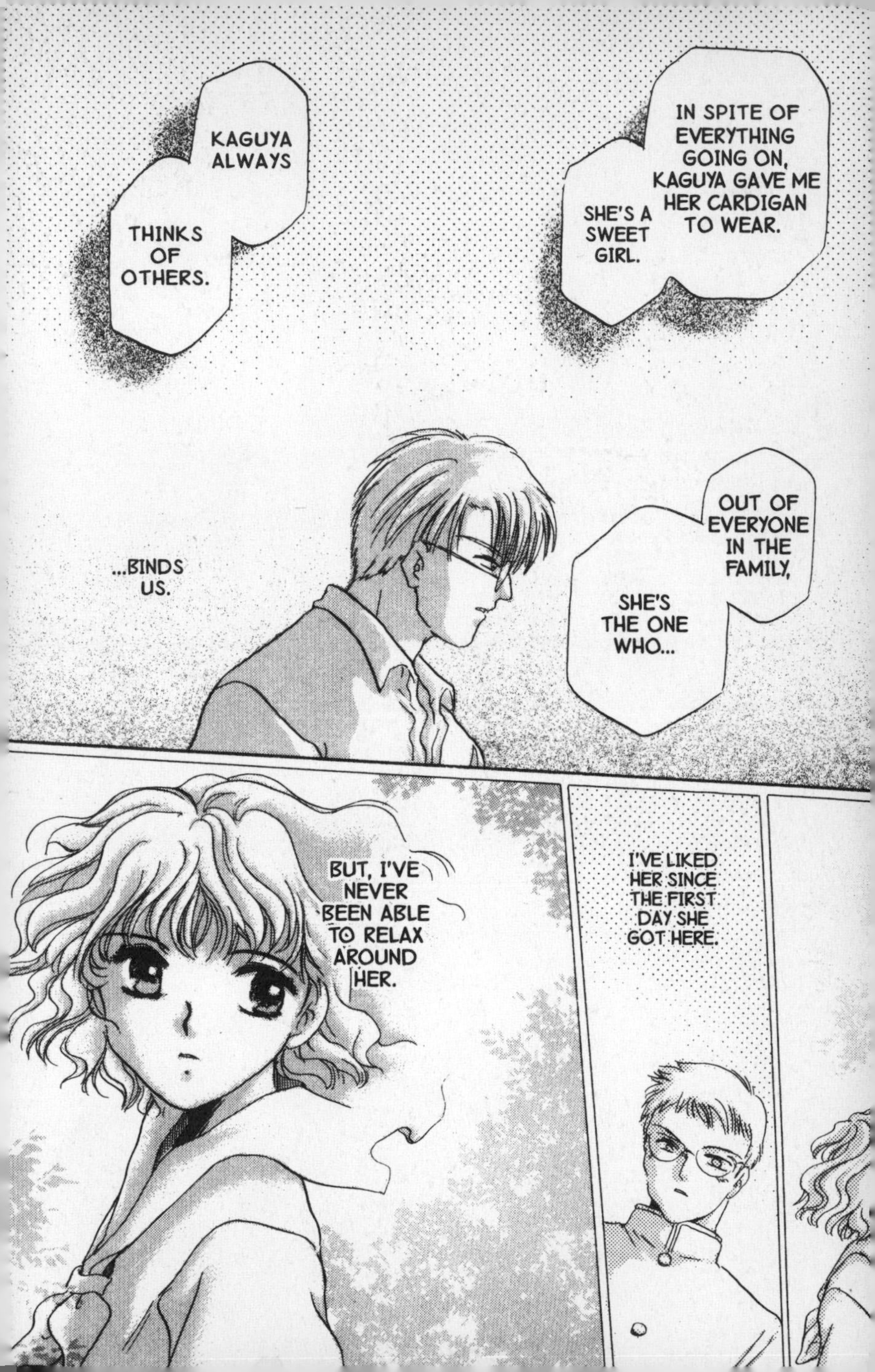
IN SPITE OF EVERYTHING GOING ON, KAGUYA GAVE ME HER CARDIGAN TO WEAR.
SHE'S A SWEET GIRL.
KAGUYA ALWAYS
THINKS OF OTHERS.
OUT OF EVERYONE IN THE FAMILY,
SHE'S THE ONE WHO...
...BINDS US.
I'VE LIKED HER SINCE THE FIRST DAY SHE GOT HERE.
BUT, I'VE NEVER BEEN ABLE TO RELAX AROUND HER.

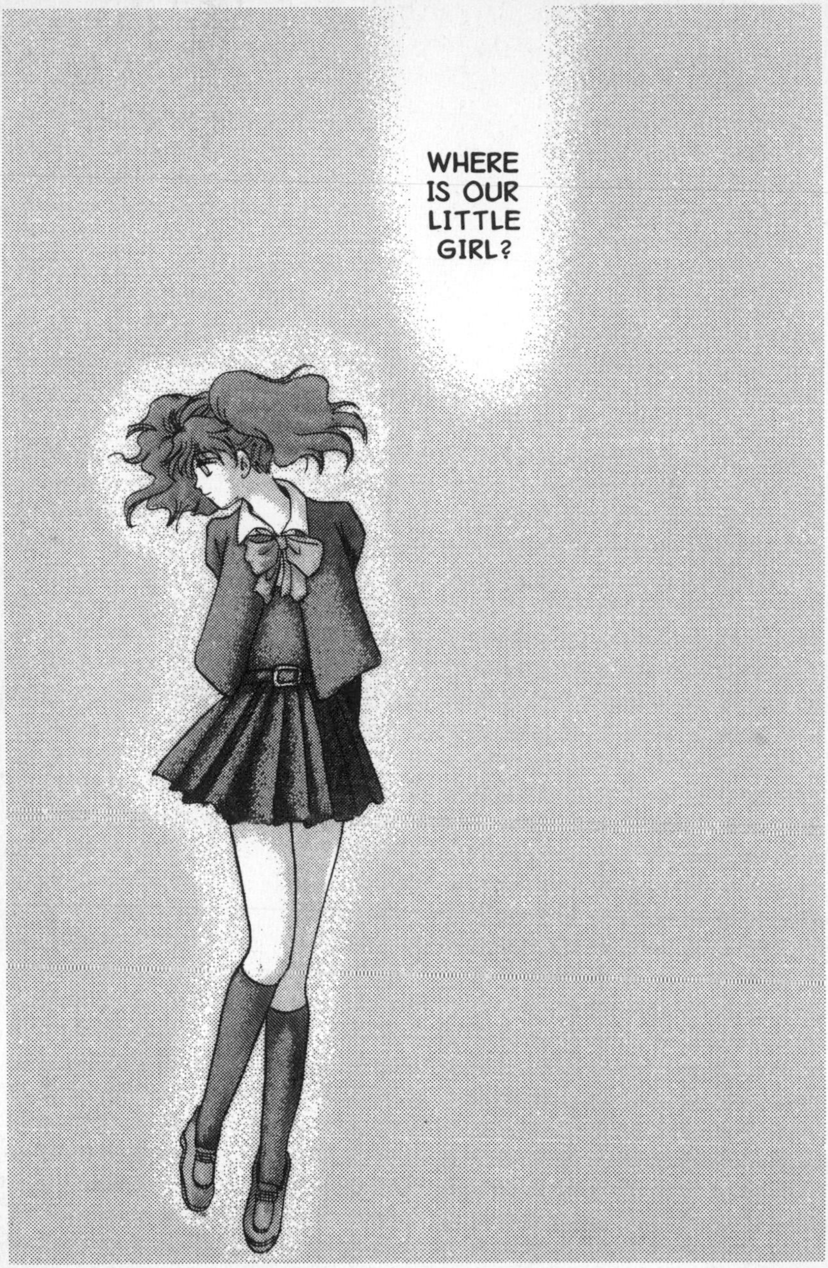
WHERE IS OUR LITTLE GIRL?

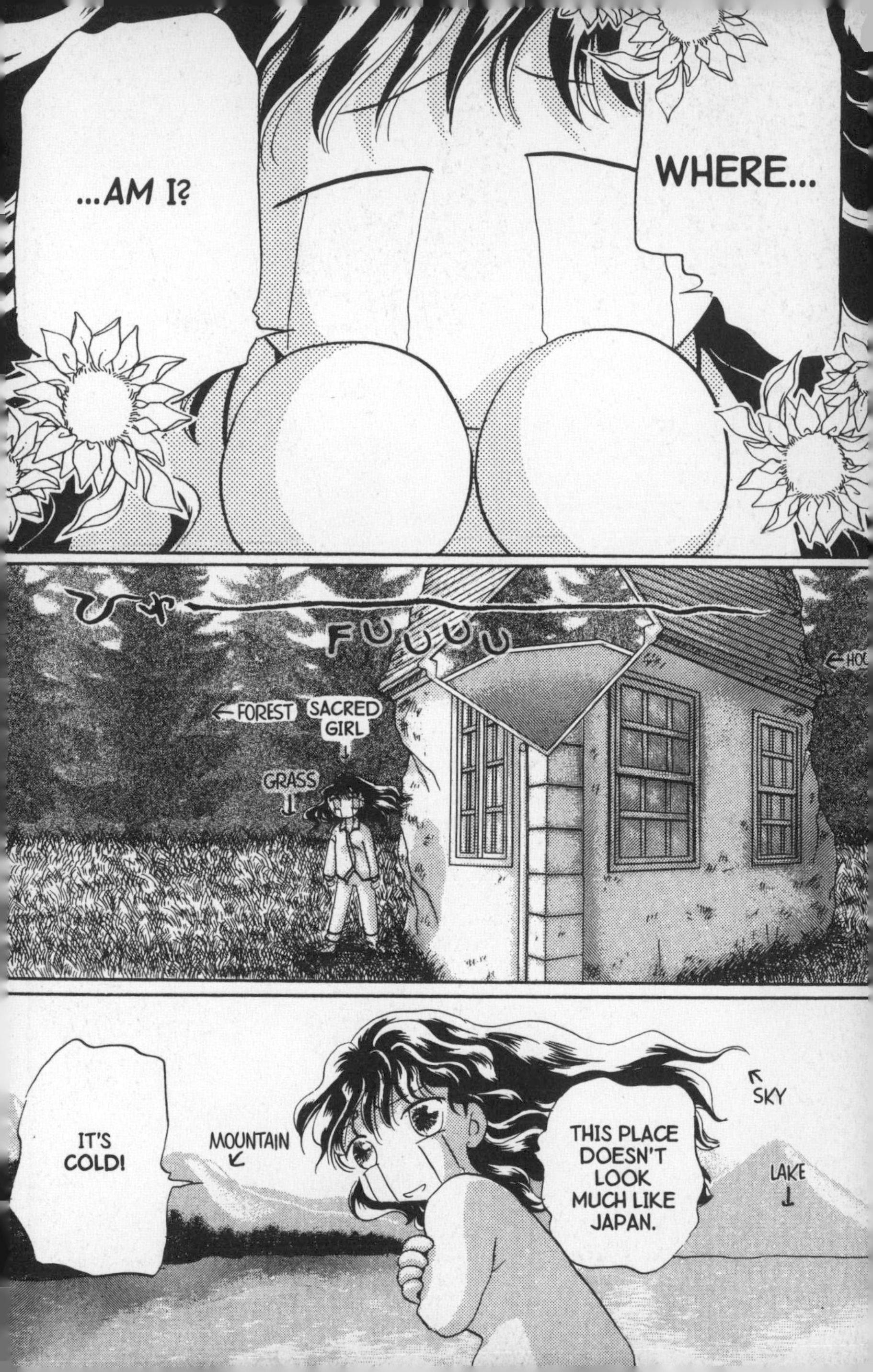
WHERE...
...AM I?
FUUUU
SACRED GIRL
← FOREST
GRASS
SKY
LAKE
THIS PLACE DOESN'T LOOK MUCH LIKE JAPAN.
MOUNTAIN
IT'S COLD!

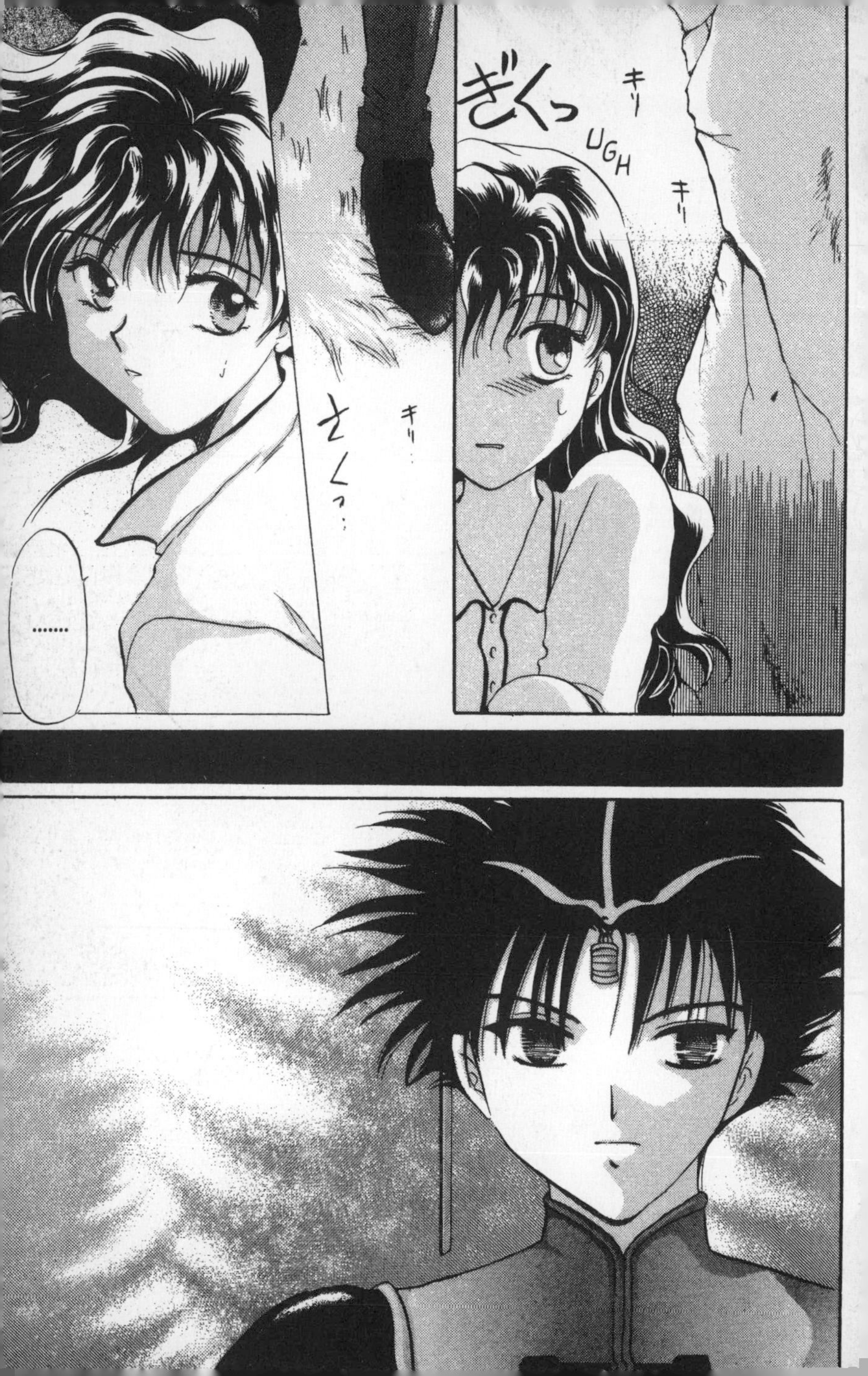
ぎくっ
キリ
UGH
キリ
キリ
さくっ
……

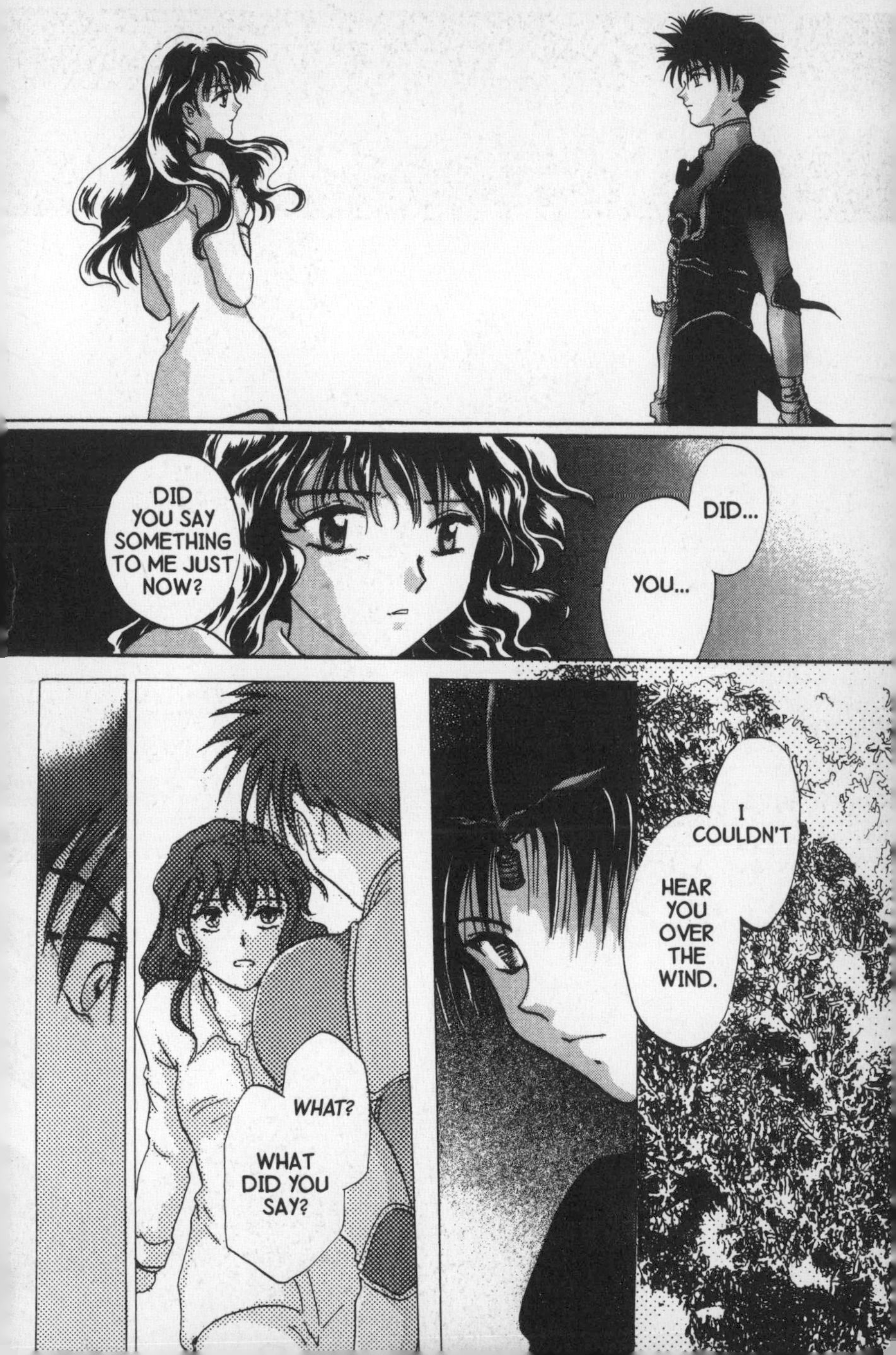
DID... YOU...
DID YOU SAY SOMETHING TO ME JUST NOW?
I COULDN'T HEAR YOU OVER THE WIND.
WHAT? WHAT DID YOU SAY?

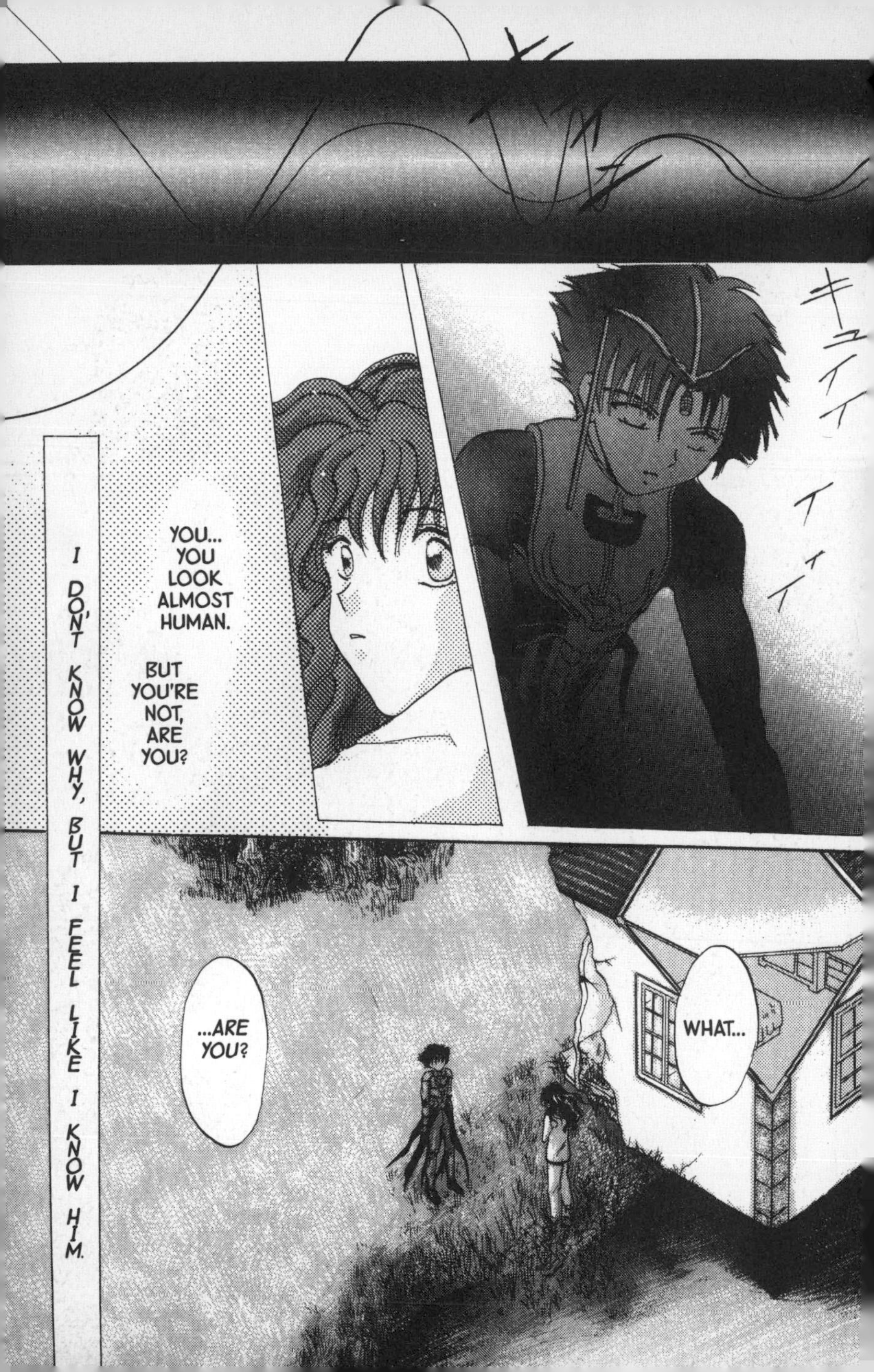
YOU... YOU LOOK ALMOST HUMAN.
BUT YOU'RE NOT, ARE YOU?
I DON'T KNOW WHY, BUT I FEEL LIKE I KNOW HIM.
WHAT...
...ARE YOU?

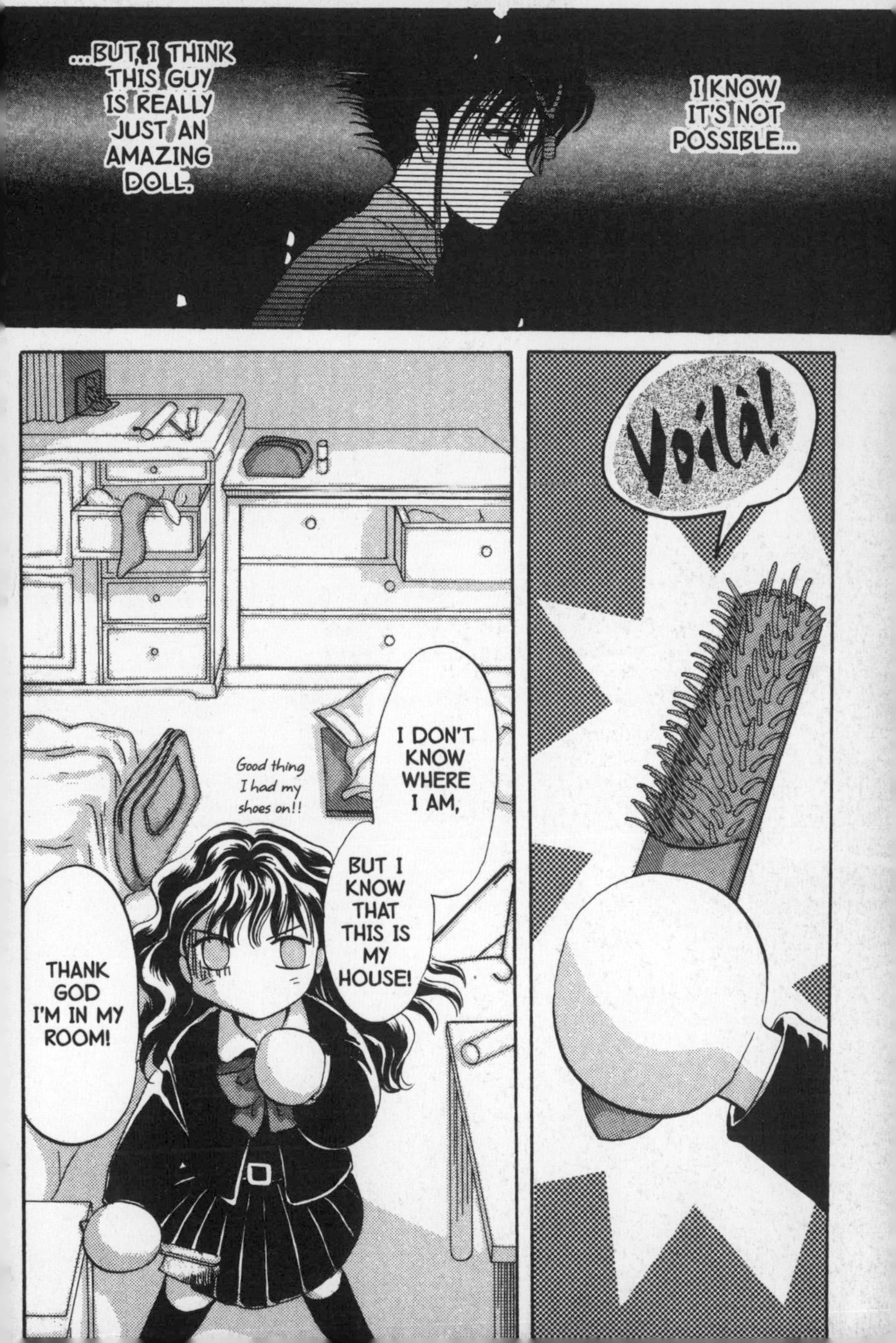
I KNOW IT'S NOT POSSIBLE...
...BUT, I THINK THIS GUY IS REALLY JUST AN AMAZING DOLL.
Voilà!
I DON'T KNOW WHERE I AM,
BUT I KNOW THAT THIS IS MY HOUSE!
Good thing I had my shoes on!!
THANK GOD I'M IN MY ROOM!

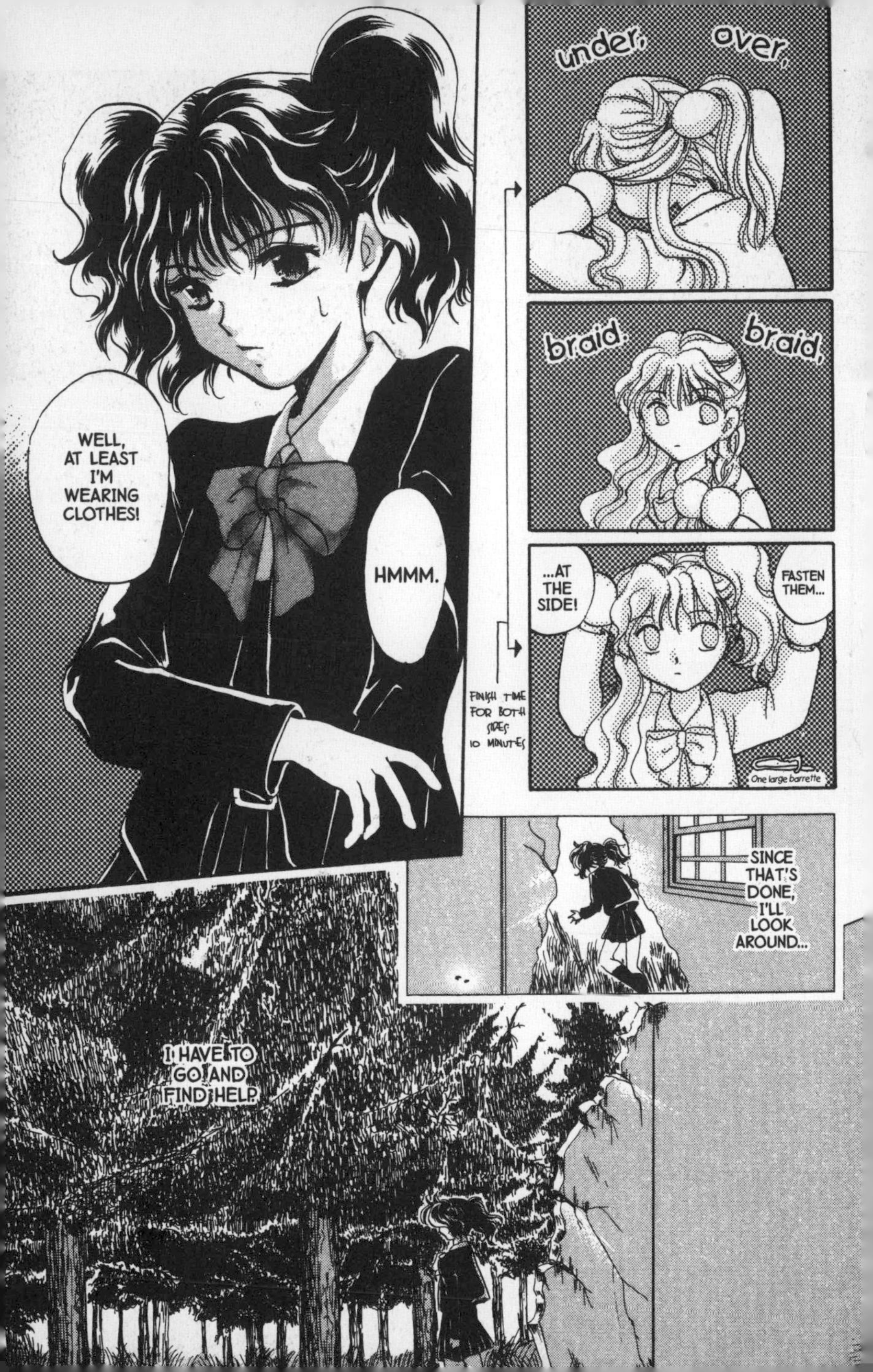
under, over,
braid. braid,
FASTEN THEM...
...AT THE SIDE!
FINISH TIME FOR BOTH SIDES 10 MINUTES
One large barrette
WELL, AT LEAST I'M WEARING CLOTHES!
HMMM.
SINCE THAT'S DONE, I'LL LOOK AROUND...
I HAVE TO GO AND FIND HELP.

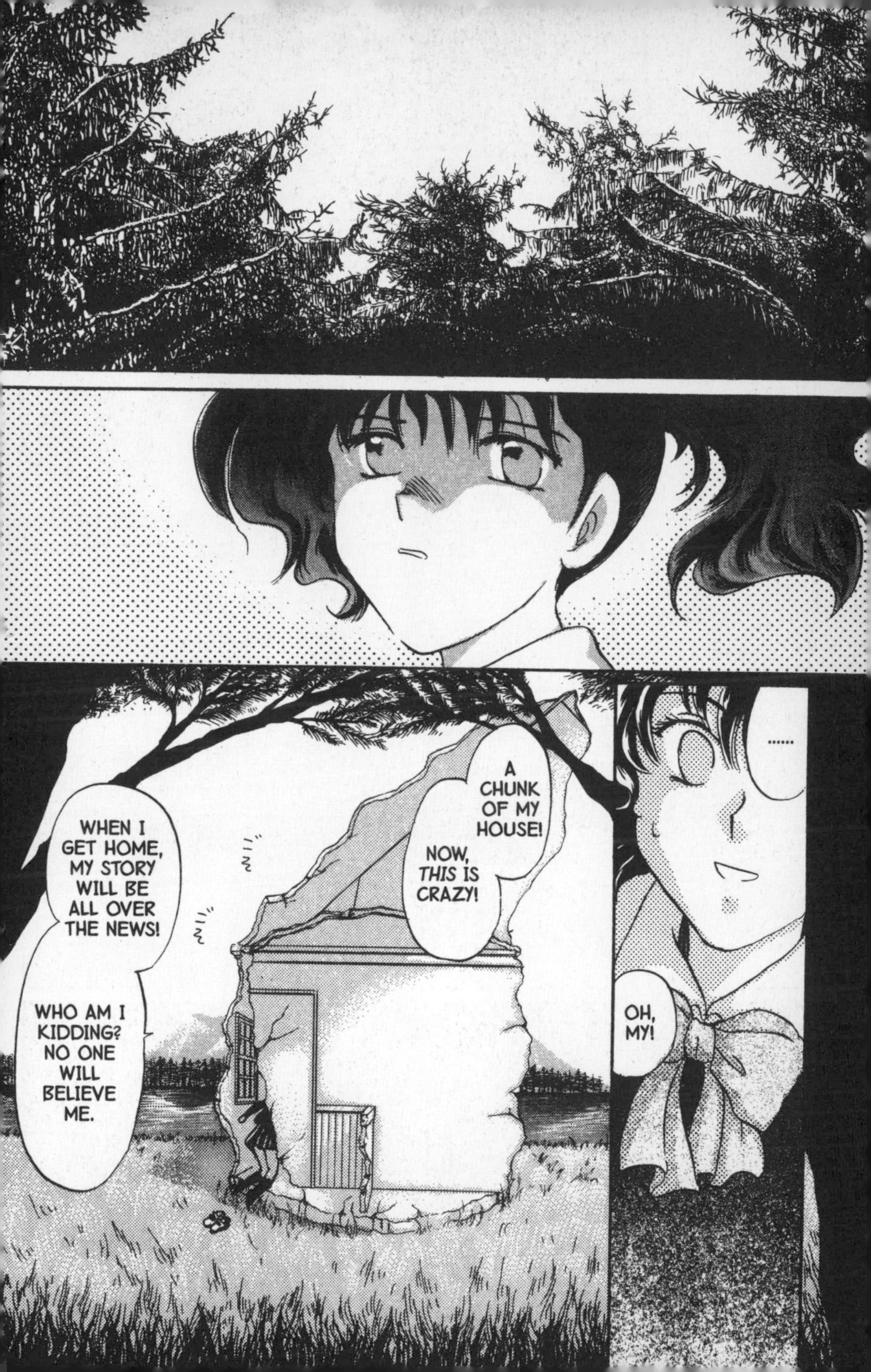
......
OH, MY!
A CHUNK OF MY HOUSE!
NOW, *THIS* IS CRAZY!
WHEN I GET HOME, MY STORY WILL BE ALL OVER THE NEWS!
WHO AM I KIDDING? NO ONE WILL BELIEVE ME.

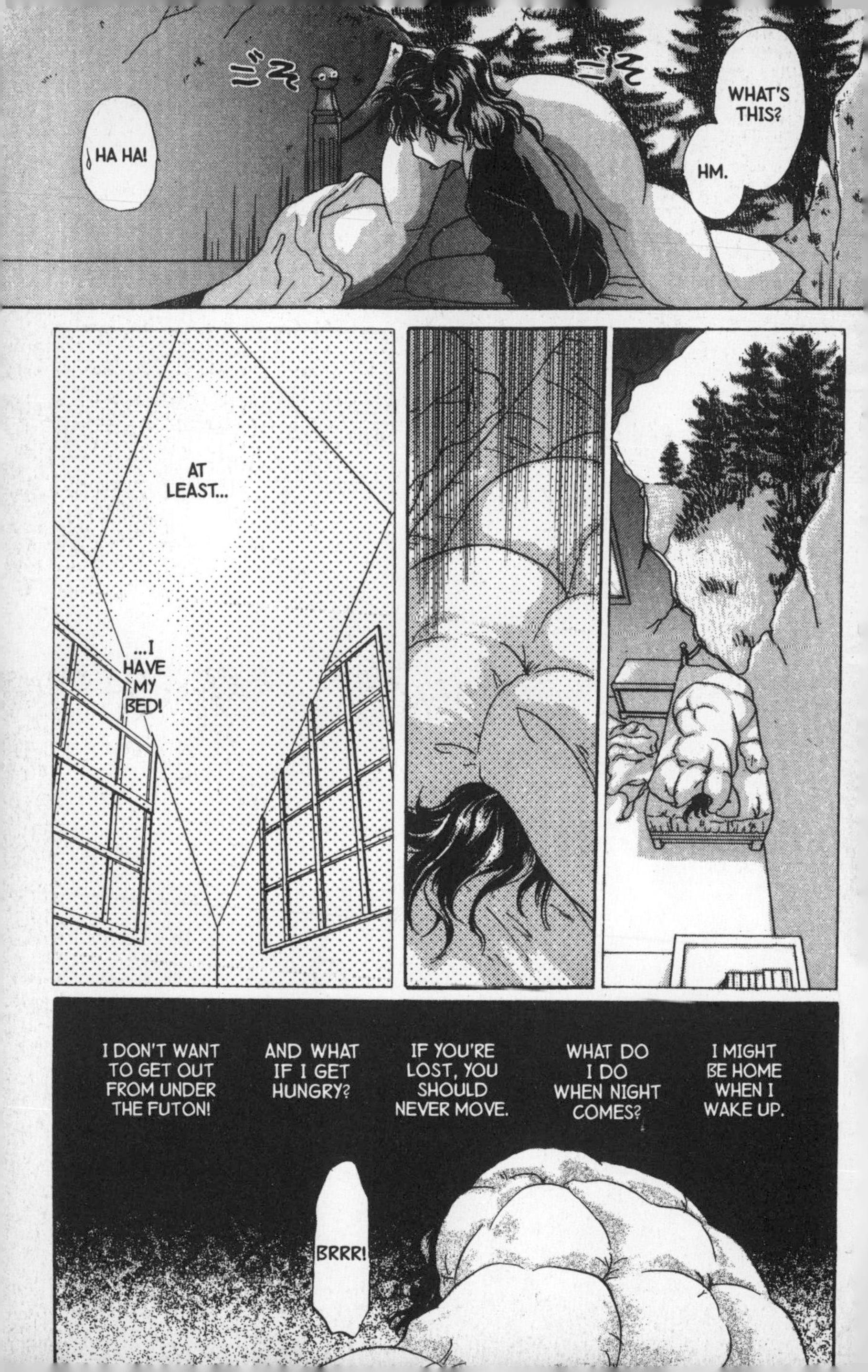
WHAT'S THIS?
HM.
♪HA HA!
AT LEAST...
...I HAVE MY BED!
I MIGHT BE HOME WHEN I WAKE UP.
WHAT DO I DO WHEN NIGHT COMES?
IF YOU'RE LOST, YOU SHOULD NEVER MOVE.
AND WHAT IF I GET HUNGRY?
I DON'T WANT TO GET OUT FROM UNDER THE FUTON!
BRRR!

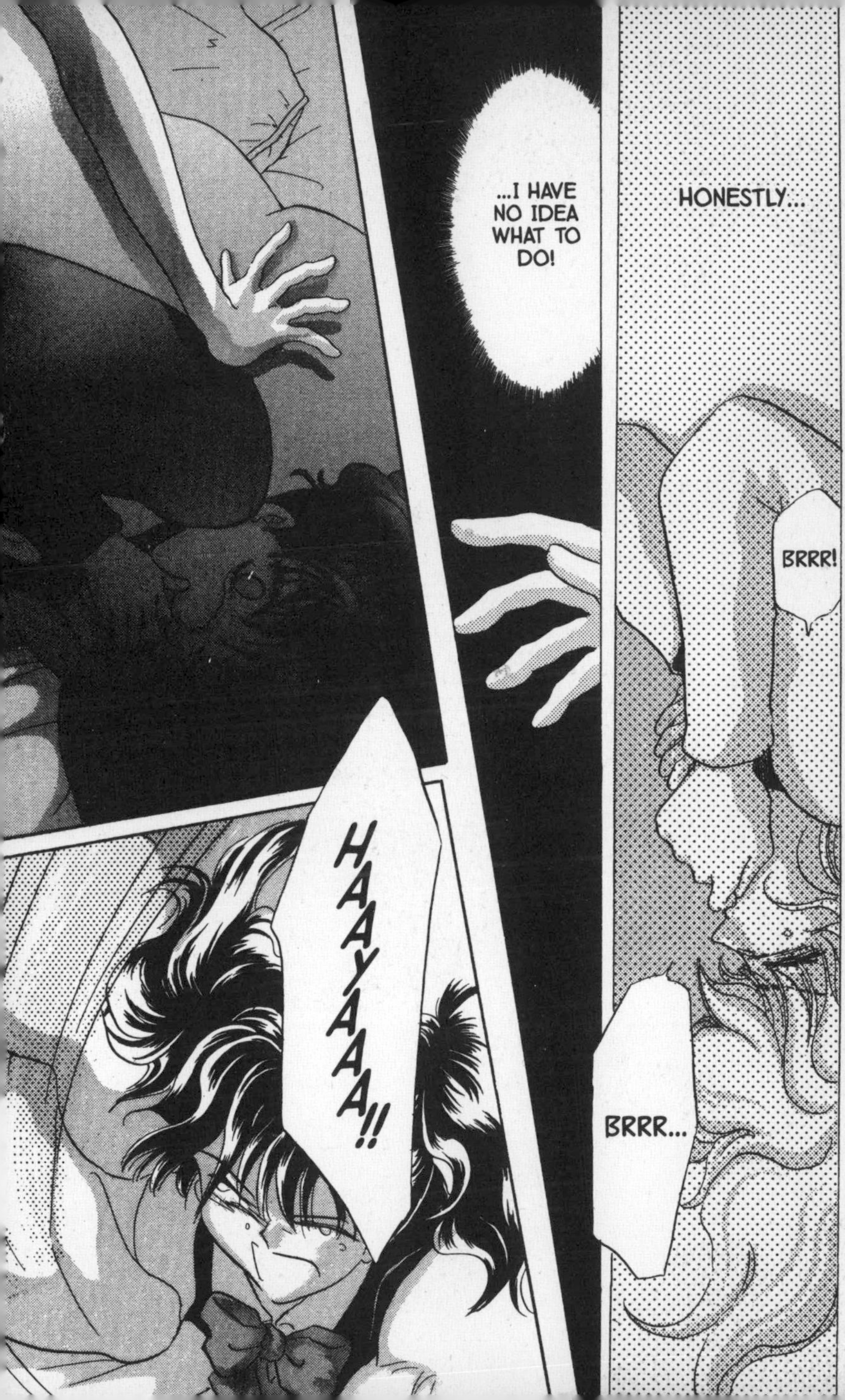
HONESTLY...
BRRR!
BRRR...
...I HAVE NO IDEA WHAT TO DO!
HAAYAAAA!!

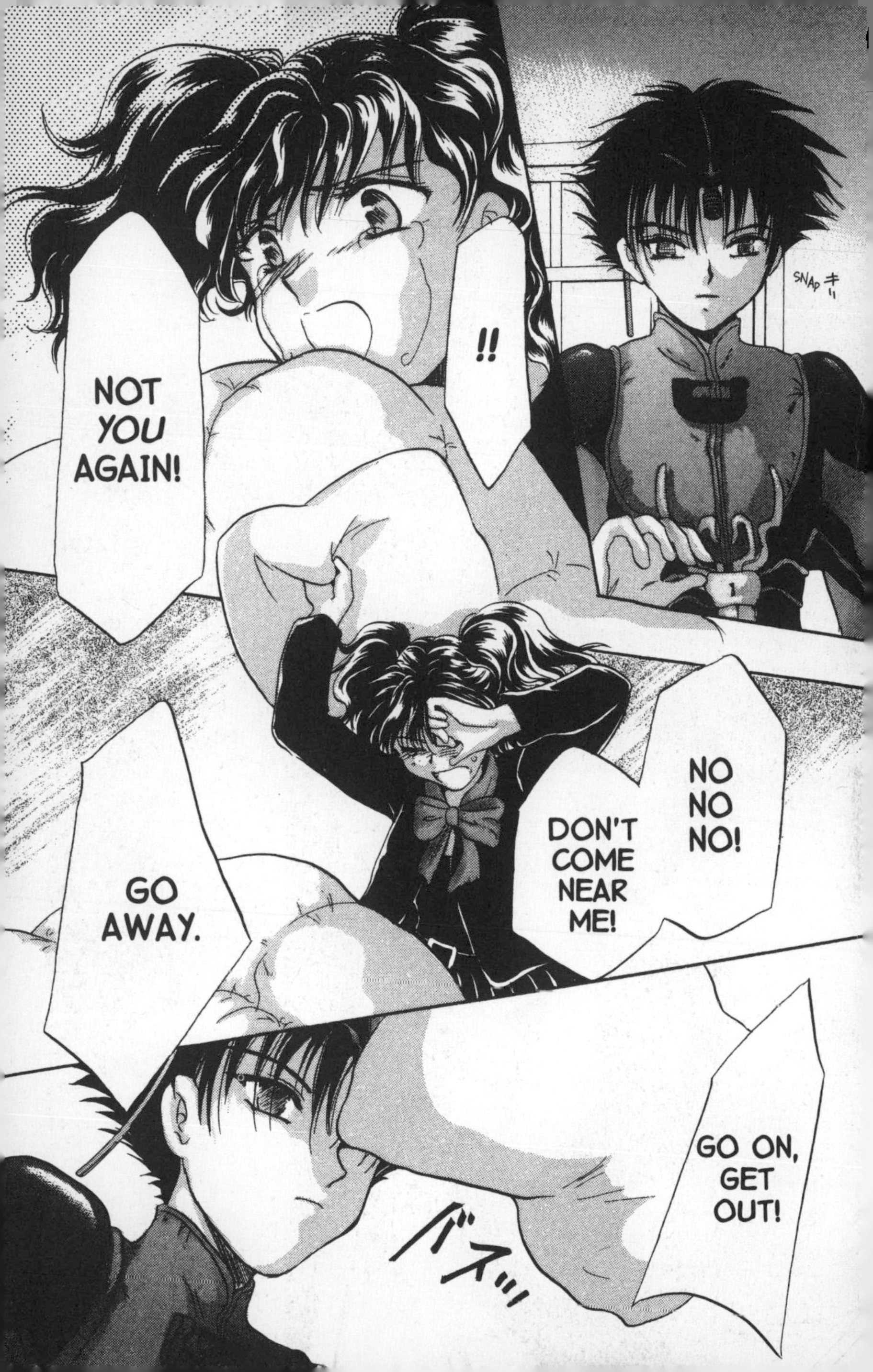

SNAP キリ
!!
NOT YOU AGAIN!
NO NO NO!
DON'T COME NEAR ME!
GO AWAY.
GO ON, GET OUT!
バスッ

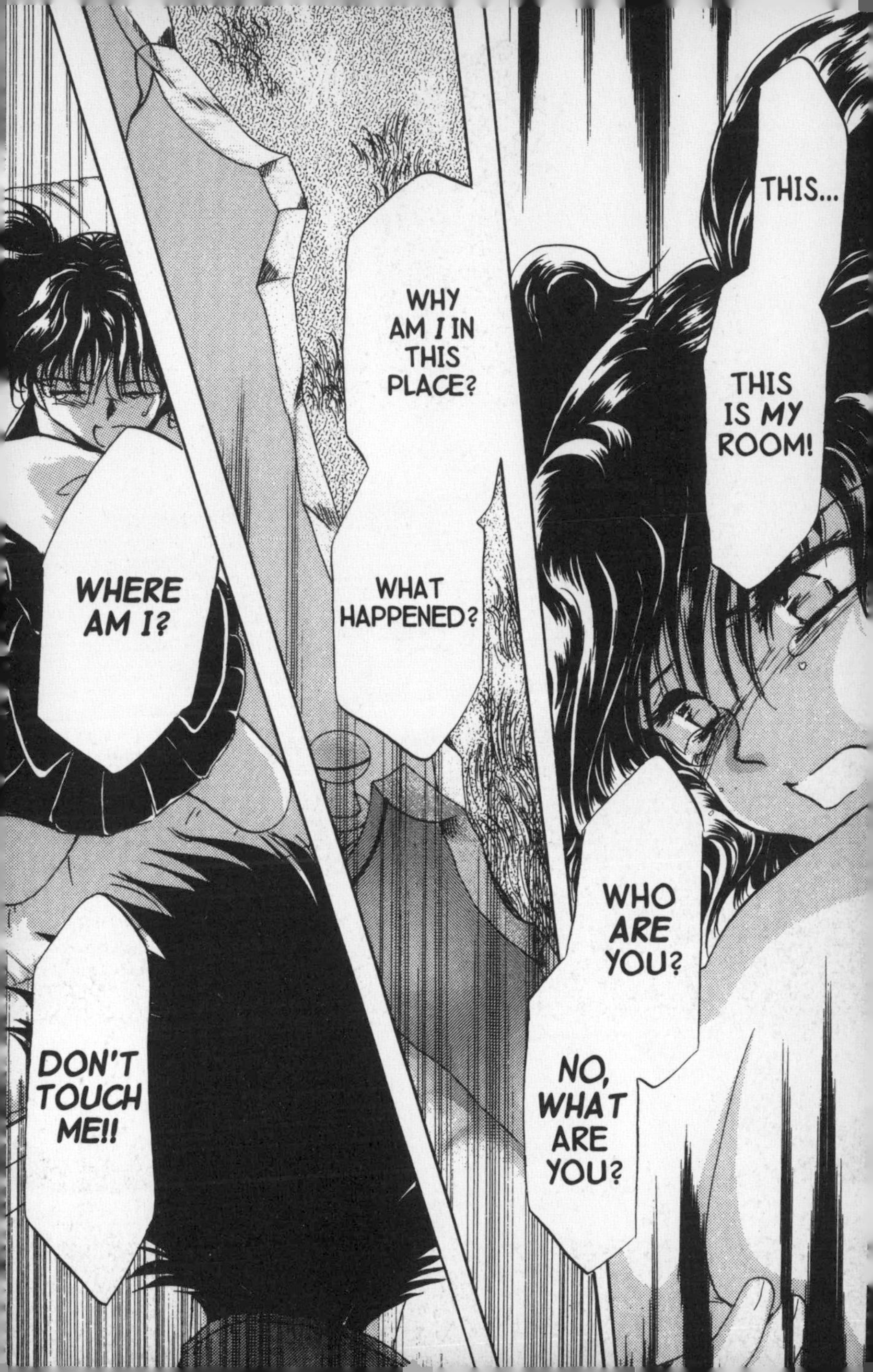
THIS...
THIS IS MY ROOM!
WHO ARE YOU?
NO, WHAT ARE YOU?
WHY AM I IN THIS PLACE?
WHAT HAPPENED?
WHERE AM I?
DON'T TOUCH ME!!

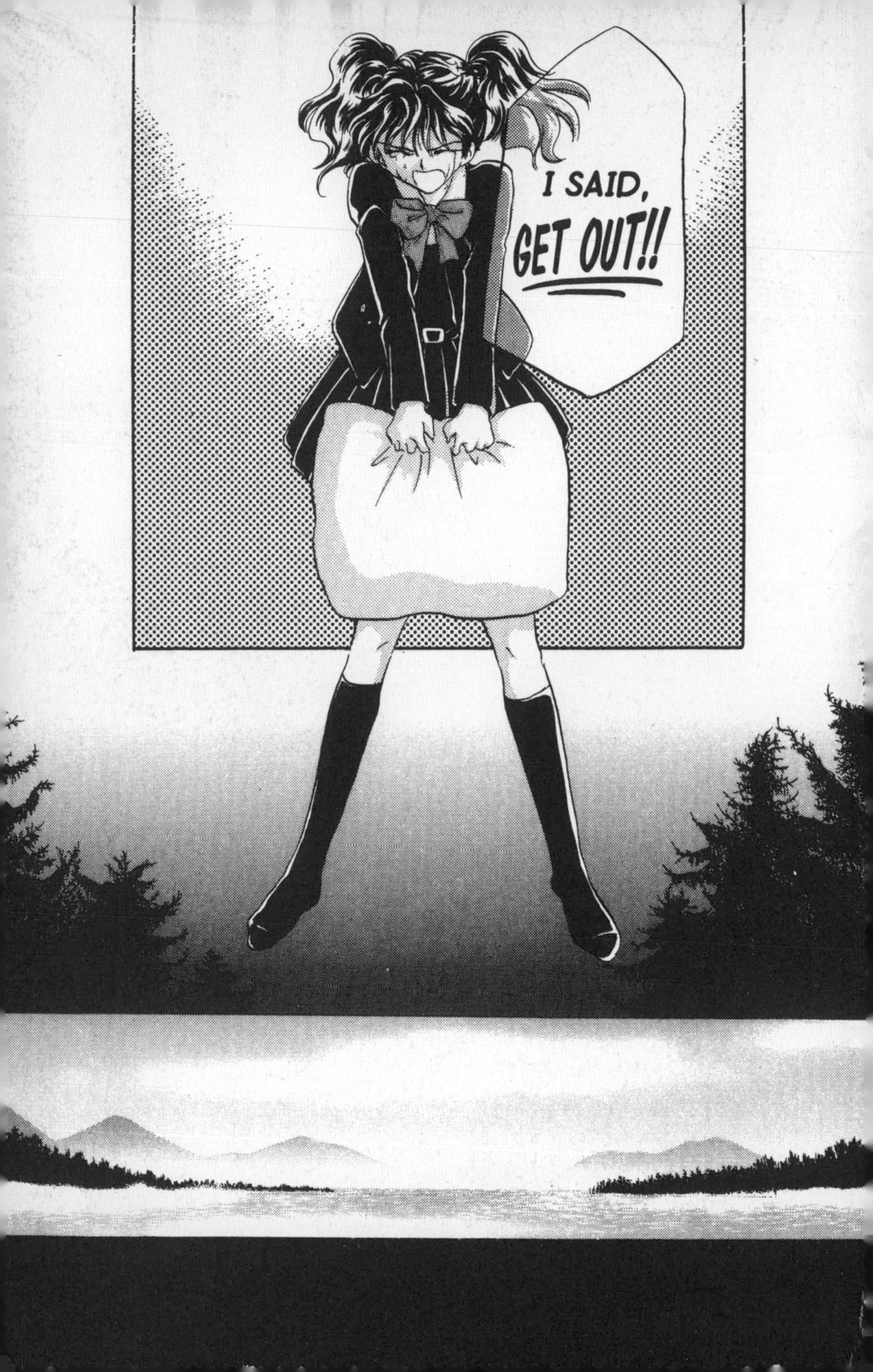
I SAID, GET OUT!!

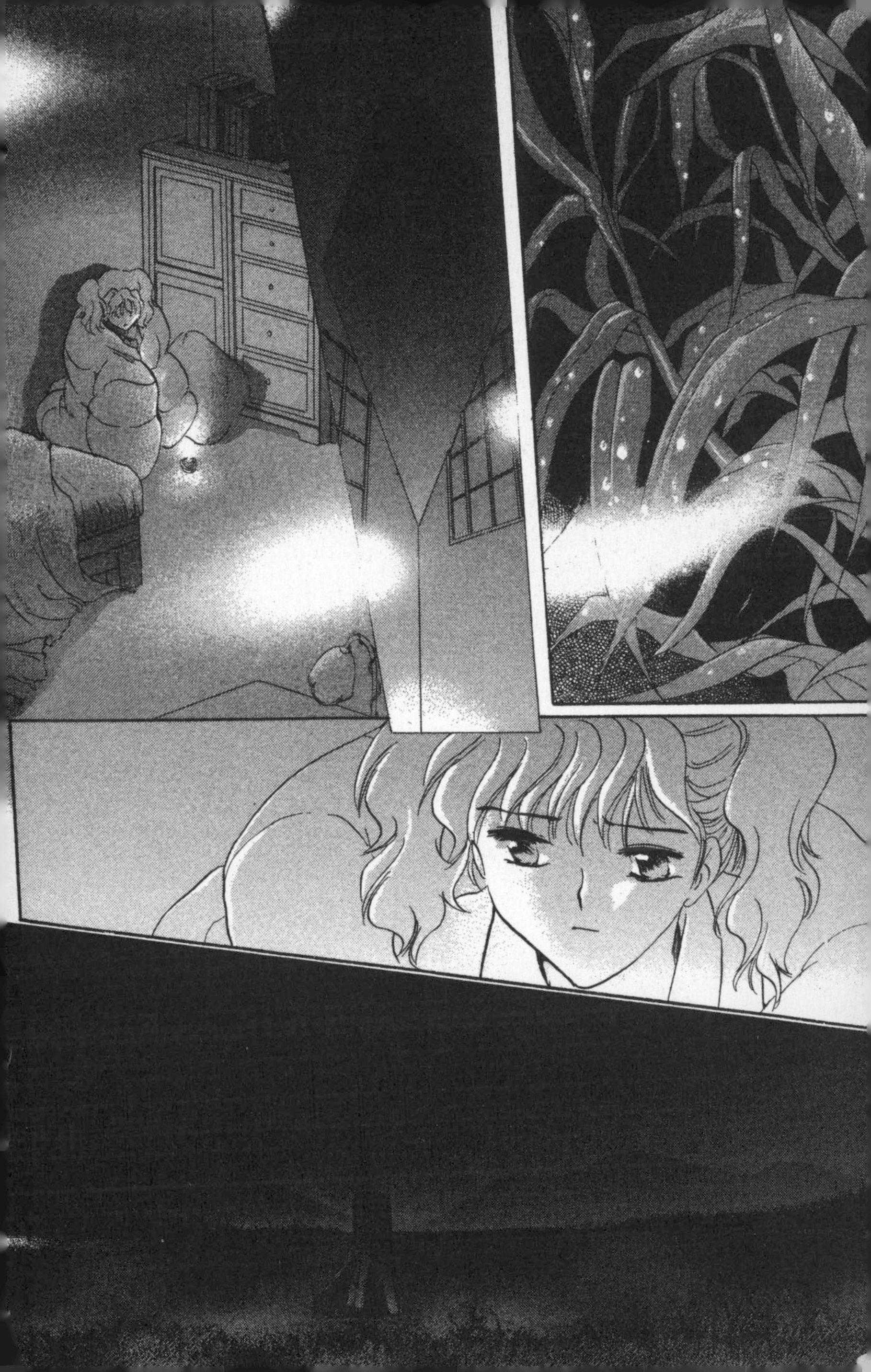

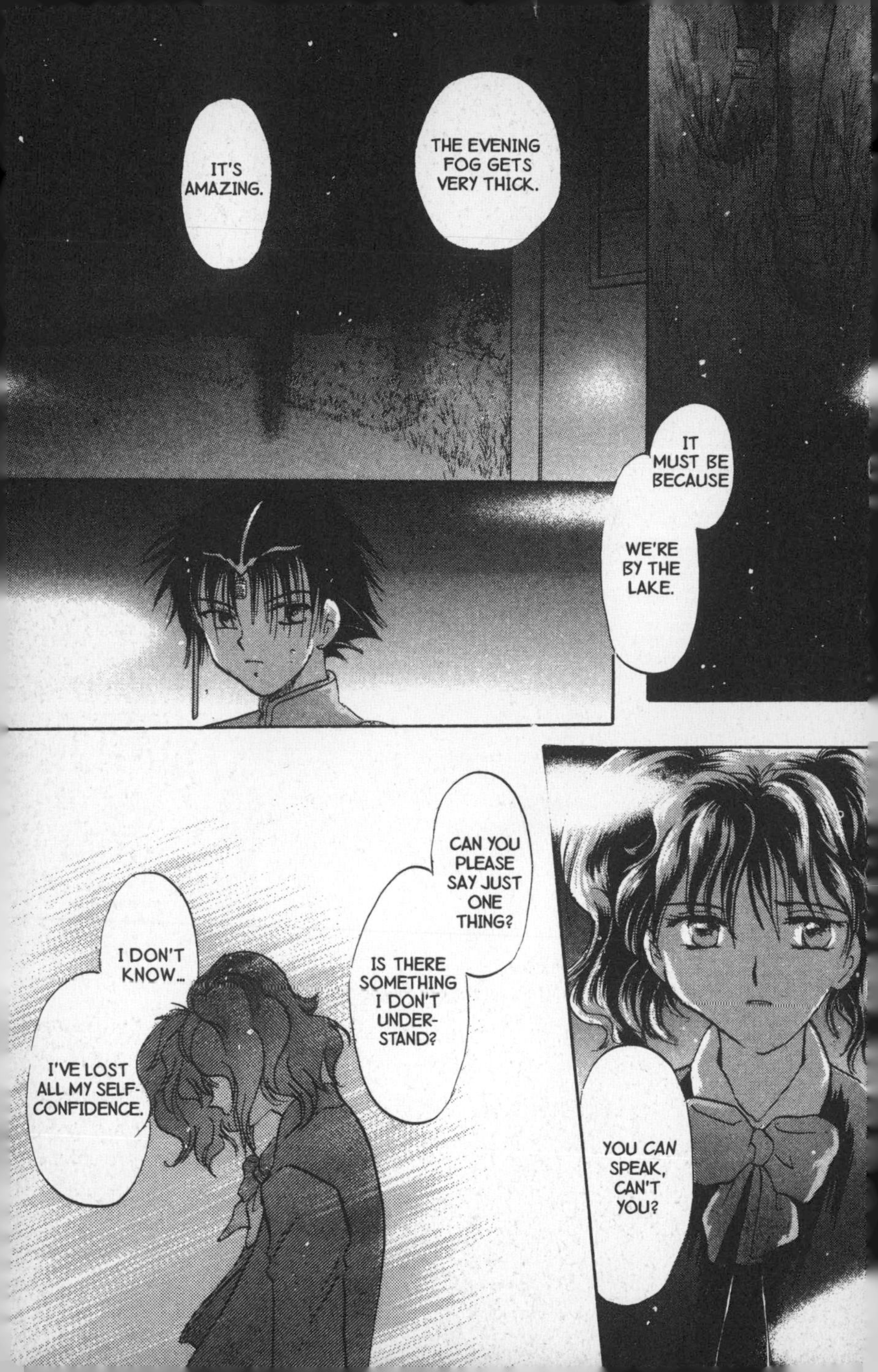
IT MUST BE BECAUSE
WE'RE BY THE LAKE.
THE EVENING FOG GETS VERY THICK.
IT'S AMAZING.
YOU CAN SPEAK, CAN'T YOU?
CAN YOU PLEASE SAY JUST ONE THING?
IS THERE SOMETHING I DON'T UNDER-STAND?
I DON'T KNOW...
I'VE LOST ALL MY SELF-CONFIDENCE.

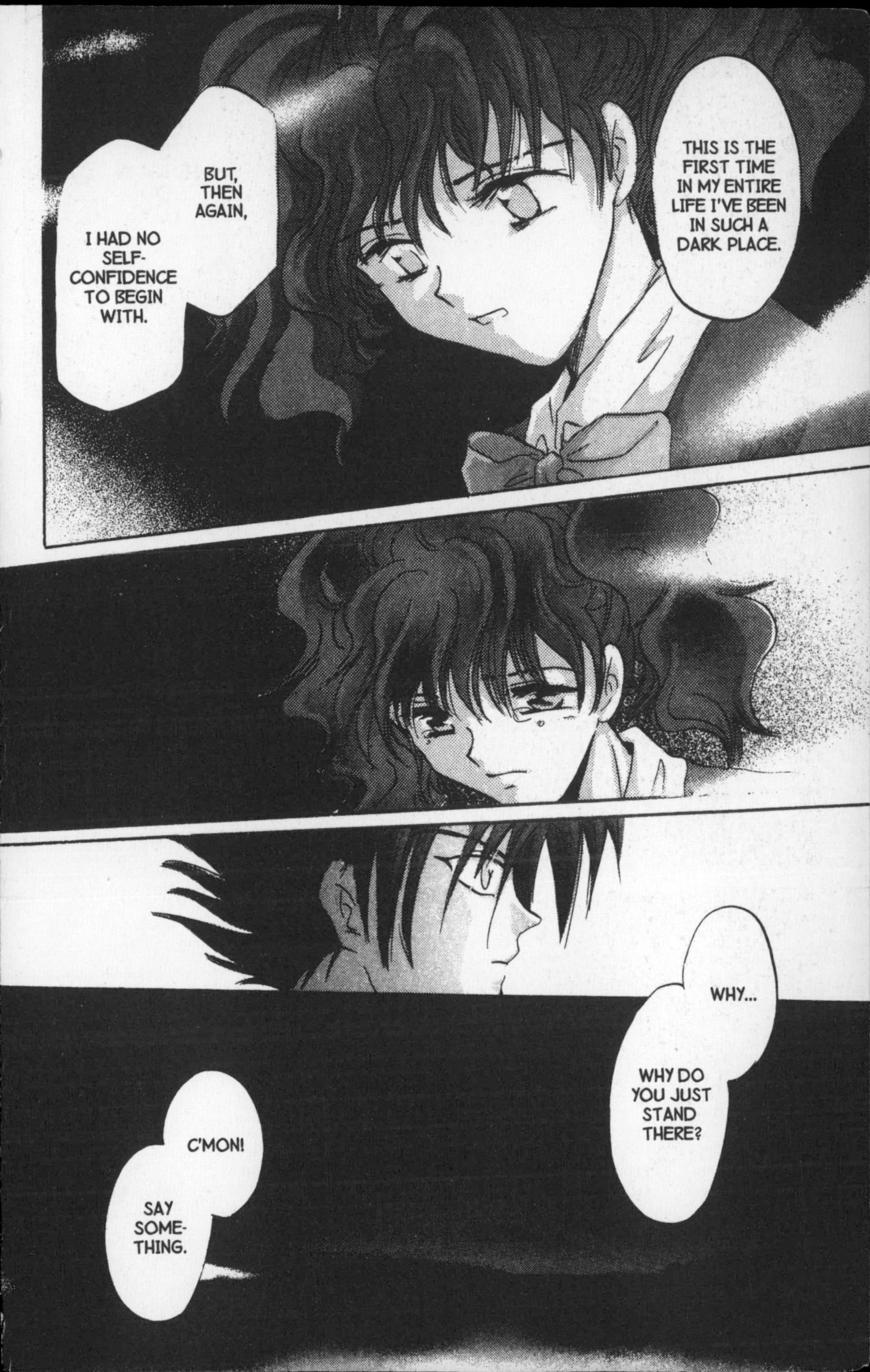
THIS IS THE FIRST TIME IN MY ENTIRE LIFE I'VE BEEN IN SUCH A DARK PLACE.
BUT, THEN AGAIN,
I HAD NO SELF-CONFIDENCE TO BEGIN WITH.
WHY...
WHY DO YOU JUST STAND THERE?
C'MON!
SAY SOME-THING.

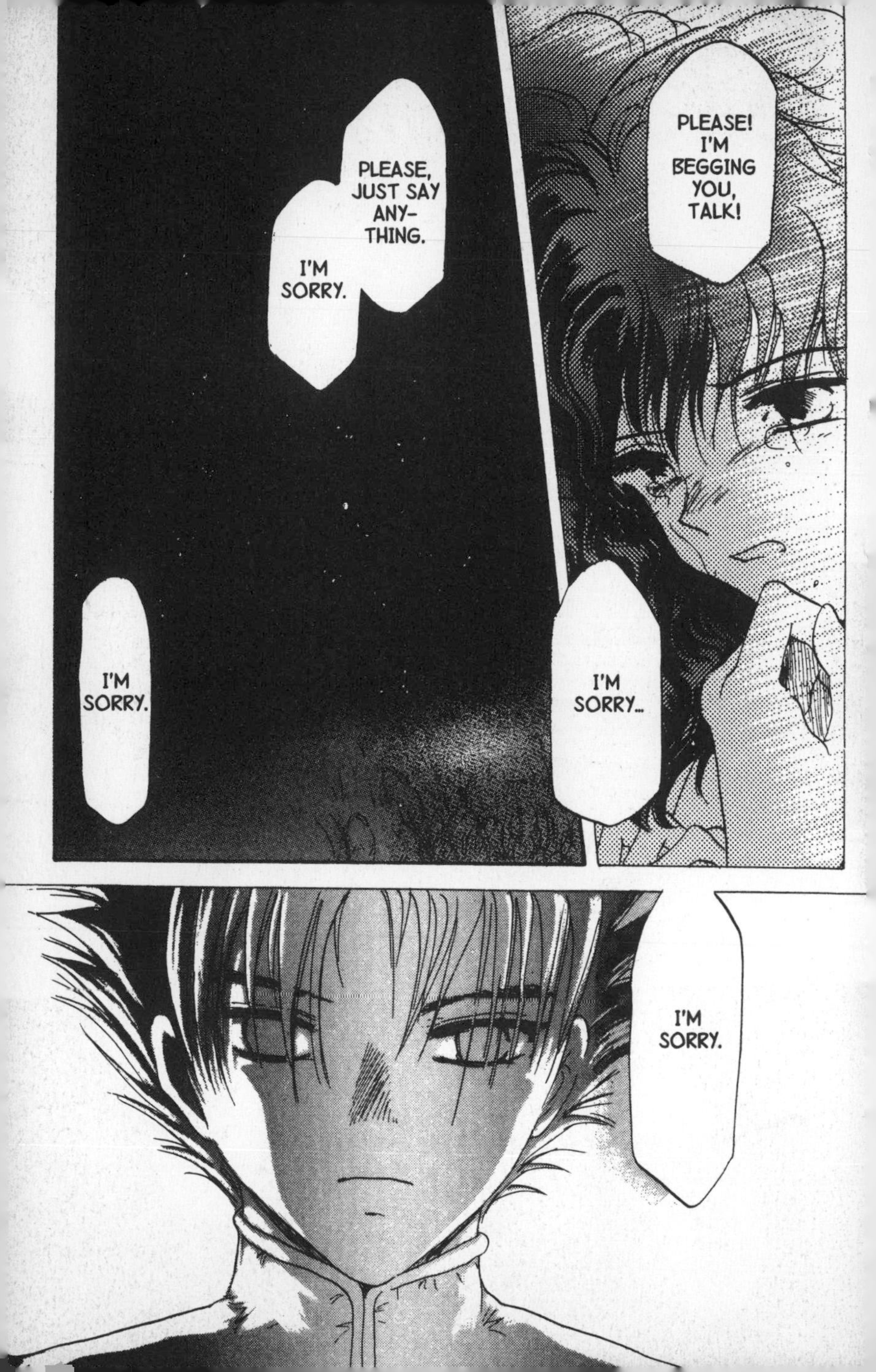
PLEASE! I'M BEGGING YOU, TALK!
I'M SORRY...
PLEASE, JUST SAY ANY-THING.
I'M SORRY.
I'M SORRY.
I'M SORRY.

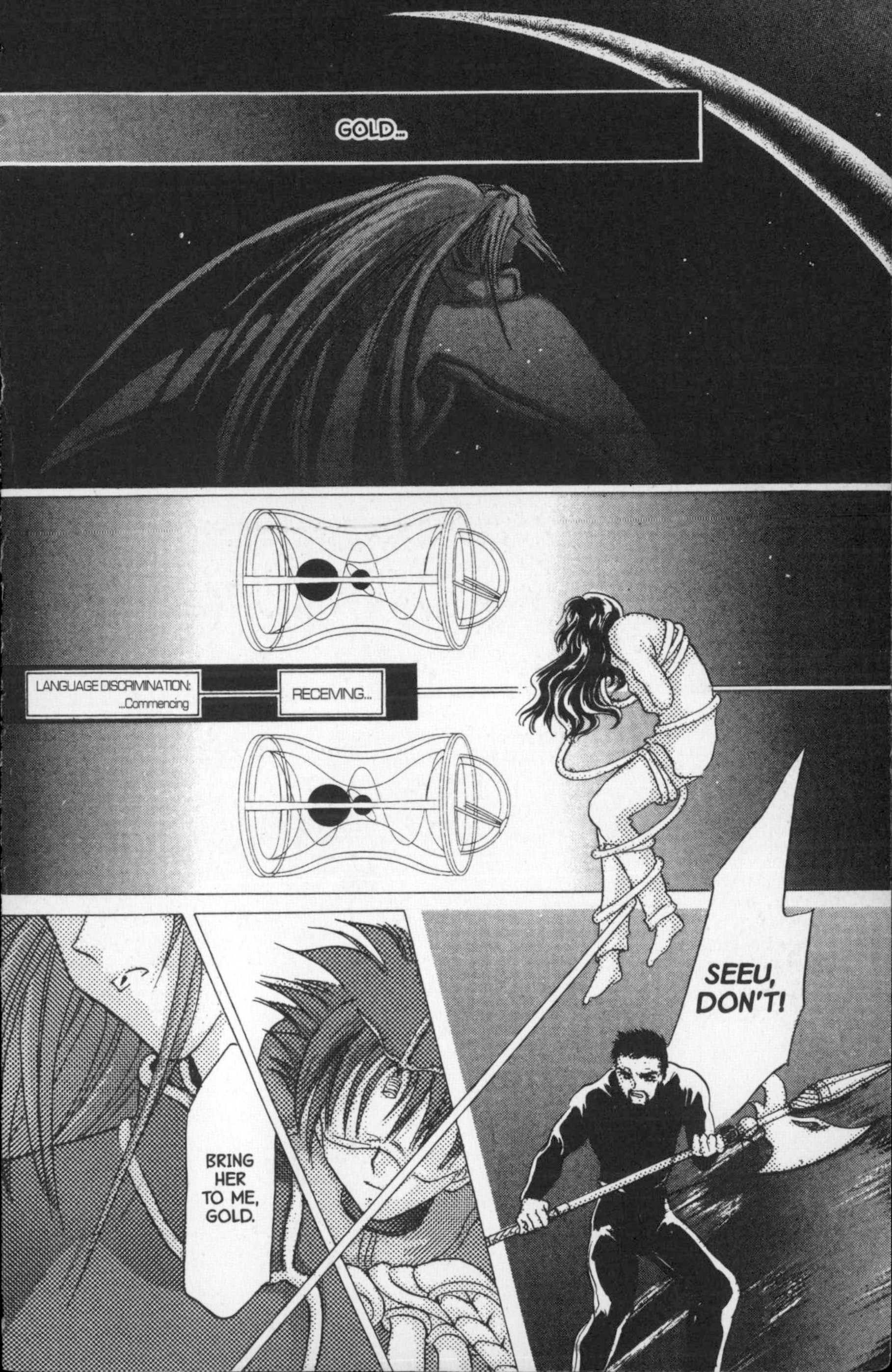
GOLD...
RECEIVING...
LANGUAGE DISCRIMINATION:
...Commencing
SEEU, DON'T!
BRING HER TO ME, GOLD.

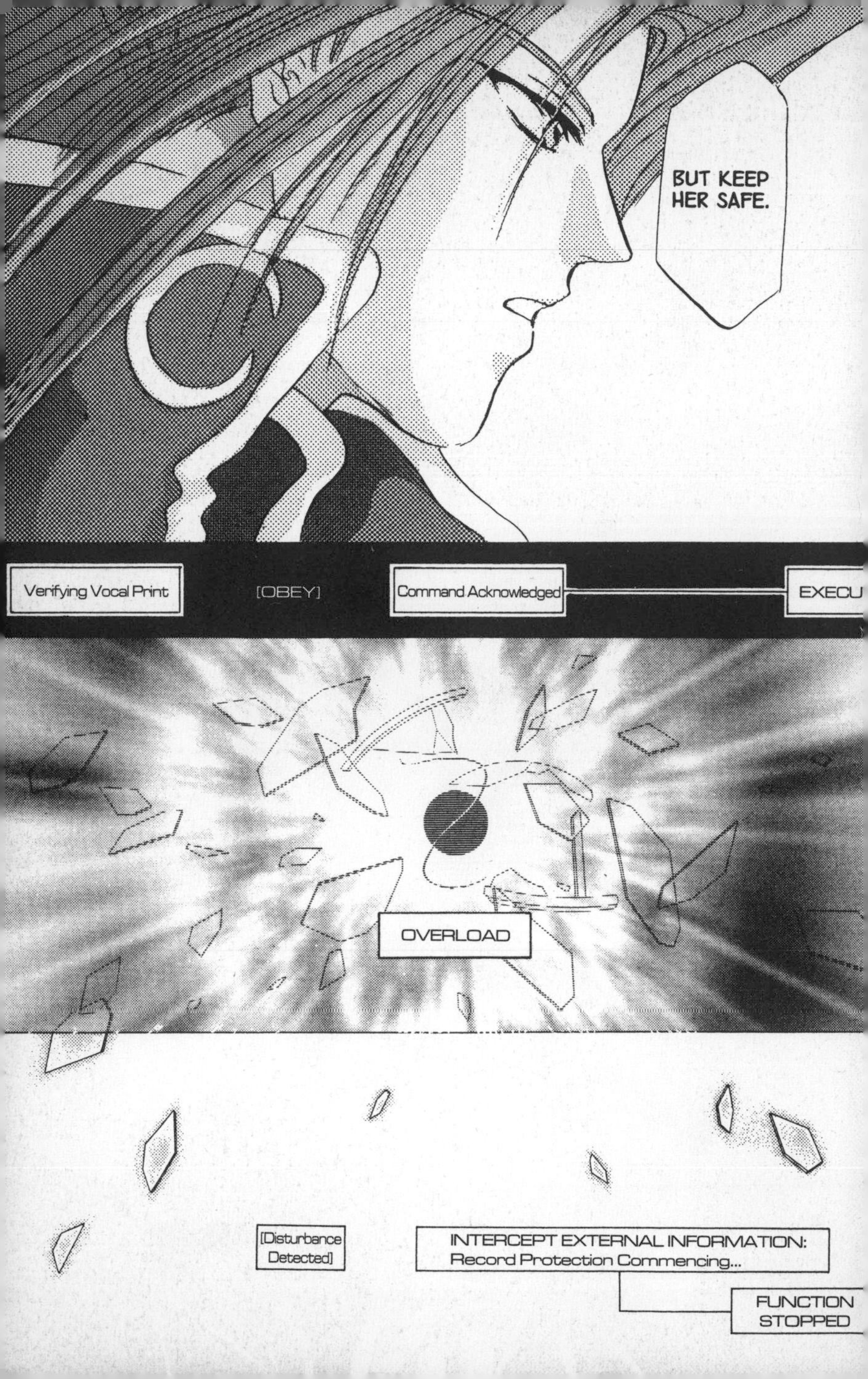
BUT KEEP HER SAFE.
Verifying Vocal Print
[OBEY]
Command Acknowledged
EXECU
OVERLOAD
[Disturbance Detected]
INTERCEPT EXTERNAL INFORMATION: Record Protection Commencing...
FUNCTION STOPPED

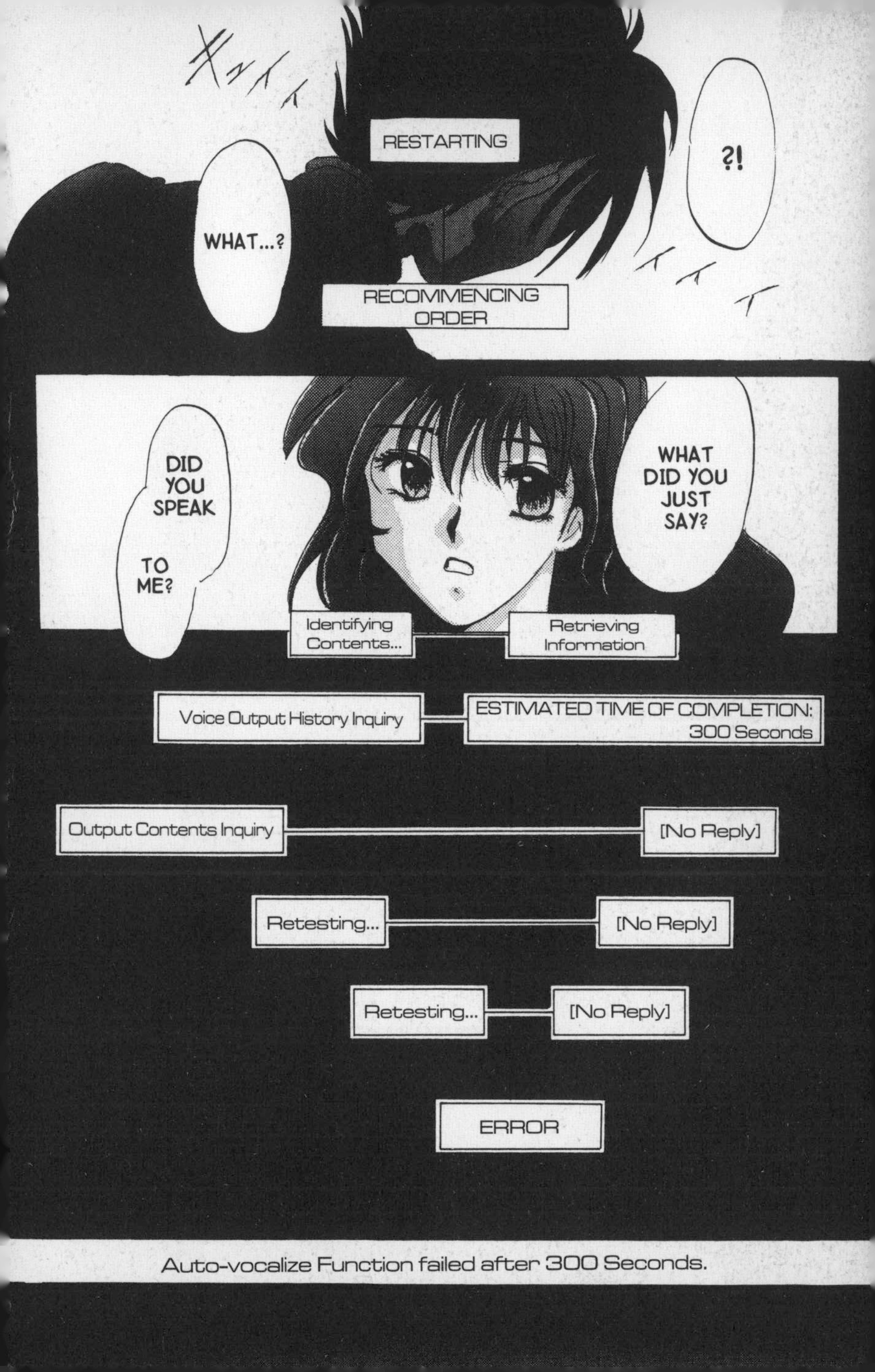
?!
RESTARTING
キュイイ
WHAT...?
イイイイ
RECOMMENCING ORDER
WHAT DID YOU JUST SAY?
DID YOU SPEAK
TO ME?
Identifying Contents...
Retrieving Information
Voice Output History Inquiry
ESTIMATED TIME OF COMPLETION: 300 Seconds
Output Contents Inquiry
[No Reply]
Retesting...
[No Reply]
Retesting...
[No Reply]
ERROR
Auto-vocalize Function failed after 300 Seconds.

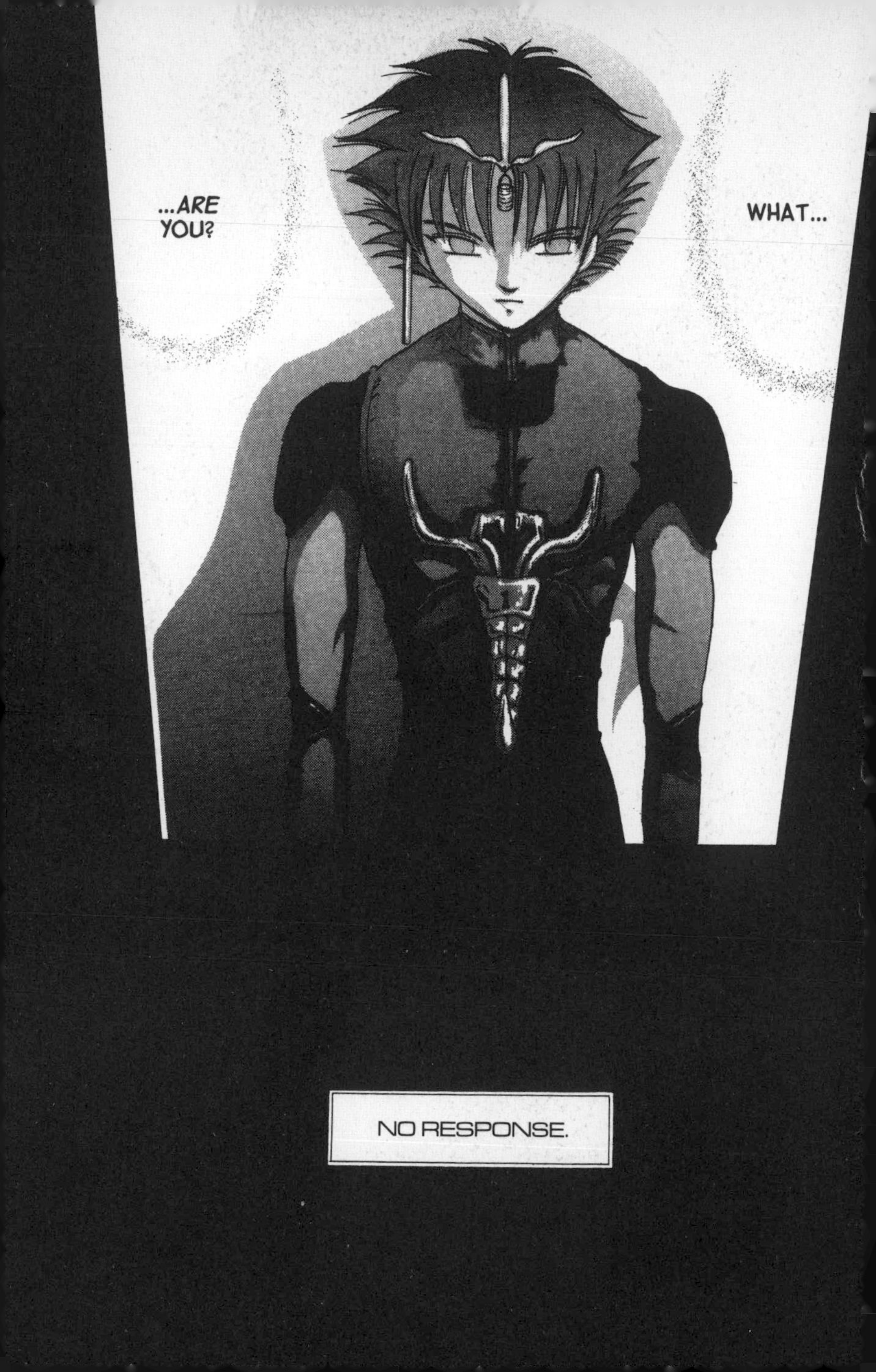
WHAT...
...ARE YOU?
NO RESPONSE.

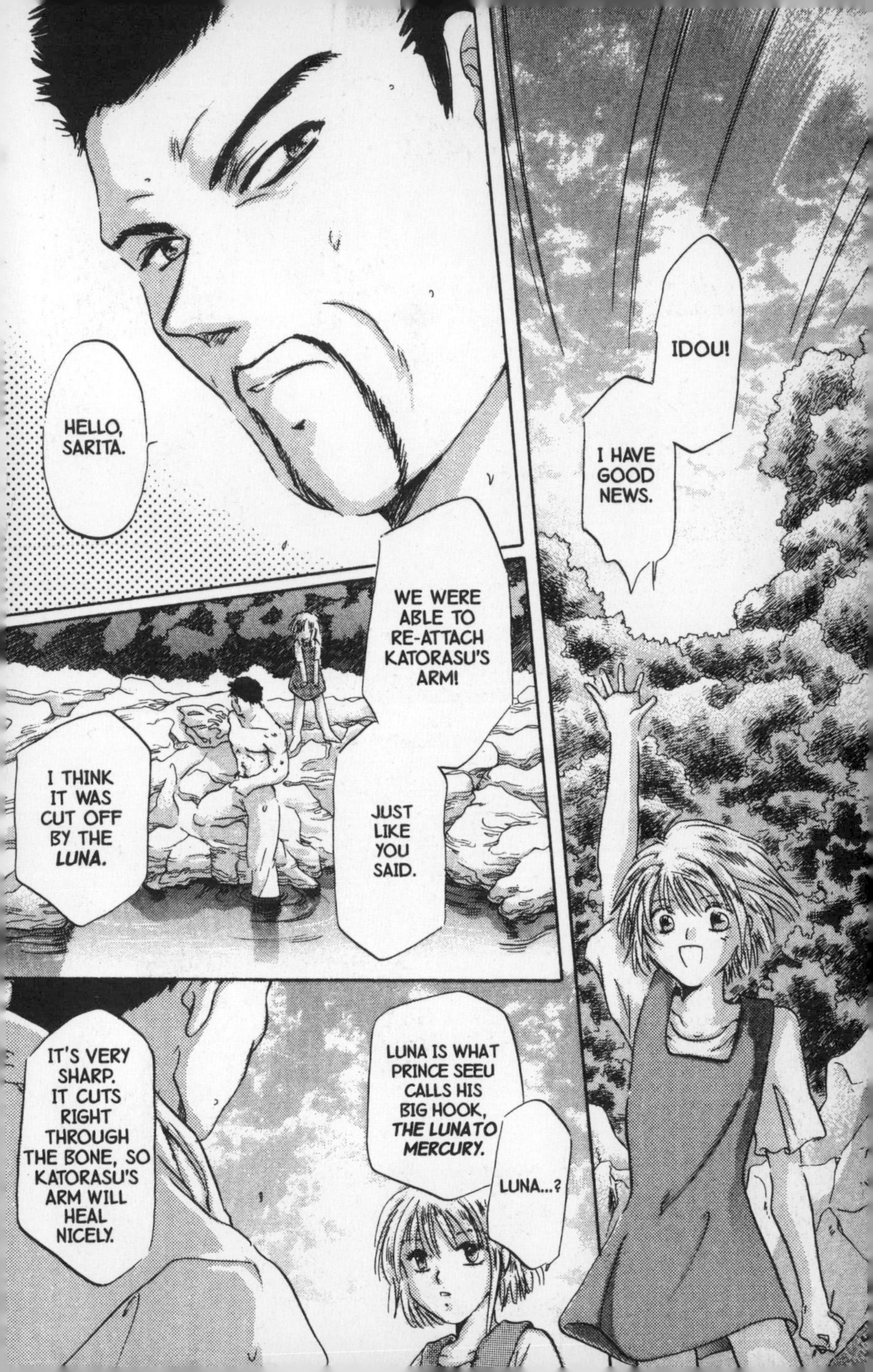
IDOU!
I HAVE GOOD NEWS.
HELLO, SARITA.
WE WERE ABLE TO RE-ATTACH KATORASU'S ARM!
JUST LIKE YOU SAID.
I THINK IT WAS CUT OFF BY THE *LUNA*.
LUNA...?
LUNA IS WHAT PRINCE SEEU CALLS HIS BIG HOOK, *THE LUNATO MERCURY*.
IT'S VERY SHARP. IT CUTS RIGHT THROUGH THE BONE, SO KATORASU'S ARM WILL HEAL NICELY.

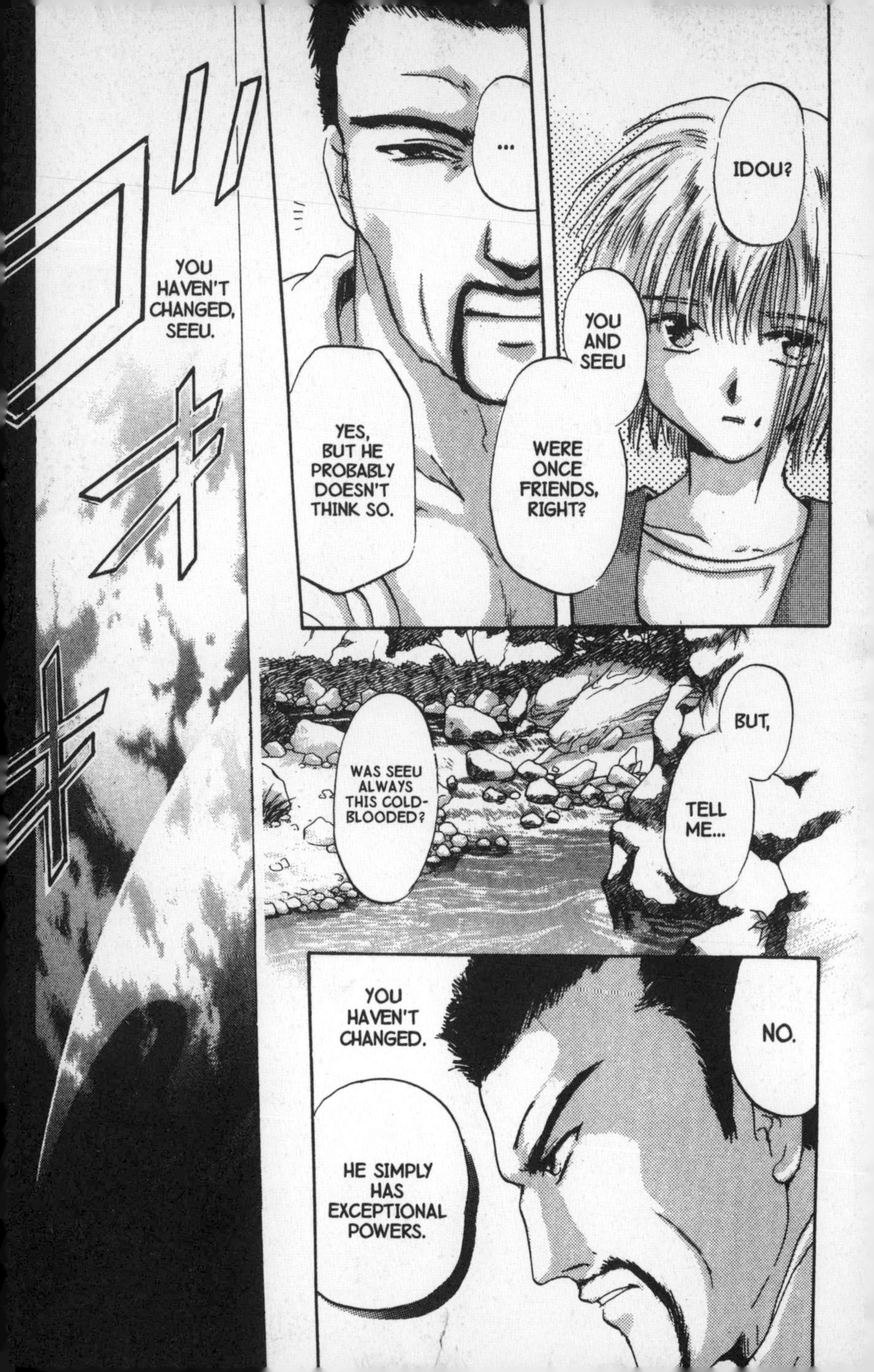
IDOU?
...
YOU AND SEEU
WERE ONCE FRIENDS, RIGHT?
YES, BUT HE PROBABLY DOESN'T THINK SO.
BUT,
TELL ME...
WAS SEEU ALWAYS THIS COLD-BLOODED?
NO.
YOU HAVEN'T CHANGED.
HE SIMPLY HAS EXCEPTIONAL POWERS.
YOU HAVEN'T CHANGED, SEEU.

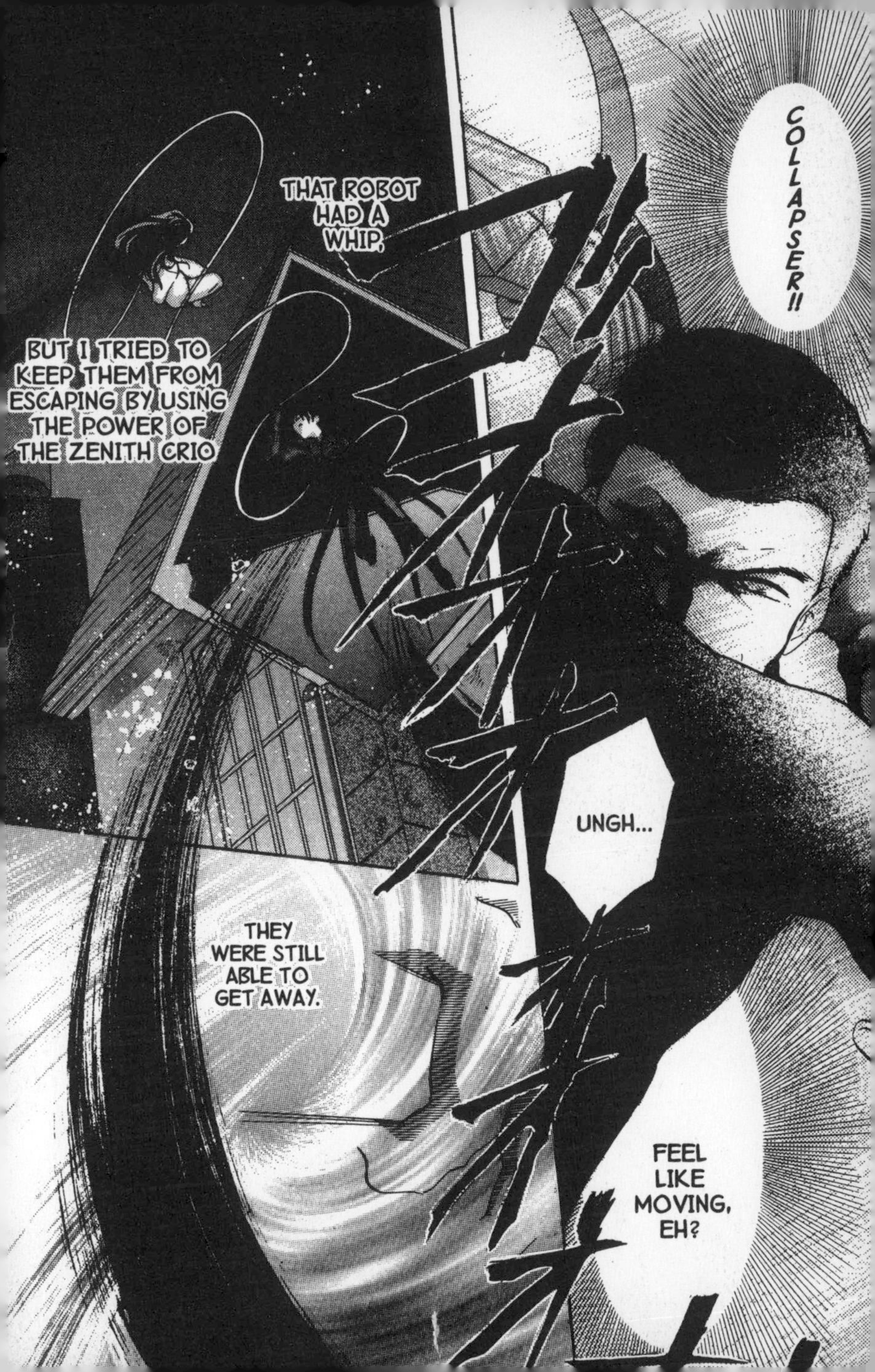
COLLAPSER!!
UNGH...
FEEL LIKE MOVING, EH?
THAT ROBOT HAD A WHIP,
BUT I TRIED TO KEEP THEM FROM ESCAPING BY USING THE POWER OF THE ZENITH CRIO
THEY WERE STILL ABLE TO GET AWAY.

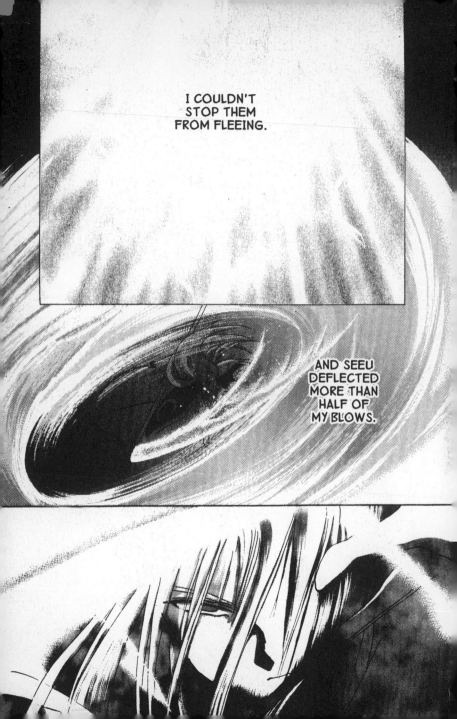

I COULDN'T
STOP THEM
FROM FLEEING.

AND SEEU
DEFLECTED
MORE THAN
HALF OF
MY BLOWS.

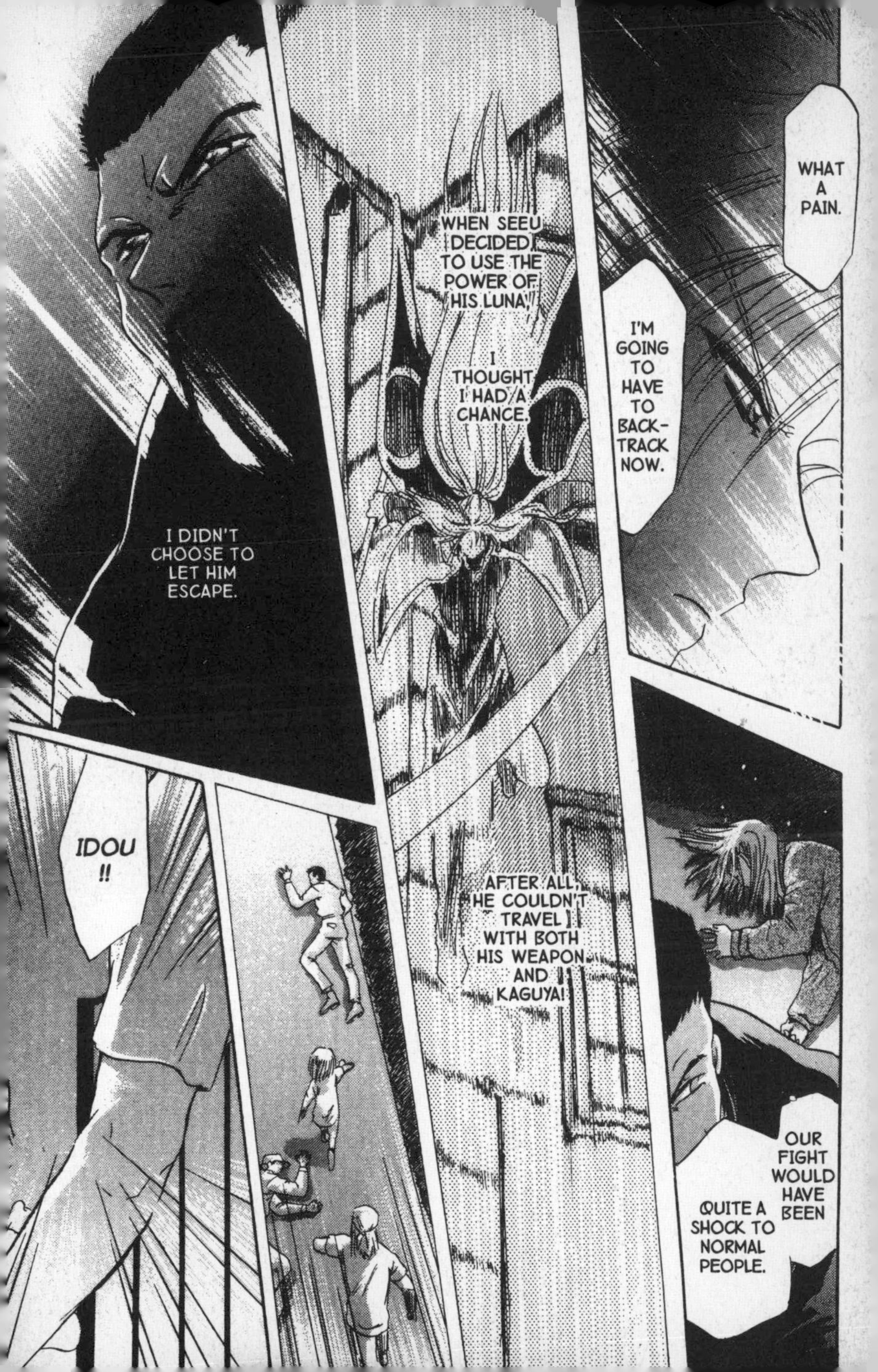
WHAT A PAIN.
I'M GOING TO HAVE TO BACK-TRACK NOW.
OUR FIGHT WOULD HAVE BEEN QUITE A SHOCK TO NORMAL PEOPLE.
WHEN SEEU DECIDED TO USE THE POWER OF HIS LUNA,
I THOUGHT I HAD A CHANCE.
AFTER ALL, HE COULDN'T TRAVEL WITH BOTH HIS WEAPON AND KAGUYA!
I DIDN'T CHOOSE TO LET HIM ESCAPE.
IDOU !!

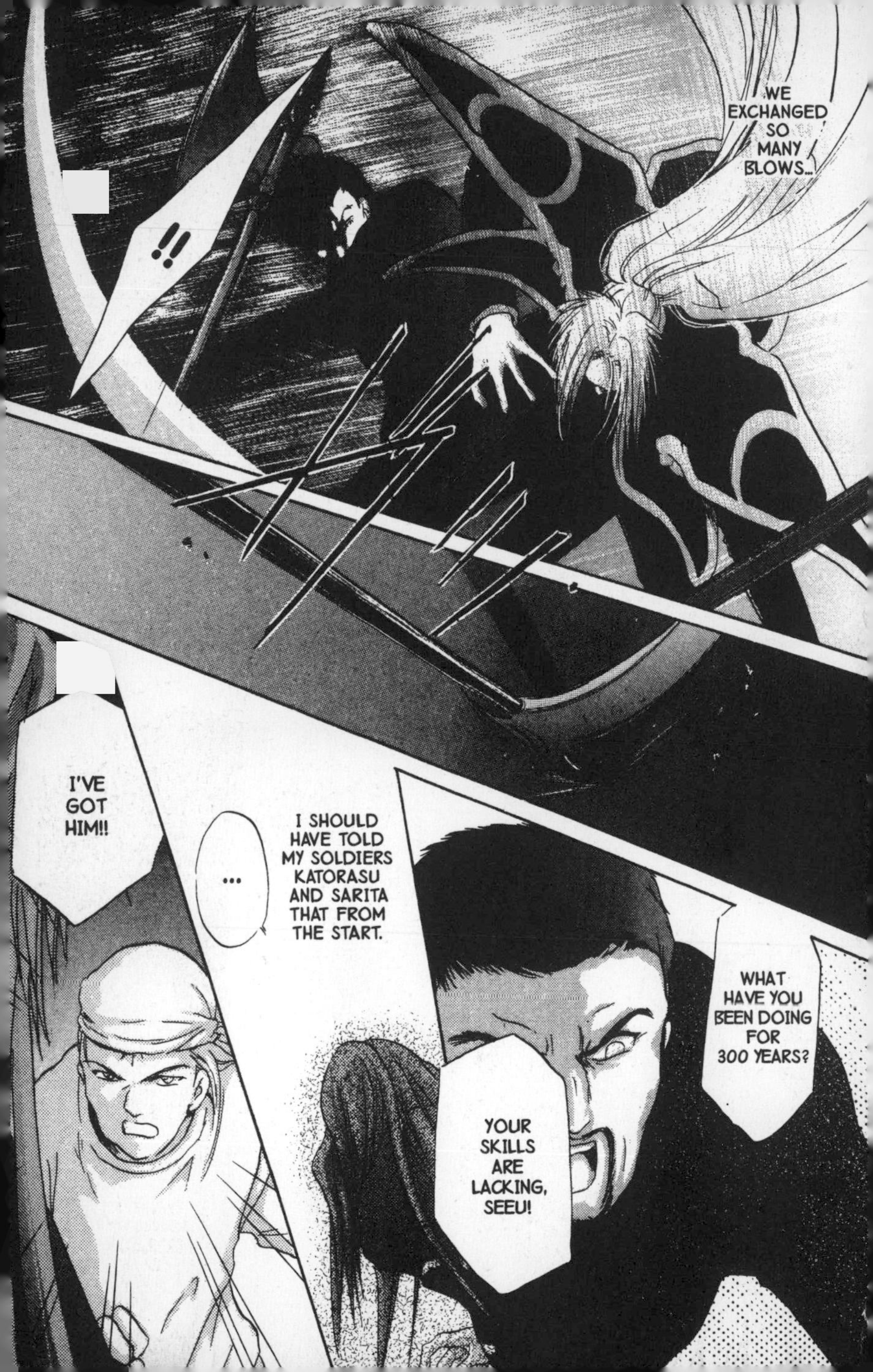
WE EXCHANGED SO MANY BLOWS...
!!
WHAT HAVE YOU BEEN DOING FOR 300 YEARS?
YOUR SKILLS ARE LACKING, SEEU!
I SHOULD HAVE TOLD MY SOLDIERS KATORASU AND SARITA THAT FROM THE START.
...
I'VE GOT HIM!!

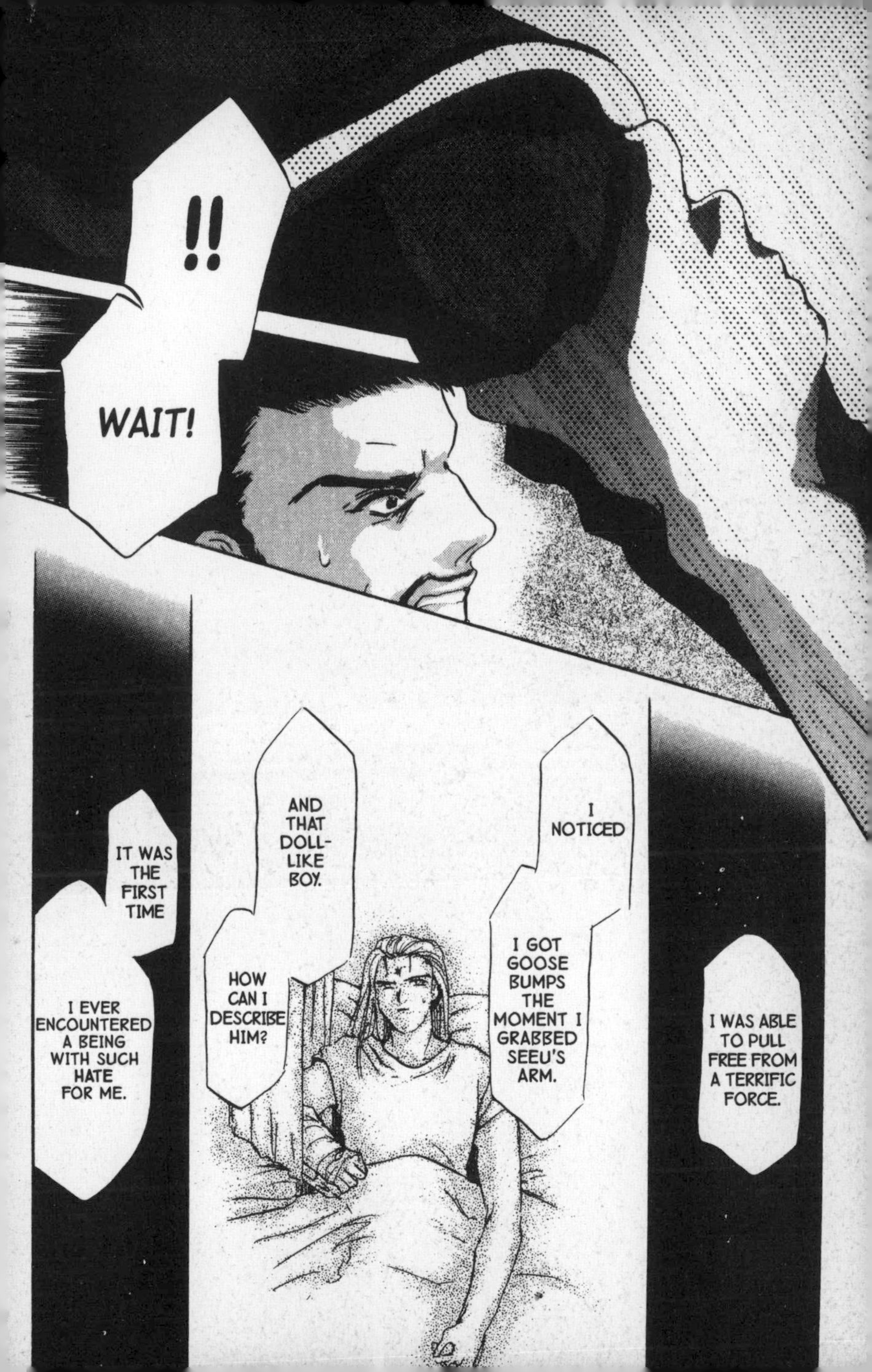
!!
WAIT!
I WAS ABLE TO PULL FREE FROM A TERRIFIC FORCE.
I NOTICED
I GOT GOOSE BUMPS THE MOMENT I GRABBED SEEU'S ARM.
AND THAT DOLL-LIKE BOY.
HOW CAN I DESCRIBE HIM?
IT WAS THE FIRST TIME
I EVER ENCOUNTERED A BEING WITH SUCH HATE FOR ME.

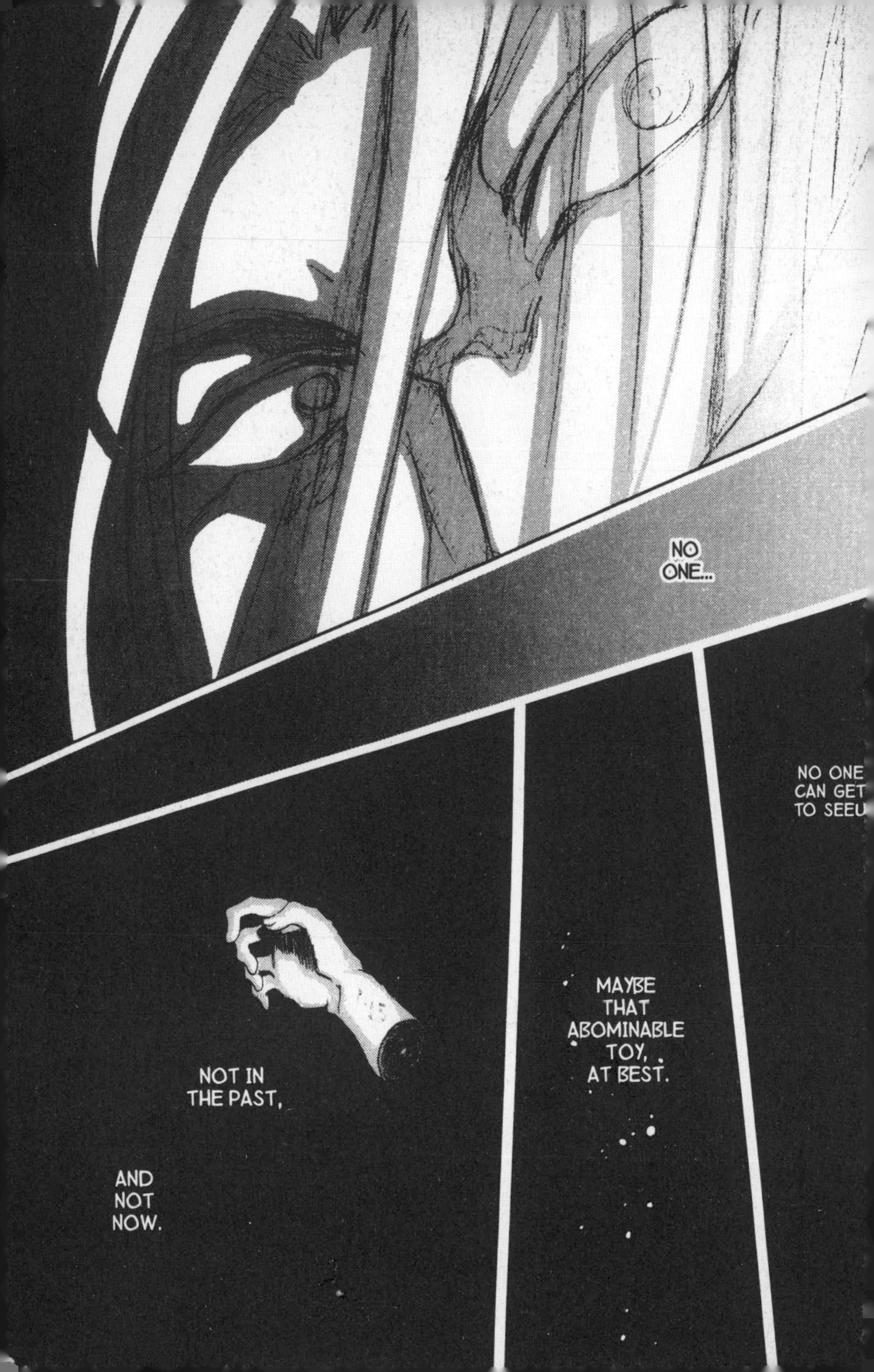
NO ONE...
NO ONE CAN GET TO SEE U
MAYBE THAT ABOMINABLE TOY, AT BEST.
NOT IN THE PAST,
AND NOT NOW.

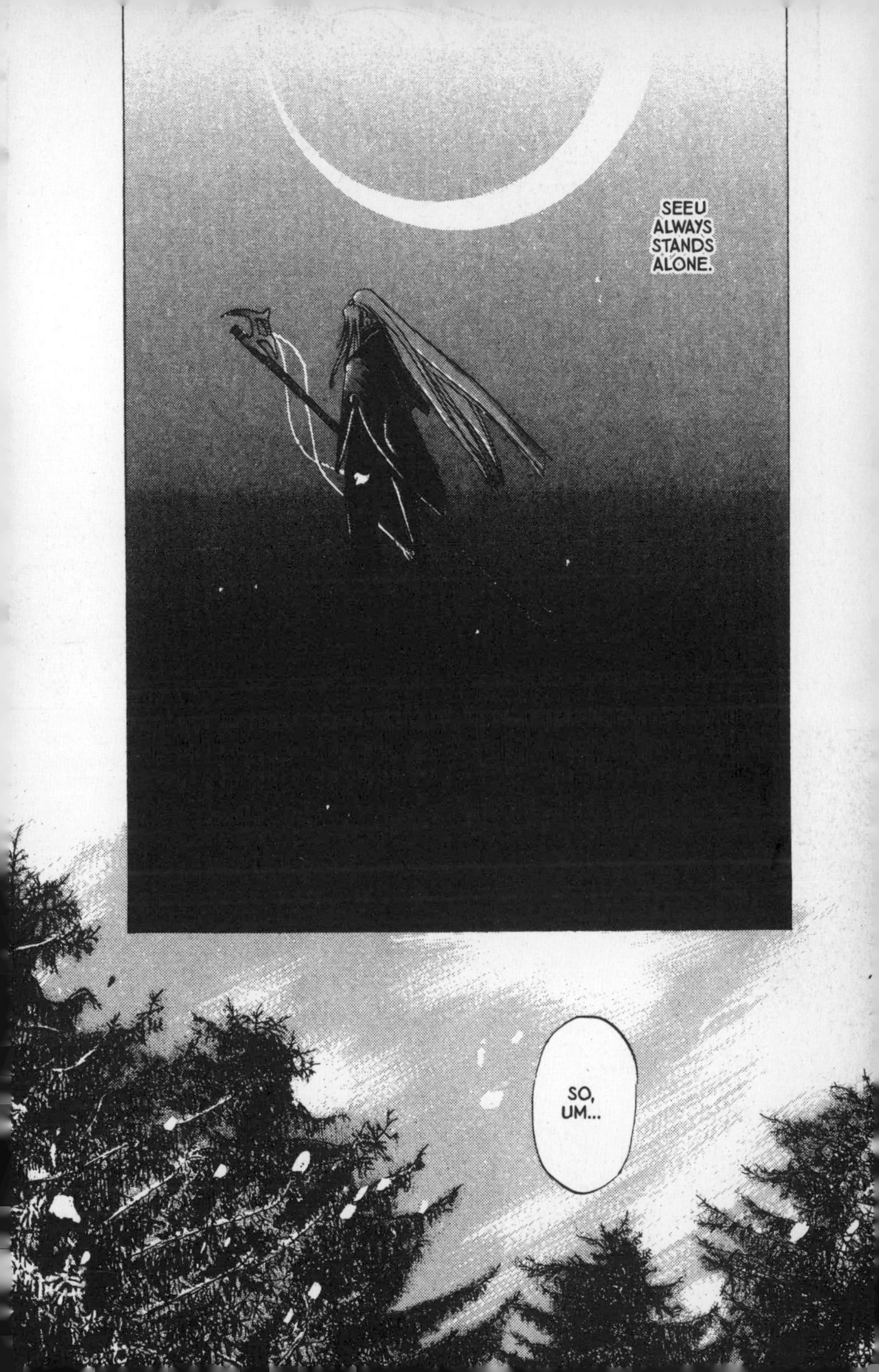
SEEU ALWAYS STANDS ALONE.
SO, UM...

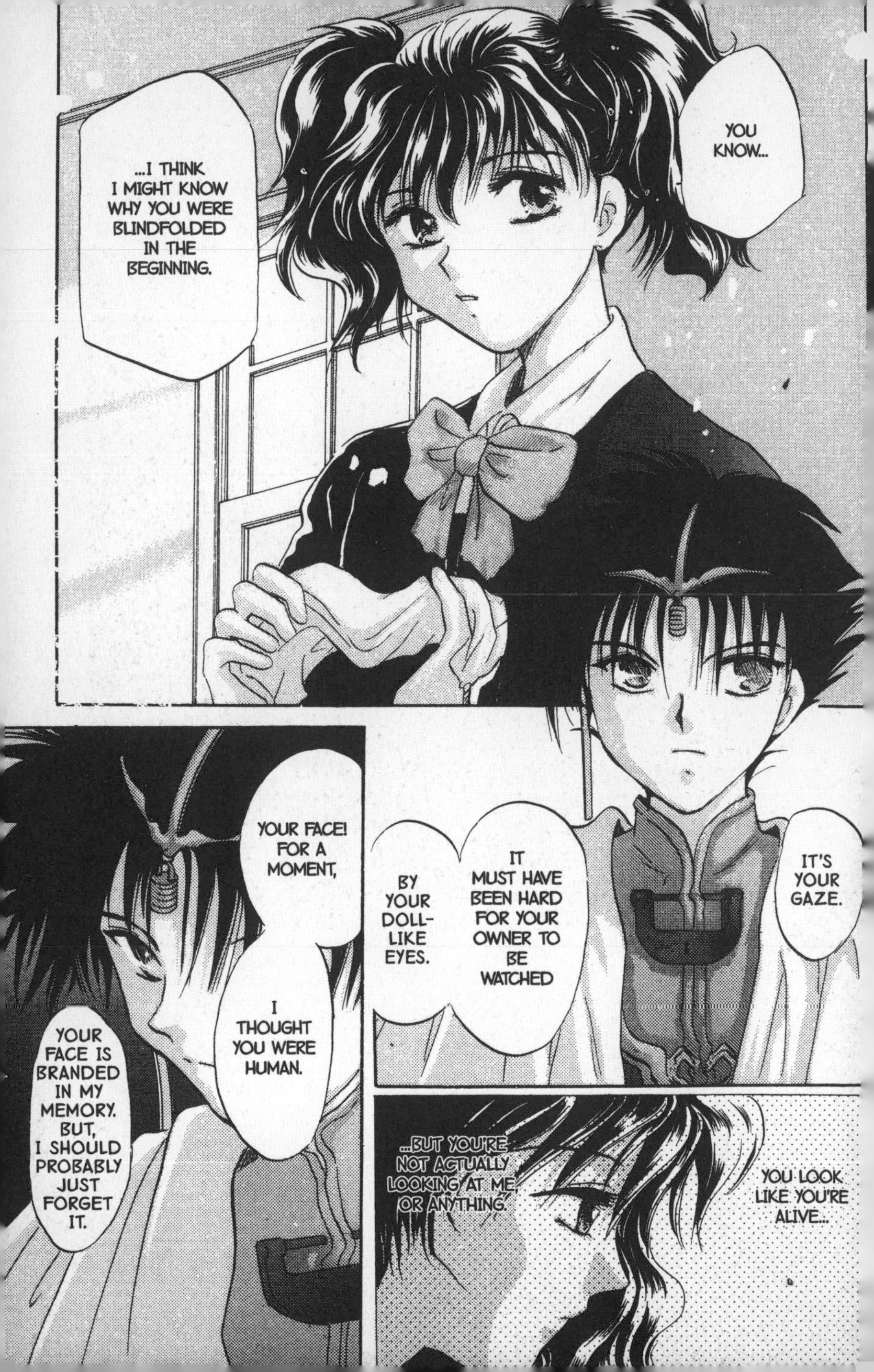
YOU KNOW...
...I THINK I MIGHT KNOW WHY YOU WERE BLINDFOLDED IN THE BEGINNING.
IT'S YOUR GAZE.
IT MUST HAVE BEEN HARD FOR YOUR OWNER TO BE WATCHED
BY YOUR DOLL-LIKE EYES.
YOU LOOK LIKE YOU'RE ALIVE...
...BUT YOU'RE NOT ACTUALLY LOOKING AT ME, OR ANYTHING.
YOUR FACE! FOR A MOMENT,
I THOUGHT YOU WERE HUMAN.
YOUR FACE IS BRANDED IN MY MEMORY. BUT, I SHOULD PROBABLY JUST FORGET IT.

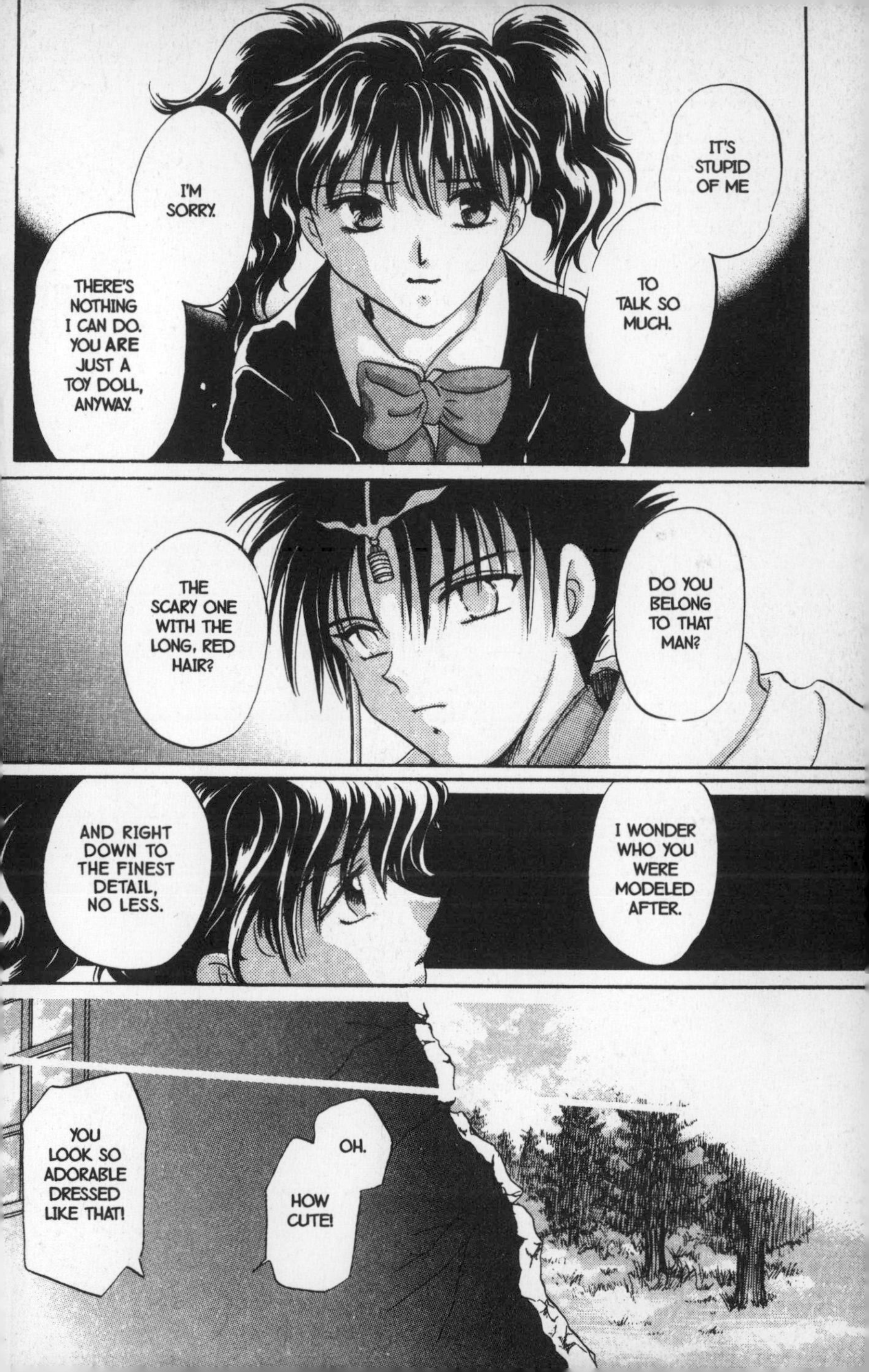
IT'S STUPID OF ME
TO TALK SO MUCH.
I'M SORRY.
THERE'S NOTHING I CAN DO. YOU ARE JUST A TOY DOLL, ANYWAY.
DO YOU BELONG TO THAT MAN?
THE SCARY ONE WITH THE LONG, RED HAIR?
I WONDER WHO YOU WERE MODELED AFTER.
AND RIGHT DOWN TO THE FINEST DETAIL, NO LESS.
OH.
HOW CUTE!
YOU LOOK SO ADORABLE DRESSED LIKE THAT!

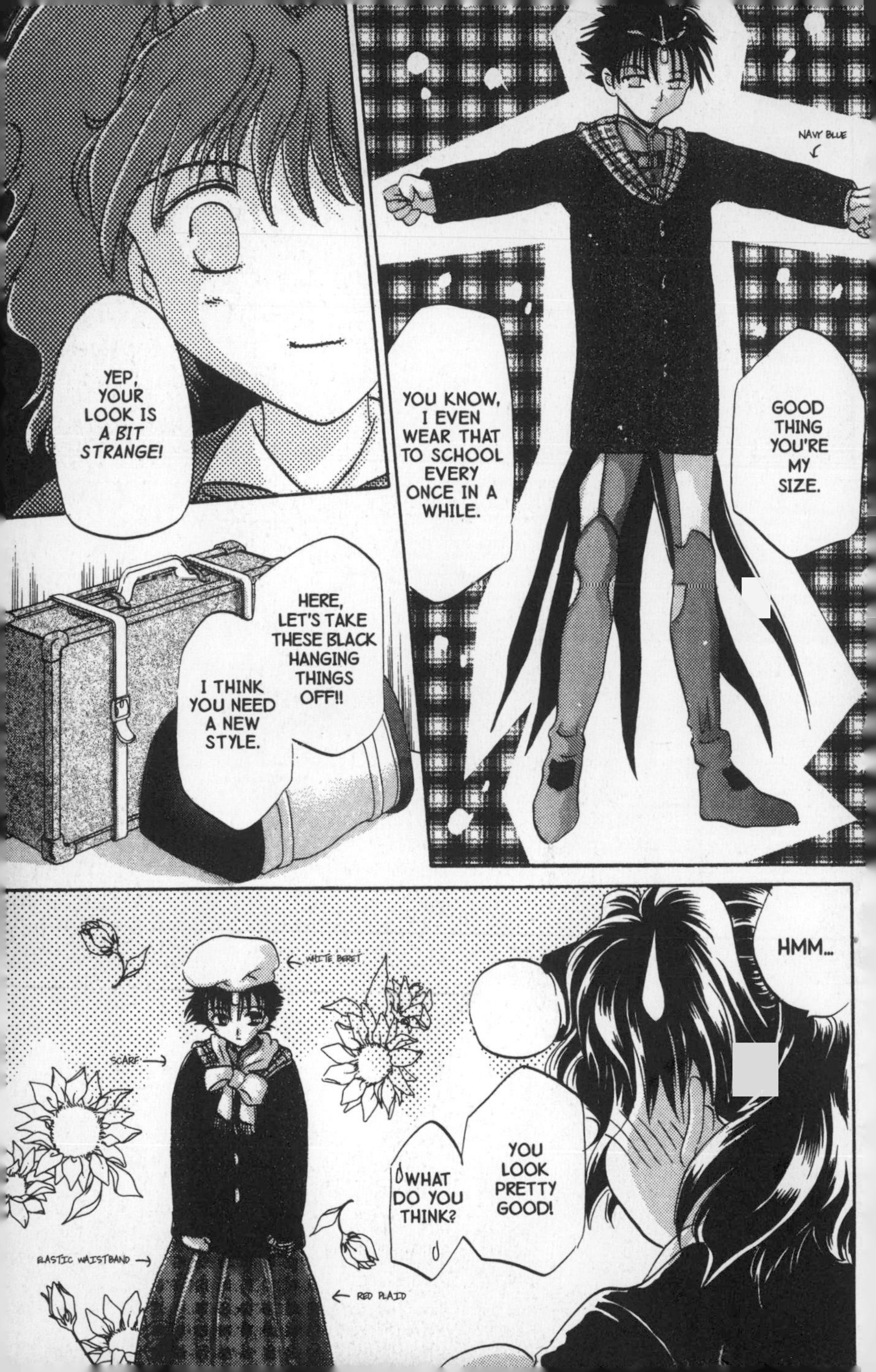
NAVY BLUE
GOOD THING YOU'RE MY SIZE.
YOU KNOW, I EVEN WEAR THAT TO SCHOOL EVERY ONCE IN A WHILE.
YEP, YOUR LOOK IS A BIT STRANGE!
HERE, LET'S TAKE THESE BLACK HANGING THINGS OFF!!
I THINK YOU NEED A NEW STYLE.
HMM...
YOU LOOK PRETTY GOOD!
WHAT DO YOU THINK?
WHITE BERET
SCARF
ELASTIC WAISTBAND
RED PLAID

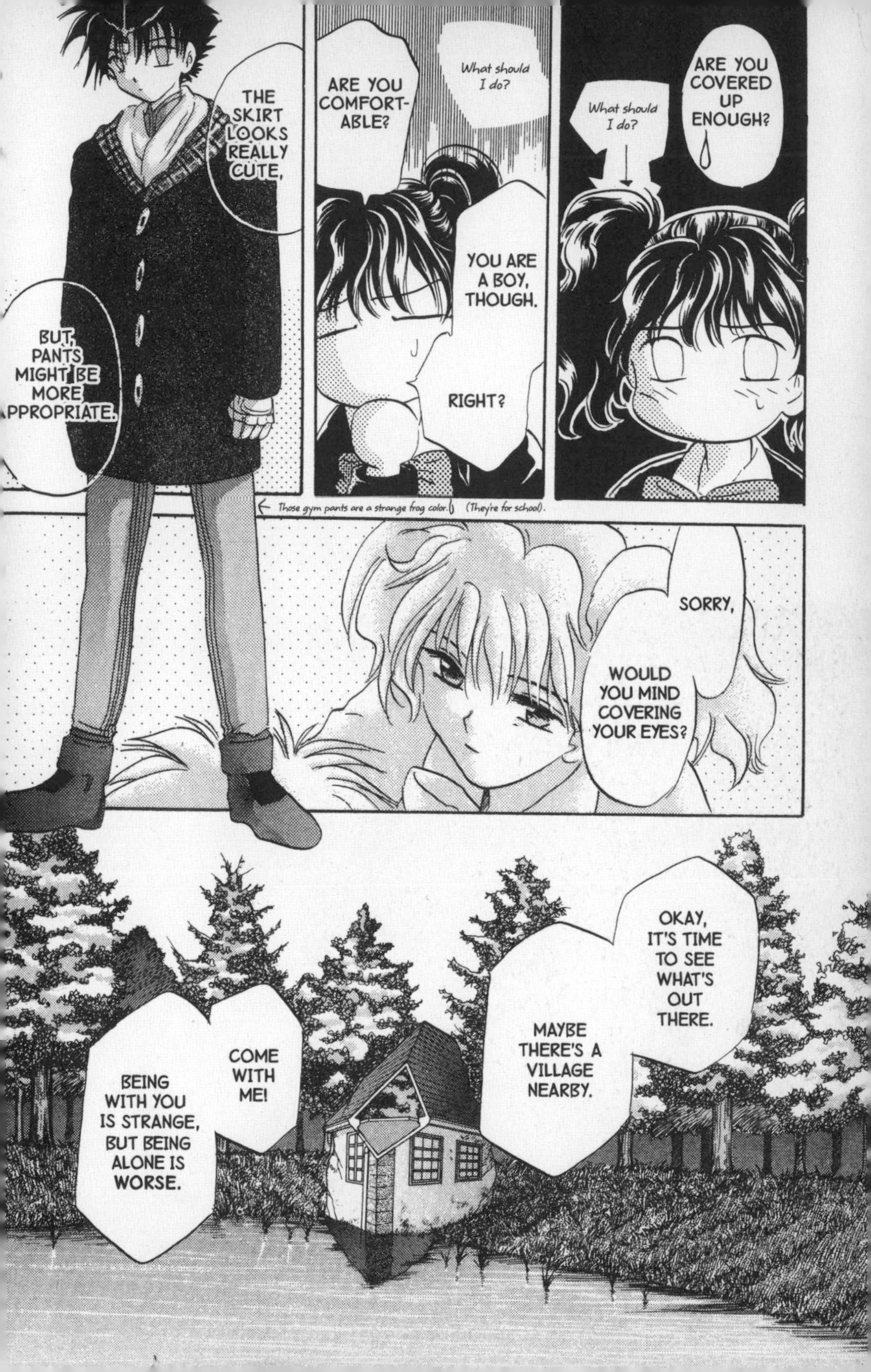
ARE YOU COVERED UP ENOUGH?
What should I do?
What should I do?
ARE YOU COMFORTABLE?
YOU ARE A BOY, THOUGH.
RIGHT?
THE SKIRT LOOKS REALLY CUTE,
BUT, PANTS MIGHT BE MORE APPROPRIATE.
← Those gym pants are a strange frog color. (They're for school).
SORRY,
WOULD YOU MIND COVERING YOUR EYES?
OKAY, IT'S TIME TO SEE WHAT'S OUT THERE.
MAYBE THERE'S A VILLAGE NEARBY.
COME WITH ME!
BEING WITH YOU IS STRANGE, BUT BEING ALONE IS WORSE.

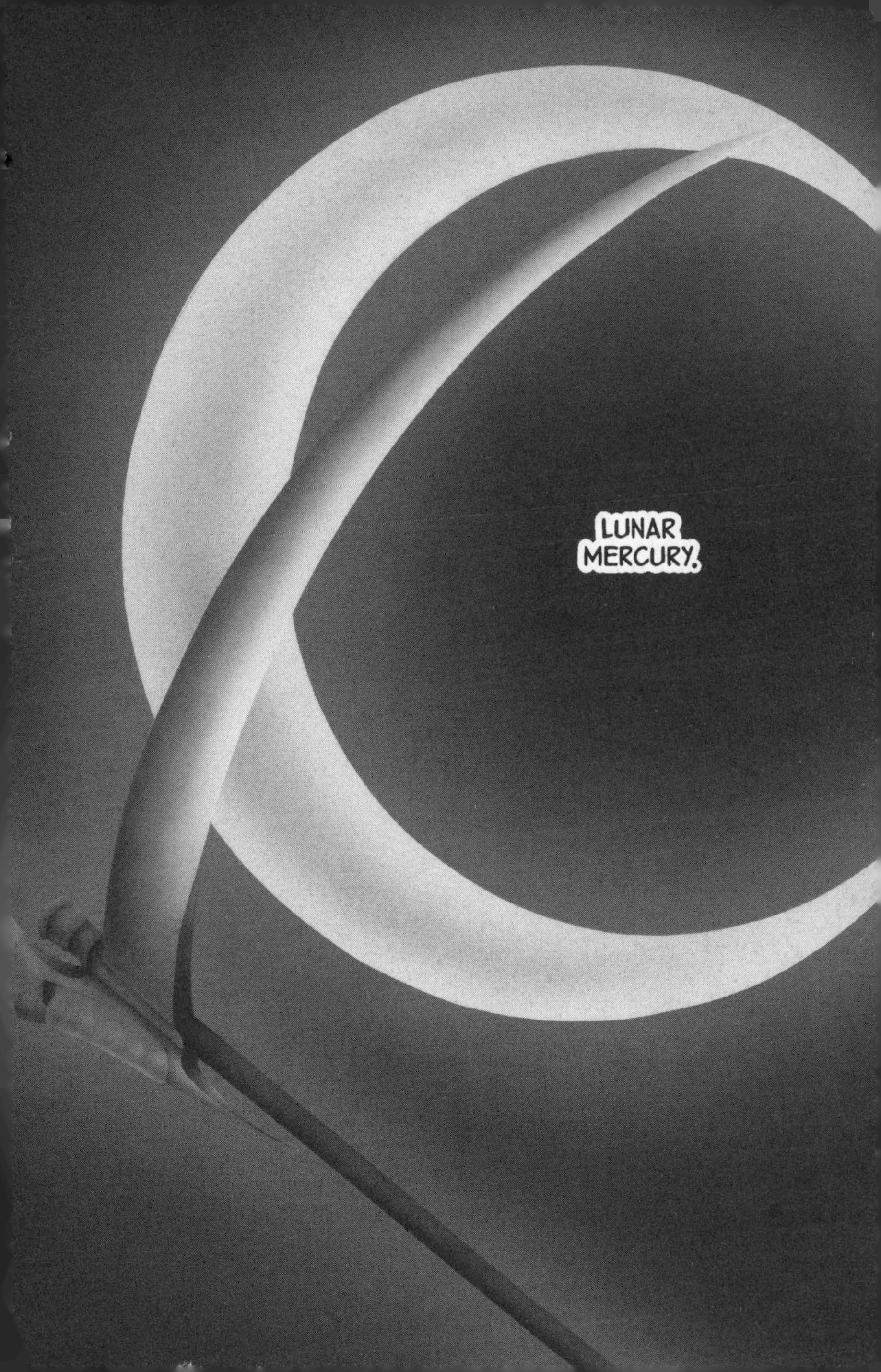
LUNAR
MERCURY.

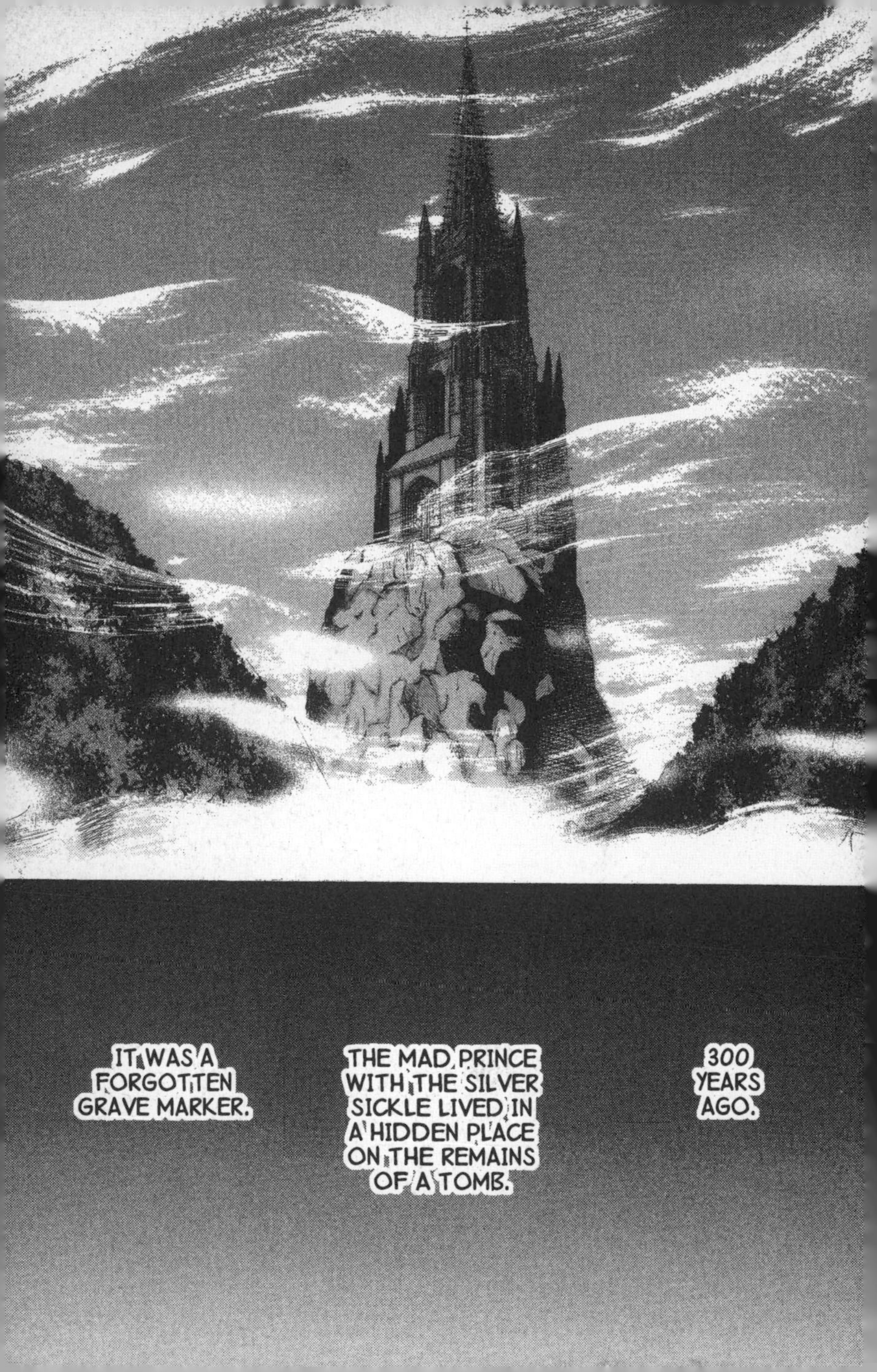
300 YEARS AGO.
THE MAD PRINCE WITH THE SILVER SICKLE LIVED IN A HIDDEN PLACE ON THE REMAINS OF A TOMB.
IT WAS A FORGOTTEN GRAVE MARKER.

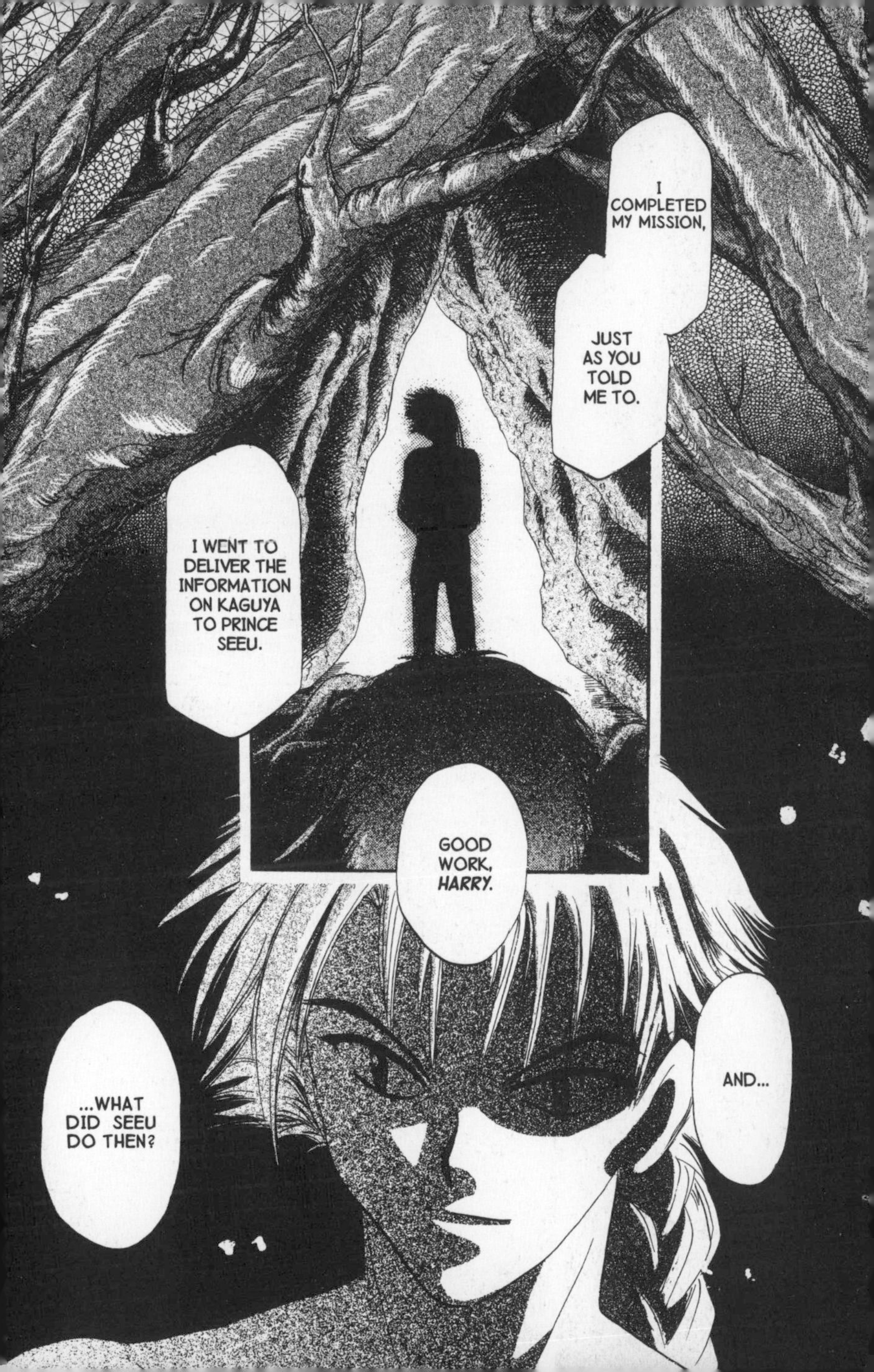
I COMPLETED MY MISSION,
JUST AS YOU TOLD ME TO.
I WENT TO DELIVER THE INFORMATION ON KAGUYA TO PRINCE SEEU.
GOOD WORK, HARRY.
AND...
...WHAT DID SEEU DO THEN?

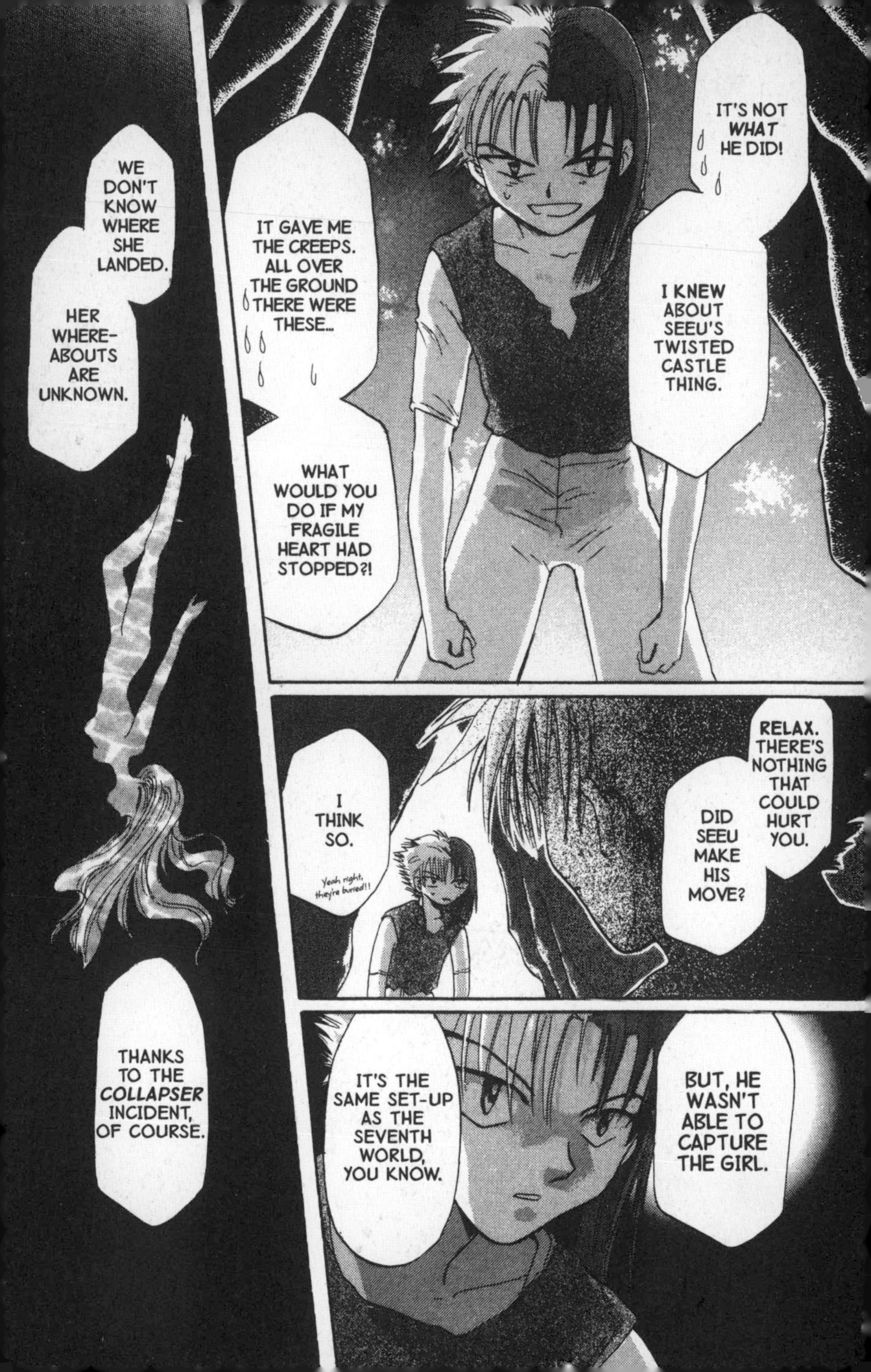
IT'S NOT *WHAT* HE DID!
I KNEW ABOUT SEEU'S TWISTED CASTLE THING.
IT GAVE ME THE CREEPS. ALL OVER THE GROUND THERE WERE THESE...
WHAT WOULD YOU DO IF MY FRAGILE HEART HAD STOPPED?!
RELAX. THERE'S NOTHING THAT COULD HURT YOU.
DID SEEU MAKE HIS MOVE?
I THINK SO.
Yeah right, they're buried!!
BUT, HE WASN'T ABLE TO CAPTURE THE GIRL.
IT'S THE SAME SET-UP AS THE SEVENTH WORLD, YOU KNOW.
WE DON'T KNOW WHERE SHE LANDED.
HER WHERE-ABOUTS ARE UNKNOWN.
THANKS TO THE *COLLAPSER* INCIDENT, OF COURSE.

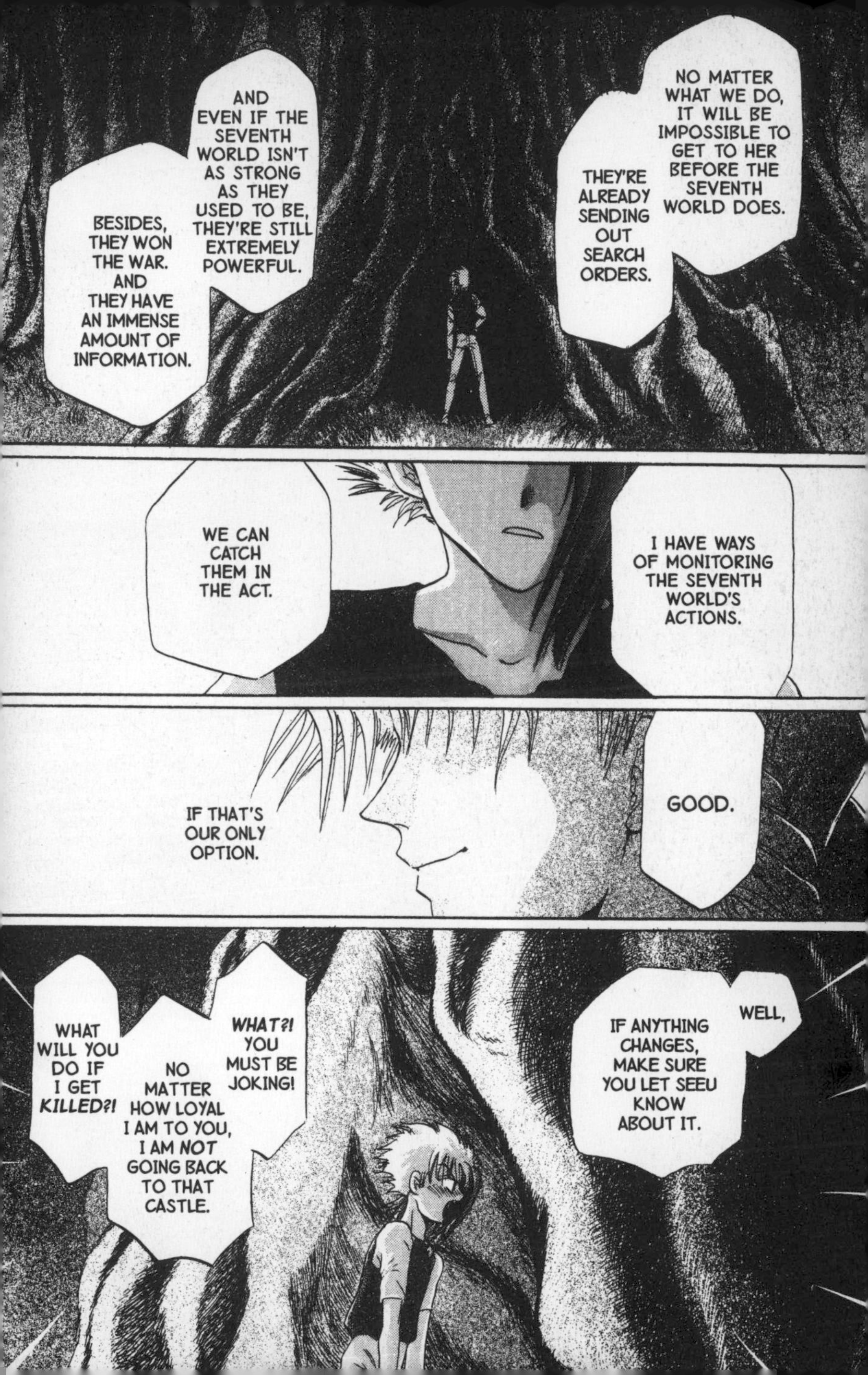
NO MATTER WHAT WE DO, IT WILL BE IMPOSSIBLE TO GET TO HER BEFORE THE SEVENTH WORLD DOES.
THEY'RE ALREADY SENDING OUT SEARCH ORDERS.
AND EVEN IF THE SEVENTH WORLD ISN'T AS STRONG AS THEY USED TO BE, THEY'RE STILL EXTREMELY POWERFUL.
BESIDES, THEY WON THE WAR. AND THEY HAVE AN IMMENSE AMOUNT OF INFORMATION.
I HAVE WAYS OF MONITORING THE SEVENTH WORLD'S ACTIONS.
WE CAN CATCH THEM IN THE ACT.
GOOD.
IF THAT'S OUR ONLY OPTION.
WELL,
IF ANYTHING CHANGES, MAKE SURE YOU LET SEEU KNOW ABOUT IT.
WHAT?! YOU MUST BE JOKING!
NO MATTER HOW LOYAL I AM TO YOU, I AM *NOT* GOING BACK TO THAT CASTLE.
WHAT WILL YOU DO IF I GET *KILLED?!*

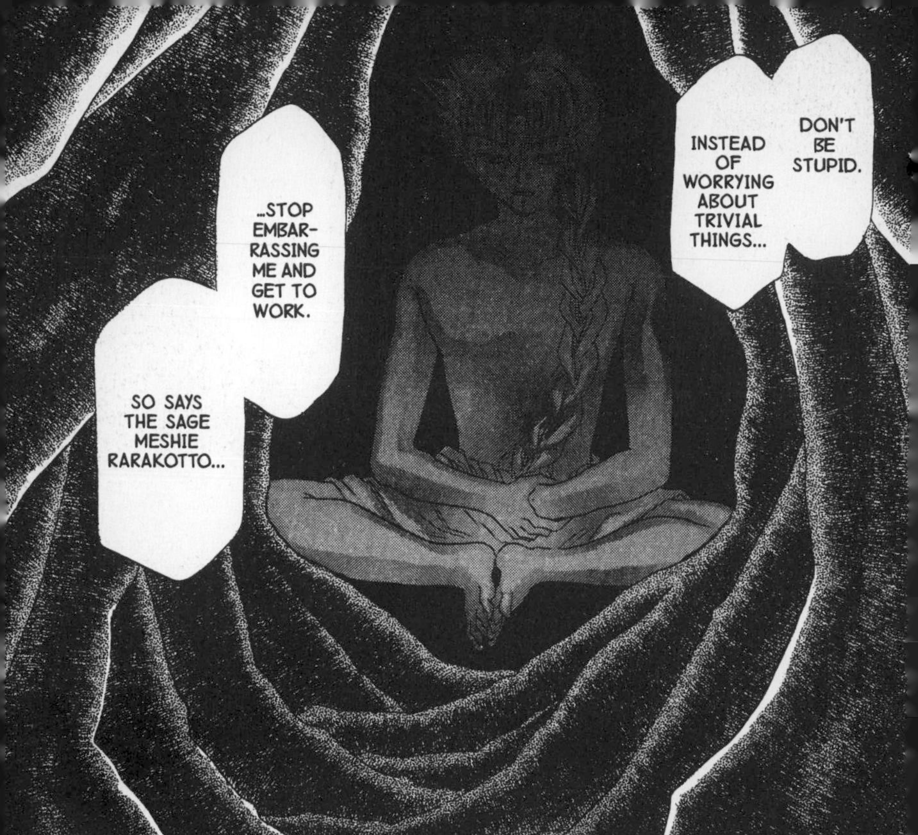
DON'T BE STUPID.
INSTEAD OF WORRYING ABOUT TRIVIAL THINGS...
...STOP EMBAR-RASSING ME AND GET TO WORK.
SO SAYS THE SAGE MESHIE RARAKOTTO...
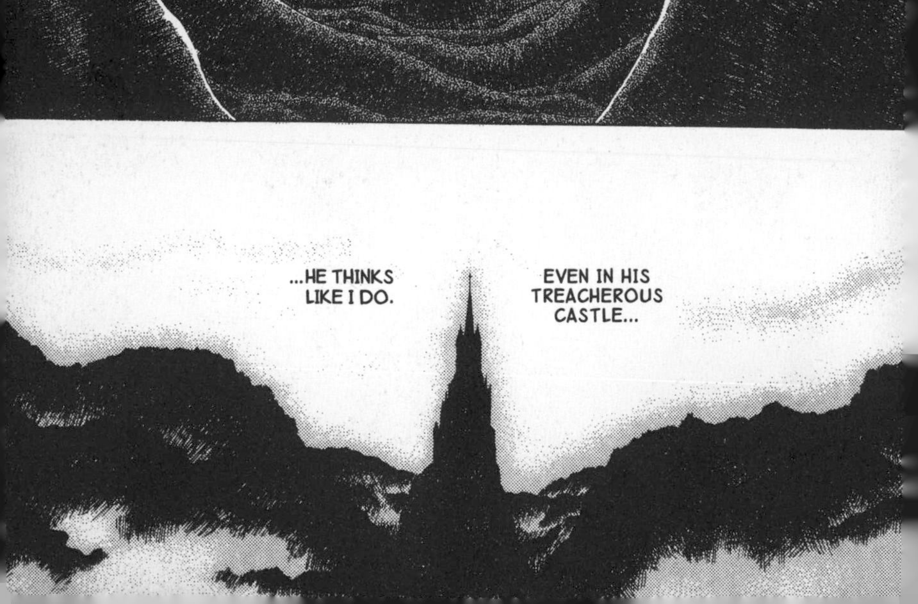
EVEN IN HIS TREACHEROUS CASTLE...
...HE THINKS LIKE I DO.

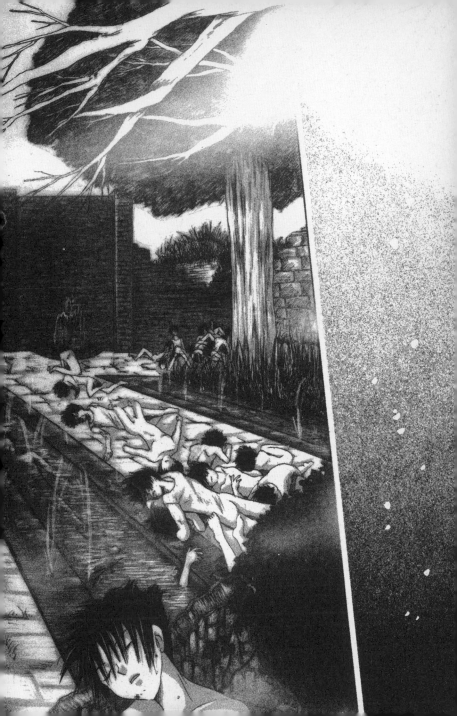

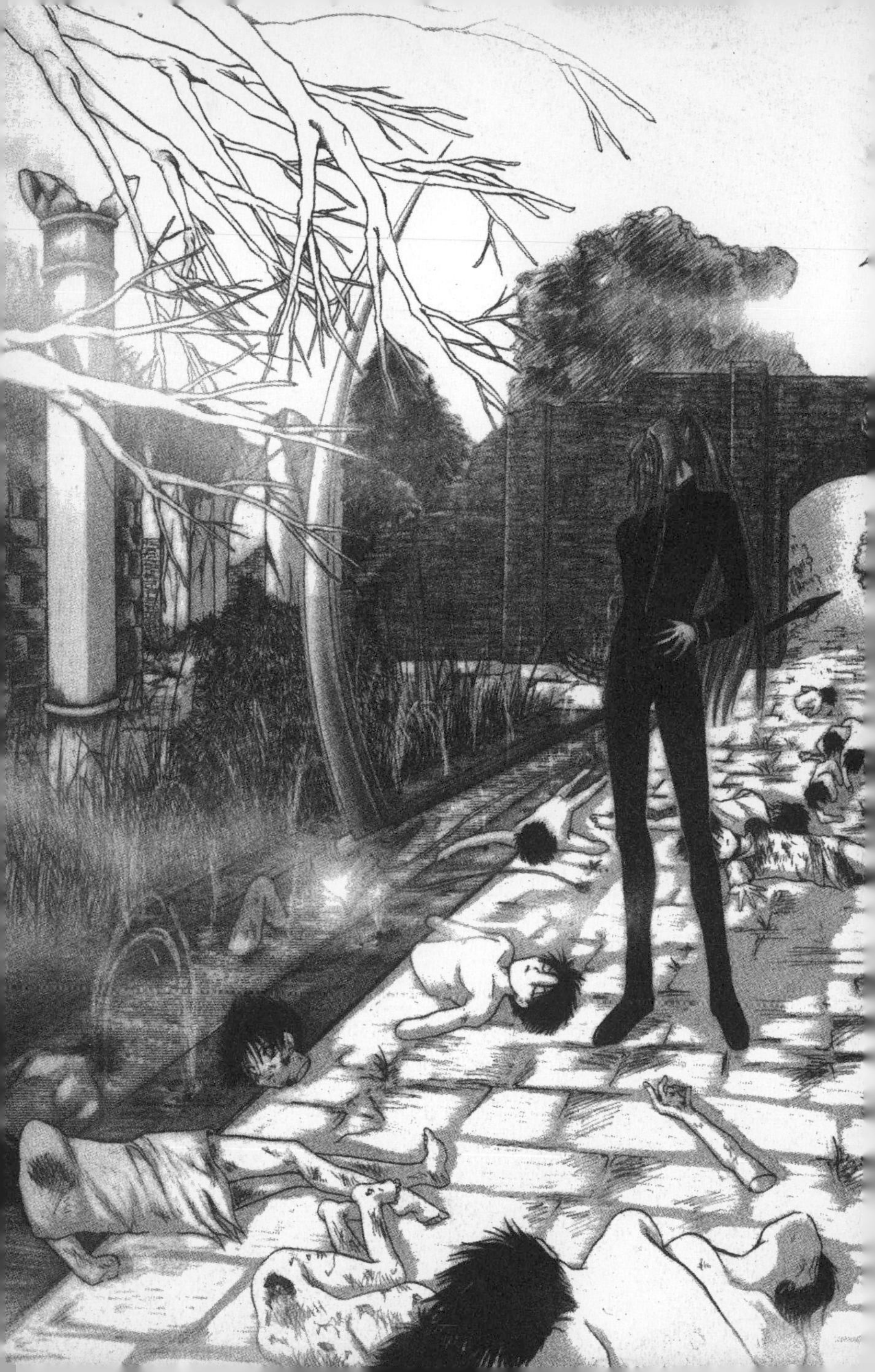

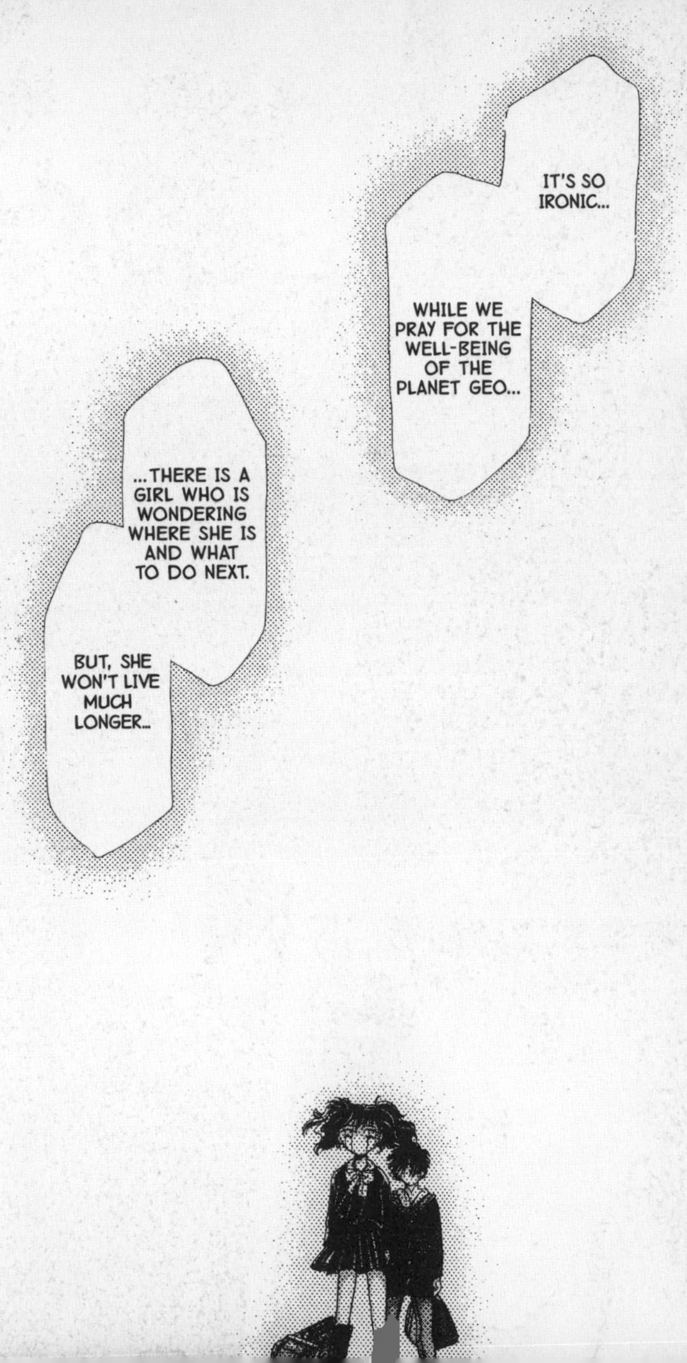
IT'S SO IRONIC...
WHILE WE PRAY FOR THE WELL-BEING OF THE PLANET GEO...
...THERE IS A GIRL WHO IS WONDERING WHERE SHE IS AND WHAT TO DO NEXT.
BUT, SHE WON'T LIVE MUCH LONGER...

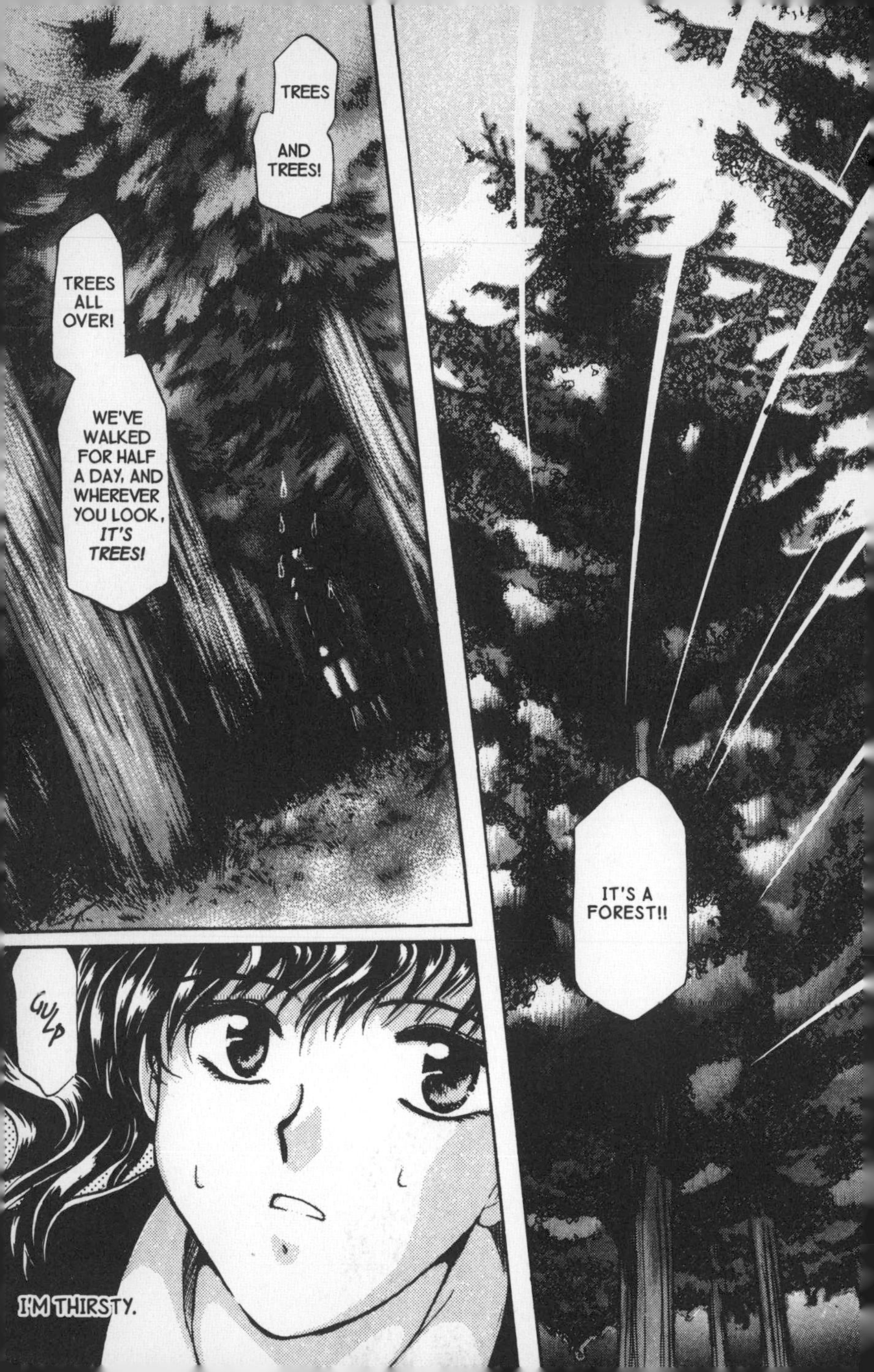
IT'S A FOREST!!
TREES AND TREES!
TREES ALL OVER!
WE'VE WALKED FOR HALF A DAY, AND WHEREVER YOU LOOK, *IT'S TREES!*
GULP
I'M THIRSTY.

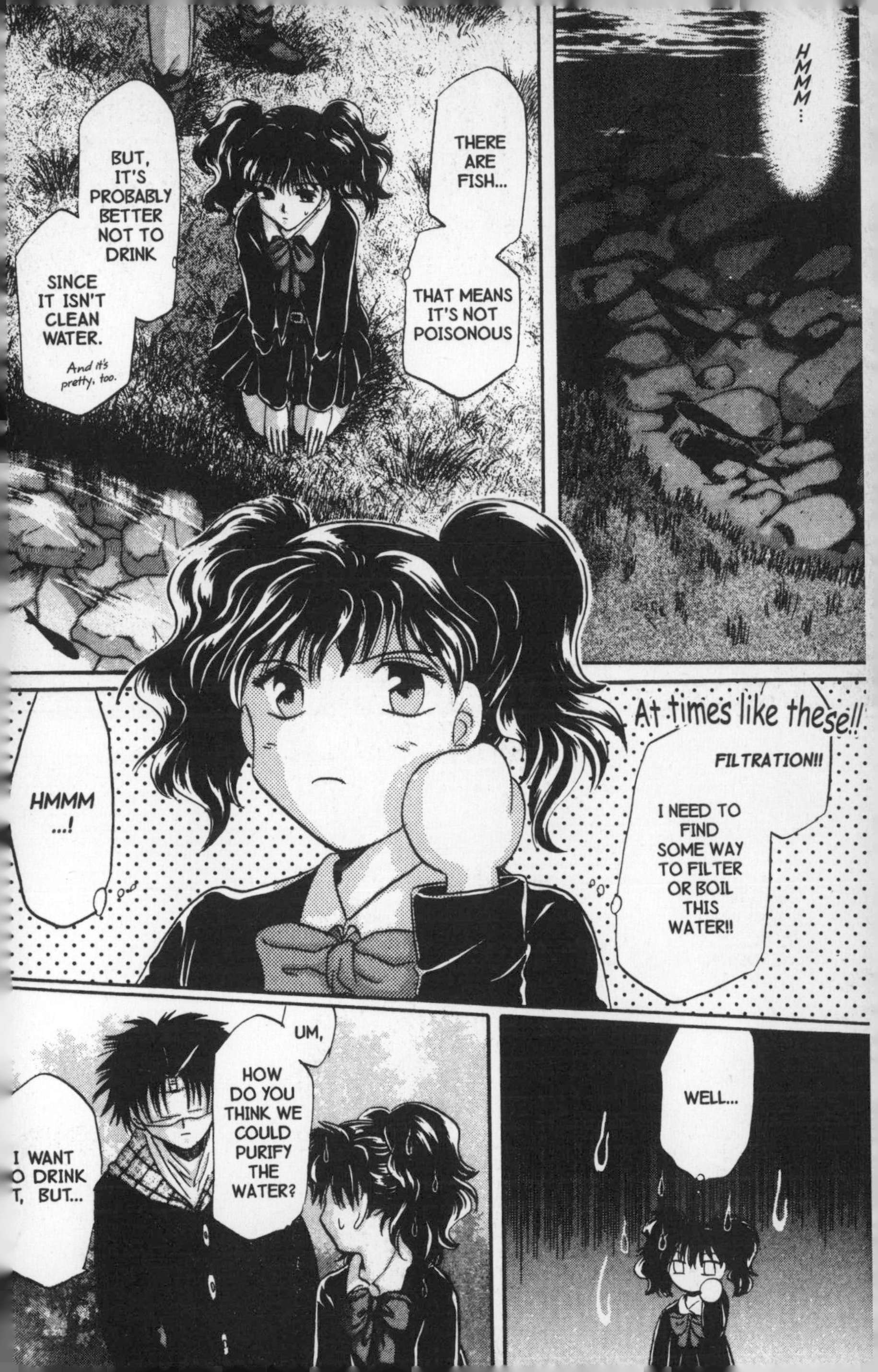
HMMM...
THERE ARE FISH...
THAT MEANS IT'S NOT POISONOUS
BUT, IT'S PROBABLY BETTER NOT TO DRINK
SINCE IT ISN'T CLEAN WATER.
And it's pretty, too.
At times like these!!
FILTRATION!!
I NEED TO FIND SOME WAY TO FILTER OR BOIL THIS WATER!!
HMMM ...!
WELL...
UM,
HOW DO YOU THINK WE COULD PURIFY THE WATER?
I WANT O DRINK T, BUT...

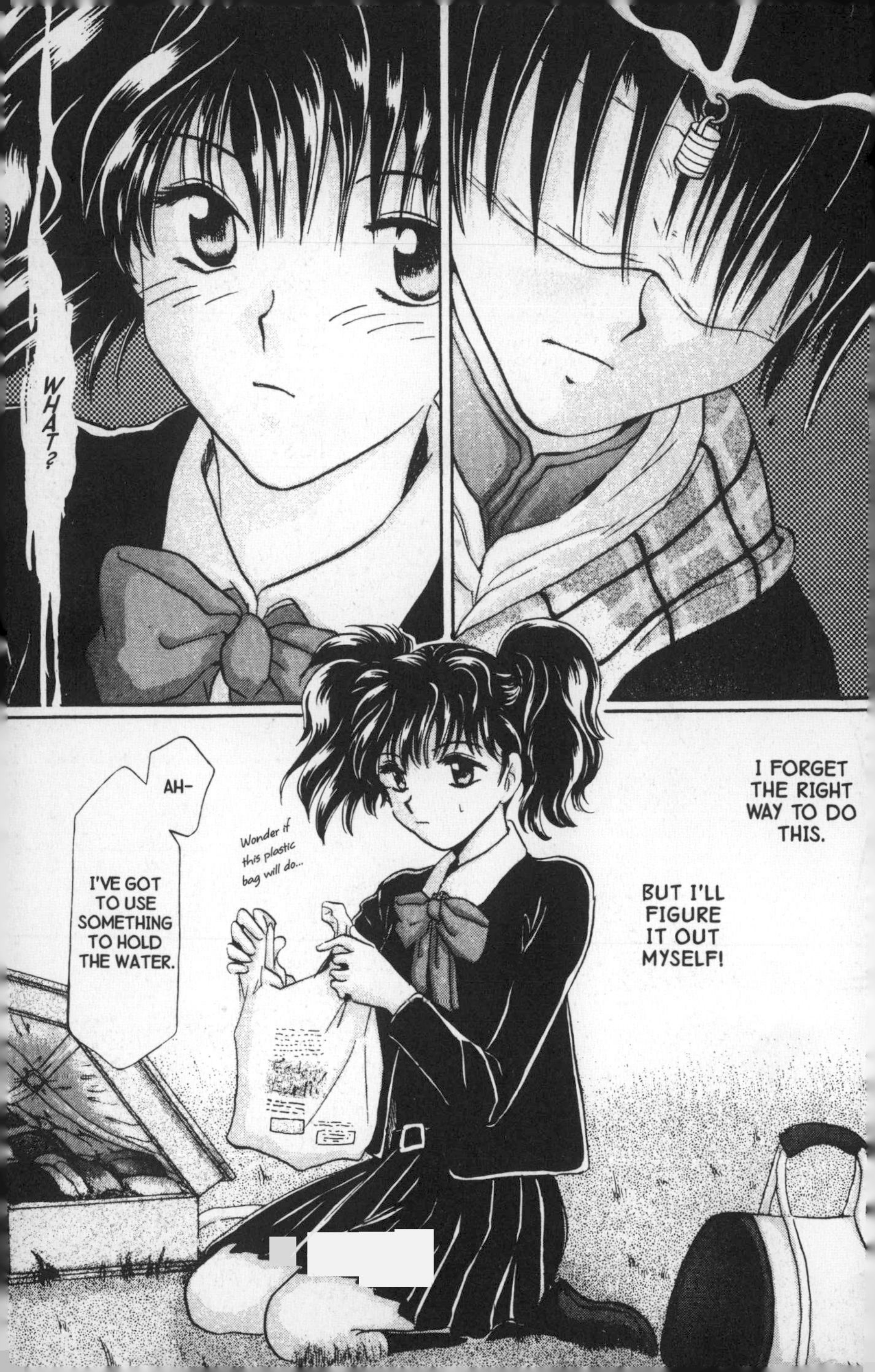
WHAT?
I FORGET THE RIGHT WAY TO DO THIS.
BUT I'LL FIGURE IT OUT MYSELF!
Wonder if this plastic bag will do...
AH-
I'VE GOT TO USE SOMETHING TO HOLD THE WATER.

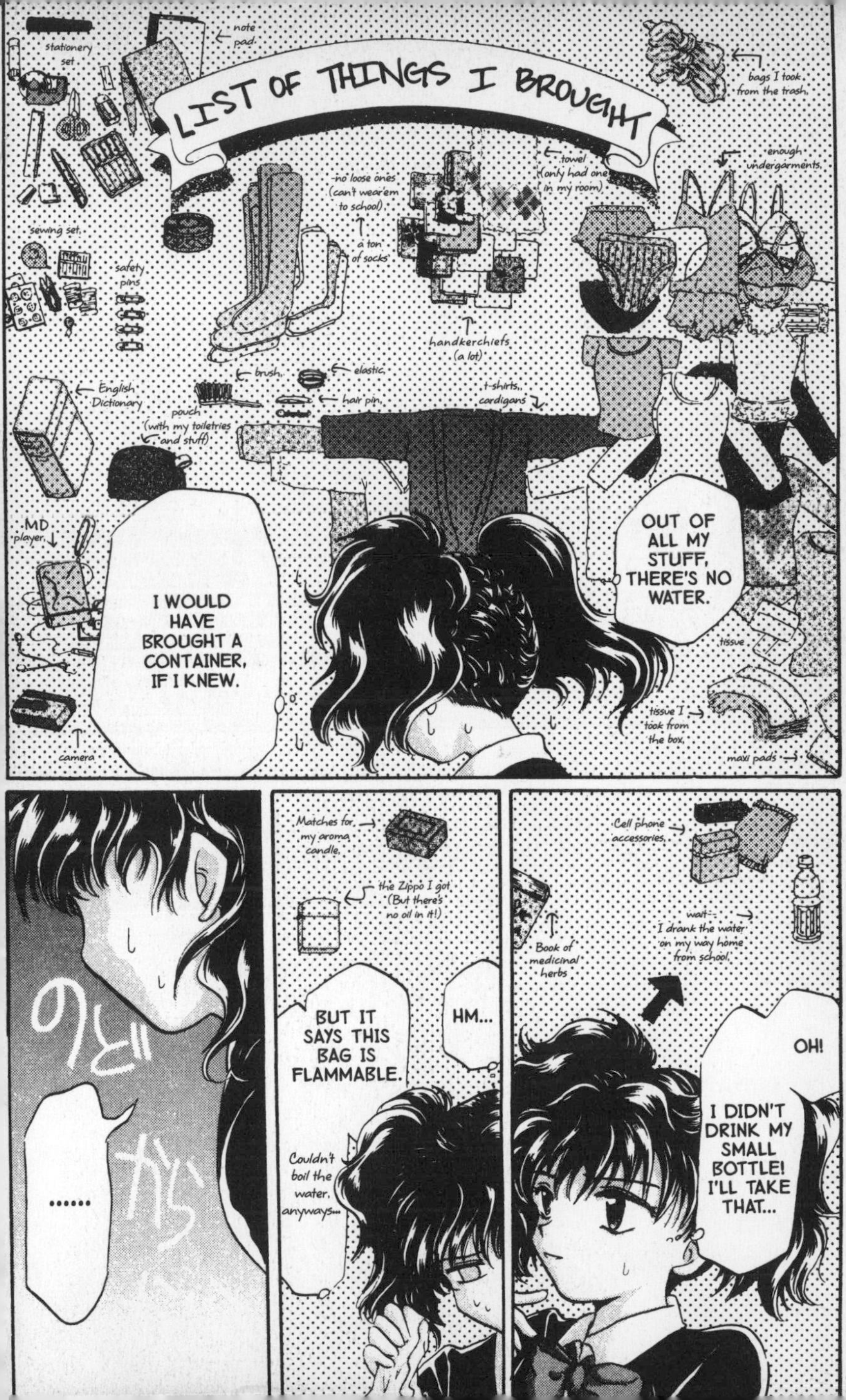
LIST OF THINGS I BROUGHT
bags I took from the trash.
enough undergarments.
towel (only had one in my room)
-no loose ones (can't wear'em to school)
a ton of socks
note pad.
stationery set
sewing set.
safety pins
handkerchiefs (a lot)
elastic.
brush.
hair pin.
t-shirts., cardigans
English Dictionary
pouch (with my toiletries and stuff)
OUT OF ALL MY STUFF, THERE'S NO WATER.
tissue
tissue I took from the box.
maxi pads
I WOULD HAVE BROUGHT A CONTAINER, IF I KNEW.
MD player.
camera
Cell phone accessories.
Book of medicinal herbs
wait-- I drank the water on my way home from school.
OH!
I DIDN'T DRINK MY SMALL BOTTLE! I'LL TAKE THAT...
Matches for my aroma candle.
the Zippo I got (But there's no oil in it!)
HM...
BUT IT SAYS THIS BAG IS FLAMMABLE.
Couldn't boil the water, anyways...
のど
から
......

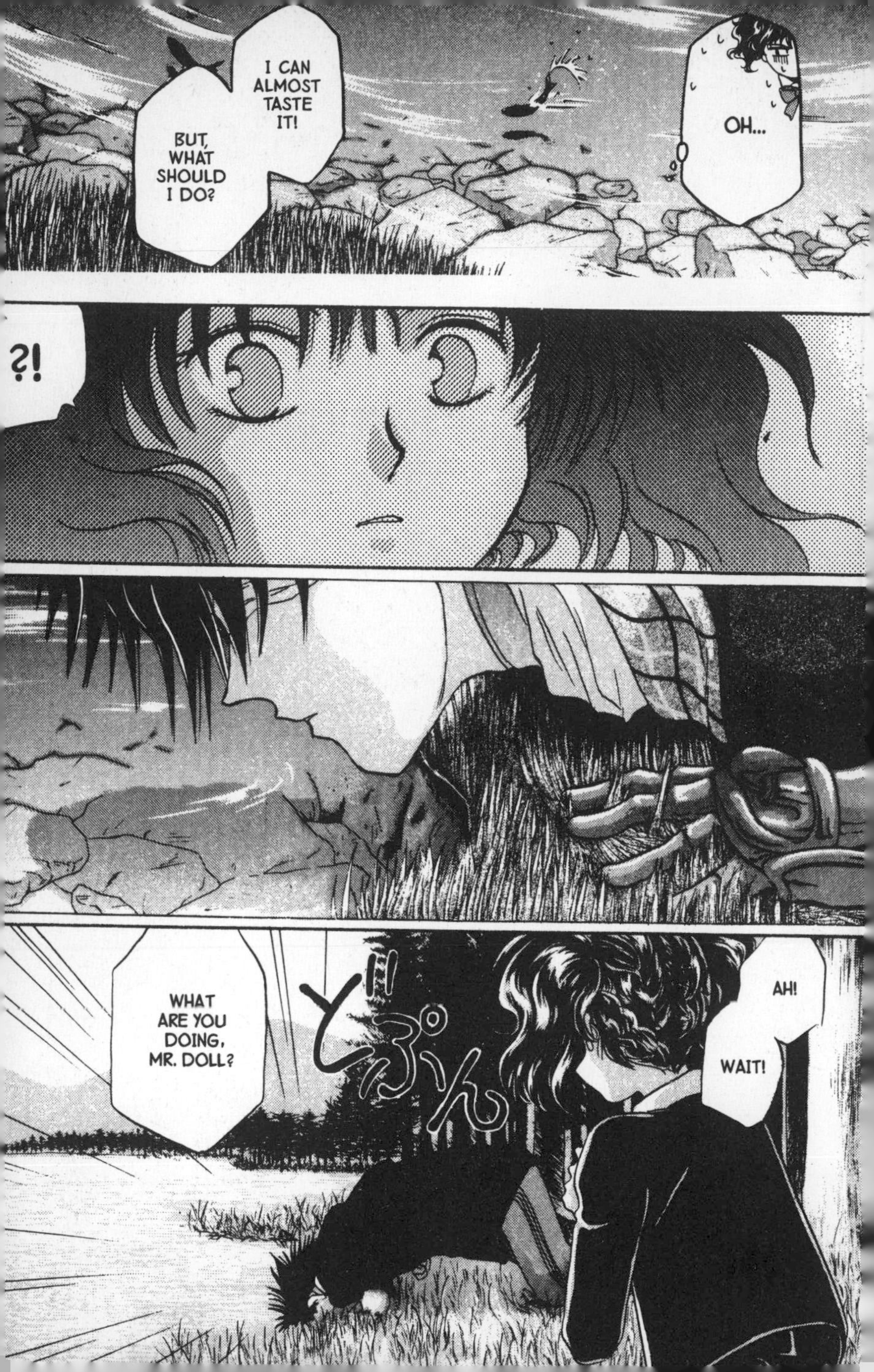
OH...
I CAN ALMOST TASTE IT!
BUT, WHAT SHOULD I DO?
?!
AH!
WAIT!
どぷん
WHAT ARE YOU DOING, MR. DOLL?

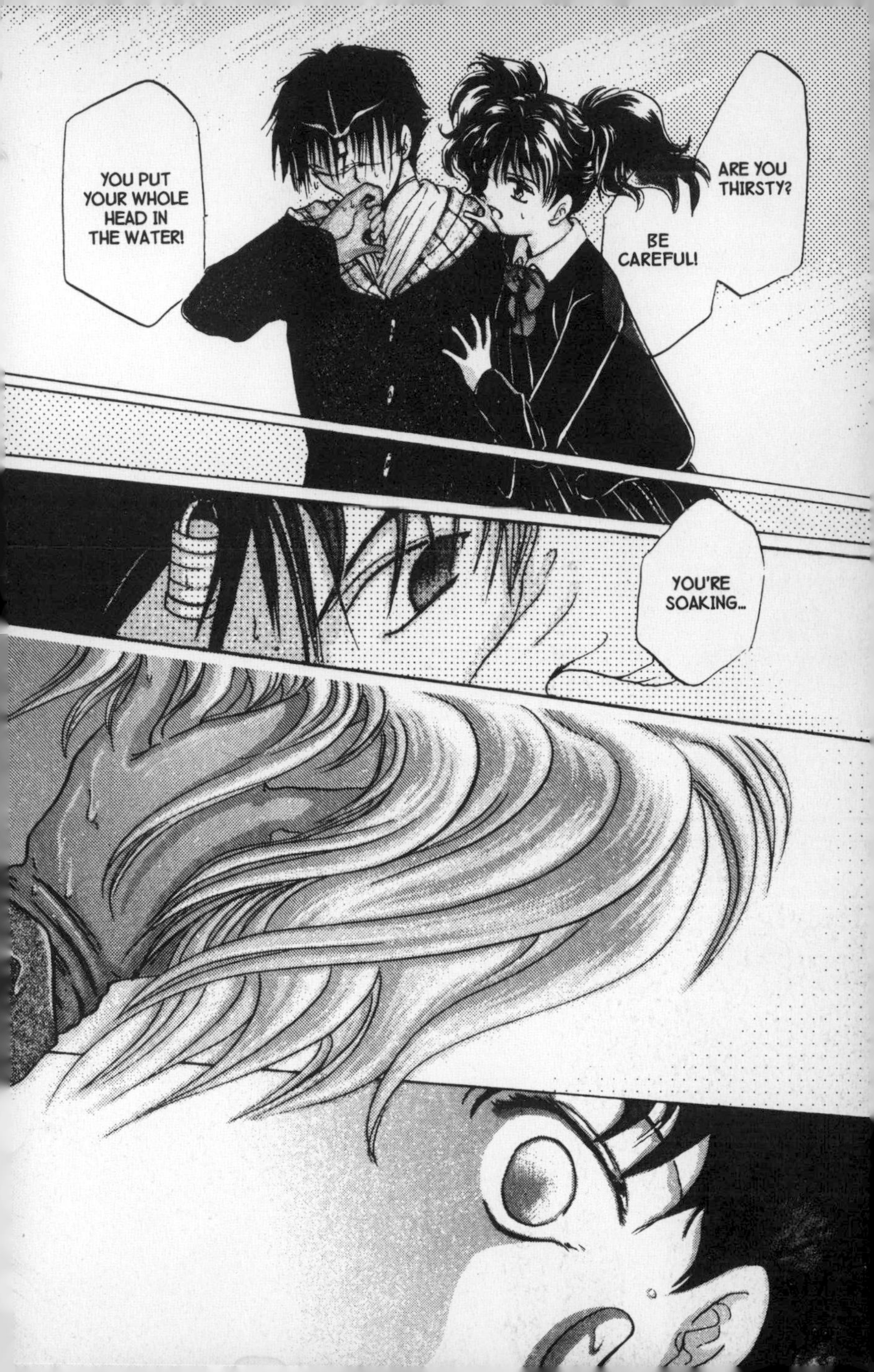
ARE YOU THIRSTY?
BE CAREFUL!
YOU PUT YOUR WHOLE HEAD IN THE WATER!
YOU'RE SOAKING...

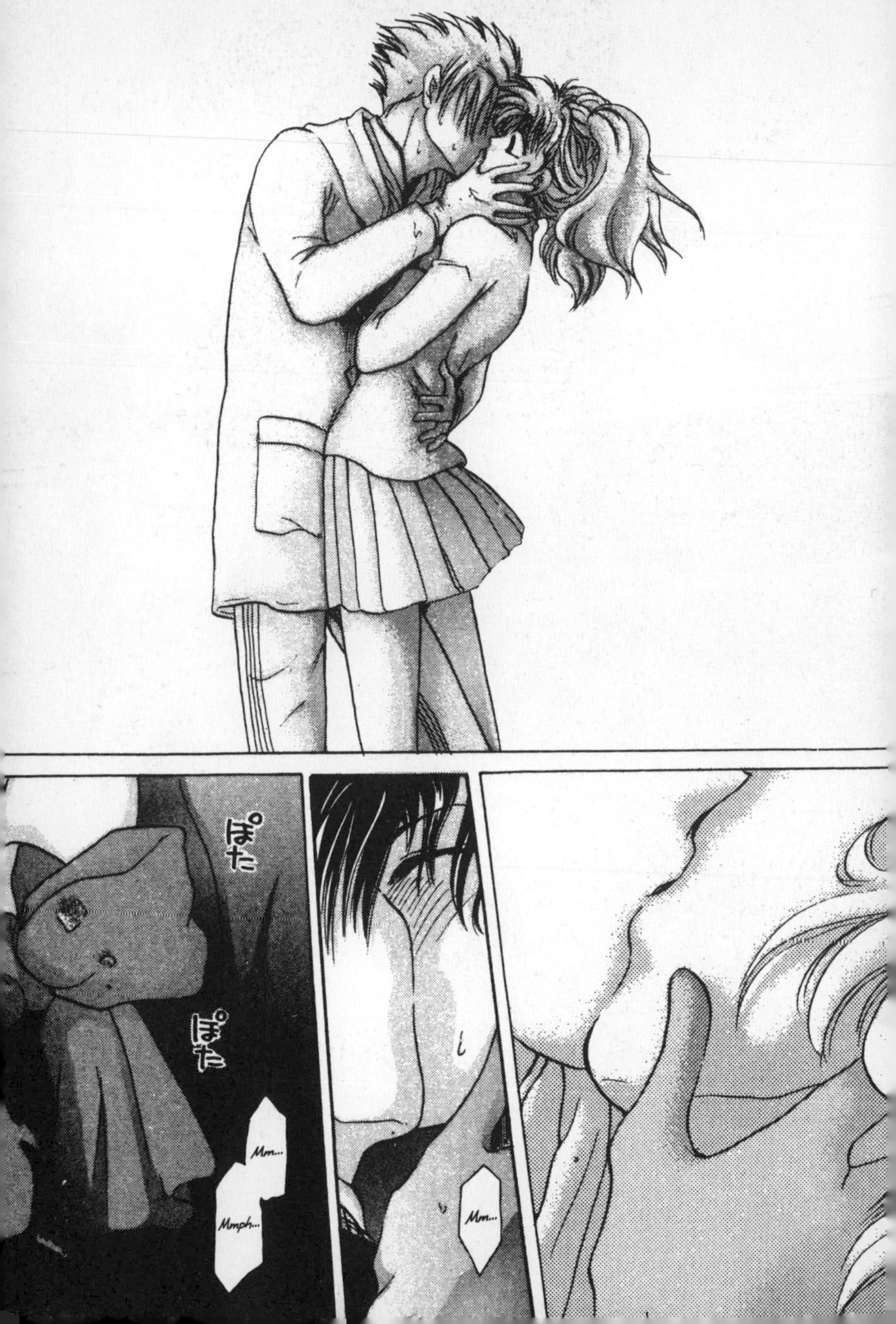
Mm...
ぽた
ぽた
Mm...
Mmph...

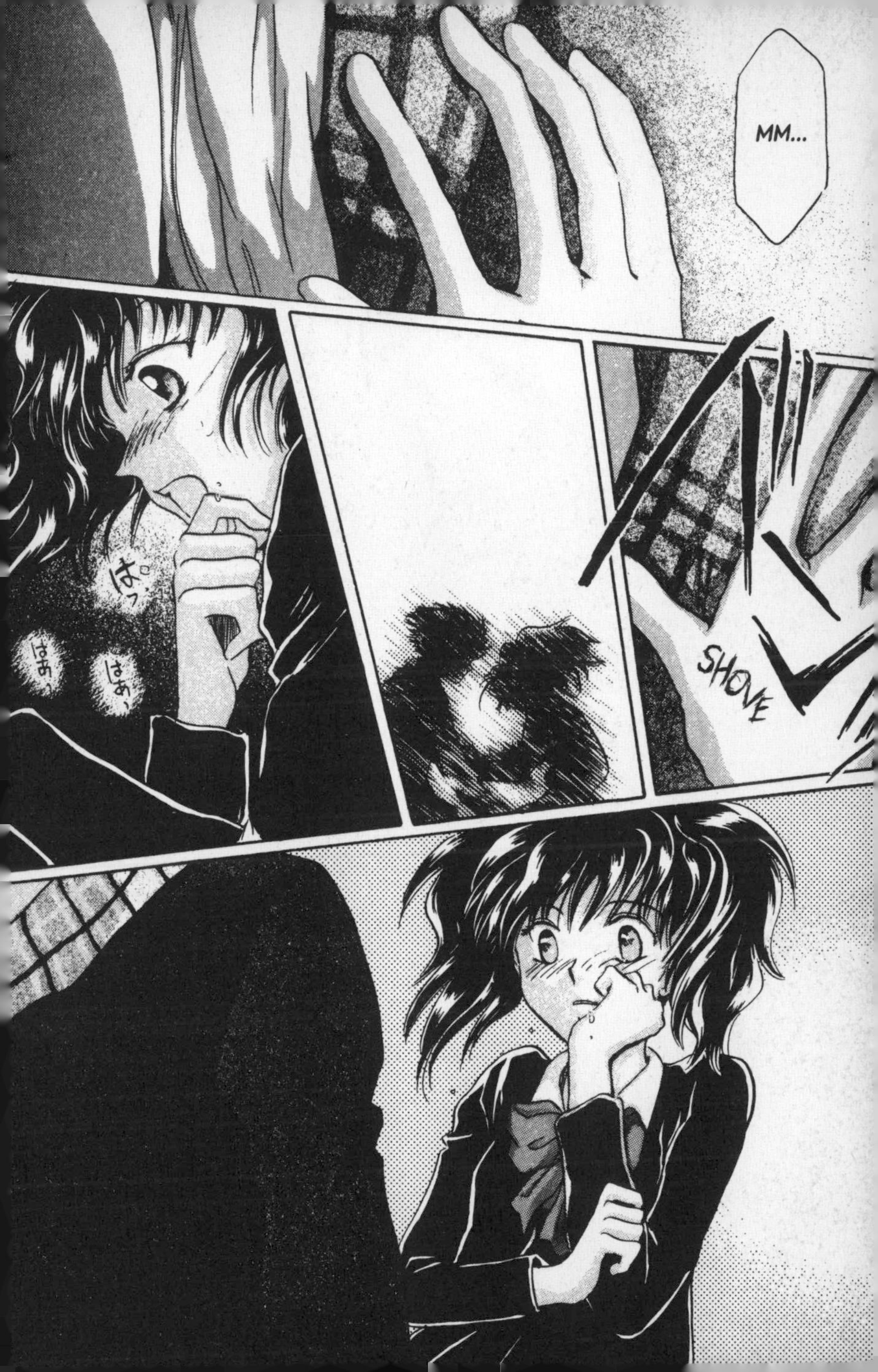
MM...
SHOVE
ぱっ
はあ、
はあ

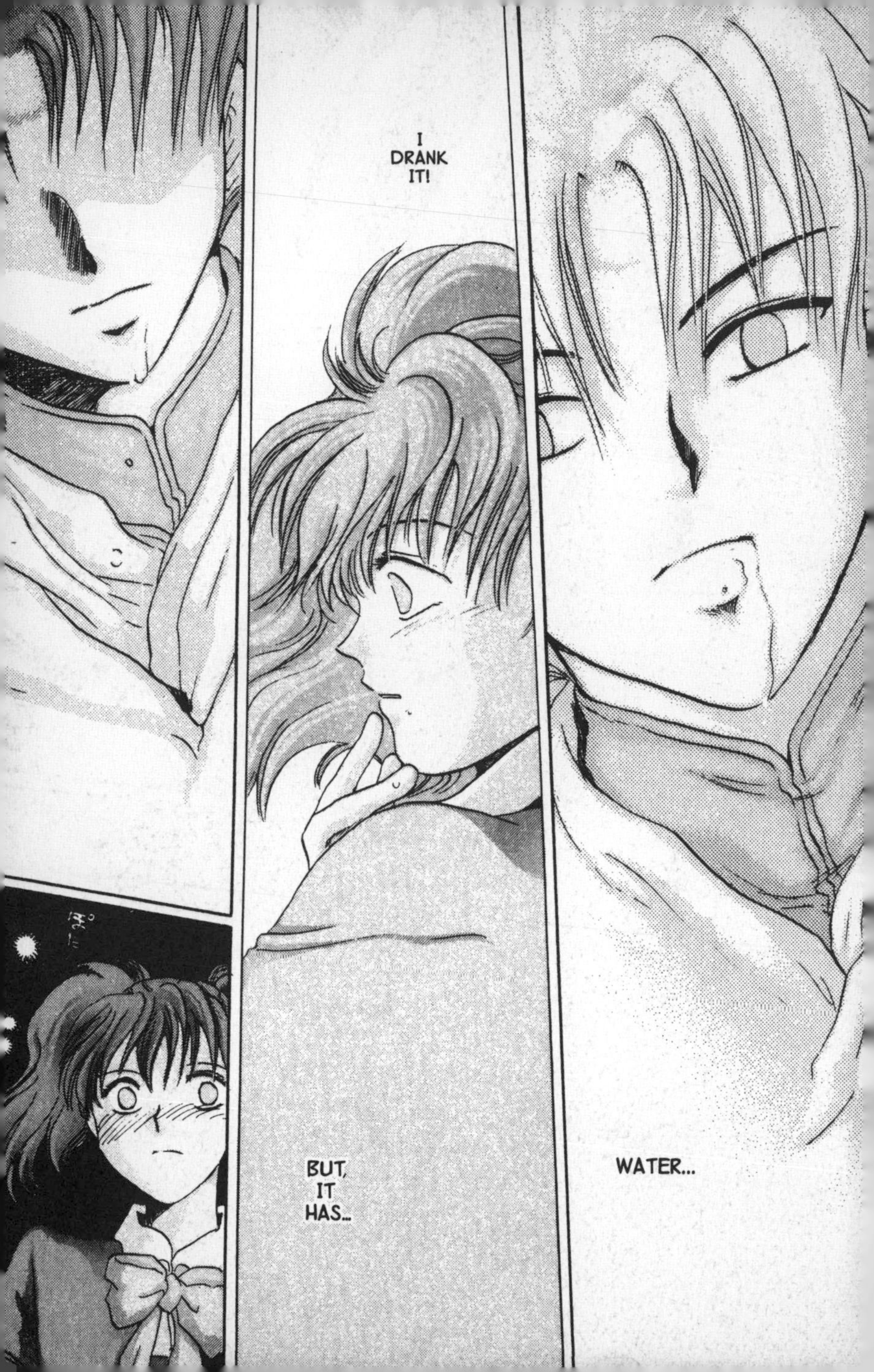
WATER...
I DRANK IT!
BUT, IT HAS...

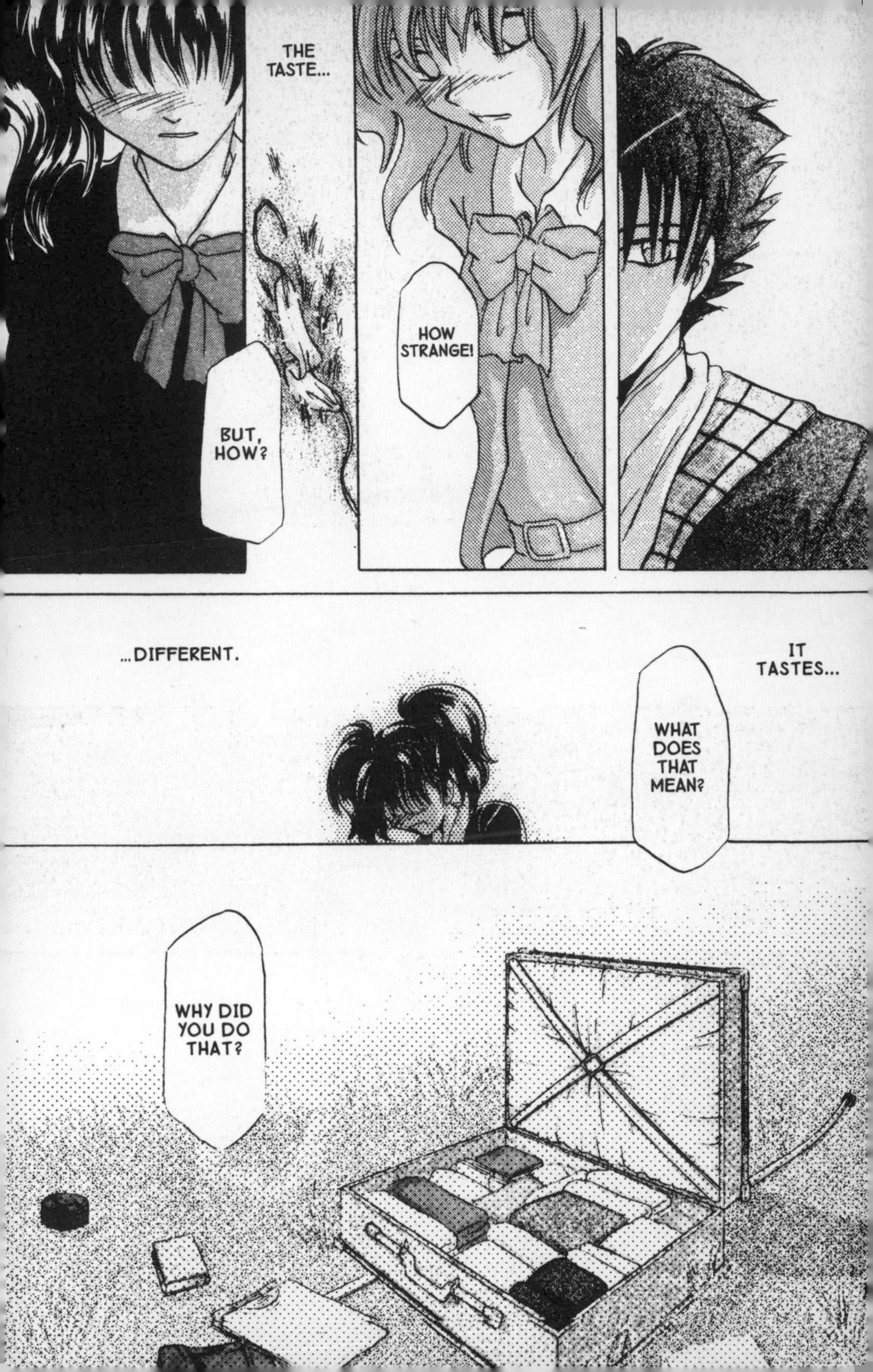
HOW STRANGE!
THE TASTE...
BUT, HOW?
IT TASTES...
...DIFFERENT.
WHAT DOES THAT MEAN?
WHY DID YOU DO THAT?

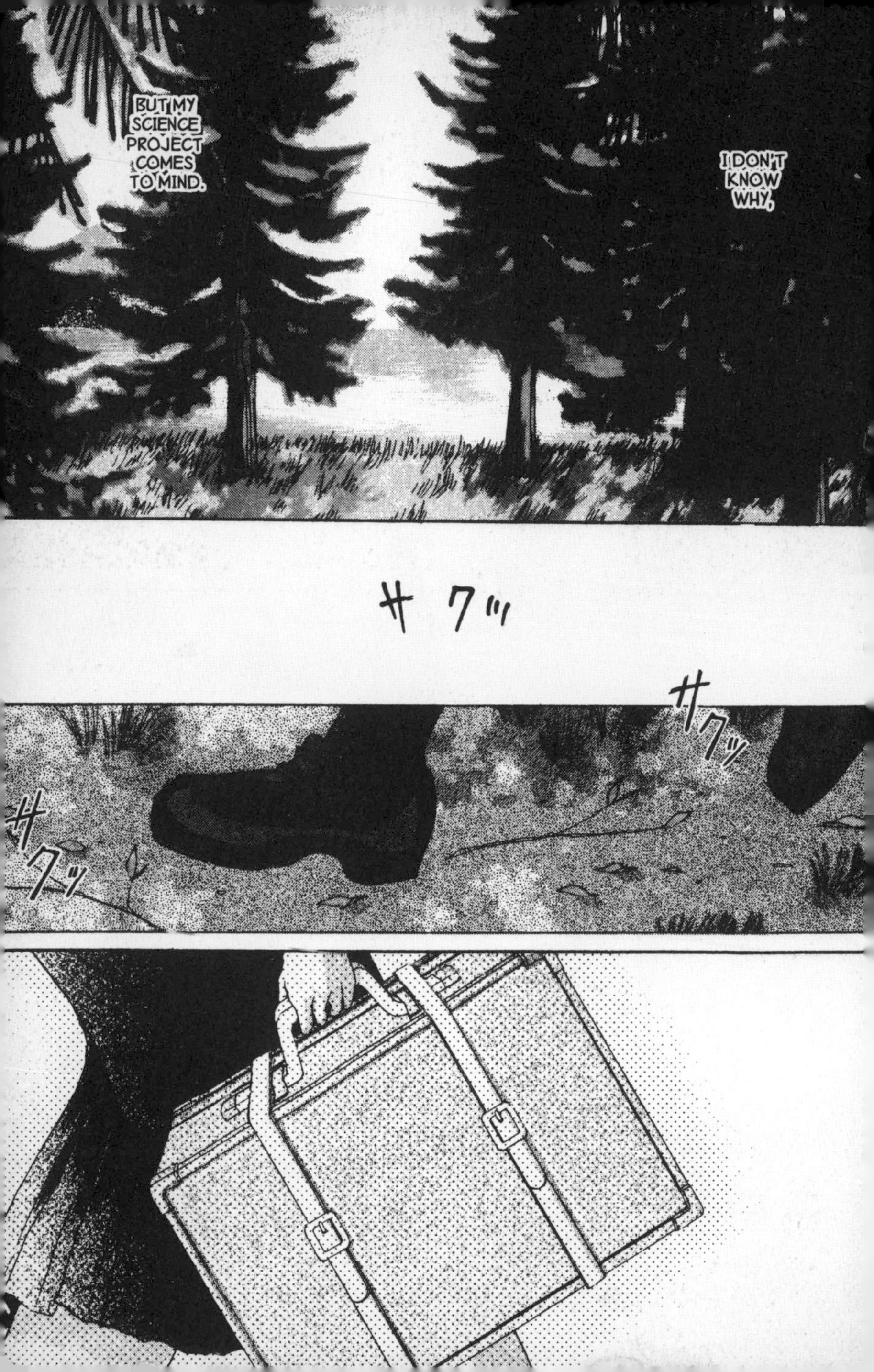
I DON'T KNOW WHY,
BUT MY SCIENCE PROJECT COMES TO MIND.
サクッ
サクッ
サクッ

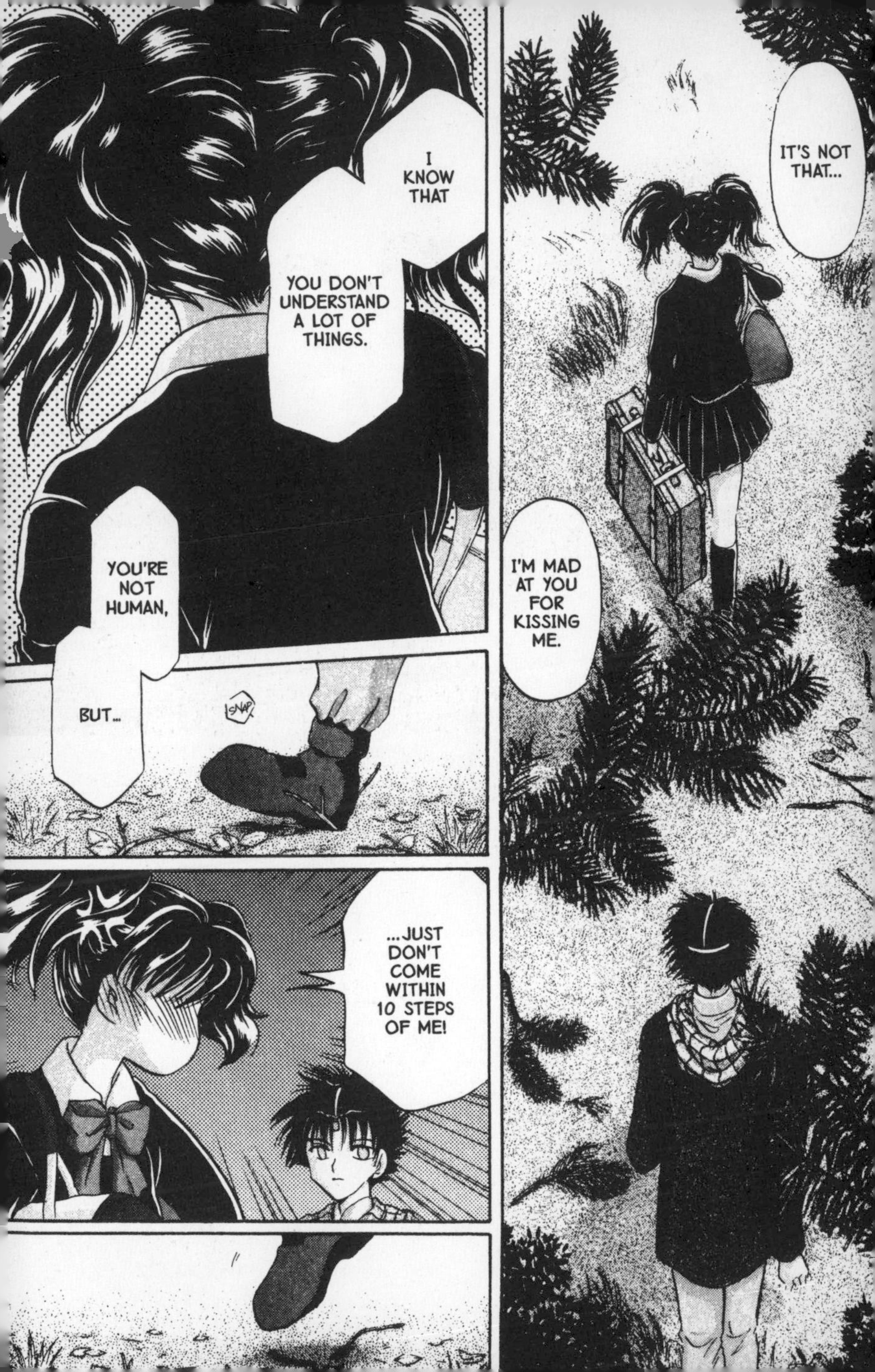
IT'S NOT THAT...
I'M MAD AT YOU FOR KISSING ME.
I KNOW THAT
YOU DON'T UNDERSTAND A LOT OF THINGS.
YOU'RE NOT HUMAN,
BUT...
SNAP
...JUST DON'T COME WITHIN 10 STEPS OF ME!

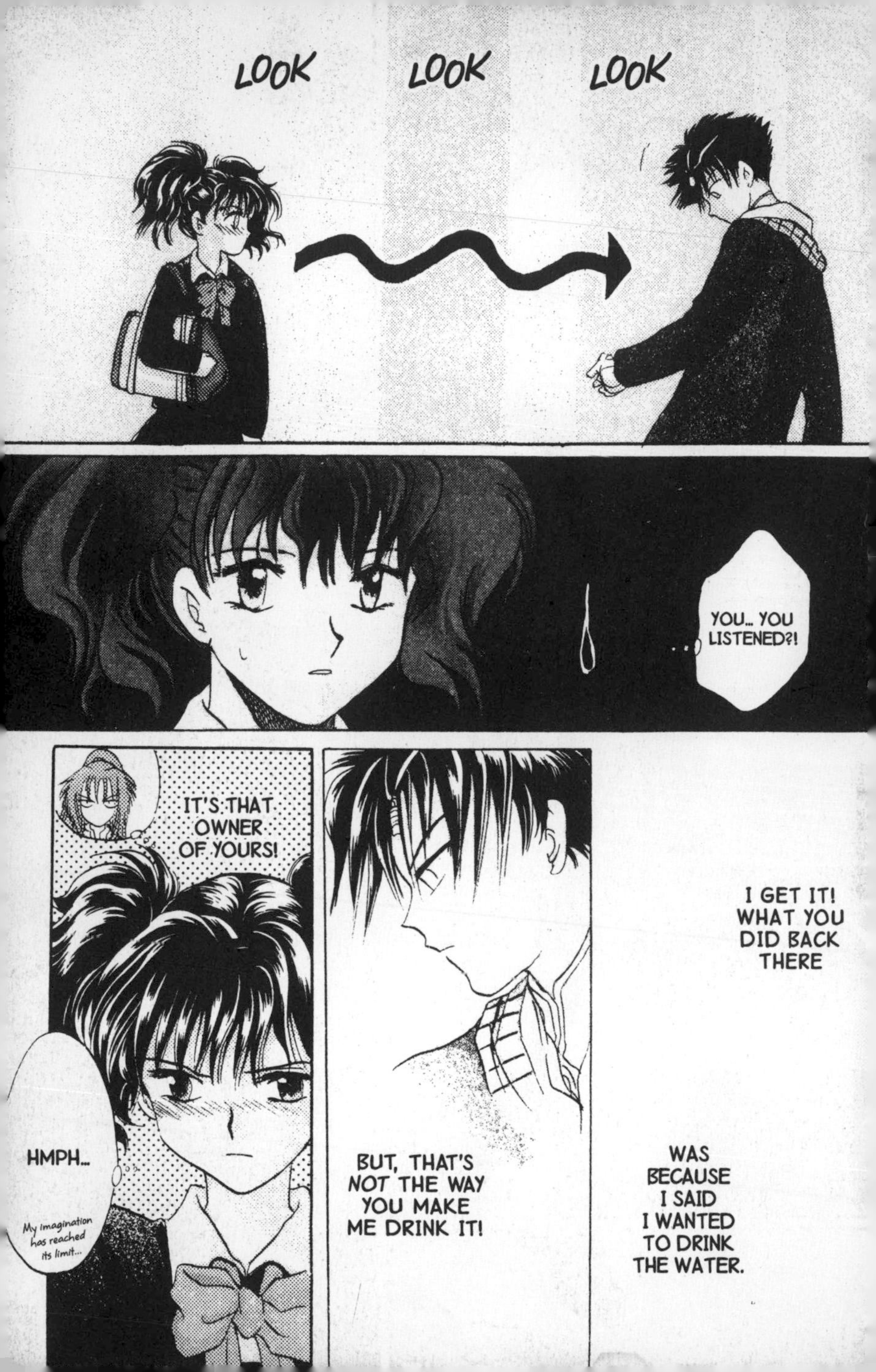
LOOK
LOOK
LOOK
YOU... YOU LISTENED?!
I GET IT! WHAT YOU DID BACK THERE
WAS BECAUSE I SAID I WANTED TO DRINK THE WATER.
BUT, THAT'S NOT THE WAY YOU MAKE ME DRINK IT!
IT'S THAT OWNER OF YOURS!
HMPH...
My imagination has reached its limit...

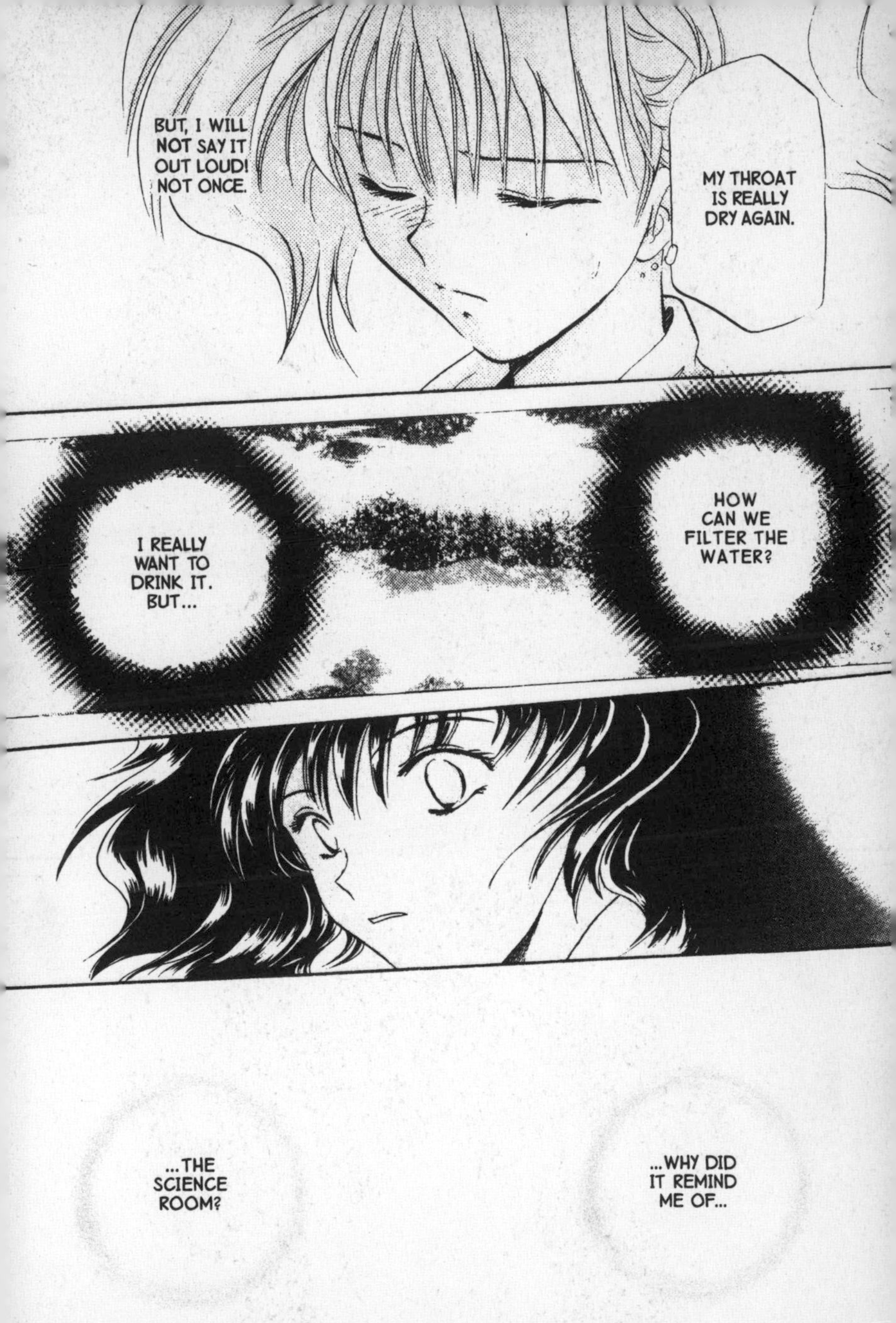
MY THROAT IS REALLY DRY AGAIN.
BUT, I WILL NOT SAY IT OUT LOUD! NOT ONCE.
HOW CAN WE FILTER THE WATER?
I REALLY WANT TO DRINK IT. BUT...
...WHY DID IT REMIND ME OF...
...THE SCIENCE ROOM?

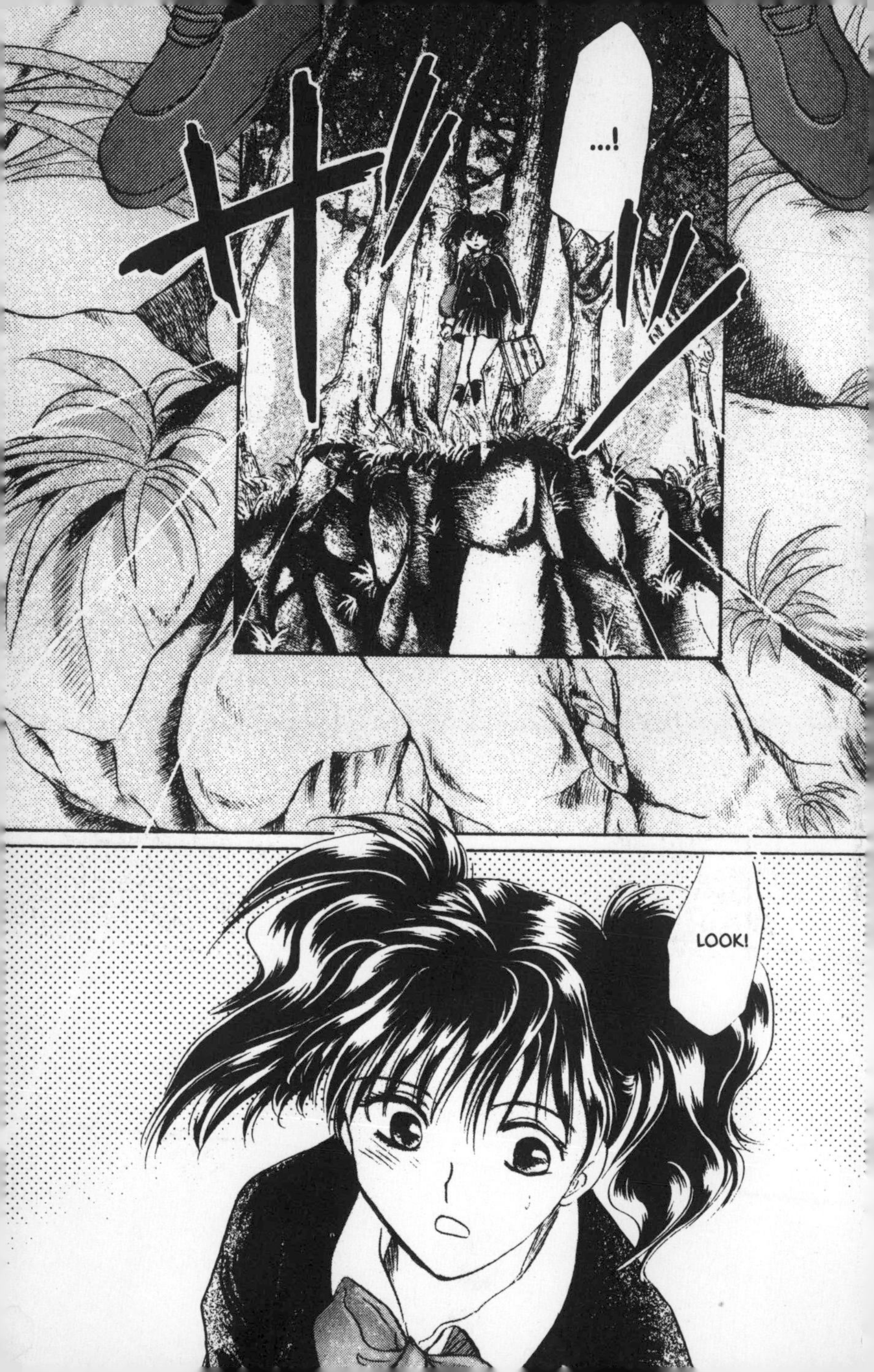
...!
LOOK!

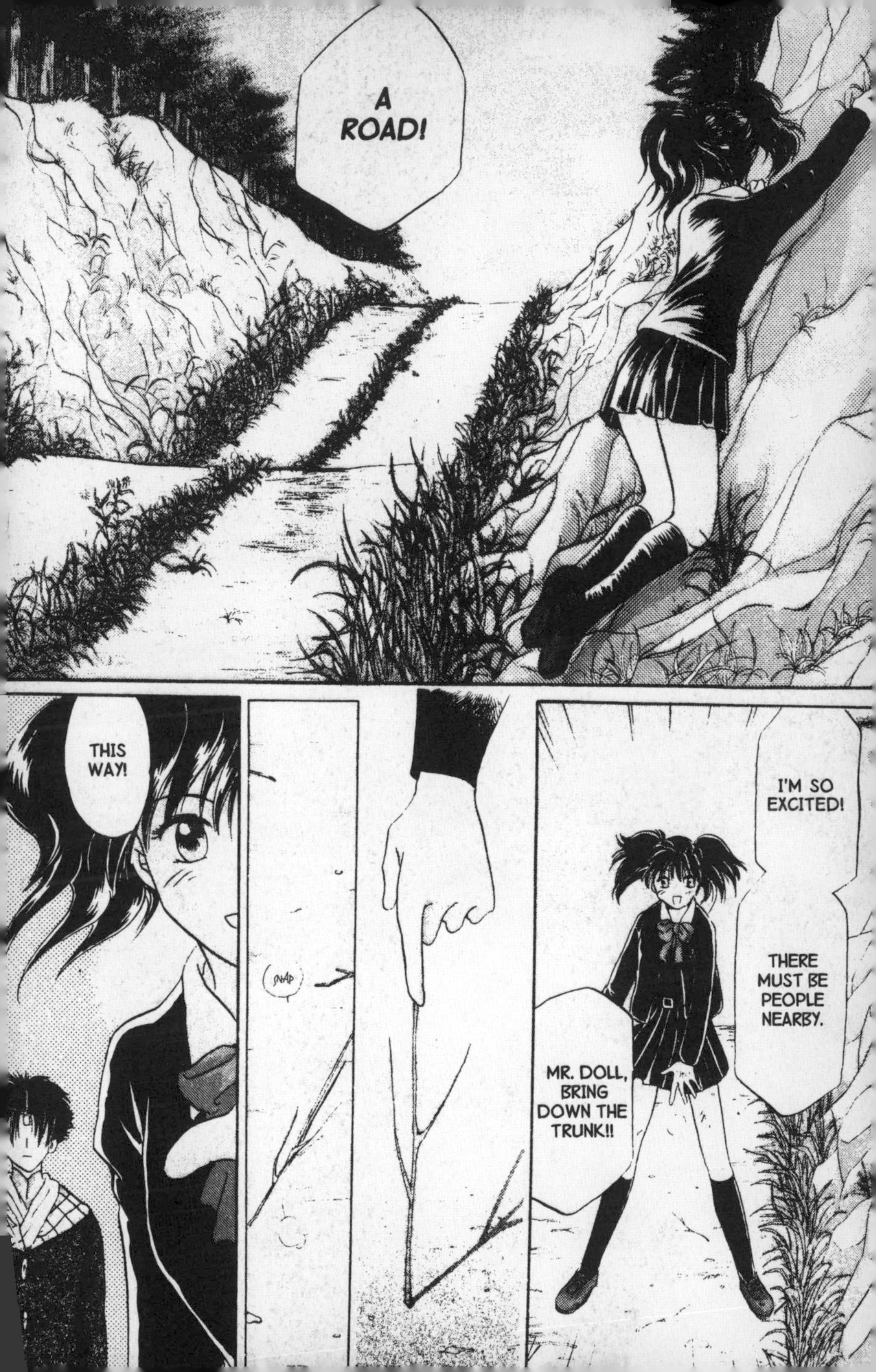
A ROAD!
I'M SO EXCITED!
THERE MUST BE PEOPLE NEARBY.
MR. DOLL, BRING DOWN THE TRUNK!!
SNAP
THIS WAY!

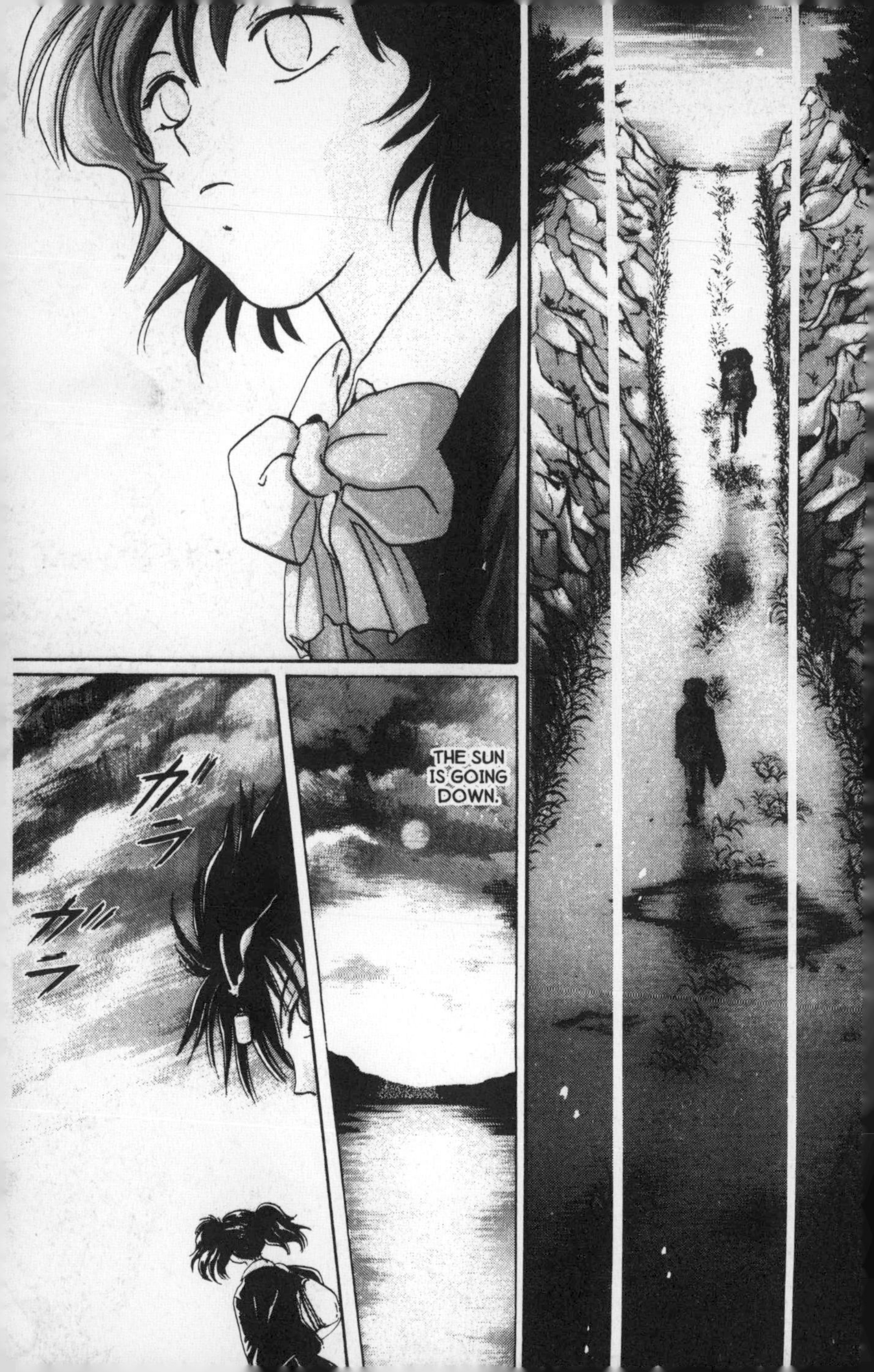
THE SUN IS GOING DOWN.
ガラ
ガラ

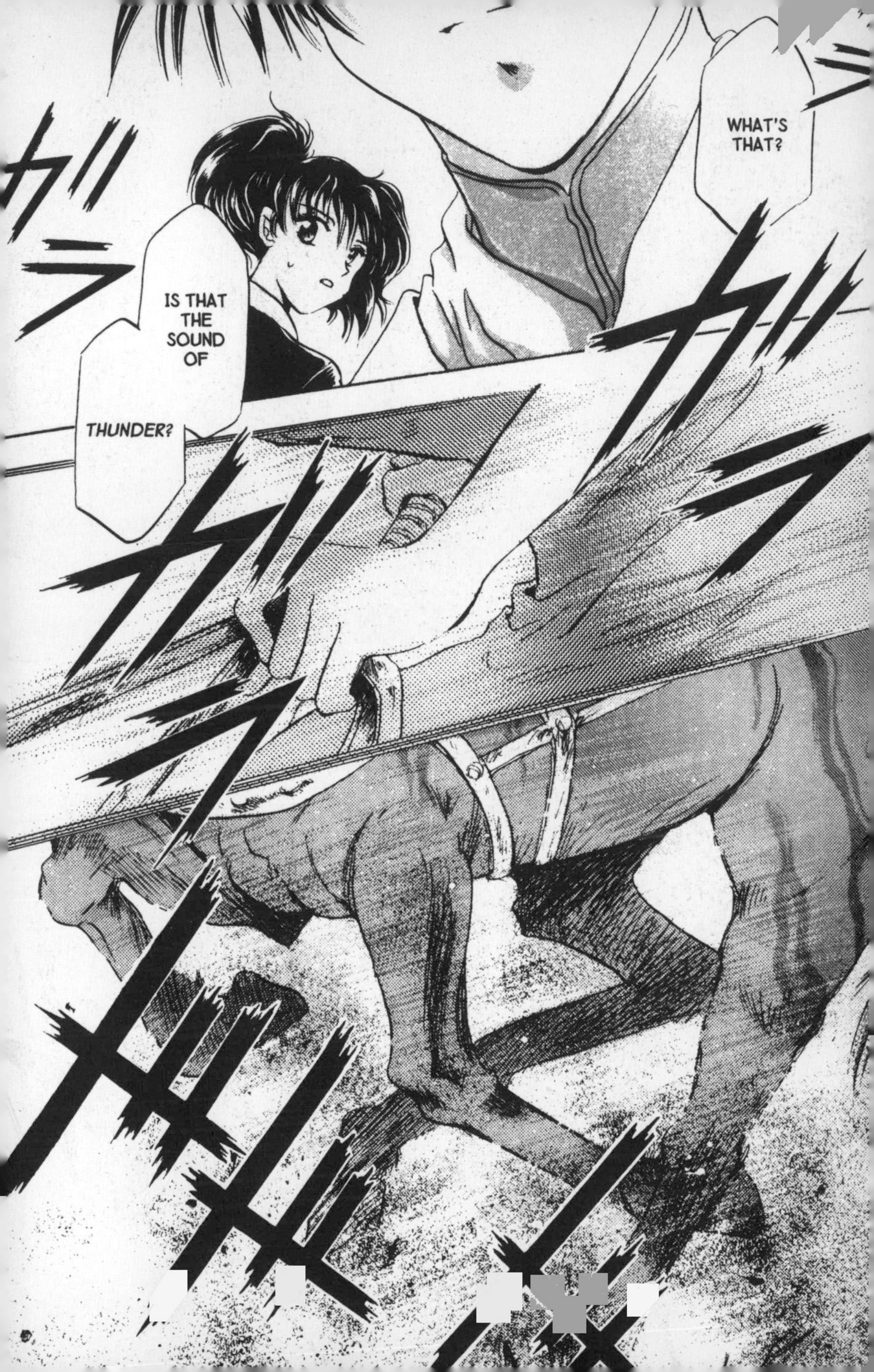
WHAT'S THAT?
IS THAT THE SOUND OF THUNDER?

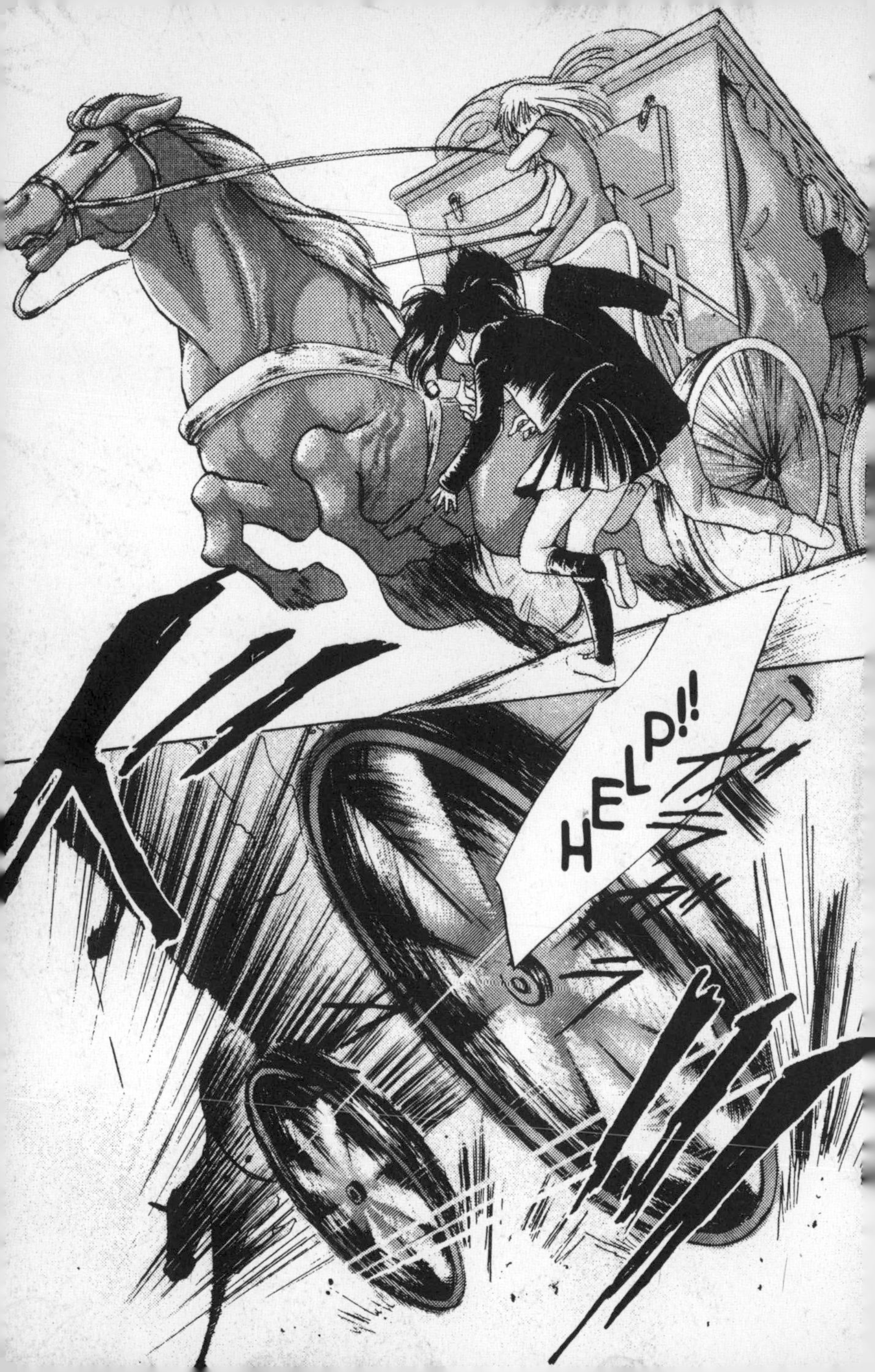
HELP!!

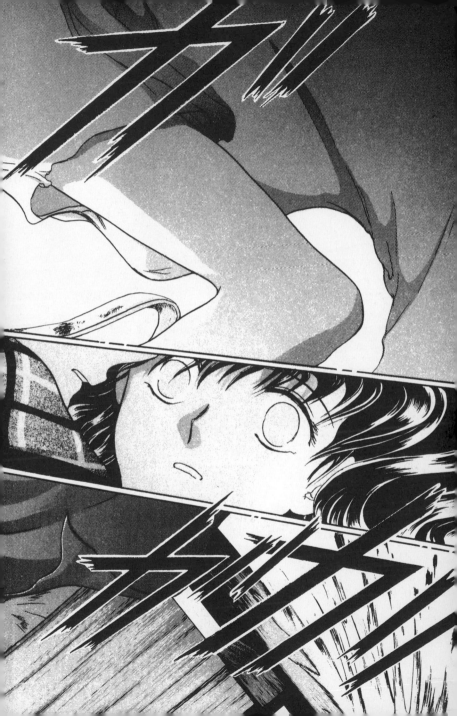

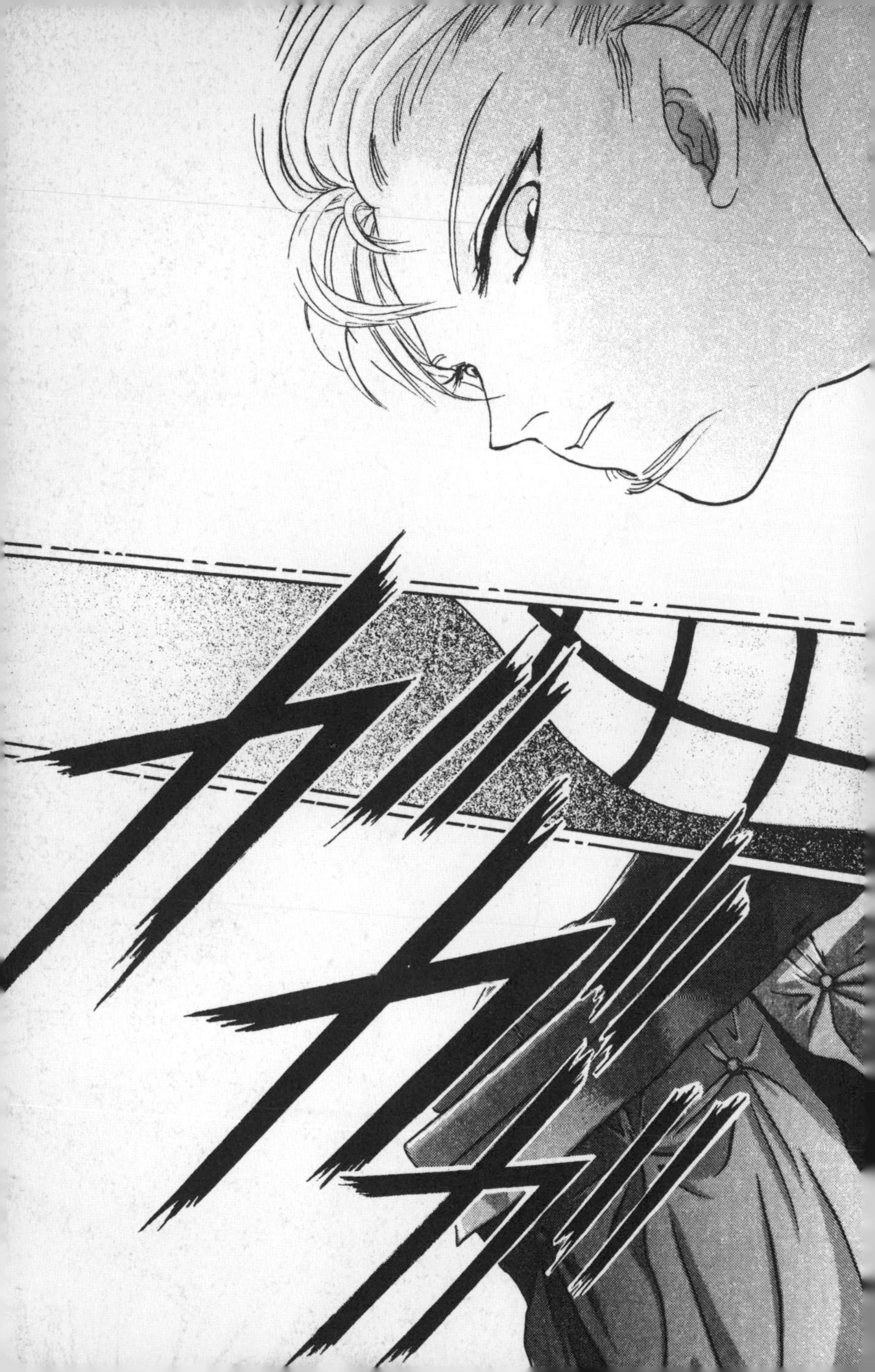

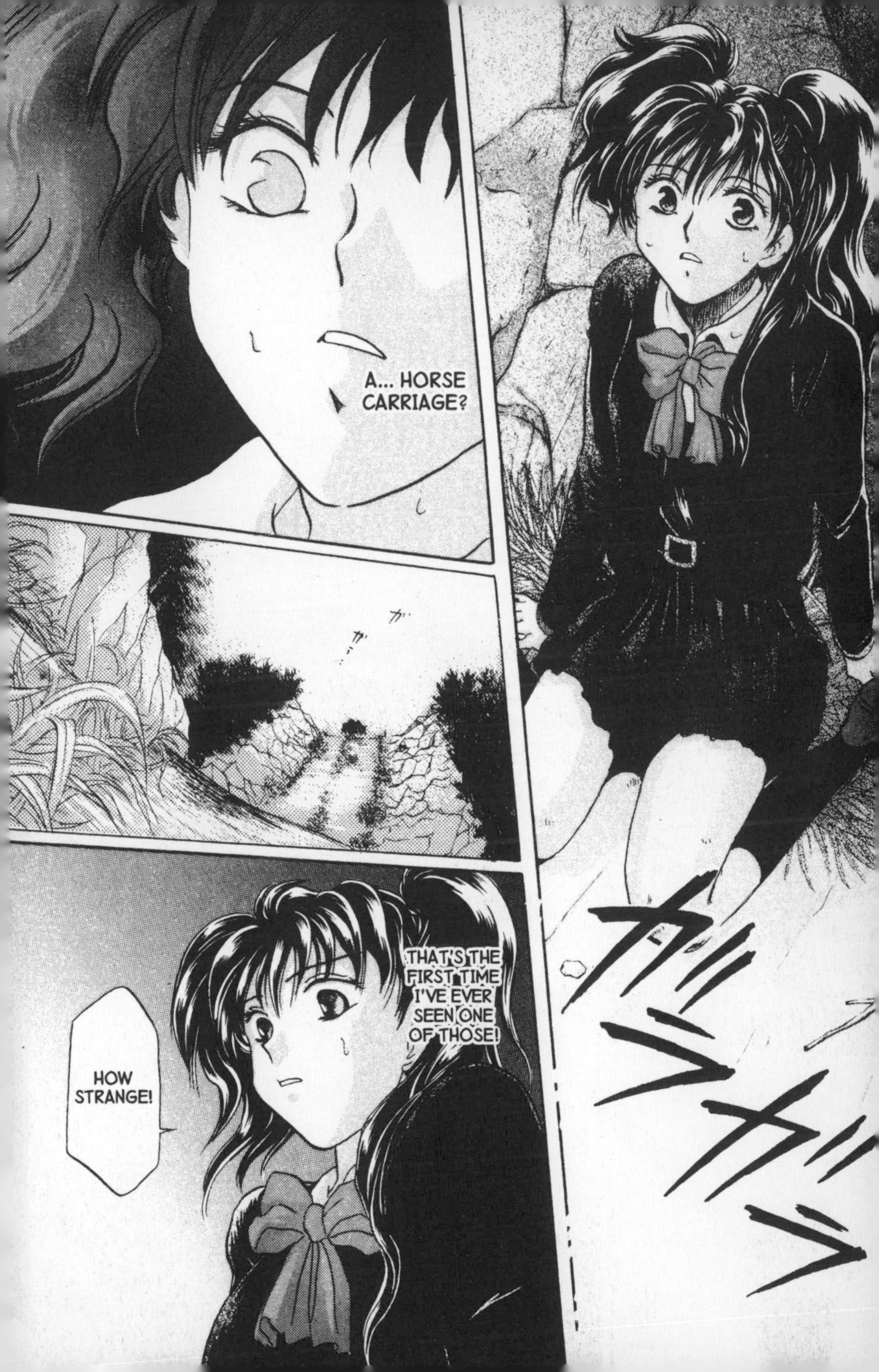
ガラガラ
A... HORSE CARRIAGE?
THAT'S THE FIRST TIME I'VE EVER SEEN ONE OF THOSE!
HOW STRANGE!

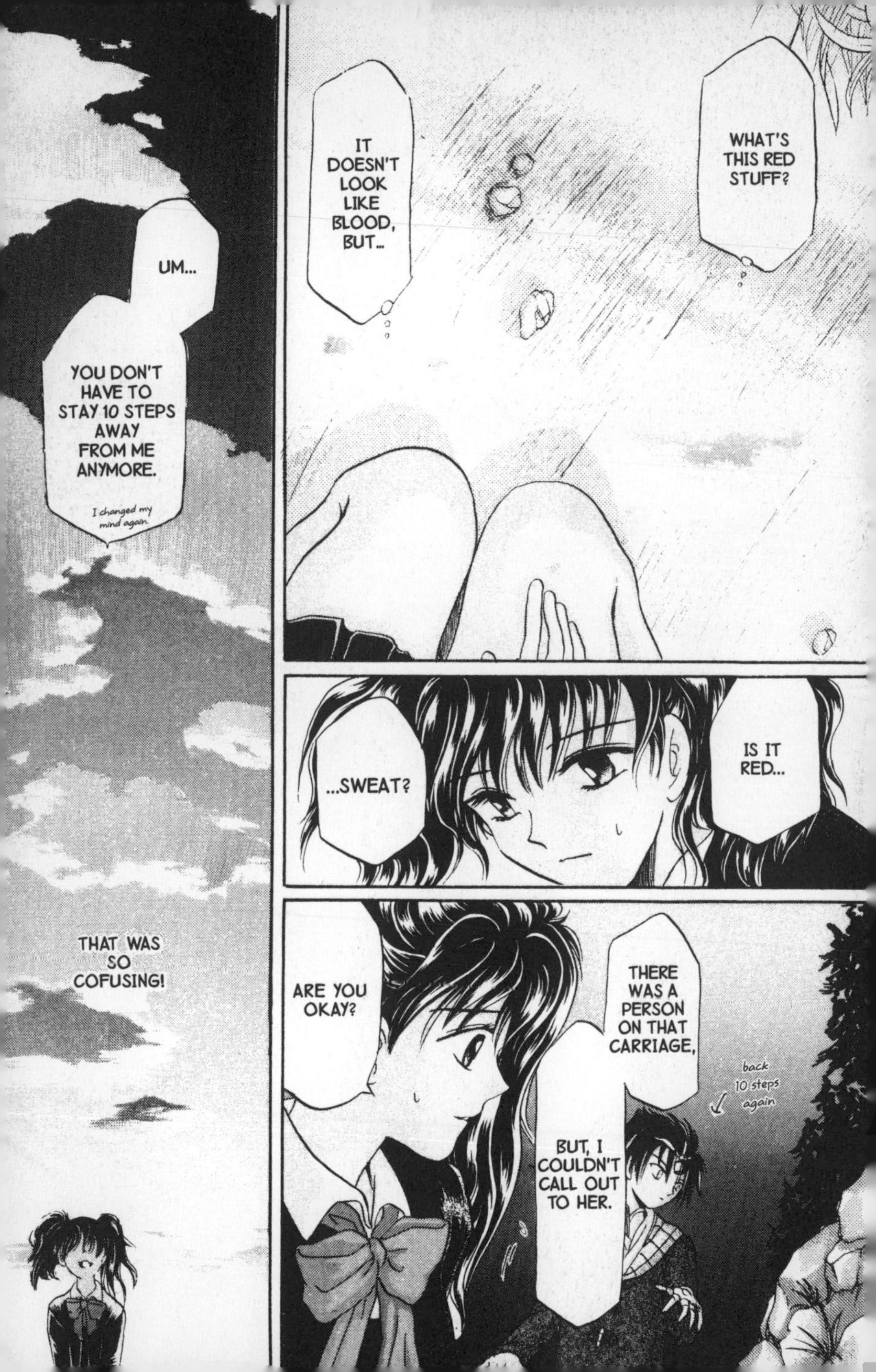
WHAT'S THIS RED STUFF?
IT DOESN'T LOOK LIKE BLOOD, BUT...
IS IT RED...
...SWEAT?
THERE WAS A PERSON ON THAT CARRIAGE,
back 10 steps again
BUT, I COULDN'T CALL OUT TO HER.
ARE YOU OKAY?
UM...
YOU DON'T HAVE TO STAY 10 STEPS AWAY FROM ME ANYMORE.
I changed my mind again.
THAT WAS SO COFUSING!

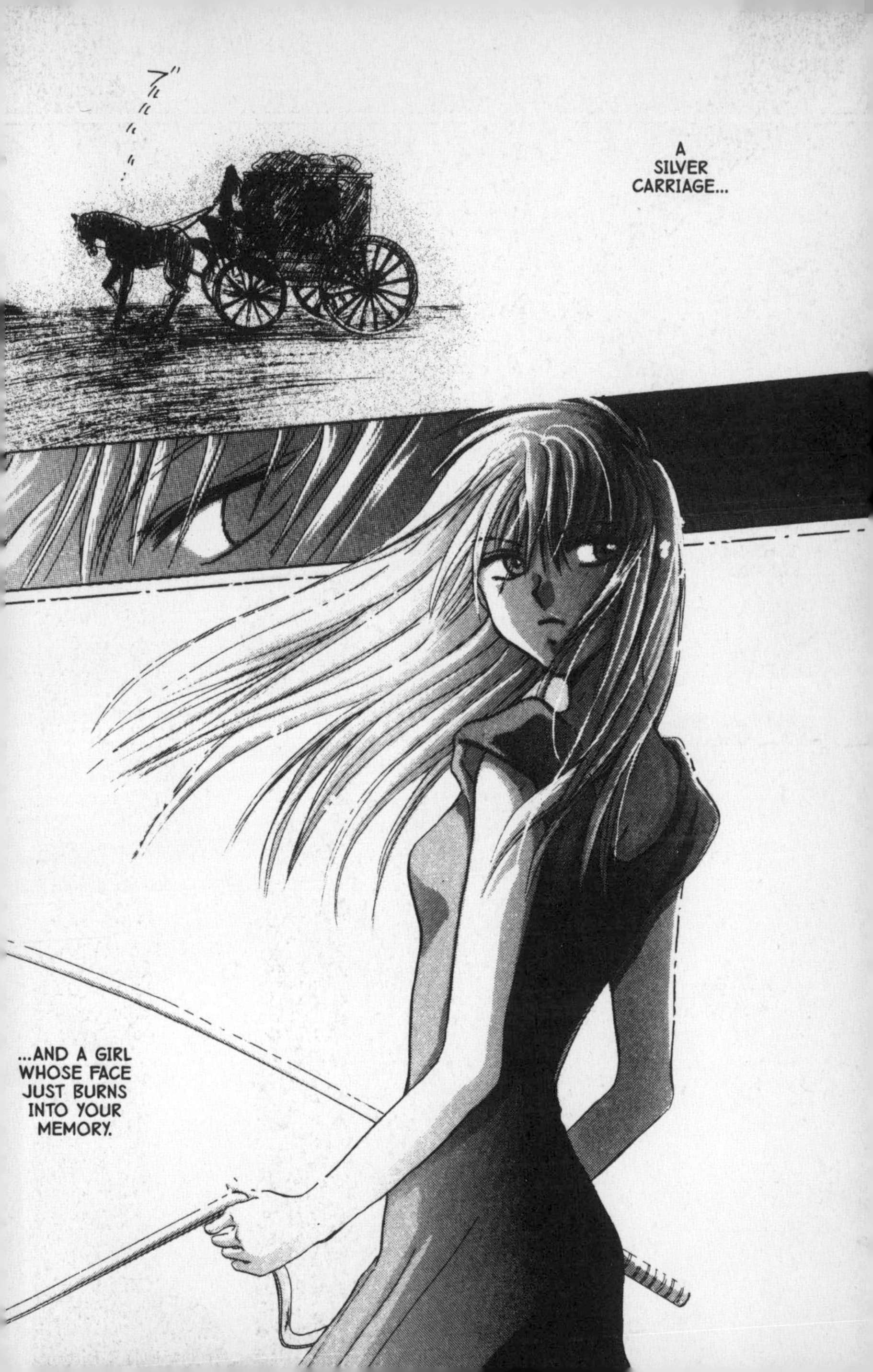
A SILVER CARRIAGE...
...AND A GIRL WHOSE FACE JUST BURNS INTO YOUR MEMORY.

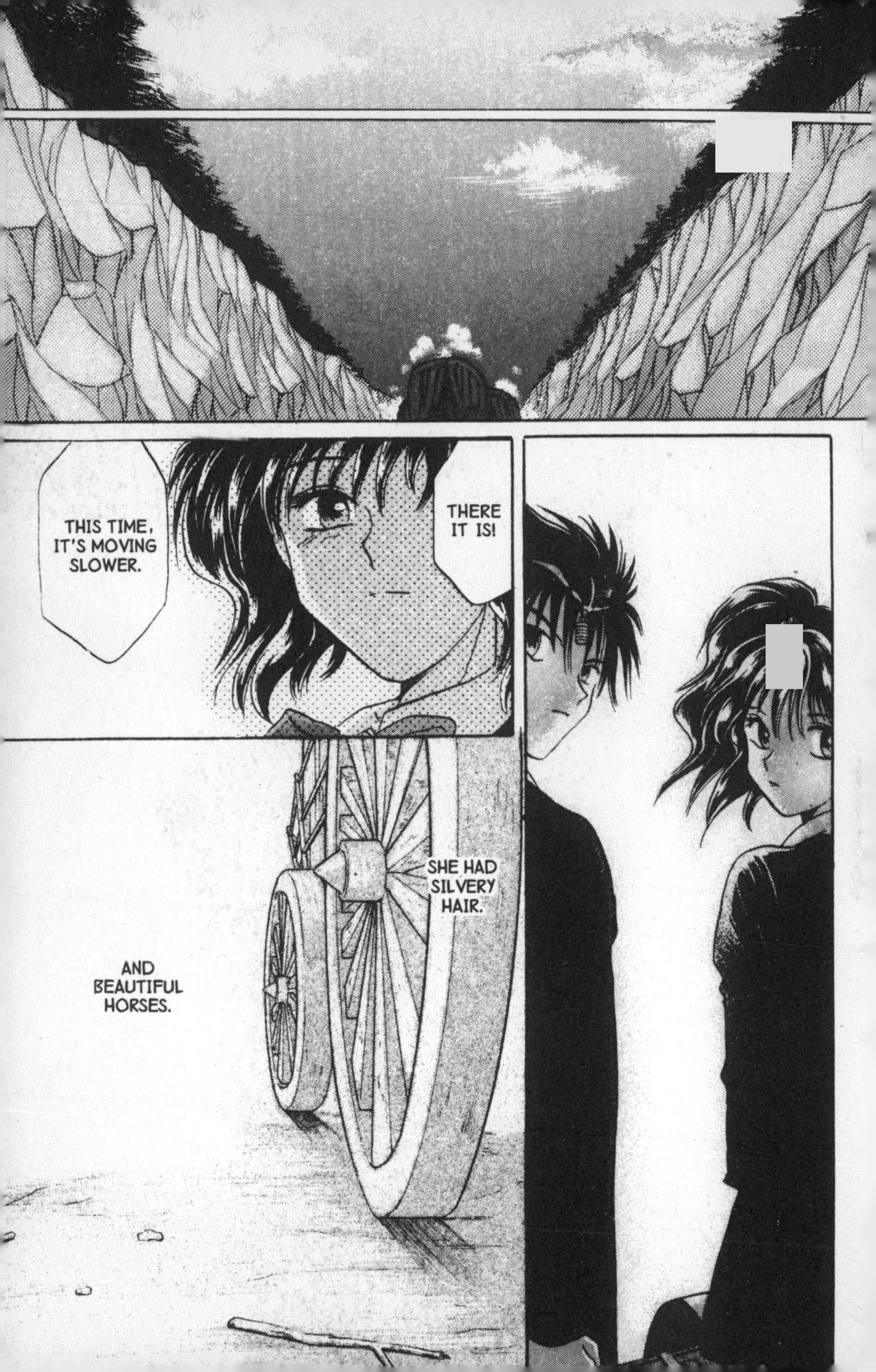
THERE IT IS!
THIS TIME, IT'S MOVING SLOWER.
SHE HAD SILVERY HAIR.
AND BEAUTIFUL HORSES.

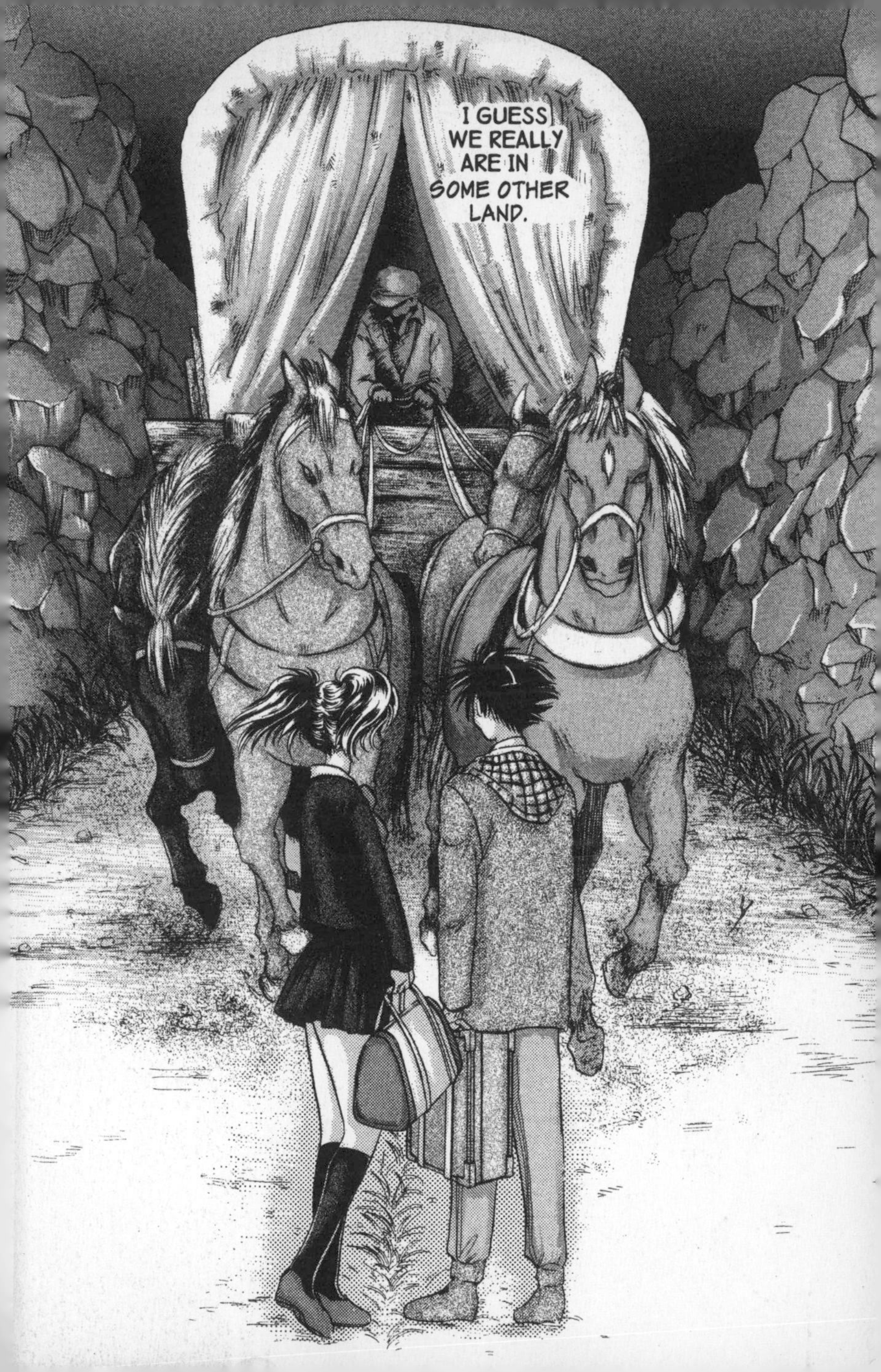
I GUESS WE REALLY ARE IN SOME OTHER LAND.

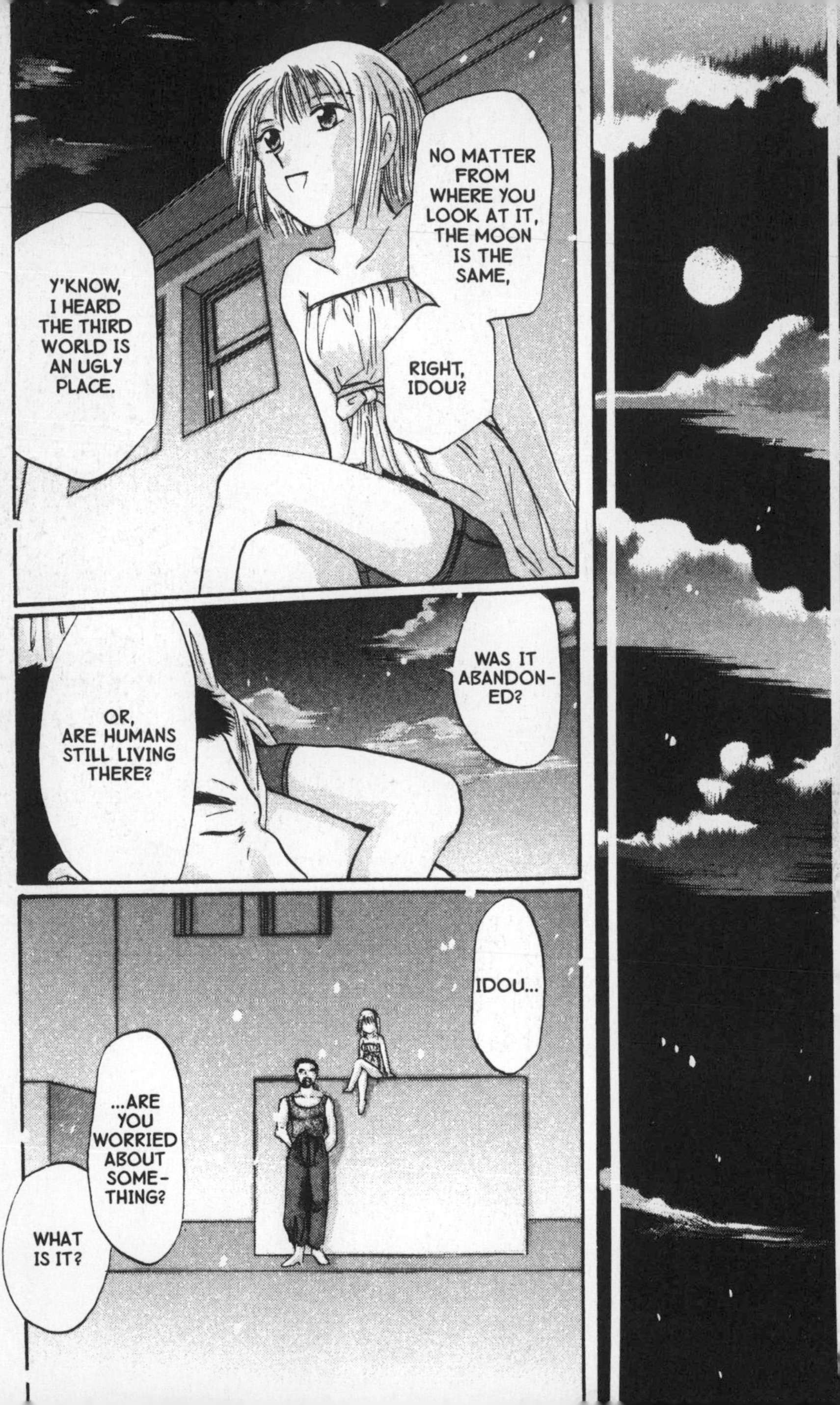

NO MATTER FROM WHERE YOU LOOK AT IT, THE MOON IS THE SAME,
RIGHT, IDOU?
Y'KNOW, I HEARD THE THIRD WORLD IS AN UGLY PLACE.
WAS IT ABANDON-ED?
OR, ARE HUMANS STILL LIVING THERE?
IDOU...
...ARE YOU WORRIED ABOUT SOME-THING?
WHAT IS IT?

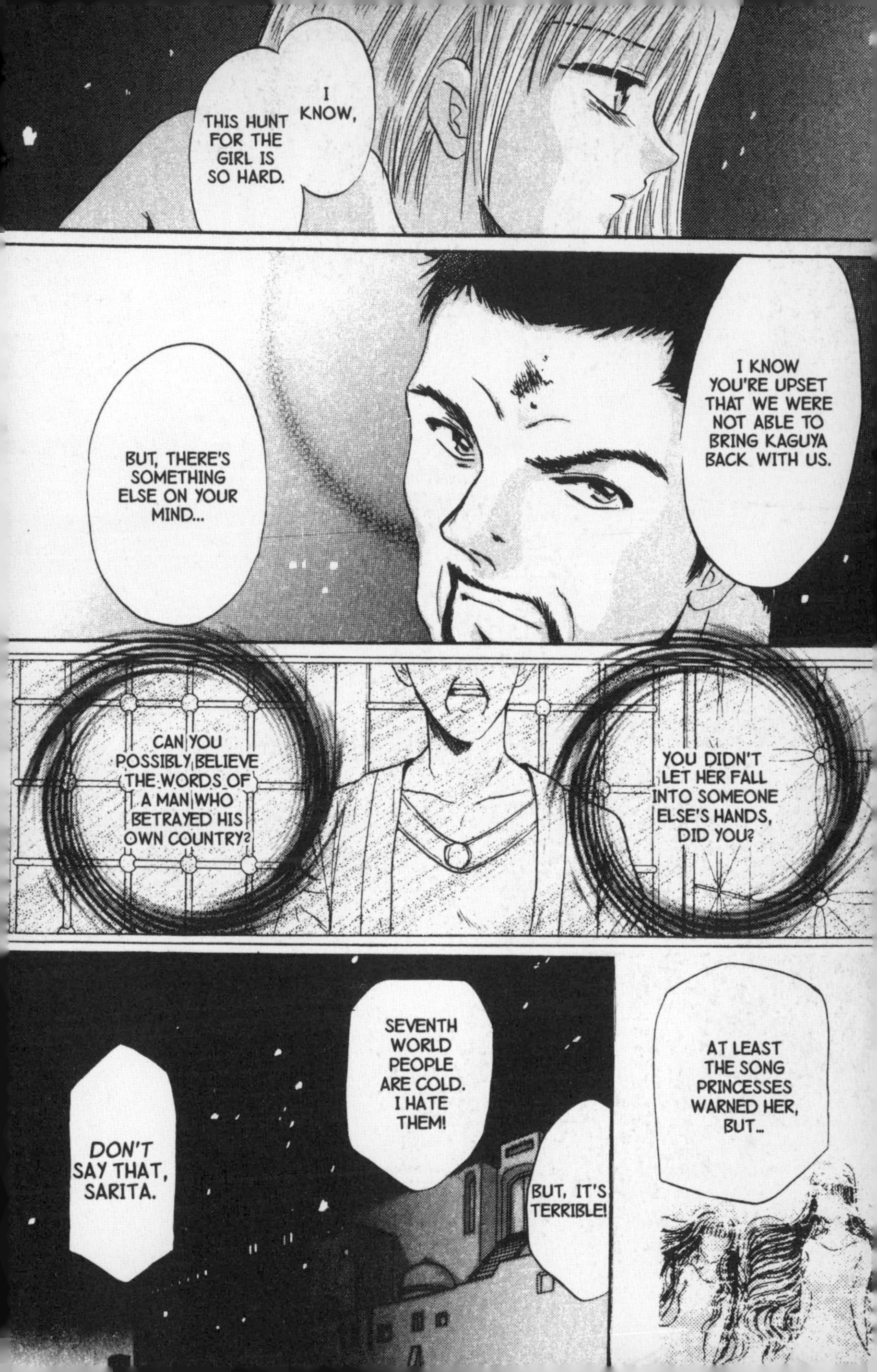
I KNOW, THIS HUNT FOR THE GIRL IS SO HARD.
I KNOW YOU'RE UPSET THAT WE WERE NOT ABLE TO BRING KAGUYA BACK WITH US.
BUT, THERE'S SOMETHING ELSE ON YOUR MIND...
YOU DIDN'T LET HER FALL INTO SOMEONE ELSE'S HANDS, DID YOU?
CAN YOU POSSIBLY BELIEVE THE WORDS OF A MAN WHO BETRAYED HIS OWN COUNTRY?
AT LEAST THE SONG PRINCESSES WARNED HER, BUT...
SEVENTH WORLD PEOPLE ARE COLD. I HATE THEM!
DON'T SAY THAT, SARITA.
BUT, IT'S TERRIBLE!

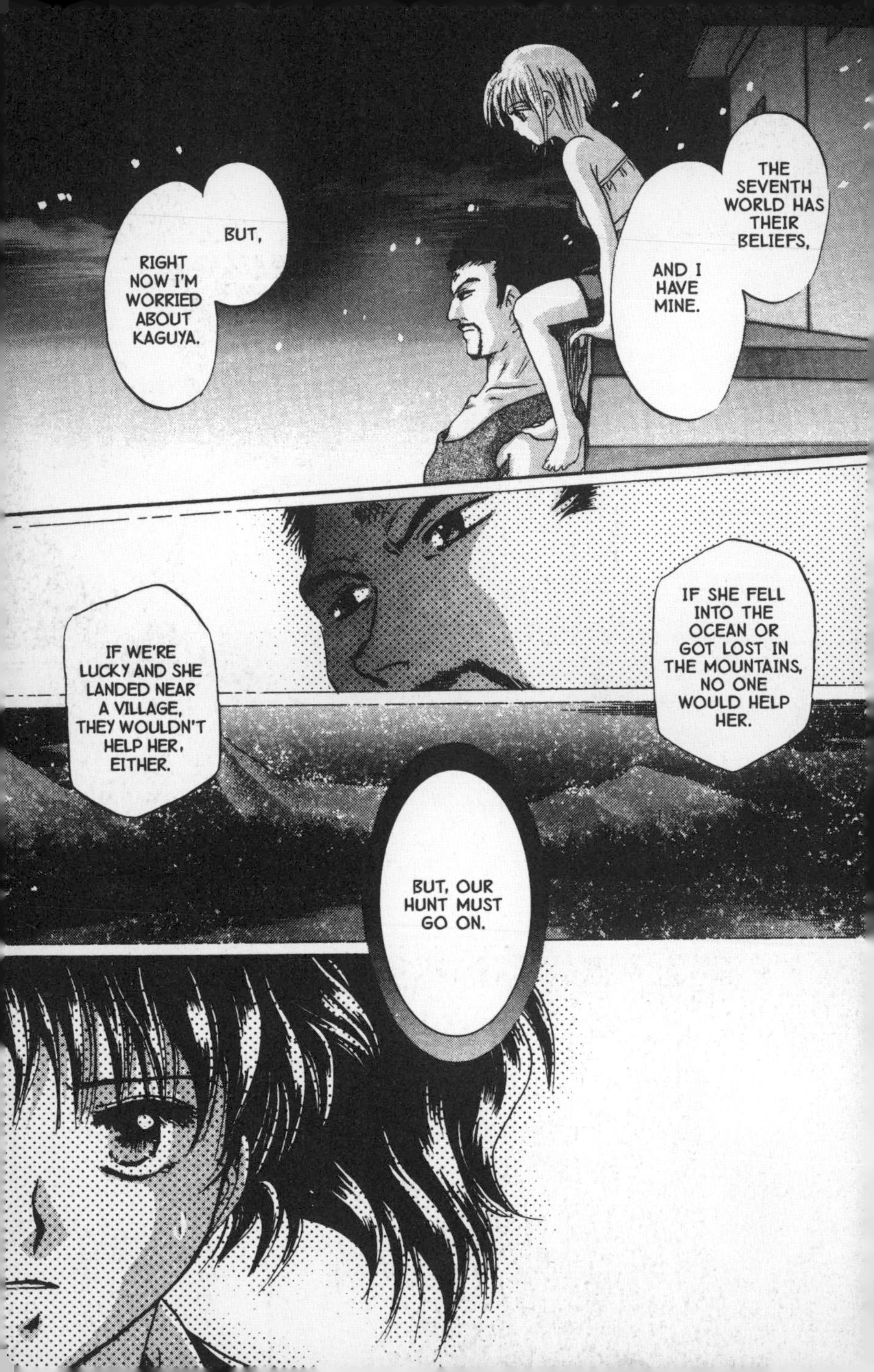
THE SEVENTH WORLD HAS THEIR BELIEFS,
AND I HAVE MINE.
BUT,
RIGHT NOW I'M WORRIED ABOUT KAGUYA.
IF SHE FELL INTO THE OCEAN OR GOT LOST IN THE MOUNTAINS, NO ONE WOULD HELP HER.
IF WE'RE LUCKY AND SHE LANDED NEAR A VILLAGE, THEY WOULDN'T HELP HER, EITHER.
BUT, OUR HUNT MUST GO ON.

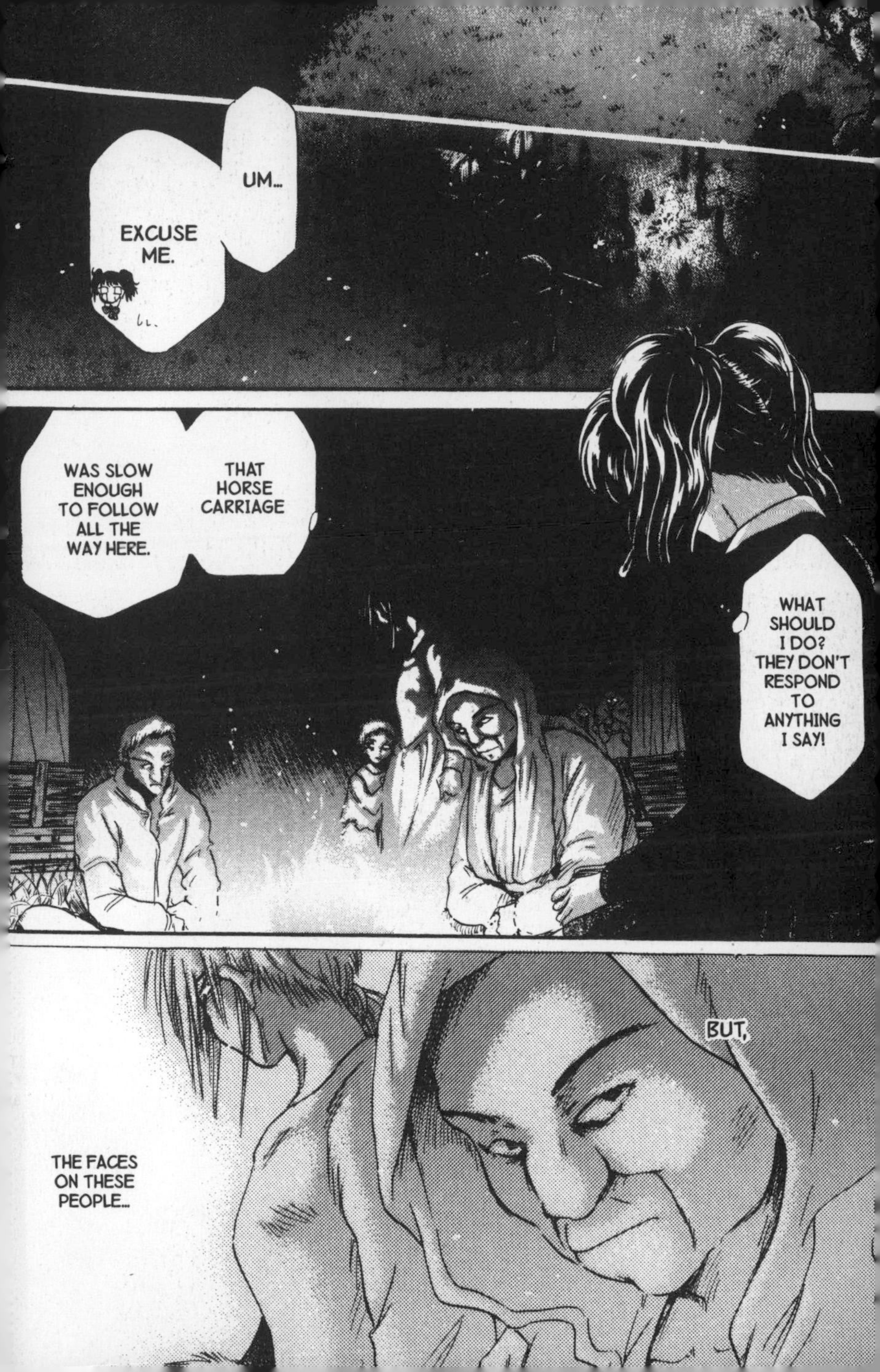

UM...
EXCUSE ME.
WHAT SHOULD I DO? THEY DON'T RESPOND TO ANYTHING I SAY!
THAT HORSE CARRIAGE
WAS SLOW ENOUGH TO FOLLOW ALL THE WAY HERE.
BUT,
THE FACES ON THESE PEOPLE...

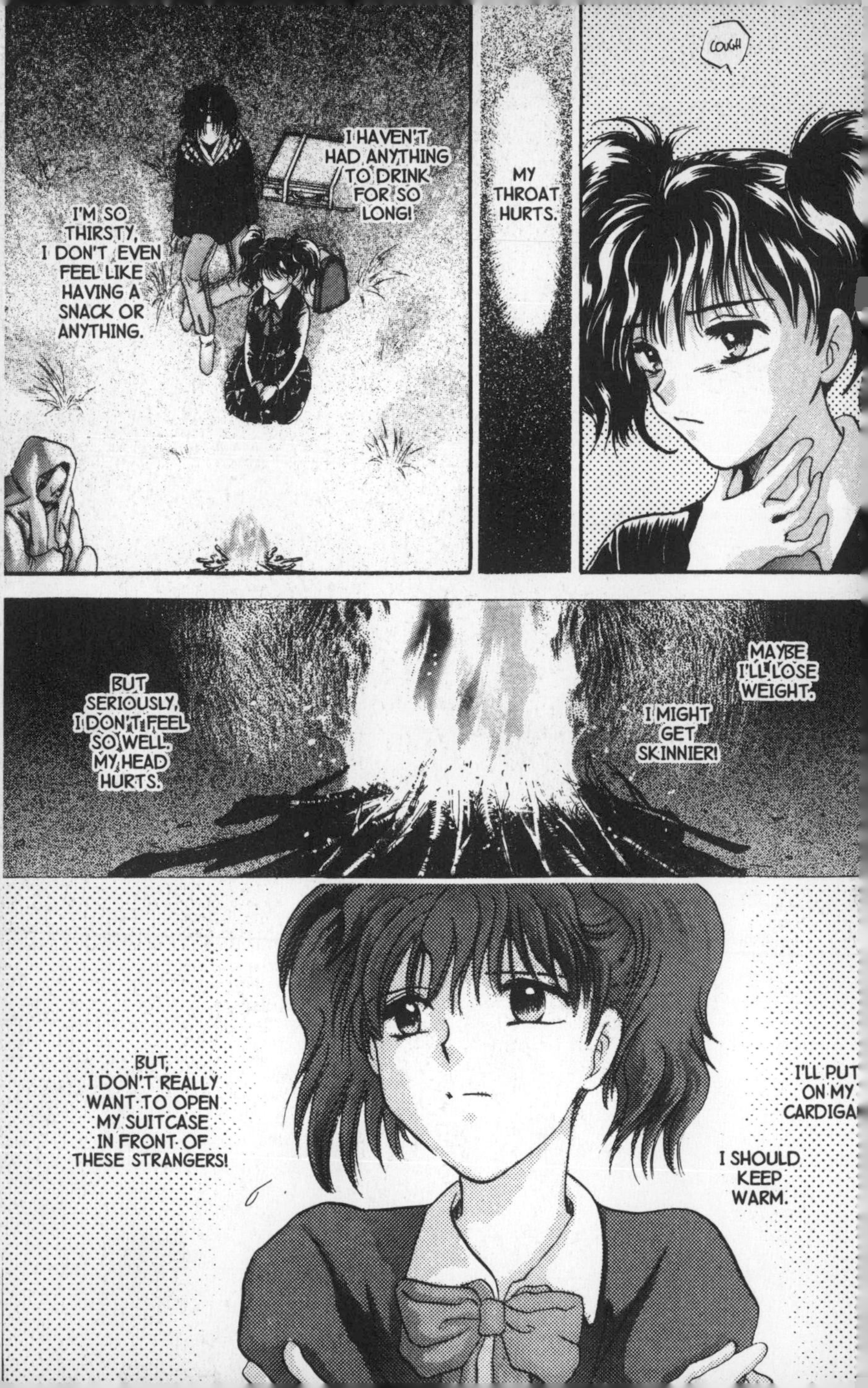
COUGH
MY THROAT HURTS.
I HAVEN'T HAD ANYTHING TO DRINK FOR SO LONG!
I'M SO THIRSTY, I DON'T EVEN FEEL LIKE HAVING A SNACK OR ANYTHING.
MAYBE I'LL LOSE WEIGHT.
I MIGHT GET SKINNIER!
BUT SERIOUSLY, I DON'T FEEL SO WELL. MY HEAD HURTS.
I'LL PUT ON MY CARDIGA
I SHOULD KEEP WARM.
BUT, I DON'T REALLY WANT TO OPEN MY SUITCASE IN FRONT OF THESE STRANGERS!

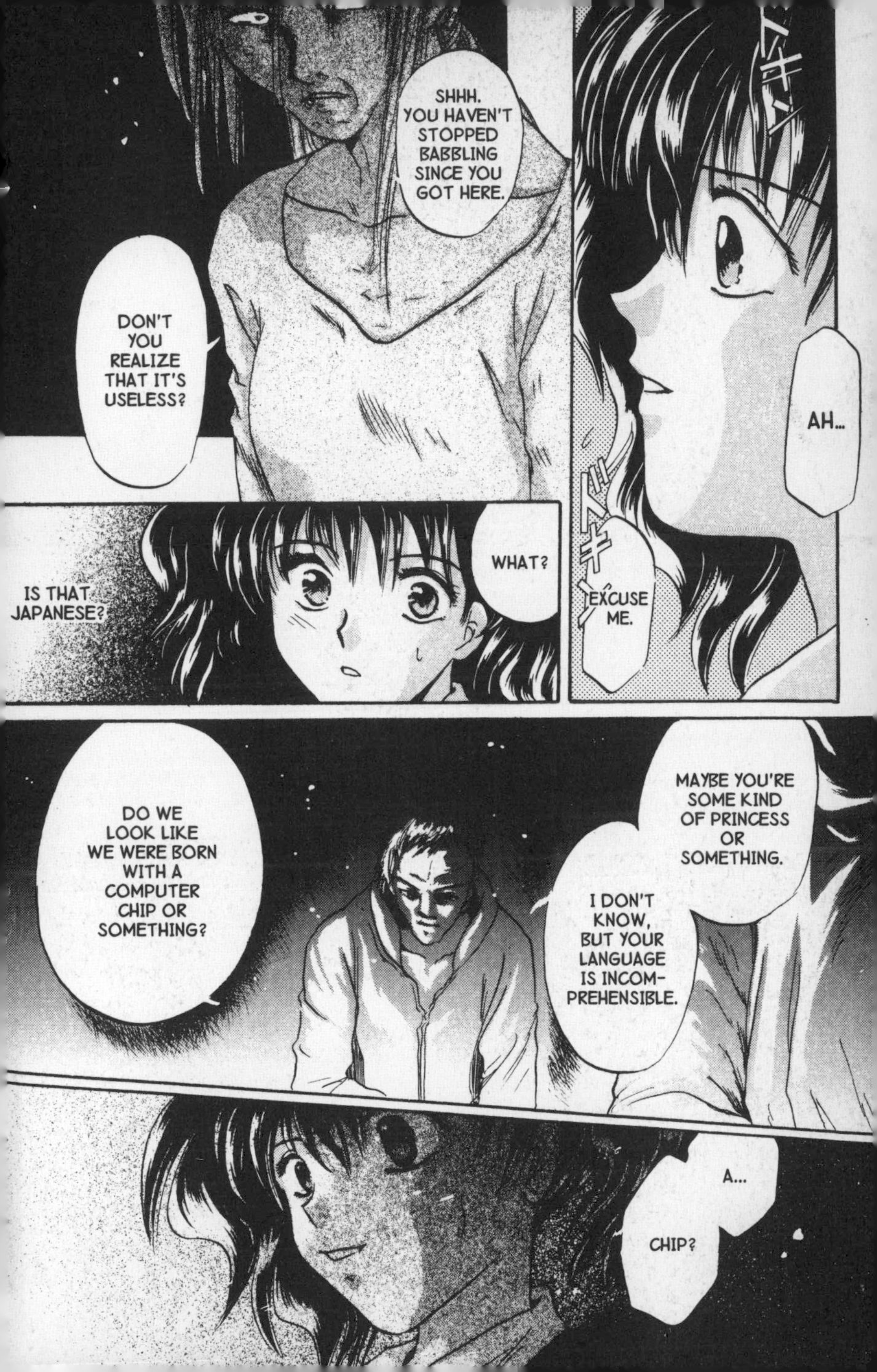
AH...
EXCUSE ME.
SHHH. YOU HAVEN'T STOPPED BABBLING SINCE YOU GOT HERE.
DON'T YOU REALIZE THAT IT'S USELESS?
WHAT?
IS THAT JAPANESE?
MAYBE YOU'RE SOME KIND OF PRINCESS OR SOMETHING.
I DON'T KNOW, BUT YOUR LANGUAGE IS INCOM-PREHENSIBLE.
DO WE LOOK LIKE WE WERE BORN WITH A COMPUTER CHIP OR SOMETHING?
A...
CHIP?

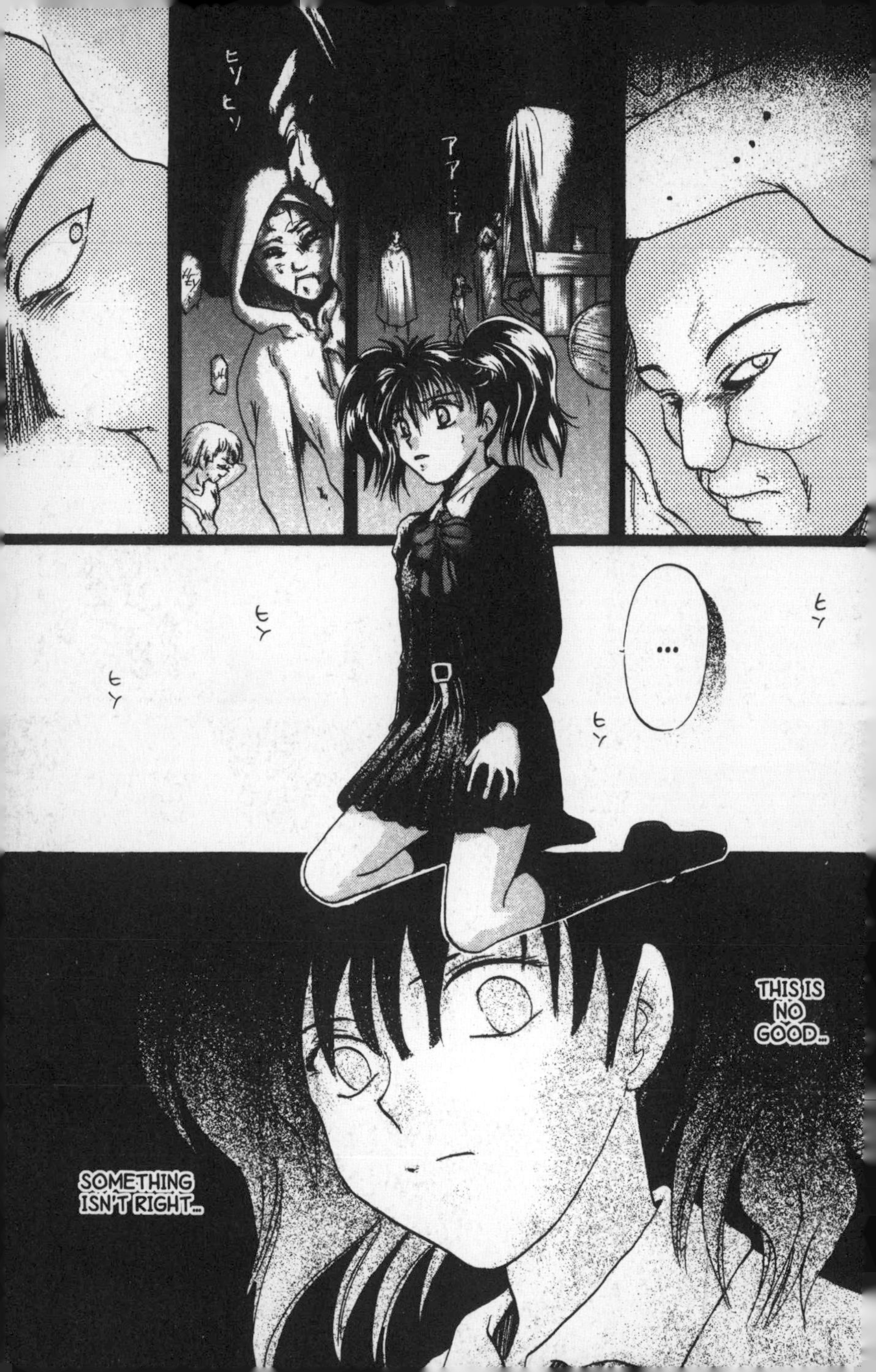
アア…ア
ヒソヒソ
ヒソ
...
ヒソ
ヒソ
ヒソ
THIS IS NO GOOD..
SOMETHING ISN'T RIGHT..

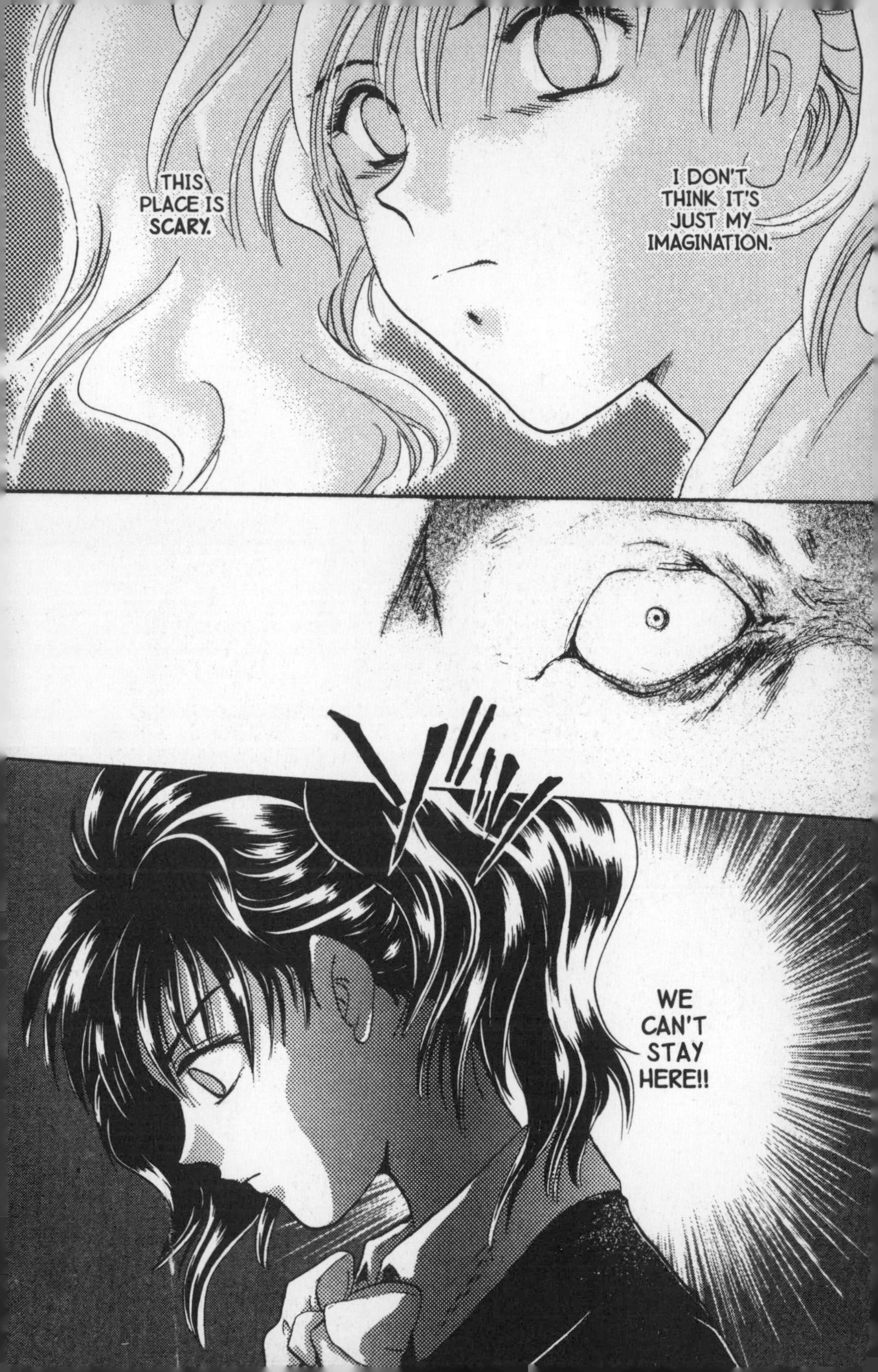
I DON'T THINK IT'S JUST MY IMAGINATION.
THIS PLACE IS SCARY.
WE CAN'T STAY HERE!!

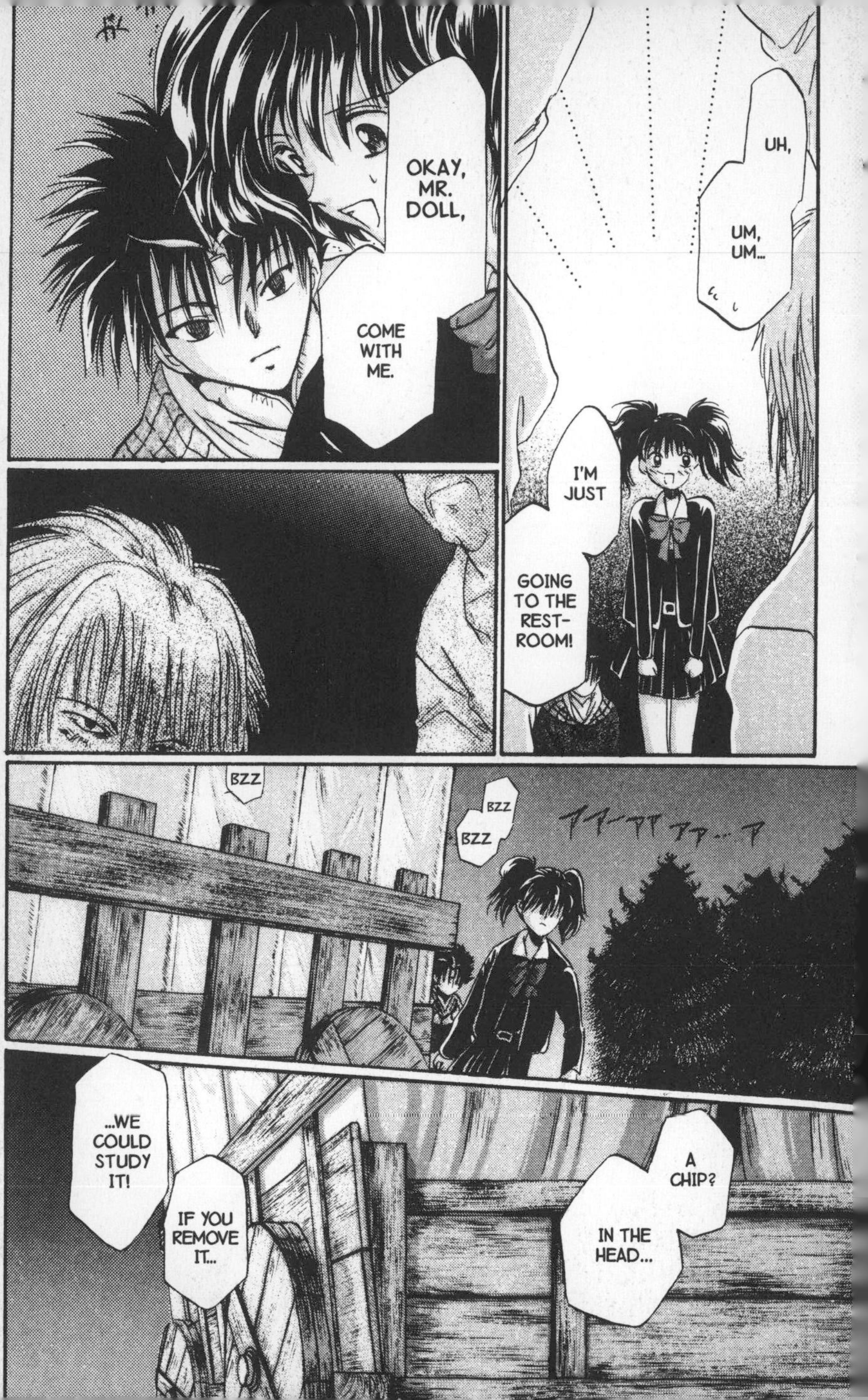
UH,
UM, UM...
I'M JUST
GOING TO THE REST-ROOM!
OKAY, MR. DOLL,
COME WITH ME.
BZZ
BZZ
BZZ
A CHIP?
IN THE HEAD...
IF YOU REMOVE IT...
...WE COULD STUDY IT!

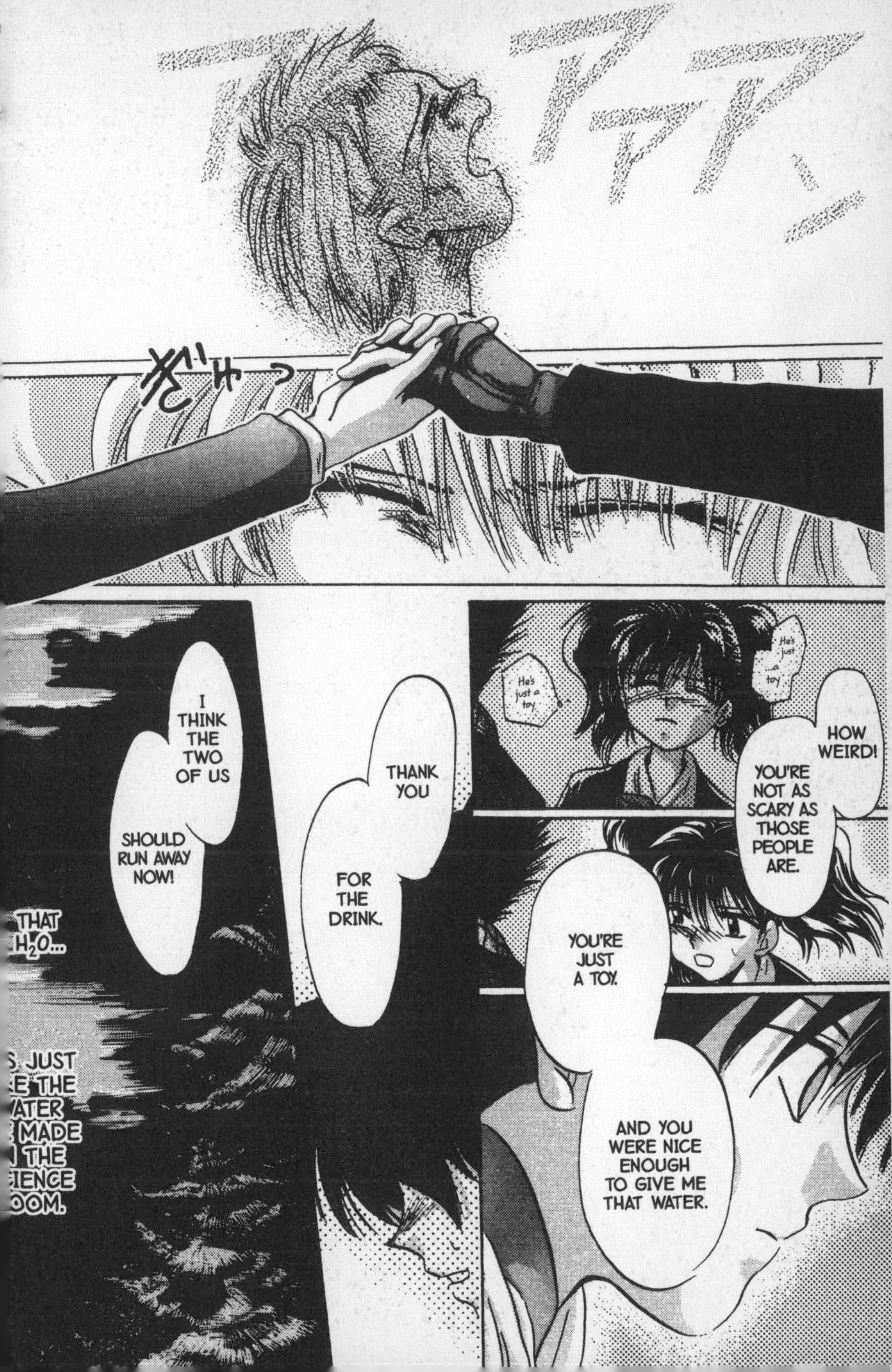
He's just ...a toy.
He's just a toy.
HOW WEIRD!
YOU'RE NOT AS SCARY AS THOSE PEOPLE ARE.
YOU'RE JUST A TOY.
AND YOU WERE NICE ENOUGH TO GIVE ME THAT WATER.
THANK YOU
FOR THE DRINK.
I THINK THE TWO OF US
SHOULD RUN AWAY NOW!
THAT H_2O...
S JUST E THE ATER MADE N THE CIENCE OOM.

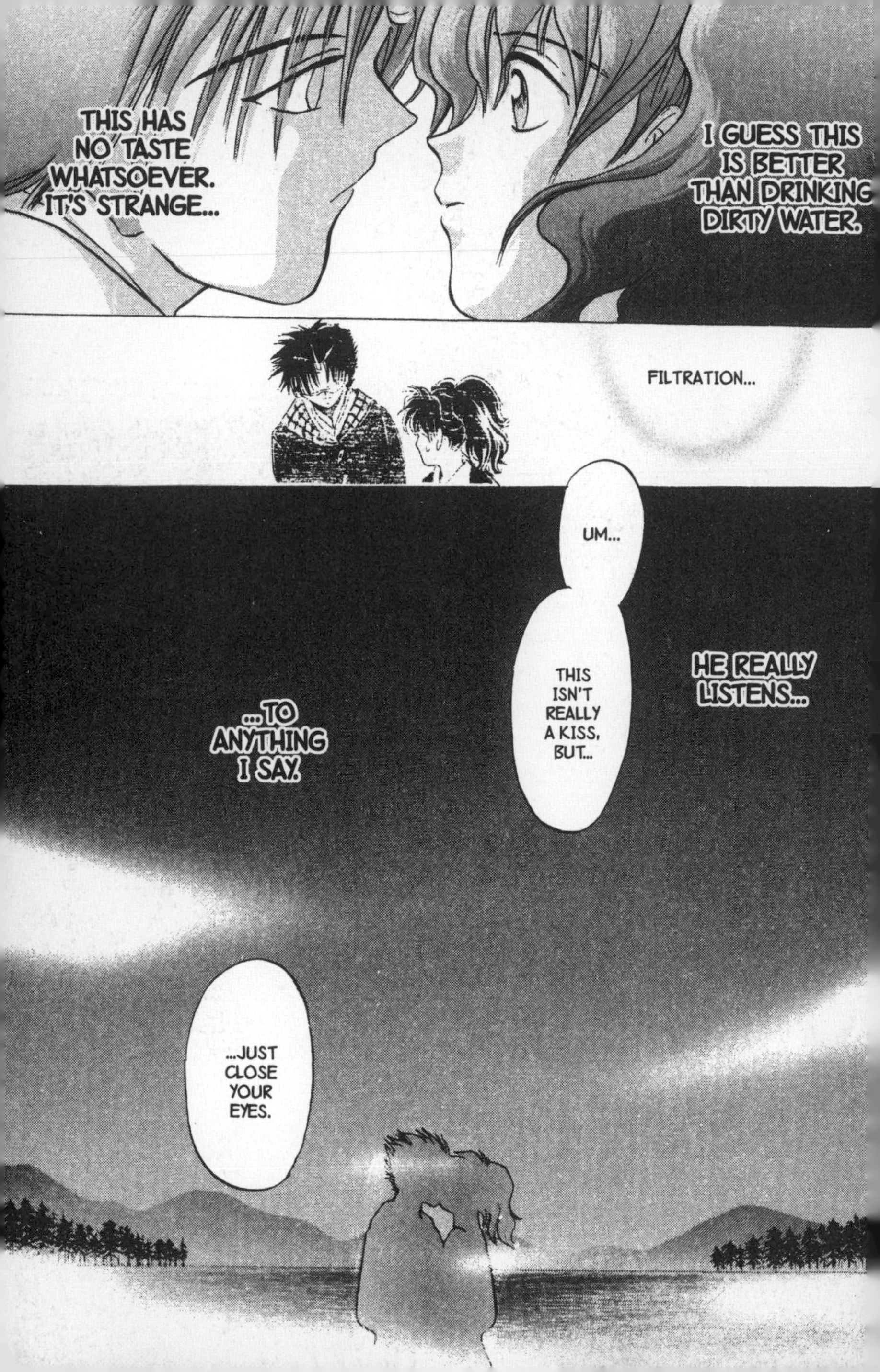
I GUESS THIS IS BETTER THAN DRINKING DIRTY WATER.
THIS HAS NO TASTE WHATSOEVER. IT'S STRANGE...
FILTRATION...
UM...
HE REALLY LISTENS...
THIS ISN'T REALLY A KISS, BUT...
...TO ANYTHING I SAY.
...JUST CLOSE YOUR EYES.

THOUGH HE'S JUST A TOY,
HIS LIPS ARE SOFT AND WARM.
IT MAKES ME UNEASY.
SHE'S NOT HERE?
MAYBE SHE RAN AWAY?
WHAT SHOULD WE DO?

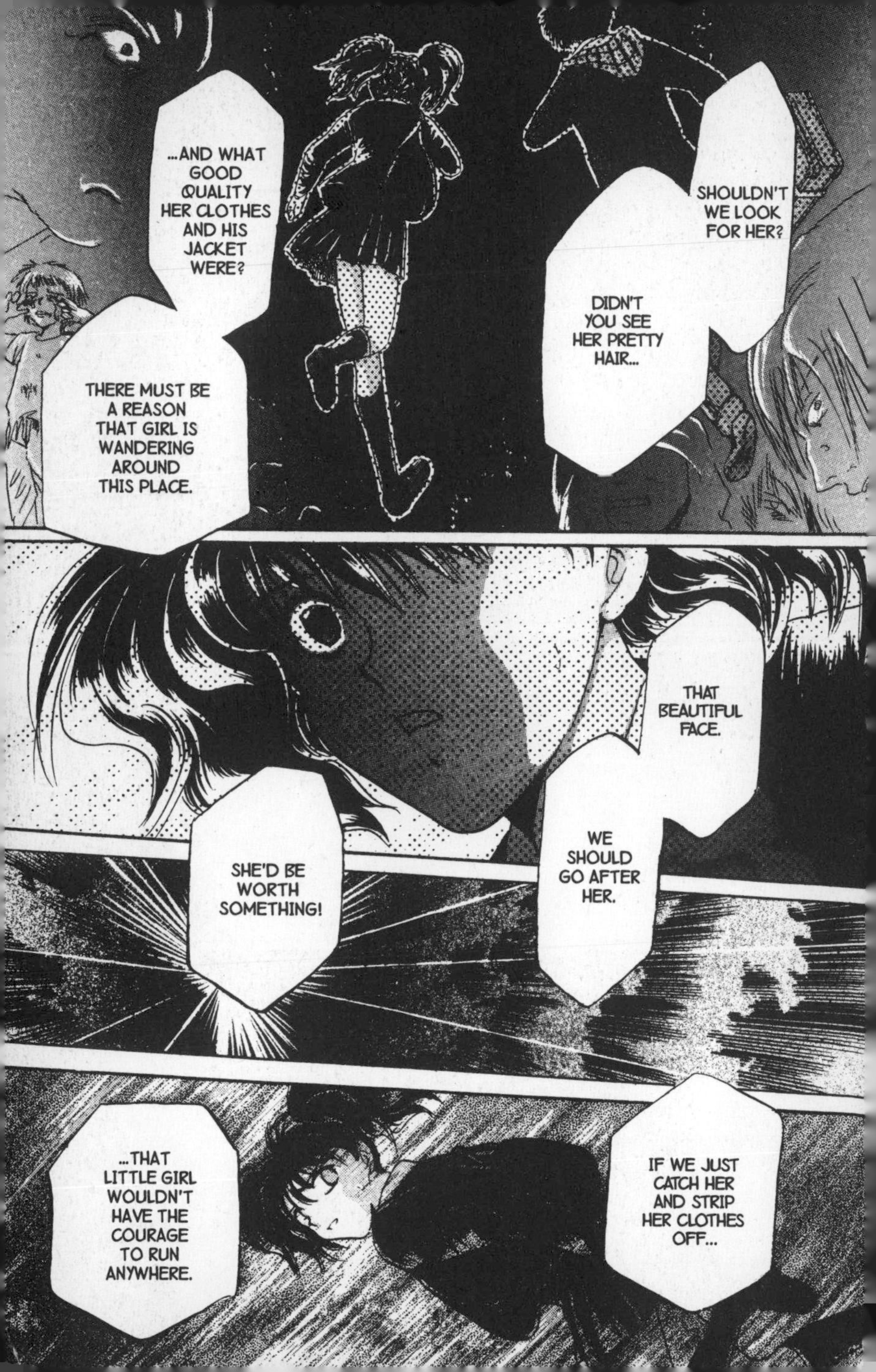
SHOULDN'T WE LOOK FOR HER?
DIDN'T YOU SEE HER PRETTY HAIR...
...AND WHAT GOOD QUALITY HER CLOTHES AND HIS JACKET WERE?
THERE MUST BE A REASON THAT GIRL IS WANDERING AROUND THIS PLACE.
THAT BEAUTIFUL FACE.
WE SHOULD GO AFTER HER.
SHE'D BE WORTH SOMETHING!
IF WE JUST CATCH HER AND STRIP HER CLOTHES OFF...
...THAT LITTLE GIRL WOULDN'T HAVE THE COURAGE TO RUN ANYWHERE.

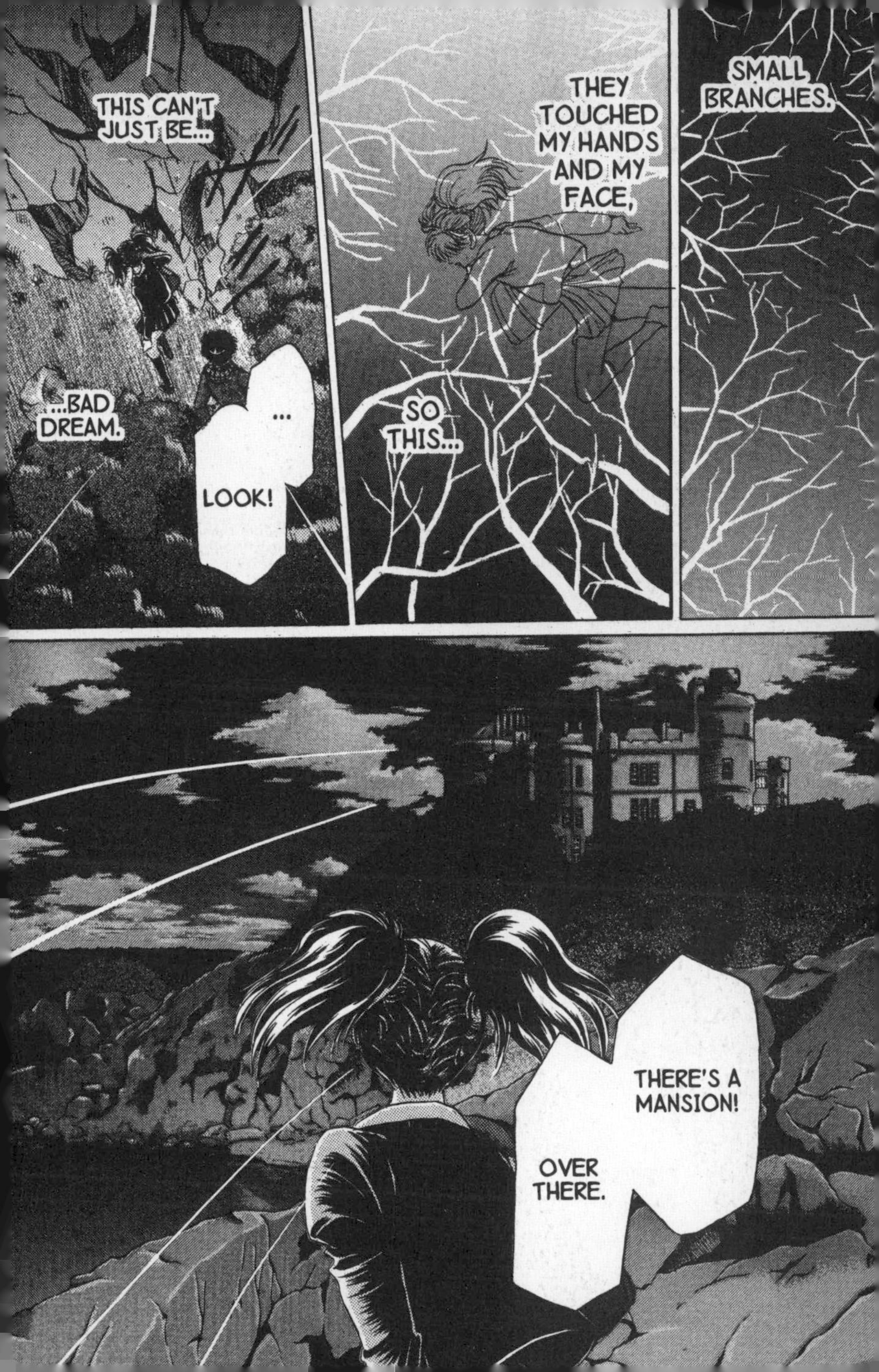
SMALL BRANCHES.
THEY TOUCHED MY HANDS AND MY FACE,
SO THIS...
THIS CAN'T JUST BE...
...BAD DREAM.
...
LOOK!
THERE'S A MANSION!
OVER THERE.

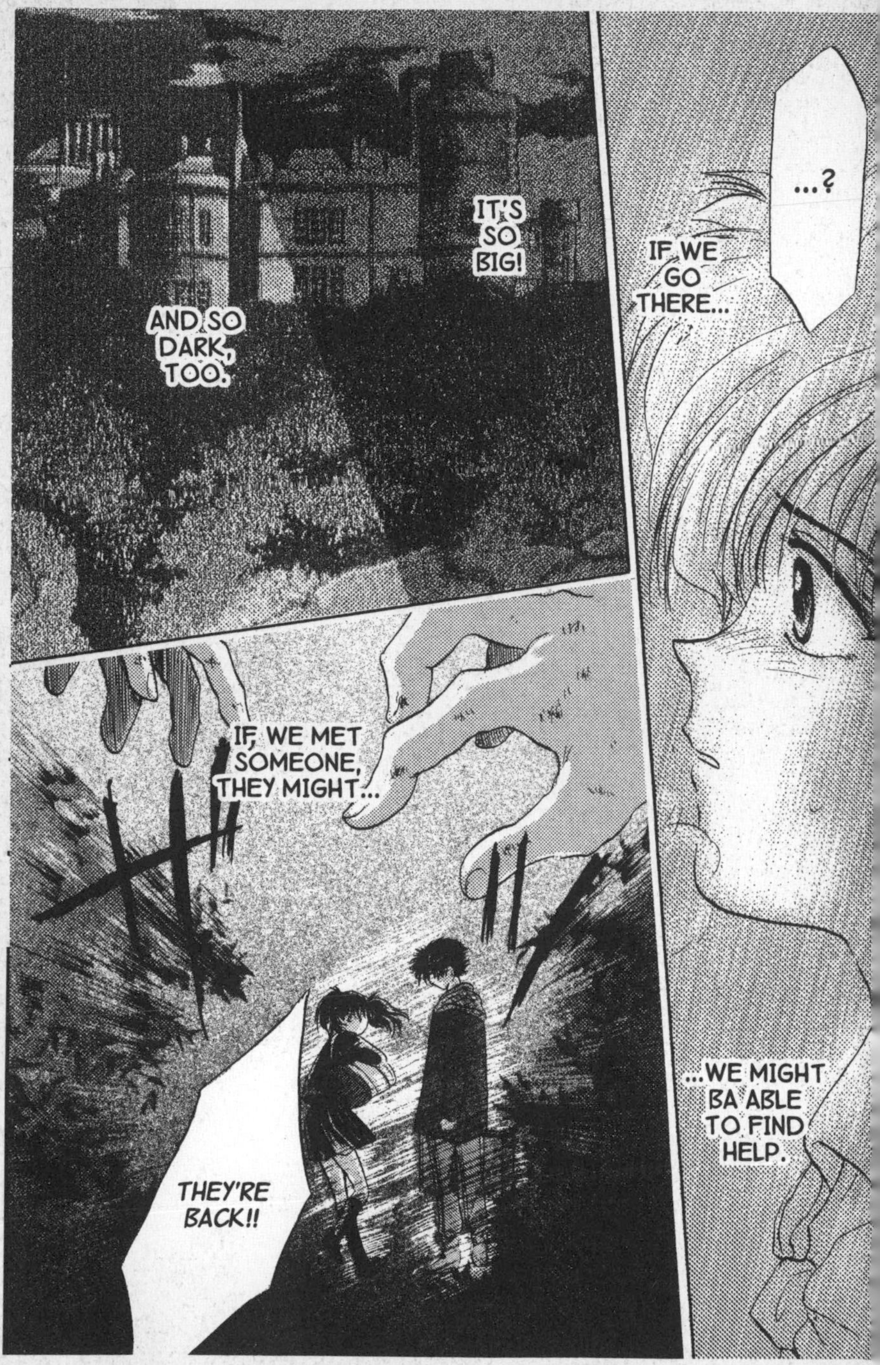
...?
IF WE GO THERE...
...WE MIGHT BA ABLE TO FIND HELP.
IT'S SO BIG!
AND SO DARK, TOO.
IF, WE MET SOMEONE, THEY MIGHT...
THEY'RE BACK!!

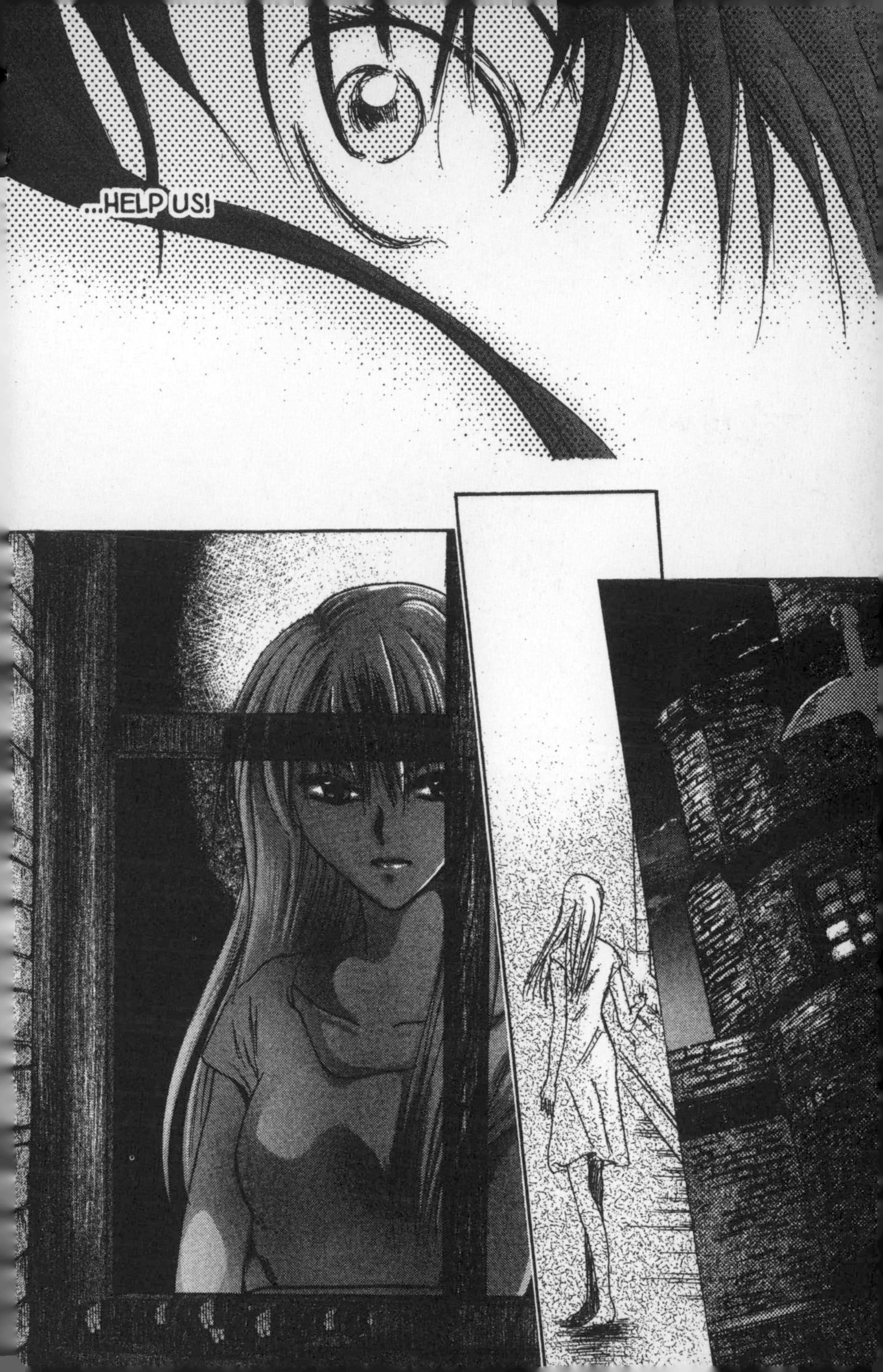
...HELP US!

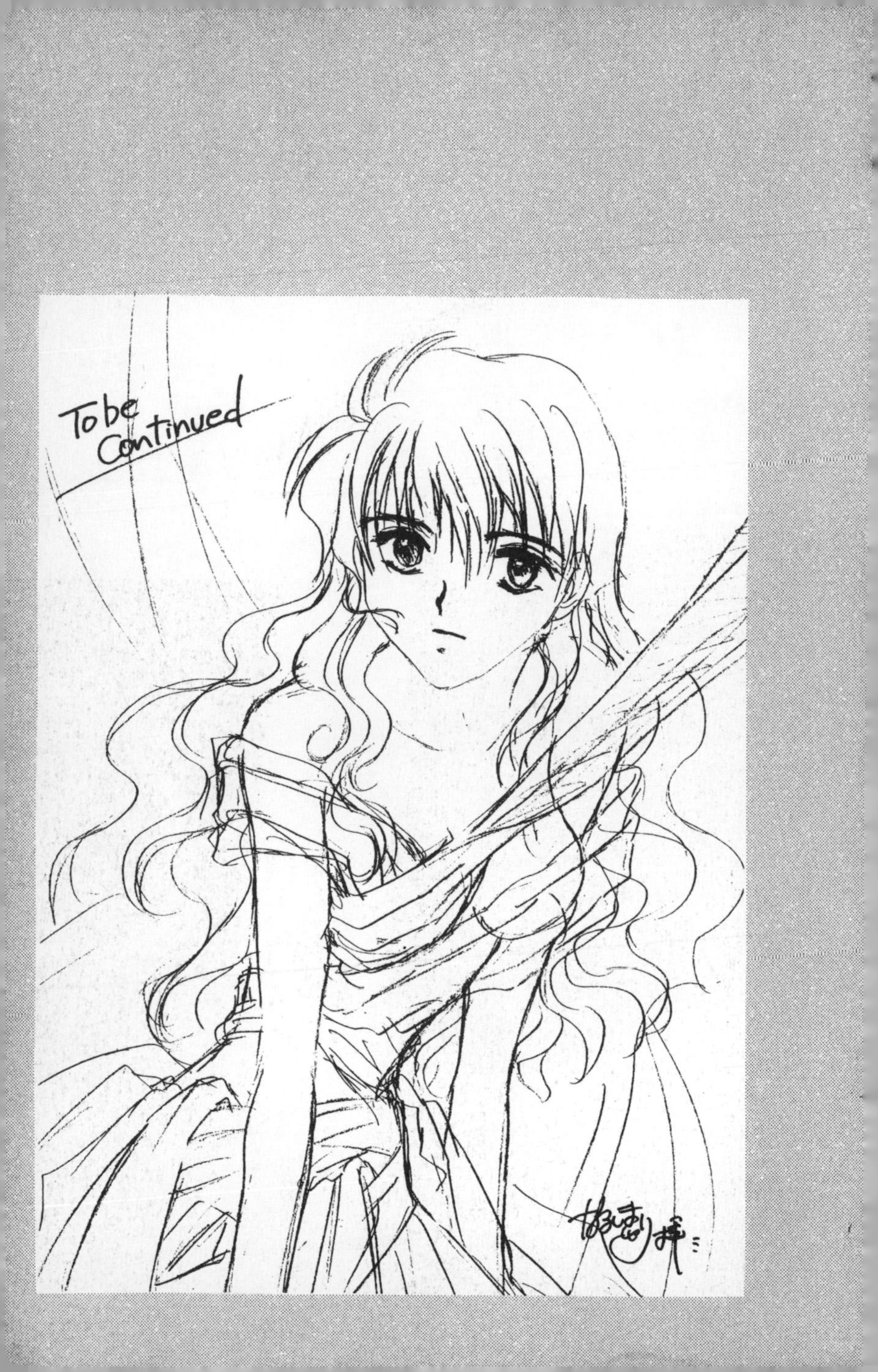
To be Continued

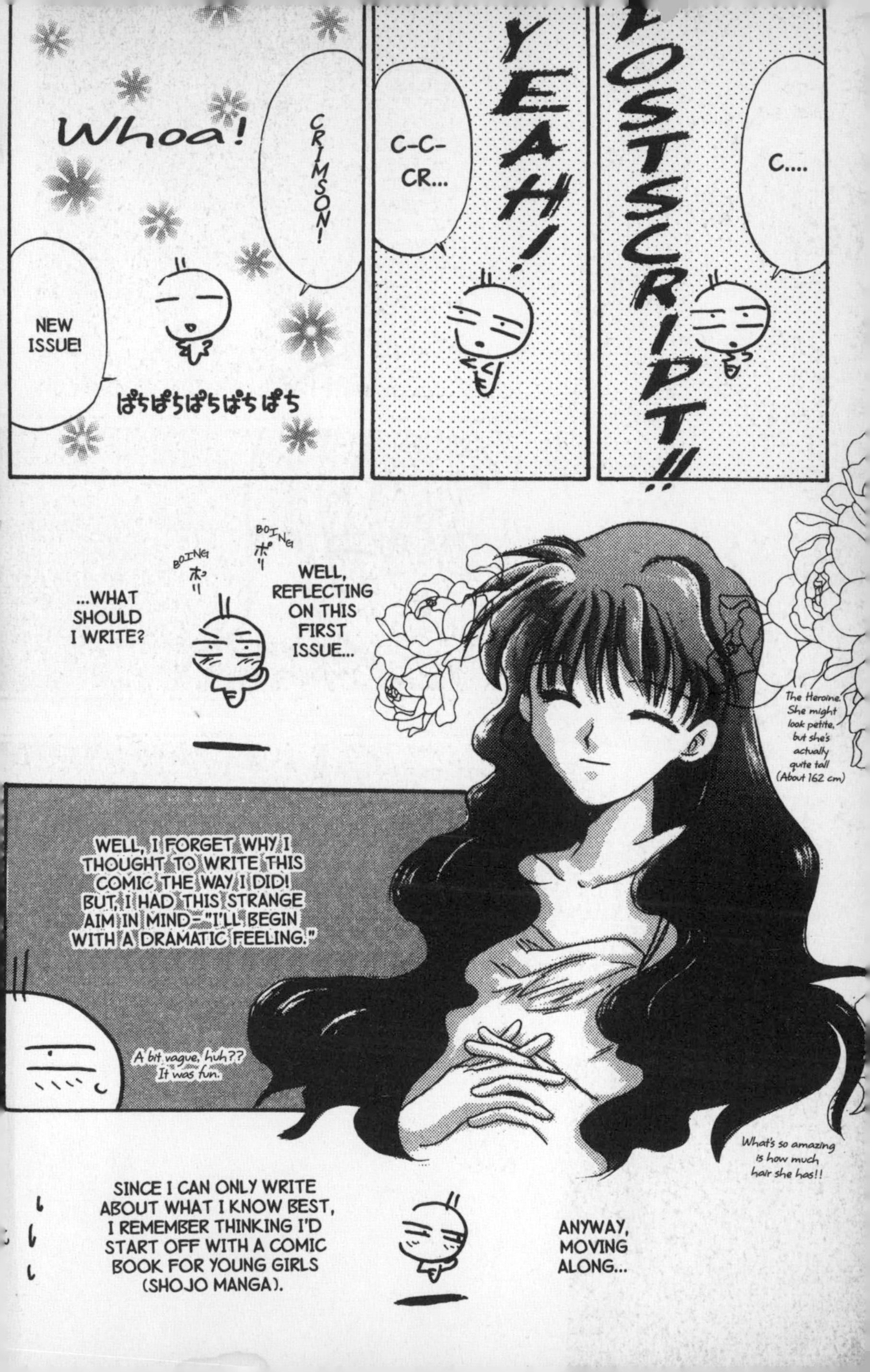
POSTSCRIPT!!
C....
YEAH!
C-C-CR...
Whoa!
CRIMSON!
NEW ISSUE!
ぱちぱちぱちぱちぱち
The Heroine. She might look petite, but she's actually quite tall (About 162 cm)
BOING
WELL, REFLECTING ON THIS FIRST ISSUE...
BOING
...WHAT SHOULD I WRITE?
WELL, I FORGET WHY I THOUGHT TO WRITE THIS COMIC THE WAY I DID! BUT, I HAD THIS STRANGE AIM IN MIND-"I'LL BEGIN WITH A DRAMATIC FEELING."
A bit vague, huh?? It was fun.
What's so amazing is how much hair she has!!
SINCE I CAN ONLY WRITE ABOUT WHAT I KNOW BEST, I REMEMBER THINKING I'D START OFF WITH A COMIC BOOK FOR YOUNG GIRLS (SHOJO MANGA).
ANYWAY, MOVING ALONG...

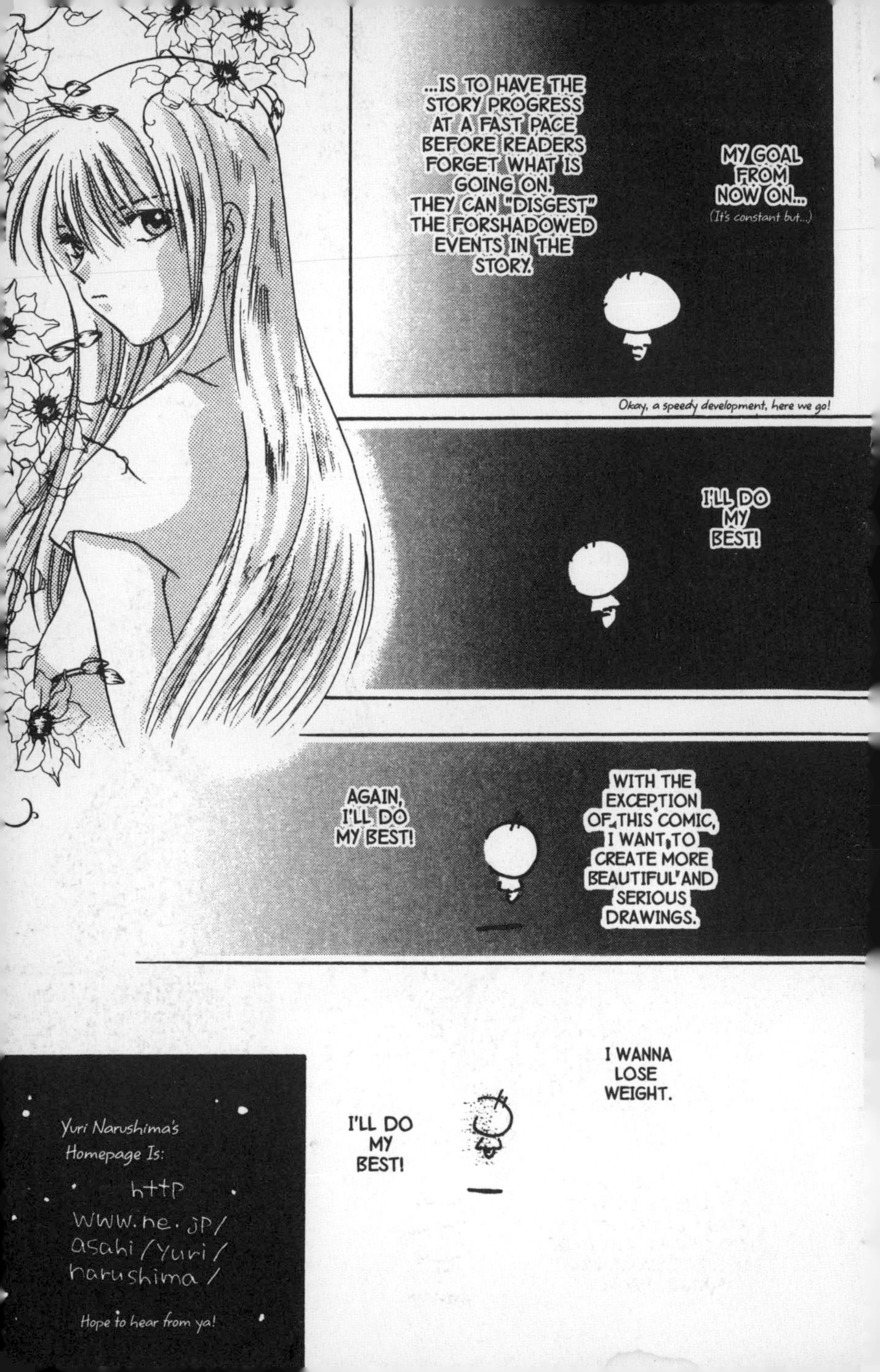
MY GOAL FROM NOW ON...
(It's constant but...)
...IS TO HAVE THE STORY PROGRESS AT A FAST PACE BEFORE READERS FORGET WHAT IS GOING ON. THEY CAN "DISGEST" THE FORSHADOWED EVENTS IN THE STORY.
Okay, a speedy development, here we go!
I'LL DO MY BEST!
WITH THE EXCEPTION OF THIS COMIC, I WANT TO CREATE MORE BEAUTIFUL AND SERIOUS DRAWINGS.
AGAIN, I'LL DO MY BEST!
I WANNA LOSE WEIGHT.
I'LL DO MY BEST!
Yuri Narushima's Homepage Is:
http
www.ne.jp/asahi/yuri/narushima/
Hope to hear from ya!

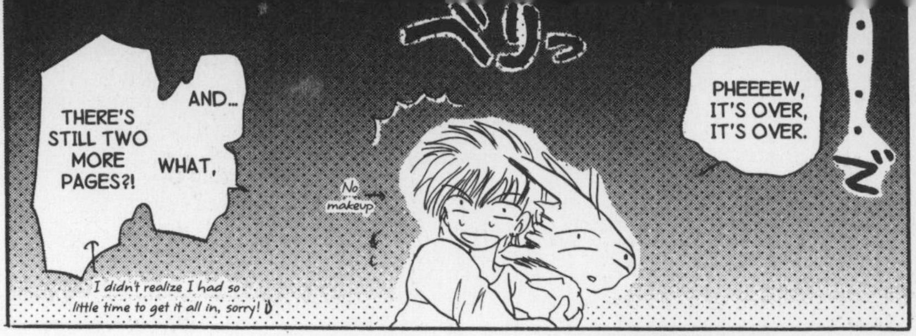

PHEEEEW, IT'S OVER, IT'S OVER.
!
Z
No makeup
AND...
WHAT,
THERE'S STILL TWO MORE PAGES?!
I didn't realize I had so little time to get it all in, sorry!

AND THAT MEANS...

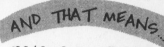

HERE ARE SOME OF MY GUIDELINE NOTES

(Some differ from the real ones though)

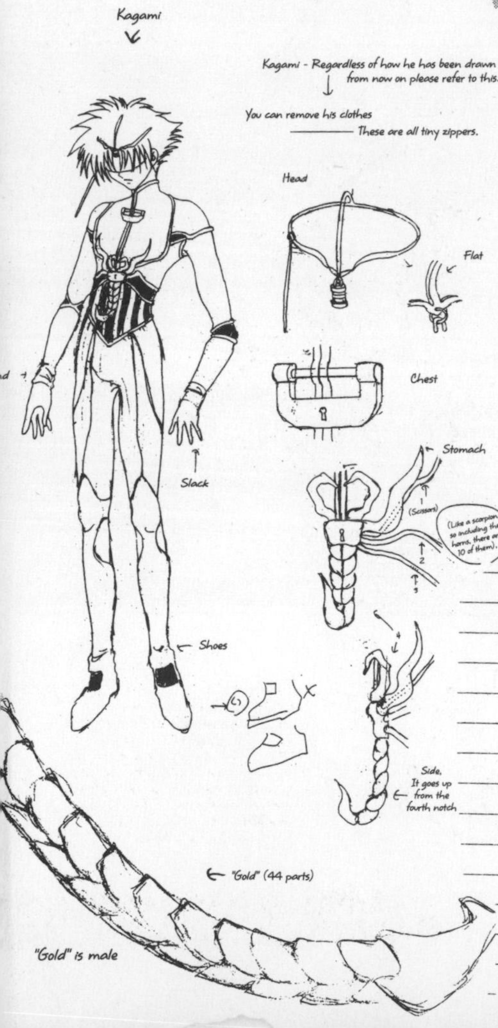

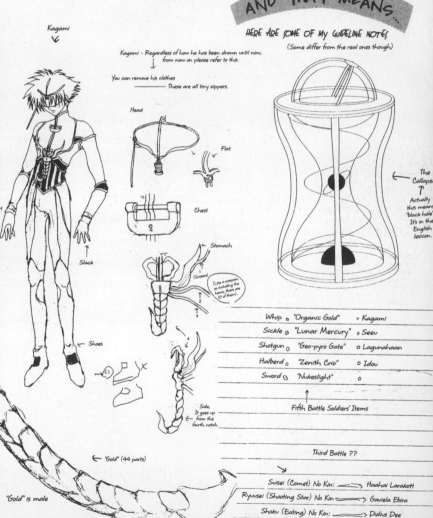

Kagami
Kagami - Regardless of how he has been drawn until now, from now on please refer to this.
You can remove his clothes
These are all tiny zippers.
Head
Flat
Chest
Slack
Stomach
1 (Scissors)
(Like a scorpion, so including the horns, there are 10 of them).
2
3
4
Shoes
Side. It goes up from the fourth notch
← "Gold" (44 parts)
"Gold" is male

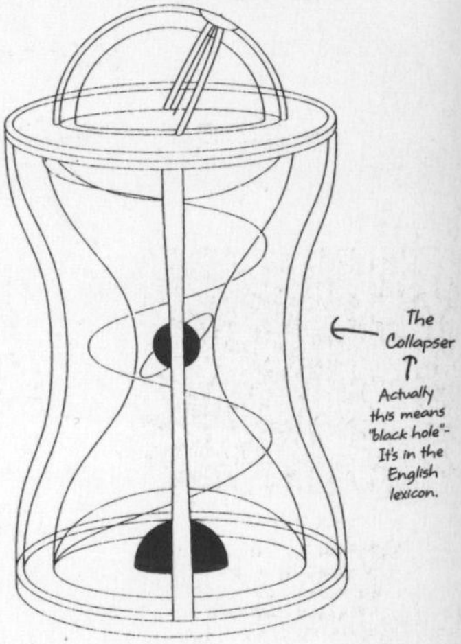

The Collapser
Actually this means "black hole"- It's in the English lexicon.

Whip	"Organic Gold"	Kagami
Sickle	"Lunar Mercury"	Seeu
Shotgun	"Geo-pyro Gate"	Lagunahaan
Halberd	"Zenith Crio"	Idou
Sword	"Nukeslight"	

↑ Fifth Battle Soldiers' Items

Third Battle ??

Suisei (Comet) No Kin: → Haahai Larakott

Ryuusei (Shooting Star) No Kin → Gaviela Ebira

Shoku (Eating) No Kin: → Didius Dee

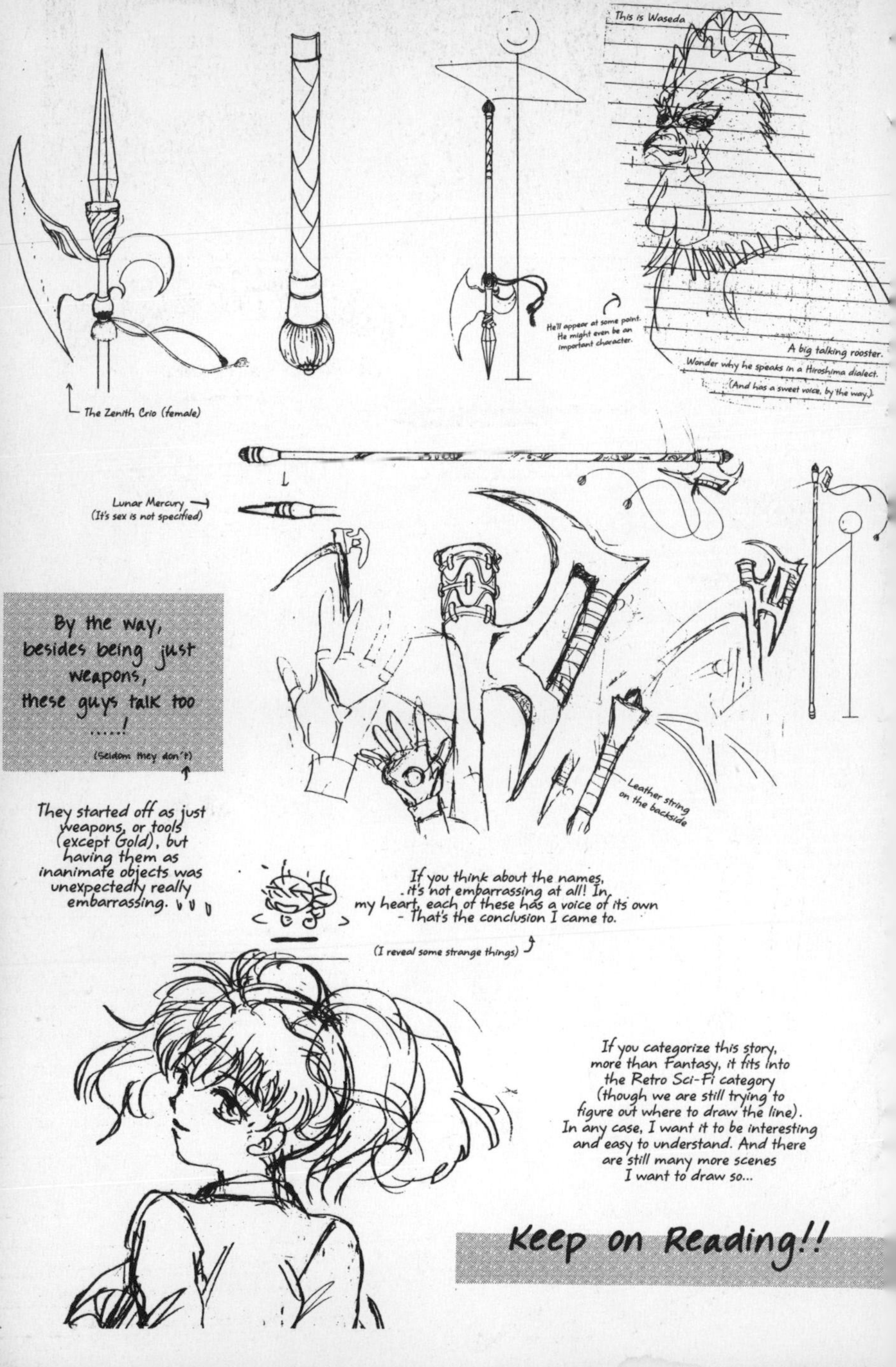
This is Waseda
He'll appear at some point. He might even be an important character.
A big talking rooster.
Wonder why he speaks in a Hiroshima dialect.
(And has a sweet voice, by the way.)
The Zenith Crio (female)
Lunar Mercury
(It's sex is not specified)
Leather string on the backside
By the way, besides being just weapons, these guys talk too .....!
(Seldom they don't)
They started off as just weapons, or tools (except Gold), but having them as inanimate objects was unexpectedly really embarrassing.
If you think about the names, it's not embarrassing at all! In my heart, each of these has a voice of its own - That's the conclusion I came to.
(I reveal some strange things)
If you categorize this story, more than Fantasy, it fits into the Retro Sci-Fi category (though we are still trying to figure out where to draw the line). In any case, I want it to be interesting and easy to understand. And there are still many more scenes I want to draw so...
Keep on Reading!!

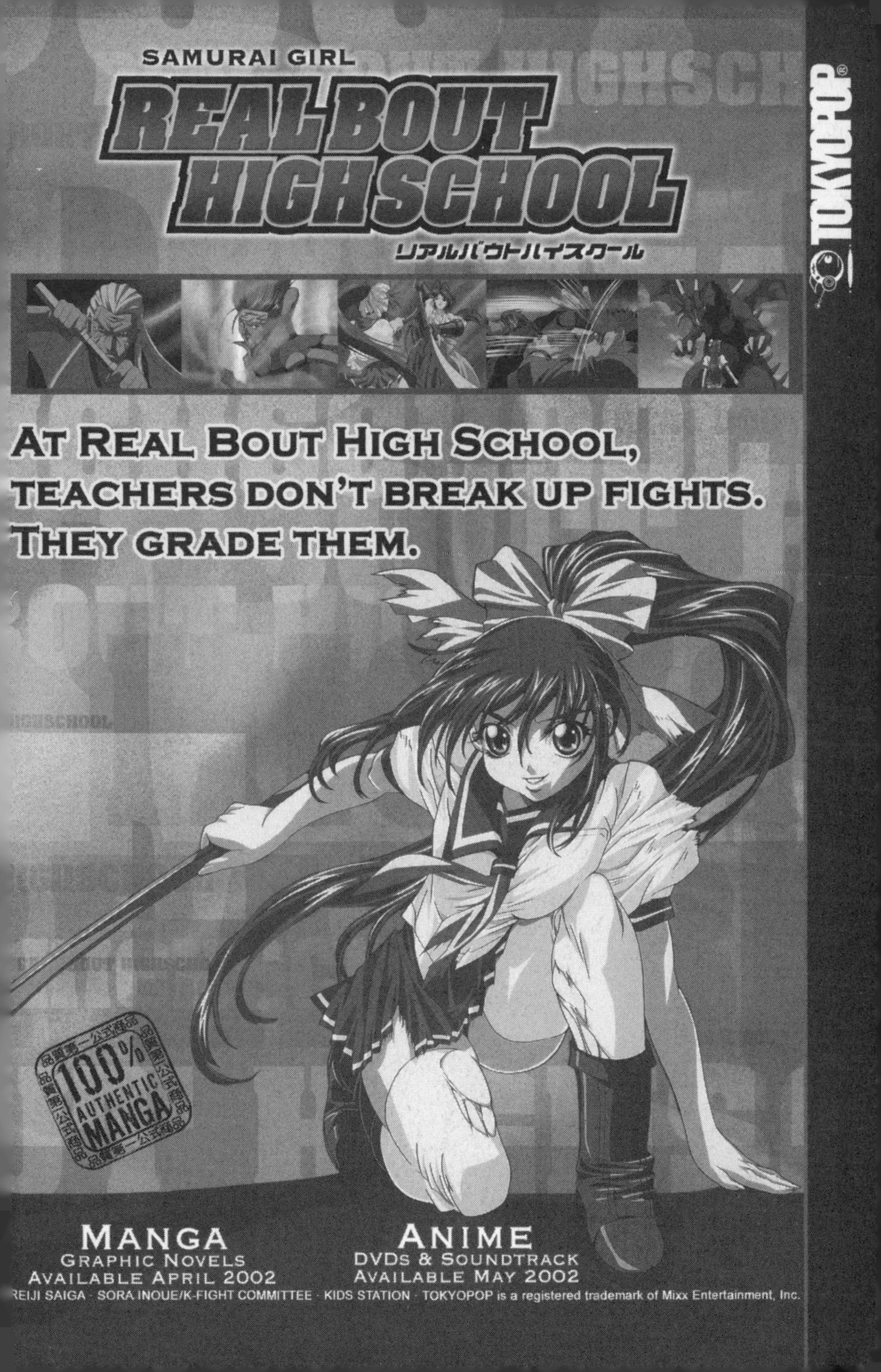
SAMURAI GIRL
REAL BOUT HIGH SCHOOL
リアルバウトハイスクール
TOKYOPOP
AT REAL BOUT HIGH SCHOOL, TEACHERS DON'T BREAK UP FIGHTS. THEY GRADE THEM.
100% AUTHENTIC MANGA
MANGA
GRAPHIC NOVELS
AVAILABLE APRIL 2002
ANIME
DVDs & SOUNDTRACK
AVAILABLE MAY 2002
REIJI SAIGA · SORA INOUE/K-FIGHT COMMITTEE · KIDS STATION · TOKYOPOP is a registered trademark of Mixx Entertainment, Inc.

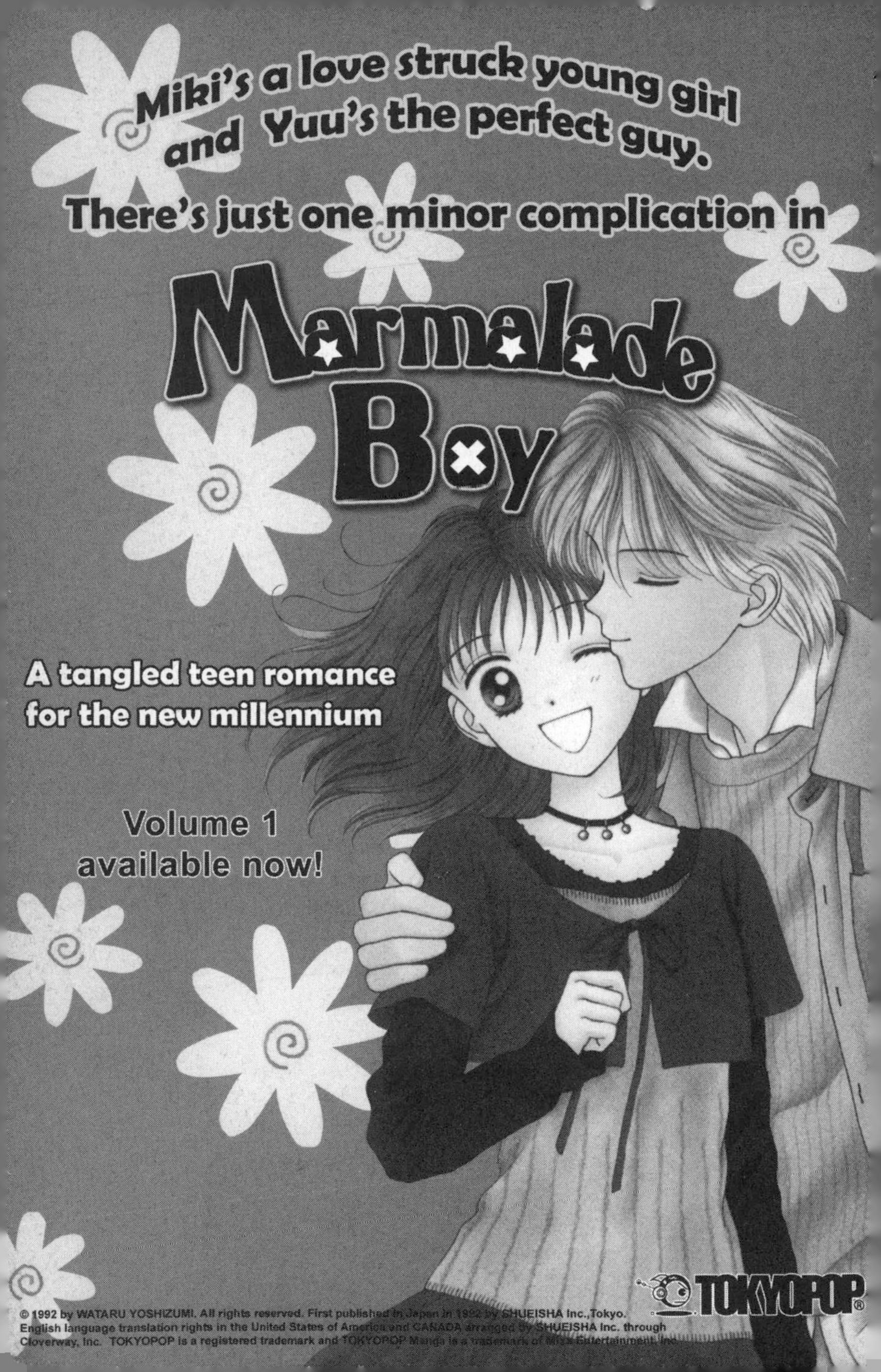

Miki's a love struck young girl and Yuu's the perfect guy.
There's just one minor complication in

Marmalade Boy

A tangled teen romance for the new millennium

Volume 1 available now!

© 1992 by WATARU YOSHIZUMI. All rights reserved. First published in Japan in 1992 by SHUEISHA Inc.,Tokyo. English language translation rights in the United States of America and CANADA arranged by SHUEISHA Inc. through Cloverway, Inc. TOKYOPOP is a registered trademark and TOKYOPOP Manga is a trademark of Mixx Entertainment, Inc.

TOKYOPOP

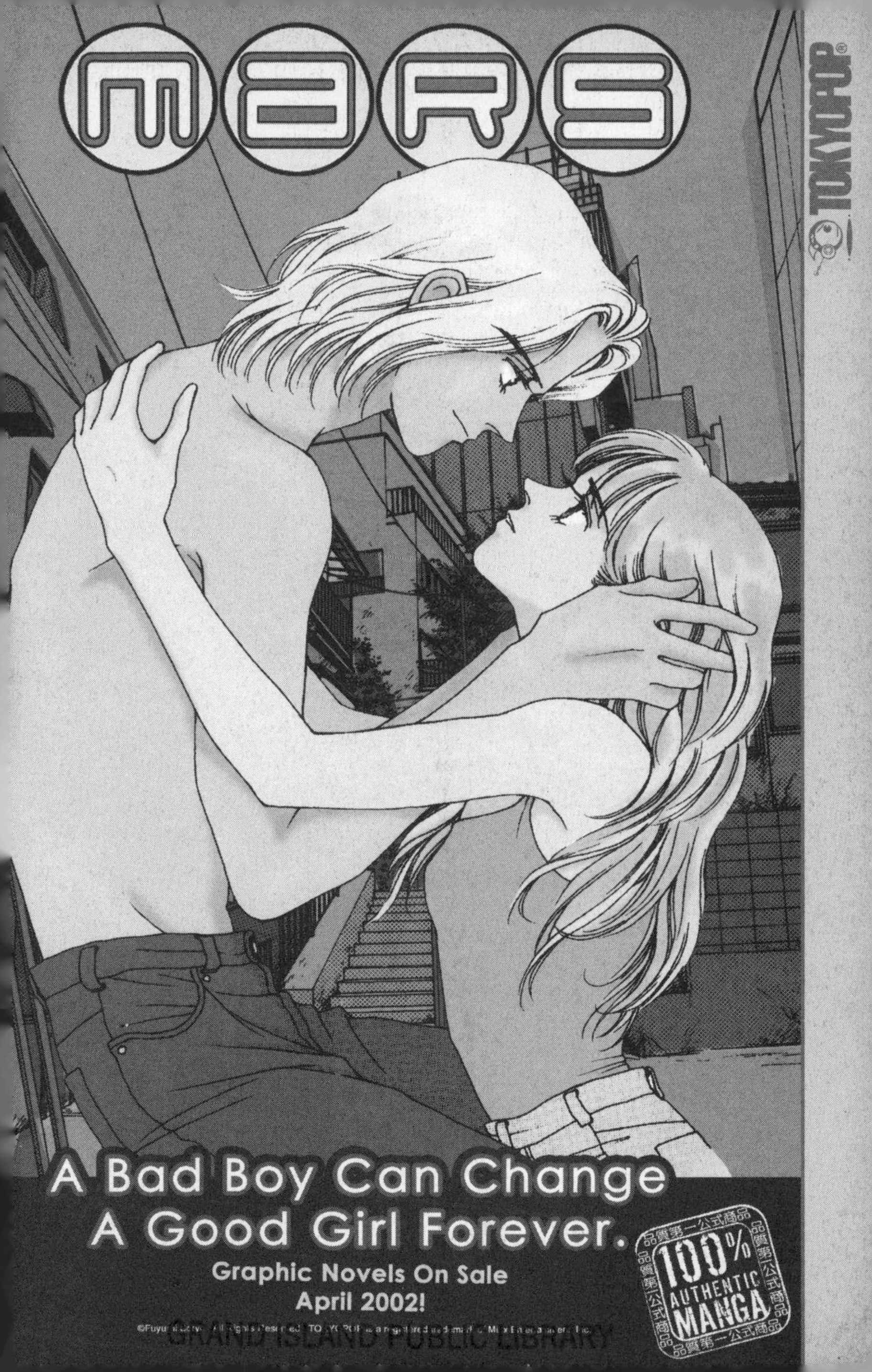
MARS
TOKYOPOP®
A Bad Boy Can Change
A Good Girl Forever.
Graphic Novels On Sale
April 2002!
100% AUTHENTIC MANGA
品質第一公式商品

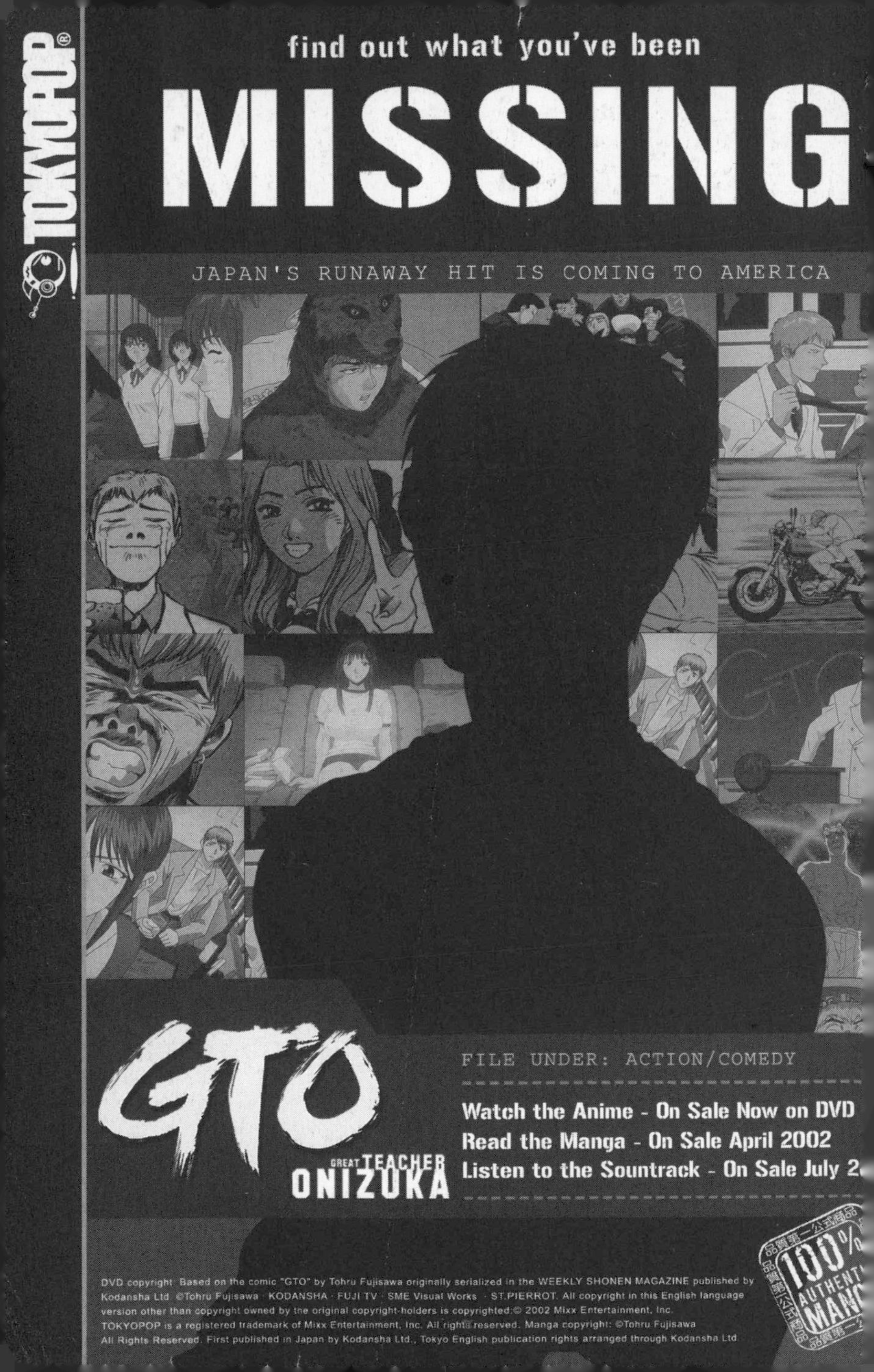
TOKYOPOP®
find out what you've been
MISSING
JAPAN'S RUNAWAY HIT IS COMING TO AMERICA
GTO
GREAT TEACHER ONIZUKA
FILE UNDER: ACTION/COMEDY
Watch the Anime - On Sale Now on DVD
Read the Manga - On Sale April 2002
Listen to the Sountrack - On Sale July 2
DVD copyright: Based on the comic "GTO" by Tohru Fujisawa originally serialized in the WEEKLY SHONEN MAGAZINE published by Kodansha Ltd. ©Tohru Fujisawa · KODANSHA · FUJI TV · SME Visual Works · ST.PIERROT. All copyright in this English language version other than copyright owned by the original copyright-holders is copyrighted:© 2002 Mixx Entertainment, Inc.
TOKYOPOP is a registered trademark of Mixx Entertainment, Inc. All rights reserved. Manga copyright: ©Tohru Fujisawa
All Rights Reserved. First published in Japan by Kodansha Ltd., Tokyo English publication rights arranged through Kodansha Ltd.
100% AUTHENTIC MANG

STOP!

This is the back of the book.
You wouldn't want to spoil a great ending!

This book is printed "manga-style," in the authentic Japanese right-to-left format. Since none of the artwork has been flipped or altered, readers get to experience the story just as the creator intended. You've been asking for it, so TOKYOPOP® delivered: authentic, hot-off-the-press, and far more fun!

DIRECTIONS

If this is your first time reading manga-style, here's a quick guide to help you understand how it works.

It's easy... just start in the top right panel and follow the numbers. Have fun, and look for more 100% authentic manga from TOKYOPOP®!